WHAT IS IN A RIM?

WHAT IS IN A RIM?

CRITICAL PERSPECTIVES ON
THE PACIFIC REGION IDEA

edited by
ARIF DIRLIK

WESTVIEW PRESS
Boulder • San Francisco • Oxford

Copyright © 1993 by Westview Press, Inc.

Published in 1993 in the United States of America by Westview Press, Inc., 5500 Central Avenue, Boulder, Colorado 80301-2877, and in the United Kingdom by Westview Press, 36 Lonsdale Road, Summertown, Oxford OX2 7EW

Library of Congress Cataloging-in-Publication Data
What is in a rim? : critical perspectives on the Pacific Region idea /
    edited by Arif Dirlik.
      p.   cm.
    Includes index.
    ISBN 0-8133-8531-8 (HC). — ISBN 0-8133-1915-3 (PB)
    1. Pacific Area—Economic conditions.   2. Pacific Area—Foreign
economic relations.   3. Pacific Area—Politics and government.
4. Pacific Area—Social conditions.   I. Dirlik, Arif.
HC681.W48   1993
330.99—dc20   93-9556
                                                                              CIP

Printed and bound in the United States of America

⊗   The paper used in this publication meets the requirements
     of the American National Standard for Permanence of Paper
     for Printed Library Materials Z39.48-1984.

10   9   8   7   6   5   4   3   2   1

To Dot Sapp,
lovingly, for her unstinting,
caring, and meticulous help over the years—
from my dissertation to the present book

Contents

THREE   Down and Out in the Realm of Miracles: Class and Gender Perspectives on the Asia-Pacific

FOUR   Cultural Formations in the Asia-Pacific

Acknowledgments

This volume is a product of a symposium held at Duke University, March 23–25, 1991, entitled "The Asia-Pacific Idea: Reality and Representation in the Invention of a Regional Structure." The symposium was made possible by contributions from The Asian-Pacific Studies Institute at Duke University, the Trent Foundation, the Office of the Dean of Arts and Sciences at Duke University, and the Duke-UNC Program in Latin American Studies. Special thanks go to Professor Nan Lin, Director of the Asian-Pacific Studies Institute, Deans Richard White and Hans Hillerbrand, and Professor Gary Gereffi of the Department of Sociology at Duke for their support.

I would like also to acknowledge the help of Mavis Mayer and the staff of the Asian-Pacific Studies Institute in making the arrangements for the symposium, which as we have learned to expect were flawless, and of Rebecca Karl, a doctoral candidate in the Department of History at Duke, who served as rapporteur for the symposium. Dorothy Sapp and Thelma Kithcart of the Department of History were as usual generous with their help in the preparation of this manuscript.

Finally, I would like to thank the participants in the symposium, not all of whom are represented in this volume, for three days of relentlessly stimulating discussion that clarified many of the issues taken up in the essays below.

Arif Dirlik

PART ONE

Setting the Scene

1

Introducing the Pacific

*P*ACIFIC RIM" and a variety of terms cognate to it, such as "Pacific Basin" and "Asia-Pacific," have become commonplaces in geopolitical vocabulary over the last decade. And yet, what these terms mean remains unclear. The immediate reference is obviously physically geographic: Pacific Rim (or Pacific Basin) refers to societies situated on the boundaries of the Pacific Ocean and within it. Discussions of the Pacific Rim, however, rarely account for all the societies thus situated, more often than not referring primarily to societies of the northern hemisphere and sometimes using the term euphemistically as a contemporary substitute for what used to be called East Asia. The terms sometimes include societies technically outside the physical boundaries of the Pacific Ocean even as some of the societies situated on the Rim or within it are left out. These usages problematize the geographic reference of the term(s). Indeed, it is arguable that the terms represent ideational constructs that, although they refer to a physical location on the globe, are themselves informed by conceptualizations that owe little to geography understood physically or positivistically; in other words, that they define the physical space they pretend to describe.[1]

The chapters in this volume inquire critically into the Pacific as representation from a variety of perspectives, thematic and area based. They are at once deconstructive and reconstructive in intention. They are deconstructive because they seek to get past representations of the Pacific as "mere" geography and to discover the ideological premises that inform the Pacific as spatial representation. They are also reconstructive, however, because they resist the reduction of the concept of the Pacific to mere representation and seek instead to identify the economic, political, and social relationships, as they have evolved historically, that account for the prominent place the idea of the Pacific occupies in contemporary geopolitical discourse. The discussions are of necessity illustrative rather than comprehensive. The multiplicity of the problems presented by the Pacific and the immense variety of the areas to which the term refers precludes any pretense to comprehensiveness. Even more important in this regard is the premise the authors share, resisting the

3

reductionism of the very concept of the Pacific: that the Pacific is as much a realm of fragmentation as of unity, which therefore deprives any effort to describe it of the narrative unity that might lend a guise of comprehensiveness to an otherwise diffuse subject. Definitions of the Pacific are part of the very struggle over the Pacific that they seek to describe. What we seek to accomplish in this volume is hence to bring to the surface some of the significant problems that present themselves to any discussion of the Pacific that seeks not an ideological constitution of the region but a recognition of the complex and contradictory relationships that shape the discourse on the Pacific.

We seek coherence not in comprehensiveness or common problems, but in a number of premises shared by the contributors: (a) that Pacific Rim (or Pacific Basin, Asia-Pacific) is an invented concept; (b) that being an invented concept does not mean the Pacific has no material basis; (c) that this material basis is defined best not by physical geography, but by relationships (economic, social, political, military, and cultural) that are concretely historical; (d) that these relationships that give meaning to the notion of the Pacific are also relationships of contradiction that disrupt the very unity that they imply; (e) that such contradictions are not to be understood without reference to global forces that transcend the Pacific, as well as relationships of hegemony and exploitation that are internal to the region; (f) that the idea of the Pacific is intended as much to express the aspirations of the people who inhabit the region as it is to contain intraregional contradictions and the relationship of the Pacific to other regions of the world; (g) that therefore the idea of the Pacific is not so much a well-defined idea as it is a discourse that seeks to construct what is pretended to be its point of departure, a discourse that is problematized by the very relationships that legitimize it.

That the Pacific is an invented concept does not mean that the region does not exist except as an idea, but that what exists does so by virtue of human interactions and the conceptualizations that endow those interactions with meaning. There is indeed a Pacific region in a different (and more meaningful) sense than the physically geographic. Motions of people, commodities, and capital over the last few centuries have created relationships that traverse the Pacific in different directions and have given rise to regional formations with shifting boundaries. These formations have varied in the area they encompass, in accordance with the nature of the relationships, restricted sometimes to portions of the area designated today as the Pacific, sometimes extending far beyond that area. Such motions continue to this day and account for the gap between the Pacific area (conceived physically) and a Pacific region conceived in terms of human activity. Emphasis on human activity shifts attention from physical area to the construction of geography through human interactions; it also underlines the historicity of the region's formation(s).

Phrased in terms of human relations, moreover, the invention of the Pacific does not imply invention by design (at least, not until the late nineteenth century), but invention haphazardly by trial and error. Europeans literally stumbled on the Pacific in 1513, and it was not until 1788 (with the completion of James Cook's last voyage) that the Pacific came into existence as we know it today. In between these dates, as well as in later years, human activity in the area was haphazard, more or less following ancient myths or educated guesses (as in the case of the geographic explorations) or commodities of one kind or another, from otter furs and sea slugs to spices and tea (as in the case of commercial ventures). By the nineteenth century such activity included large-scale human motions, such as the Chinese diaspora into Southeast Asia and across the Pacific. As a prominent historian of the Pacific wrote:

> Of the factors in the change from "South Sea" [the original name given to the Ocean by Balboa in 1513] to "Pacific" the progress of geographic discovery was important, especially as the northern bounds of the ocean were traced out; and except for rather vague knowledge in western Europe of the earlier Russian probes to Alaska, this had to wait for Cook. But probably more important were changes not just in the delineation of the Ocean, but in its patterns of trade.[2]

That the invention of the Pacific was haphazard does not mean it had no logic to it. The Pacific and the areas situated on the rim were initially filled out by peoples moving out of Asia, and there had been all along movements of commodities and people in the area, at least locally. But the filling out of the Pacific from the sixteenth century on had a more compelling logic to it, whether we speak of geographical discovery or the pursuit of commodities: the logic was the logic of the capitalist world economy spreading out of Europe to conquer the world. The modern formation of the Pacific was dynamic in its transformative powers, persistent in its logic, and total in the sense that it affected all areas of life, from economic relations to culture (from missionaries to contemporary consumer culture). The important point is that the Pacific in the end would be a EuroAmerican invention (first of Europeans and then of the transplanted Europeans of the Americas), that what we today regard as the Pacific region was formed by forces that originated outside of the region. This does not mean that the inhabitants of the region had nothing to contribute to the region's formation, which they did, but only in resistance to the EuroAmerican conquest. Again to quote Spate: "The outsiders named the Ocean, gave it bounds, and in a not trivial sense 'the Pacific' as a concept is a EuroAmerican artifact. But it was not just 'made in Europe'; the local materials were not inert."[3] Nevertheless, dynamic forces emanating from EuroAmerica, from the secular growth of capitalism to contingent political rivalries, were projected onto the Pacific and played the central part in its formation as a region as well as in its conceptualization.

The Pacific was invented by EuroAmericans in another sense: as a concept. From the very beginning, it was the Europeans who gave meaning to the area in terms of European (later EuroAmerican) concepts, visions, and fantasies. Just as they reconstructed the area in accordance with the logic of European capitalism and politics, Europeans and EuroAmericans projected on the area their myths, fantasies, and visions. To be sure, this process was not without its own internal contradictions and conflicts. The Pacific served as much to deconstruct inherited European myths (such as the existence of a southern continent) as to create new visions. But at a certain level, Eurocentrism and capitalism are indistinguishable. The Pacific in this regard has served an ambiguous purpose, reflecting the contradictions of capitalism itself: at once a "paradise" that offered relief from the harshness of life under capitalism and a frontier of capitalism that awaited the transformative powers of European dynamism. The beachcomber and the entrepreneur are two sides of the same coin. But in the end, it was the Pacific that was incorporated into the narrative of capitalism (by definition a Eurocentric narrative, even to this day when capitalism is deterritorialized), rather than the other way around. Hence the resistance to the discourse of the Pacific, described in some of the chapters that follow, in the name of localized regionalisms. To define, as to name, is to conquer. EuroAmericans were responsible not only for mapping the Pacific, but also for attaching names to the maps. Today, even Pacific peoples, in order to locate themselves in the area, have to go by EuroAmerican maps—and the new names. To use a distinction suggested by Joseph Levenson, a historian of China, the confrontation of the EuroAmerican and the Asian Pacifics entailed a vocabulary change for one and a language change for the other. From mai-tais to taboo and tattoo, a whole range of vocabulary has entered EuroAmerican languages. But for the people of the Pacific the confrontation has entailed the rephrasing of metaphysical and historical experience in a new language.

This transformation, however, does not negate the strong Asian presence in the Pacific, which justifies the use of the term "Asia-Pacific" throughout this volume. If the "Pacific" was a EuroAmerican invention, the invented region had an Asian content, which presents us with the central contradiction of the Pacific region. Asian peoples through their motions have played a highly significant part in the filling out of the region (including the initial peopling of the Americas). The China trade and visions of China were not only responsible for luring Europeans to the discovery of the Pacific, but provided the nodal point for much of the early economic activity in the area, from the Manila galleons to the pursuit of sea slugs, through which the Pacific was to emerge as a region. The Asian presence in the region is presently more prominent than ever with the post–World War II economic emergence of societies in East Asia that for the first time have begun to challenge the nearly five century long EuroAmerican domination of the region. It may be arguable that this challenge has only brought to the surface contradictions that have been implicit in the region's formation from the beginning.

The Pacific is a EuroAmerican success: an area of the world that did not even exist as an entity in human consciousness until only about two hundred years ago has been created in the image of EuroAmericans. The capitalist world system of which the Pacific as we know it today is a product presently draws sustenance from the creation of the Pacific; it has produced some of the most successful examples of capitalist development that now in their turn inject new energy into the system. Asian-Pacific capitalism has produced new models of development that may be held before the struggling societies of the non-EuroAmerican world as proof of the success of capitalism; much the same as Asian Americans are held up before other less successful minorities within the United States as a "model minority."

The Pacific is also a failure, however, because these Asian-Pacific offsprings of capitalism in their success challenge the dominion of their progenitors, introducing a new conflict into the capitalist world system. The model of capitalism they represent, so-called communitarian capitalism, as it is held up before the Third World as a new model of development, also asserts with confidence its superiority to the "individualistic capitalism" of EuroAmerican societies.[4] Likewise, the premodern ideological legacies of successful East Asian capitalist societies, once viewed by one and all as cultural obstacles to development, are now re-presented as sources of East Asian dynamism, challenging the ideological hegemony of EuroAmerican culture. The competition has once again brought to the surface the Europe/Asia (or West/East) cultural confrontation that has played a part all along in the Pacific's cultural formation; the concern with the economic threat from Asia-Pacific to the European and U.S. economies finds explicit expression in a resurgent "yellow peril" vocabulary.[5]

The success/failure of EuroAmerican capitalism in reconstituting the Pacific is also visible in the intraregional division of the Pacific into First and Third worlds. The Pacific contains within its boundaries some of the most successful examples of capitalist development in the world. It also contains some of the sorriest products of the capitalist world system; the Philippines and Indonesia, as well as many of the island societies of the Pacific once responsible for the image of the Pacific as an earthly paradise, now survive as nuclear and chemical dumps for the First World, inhabited by people who have been disoriented completely by their economic and cultural incorporation into the world system.

The discourse on the Pacific as part of a global discourse is a discourse of the powerful who seek to reconstitute the Pacific once again in their image; this time around not just a EuroAmerican image, but a homegrown image that is nevertheless no less the product of a discourse of capitalism. In its most recent manifestation, which is the manifestation in which it entered global consciousness, this discourse began to emerge sometime in the 1960s, accompanied by the first tentative efforts to institutionalize a Pacific region. Writers on the subject agree that the issue of a Pacific community originated in Japan, was picked up in the United States in the 1970s, and has been kept alive over the years by Australian efforts. One Filipina scholar describes the Pacific community idea as "a baby whose putative parents are Japanese and American and whose midwife is Australian."[6] Starting with semiofficial efforts on the part of scholars and business and government officials in the 1960s, efforts to institutionalize a Pacific community gathered momentum in the 1970s and 1980s with the closer involvement of governments. The first concrete steps toward cooperation were taken in the Asia-Pacific Economic Council (APEC) meeting in Seoul, Korea, in fall 1991.

What gave rise to a Pacific discourse in the 1960s is more problematic. It is possible that the Vietnam War and U.S. efforts to sustain power in the Pacific played a key role in the new attention to institutionalizing the Pacific region. Even if that were the case, however, the effort was given a new meaning with the emergence of Japan in the 1960s as a world economic power, to be followed closely by the other "miracles" of Asia in Taiwan, Singapore, and South Korea. Japanese initiatives toward the formation of a Pacific economic community also suggest a concern for an Asia-Pacific economic organization that would parallel initiatives in Europe toward a European economic community. The initiatives of the 1960s, in other words, would seem to have coincided with what would appear to be in hindsight a regionalization of the capitalist world economy into competitive blocs.[7]

What has made these efforts at institutionalization difficult in the Pacific has been the diversity of Pacific societies and the mutual suspicions that are the legacies of a past of imperialism and colonialism. Intraregional groups (or subregional groupings) continue to this day to interfere with and undermine an all-encompassing Asia-Pacific idea. Among a variety of such subregions, themselves tentative and diffuse, are: a North American free trade area, a South Pacific area, an East Asian free trade zone, a Northeast Asian free trade zone, a "Greater China" area, and the most successful subregion so far, the Association of Southeast Asian Nations (ASEAN). Intraregional groupings such as ASEAN are suspicious of the Pacific community idea because they see in it an effort to limit the less powerful Asian societies' autonomy in dealing with the outside world. Under conditions of unequal development, the efforts of societies such as the United States and Japan, themselves transregional world economies, to establish a Pacific community appear easily and justifiably as efforts to reserve for themselves a Pacific domain and restrict the autonomy of other (weaker) societies in the region while preserving their own autonomy as world powers.

The Pacific discourse, then, appears from these alternative perspectives as a discourse intended to suppress contradictions fundamental to the Pacific as a regional construct. The authors of the chapters in this volume seek from different perspectives to bring to the surface some of the central contradictions imbedded in the Pacific discourse as products of its formation historically. In the introduction here, I can only summarize the more prominent of these contradictions:

1. Contradiction between area and region: this is the contradiction between the Pacific as physical geography and the Pacific as a product of human activity that I have discussed above. It is the latter that gives meaning to the concept of the Pacific—but also problematizes it. In the Pacific's formation, and to this day, not all areas of the Pacific are included within the region. At the same time, areas outside of the Pacific's boundaries have played a significant part in its formation. Bostonians were active in the Pacific before there was a U.S. West Coast; and such a key player in the Pacific today as Australia was a product of the region's formation initially.

2. Contradiction between the Pacific as EuroAmerican invention and its Asian content, both in terms of people's movements and in terms of Asia (East Asia) as a node in the movement of commodities. These motions, which in a concrete sense helped in the formation of the Pacific as a region also continue to be a source of opposition and division, economically, politically, and culturally. I need not say more about this contradiction here, because as the "principal contradiction" of the Asia-Pacific region, or idea, it enters in a basic sense all the contradictions enumerated here.

3. Contradiction between fantasy and actuality: there is a Pacific of actuality. But there is also a Pacific of fantasy. The one has nourished the other. European fantasies of immense wealth in the Pacific were responsible for luring Europeans to the Pacific. The same Pacific, however, has served to extend the frontiers of capitalist development. This fantasy presently drives capitalist utopianisms. The irony here (or is it tragedy?) is that EuroAmerican expansion into the Pacific has led to the destruction of the very "paradise" that EuroAmericans fantasized about—from the destruction of entire peoples physically and culturally (especially in the South Pacific) to ecological destruction.

4. Contradiction between Asia-Pacific and the world system of which Asia-Pacific is a region. This is a contradiction within capitalism. The contradiction has become especially conspicuous as capitalism has become deterritorialized with the emergence of what has been called "global capitalism" or "flexible production"; that capitalism, in other words, that is based on a "new international division of labor" in production and is no longer nationally based but located in the narratives of transnational corporations. The Asia-Pacific idea as a conceptual construct that emerged in the 1960s may well be a product of efforts to "reterritorialize" capital, by establishing realms of control for transnational capital in constant competition internally. The effort has also brought to the surface different modes of produc-

tion and organization within the capitalist mode of production (products of the development of capitalism itself from individualistic to managerial capitalism) that are presented nevertheless in terms of an older cultural vocabulary, especially the vocabulary of Eastern-Western cultures (themselves, ironically, products of a European cultural expansionism fueled by capitalist development).

5. Contradictions between region, subregion, and nation: vis-à-vis the capitalist world system, Asia-Pacific might represent an effort to define and control one area of the world as a preserve of economic powers of world scope (such as the United States and Japan). Viewed from within the region, efforts to define or institutionalize a Pacific region appear also as attacks on subregional groupings (and divisions of labor), as well as attacks on the autonomy of nations to determine their fate. In a situation of inequality, a regional "community" serves only to disguise the subjection of individual nations and ethnic groups to the imperatives of a regional economy dominated by the powerful. The Filipina writer quoted above observes that an earlier term for the Pacific community was "co-prosperity sphere." That the initiatives for a Pacific community have come from the OECD nations within the Pacific underlines the plausibility of this fear. Again, the global capitalism of the present reveals how real this fear is. The Pacific First World supplies the capital; the Pacific Third World supplies the labor. The situation has been complicated by the entry into the scene of the Pacific Second World, the so-called socialist society of China, which uses socialism to control labor costs so as to make China competitive with other Pacific societies.

6. The contradiction, therefore, is not just between region, subregions, and nations, but between capital and classes/genders. The terminology of First, Second, and Third worlds becomes irrelevant as parts of Log Angeles become a Third World, and Manila and Hong Kong turn into centers of capital. As the transnational corporations become genuinely transnational, the terminology of imperialism (and of Leninist Marxism) becomes largely irrelevant, because the managers of capital become authentically international. So does the working class, in actuality if not in consciousness. The "new international division of labor" recruits its laborers where it can and moves around laborers as it moves around capital. Most conspicuous in Asia-Pacific production are women from this or that Pacific Third World who, faced with the choice between starvation and exploitation, move around the area, selling everything from their labor to their bodies. Of a Sunday afternoon, downtown Victoria island in "miracle" Hong Kong is a veritable sea of Filipinas, who also fuel the sex industries of Japan. Sexual fantasy has been a component of the Pacific fantasy ever since the first European set foot in Tahiti; sex tourism is today one of the booming industries of Asia-Pacific.

7. Cultural contradictions at various levels: between the EuroAmerican Pacific and the Asian Pacific, between different cultural formations within

the Asia-Pacific, and between regional forces of cultural homogenization and local resistances to it; all articulated within the context of a consumer culture that has spread throughout the area from the capitalist nodes in Los Angeles, Tokyo, and Hong Kong. We have already referred to the first contradiction between EuroAmerican and Asian-Pacific cultures. Examples of the second type of contradiction are dissonances between the "Confucian" cultures of East Asia, the Islamic and Buddhist cultures of Southeast Asia, and the Hispanic cultures of the Philippines and Latin America. In the midst of these broader cultural dissonances are efforts, such as those among the many ethnic groups in the area and on the Pacific islands, to assert some measure of local cultural identity.

NOTES

1. For a more comprehensive discussion of the issues raised in this introduction, see Arif Dirlik, "The Asia-Pacific Idea: Reality and Representation in the Invention of a Regional Structure," *Journal of World History* 3, no. 1 (Spring 1992): 55–79.

2. O.H.K. Spate, "'South Sea' to 'Pacific Ocean,'" *Journal of Pacific History* 12 (1977): 210.

3. O.H.K. Spate, *Paradise Lost and Found,* vol. 3 of *The Pacific Since Magellan* (Minneapolis: University of Minnesota Press, 1988), 211.

4. See the discussion in *New Perspectives Quarterly* (NPO) 9, no. 1 (Winter 1992), especially the interview with Lee Kuan Yew, the foremost proponent of a "Confucian capitalism" as the former prime minister of Singapore. There is more than irony in the representation as a model of "communitarian capitalism" of the fascist state Lee Kuan Yew brought into existence in Singapore.

5. For an example, see Ian Buruma's review of Michael Crichton's *Rising Sun,* "It Can't Happen Here," *New York Review of Books* 39, no. 8 (April 23, 1992): 3. According to Buruma, *Kirkus Reviews* found in *Rising Sun,* "the return of the 'Yellow Menace'"—in a "three-piece suit."

6. Valera Quisumbing in Jose P. Leviste, Jr., ed., *The Pacific Lake: Philippine Perspectives on a Pacific Community* (Manila: Philippine Council for Foreign Relations, 1986), 81.

7. For a history of the discourse on the Pacific and efforts to institutionalize a Pacific community, see the appendix in Leviste, *The Pacific Lake.* Hadi Soesastro and Han Sung-joo, eds., *Pacific Economic Cooperation: The Next Phase* (Jakarta: Centre for Strategic and International Studies, 1982) also contains a summary history of these efforts, as well as contributions by those who have played key roles in the process. For the U.S. perspective, see W. W. Rostow, *The United States and the Regional Organization of Asia and the Pacific, 1965–1985* (Austin: University of Texas Press, 1986).

ALEXANDER WOODSIDE **2**

The Asia-Pacific Idea as a Mobilization Myth

*T*HE RECENT HISTORY of the Asia-Pacific region has been converted into a myth, or sacred narrative, which invites the fulfillment of a certain kind of future, rather than just explaining and justifying one version of an ideologically contested past. Political, economic, and academic elites on both sides of the Pacific use the myth to protect programs and policies in the present to which such elites have become attached, and to mobilize people for their future achievement. Relatively commonplace observations of contemporary reality become transmuted into visions of governments' (or universities') sense of the future meaning of reality in relation to themselves and to the peoples they govern or instruct.

Such visions have their fervidly utopian side, as expressed in books like the U.S. futurologist John Naisbitt's *Megatrends 2000*, published in 1990. In Chapter 6 of his book, entitled "The Rise of the Pacific Rim," Naisbitt and his co-author make relatively modest predictions about the immediate future in Asia: Japan rather than France will lead the world in the 1990s in fashion, design, and the arts; Korea, "heir to the samurai's crown," may overtake Japan economically by the year 2010; "the whole world is moving toward greater democracy and China will follow," despite what happened in China in June 1989; in the world economy, "education is the Pacific Rim's competitive edge," and allegedly greater investment in education will allow Asian-Pacific countries to maintain their economic ascendancy.[1] But Naisbitt's ultimate conclusions storm the futurological heavens with their optimism: "On the threshold of the millennium, long the symbol of humanity's golden age, we possess the tools and the capacity to build utopia here and now. ... The Pacific Rim has rewritten the history of economic development, jumping right over the industrial period and into the information economy, where the important resources do come not from the ground but from people."[2] Naisbitt, evidently, is widely read in the Asian countries he describes or invents. His earlier *Megatrends* book, for example, was quickly translated into

13

Chinese and published in China by the prestigious Chinese Social Sciences Publishing House.[3]

Apart from its utopia builders, the Pacific Rim prophetic culture also has its less euphoric medicine men, obsessed with the need to find cures for stagnating economies on the Western side of the rim. A good recent example of a minimum version of such reformism may be found in S. B. Linder's book, *The Pacific Century: Economic and Political Consequences of Asian-Pacific Dynamism*, published in 1986. Asserting that the Pacific region is too "heterogeneous" to rely on "particularized growth theories," Linder rejects the claims that Asian-Pacific economic prosperity is due to Confucianism or to the Japanese national character or to East Asia's supposed traditional reverence for education (for which Linder's index does not even have a reference). Rather, Linder sees the secret of Asian-Pacific economic dynamism as being nothing more than the region's apotheosis of export-oriented market economies, relying upon historic policies that once gave the rich Western countries their own affluence. "It is exciting to see these policies succeeding again."[4] However valid it might be, the self-congratulatory argument that Japanese or South Korean economic success might come in effect from an adoption of the principles of the nineteenth-century British economy, is clearly meant to be confidence building for Westerners. Beleaguered nineteenth-century Chinese conservative intellectuals' rhetorical supposition that Western chemistry had all been invented by *Zhuangzi* was meant to comfort them in the same way.

We meet a more extreme version of the sort of reform proposals the Pacific Rim prophetic culture inspires in recent books like the veteran U.S. journalist Robert Elegant's *Pacific Destiny*, published in 1990. Elegant concludes this huge book:

> We must now take a profound lesson from the patient perseverance that is central to the Asian ethos: the tenacious accretion of power and virtue that lies beneath the dazzling surface of present-day Asians. ... Asian societies do change, sometimes dramatically. But they change only after attaining an almost mystical consensus regarding their new course—and the old values endure. Individualistic Westerners living in laissez-faire societies are unaccustomed to arriving at fundamental decisions by such patient and profound processes.

To hold their own in the Asia-Pacific region, Elegant counsels, Western countries do not need "authoritarianism, which could cripple initiative, but a structured consensus such as normally prevails in wartime."[5]

Despite this apocalyptic language, Elegant, Linder, and Naisbitt are agreed that, in Naisbitt's words, "The rise of the East need not mean the decline of the West."[6] Writers like Elegant are really vulgar latter-day mercantile Leibnizes; they preach the need for a synthesis, or convergence, of Asian and Western economic planning behavior, just as Leibniz's far more sublime

Novissima Sinica once pleaded for an East-West synthesis in natural theology, to be aided by the stationing of Confucian missionaries in Europe.

This particular renewal of the old dream of convergence implies that the West should conform at least in part to an "Asian" example. Technically, moreover, the idea of an Asia-Pacific economic community itself seems to have originated in Asia, in Japan in the middle of the 1960s. As the Beijing economist Luo Yuanzheng, himself the author of significant Chinese books and articles on the subject, has pointed out, Japanese politicians, and famous Japanese economists like Kojima Kiyoshi, proposed the notion of a Pacific Ocean free trade zone in the 1960s, only to meet with a rebuff from the United States and caution elsewhere; the U.S. attitude underwent a "major" change and became far more receptive only in the late 1970s.[7] Yet the paradox is that the Pacific Rim prophetic culture, like much of the rest of Pacific Rim thought, is as Arif Dirlik has rightly argued, a "EuroAmerican construct" whose imaginative hegemony is in Western hands.[8] It is surely significant that most of the roots of such thought may be traced back in the West to a time when no Japanese-made or Korean-made machines of any kind offered the slightest threat to Western countries' manufacturers.

If we merely confine ourselves to Britain's hegemonic "invention" of Japan before World War I, we could cite Alfred Stead's book *Great Japan: A Study of National Efficiency* (1905), in the preface of which a former British prime minister (Lord Rosebery) praised the Japanese for their patriotism and self-discipline; or *A Modern Utopia* (also 1905), by H. G. Wells, in which the members of Wells's ideal ruling elite were called "samurai"; or *Universities and National Life* (1911), by the British cabinet minister R. B. Haldane, who also urged British students to imitate the "disciplinarianism" of the Japanese.[9] Despite the Pacific Rim futurologists' exhilarating reminders of the inadequacy of our inherited conceptual schemes and paradigms for understanding the future, the main modes of their own thought are hardly new.

Three principal such modes are easily detected. The first one might be called Saint-Simonianism, in honor of the French thinker of the early nineteenth century who located the golden age in the future, not the past, and anticipated a future industrial civilization, ruled by an elite of scientists and engineers, undergoing repeated progressive transformations in which supposedly more primitive political struggles disappeared or were marginalized. The second mode of thought could obviously be said to be a genteel social Darwinism—the belief in a competitive struggle between civilizations in varying degrees of economic fitness—minus the original social Darwinism's tedious fascination with national physique sizes, and with the possibility of peace and prosperity for all through convergence benignly substituted for the older, more brutal outcome of the wholesale elimination of unfit civilizations. (Linder, for example, says that there must be "adjustment without tears.") The third mode of thought, as Elegant's moonshine about the "al-

most mystical consensus" of the "Asian ethos" suggests, is Orientalism. A series of reductive analytical categories is applied to Asian societies, with the
object of savoring the exotic profundity of their differences from the West
and then making this a stimulus to mission-oriented action of some kind; although again a hope of redemption through convergence softens the process.

One could add to these three modes the chief U.S. extension of them, particularly of the Saint-Simonian mode: a cybernetics-flavored managerialism
that stresses "communications" research and seeks to control the effects of
technological change through the measurement of "feedback" information
about the intended and unintended consequences of such change. If Asian
societies enjoyed the "mystical" powers of consensus building that Robert
Elegant and others attribute to them, they would presumably have only a
weak interest in such forms of political management. In fact such techniques,
dressed up as theory, have become a major U.S. export to Asia. In the 1960s,
for example, the U.S. National Aeronautics and Space Administration mobi-
lized U.S. "communications" researchers like Raymond Bauer to study such
unintended and potentially damaging "second order consequences" of the
terrestrial expansion of the NASA space exploration empire as the displacement of local businesses by NASA land acquisitions. "Social indicators" research was born. The Chinese National Statistics Bureau transferred it, giving full credit to NASA and to Raymond Bauer, to China in the early 1980s;
by 1987 the Chinese Ministry of Public Security had its own "Public Security
Statistical Indicators System," complete with 470 separate "indicators" of
"social order," "public security," and "safeguard prerequisites."[10]

Of course not all these inspirations are fully shared by everyone who
writes about the Pacific Rim. But the cardinal modes of Pacific Rim thought,
whether they are found in the heads of Western economists or Chinese police
officers, usually do serve the overall purposes of what Gao Fang—a politics
professor at People's University in Beijing, and one of the few serious present-day Chinese critics of U.S. futurologists like Alvin Toffler—calls international capitalist utopianism.[11] The Pacific Rim prophetic culture in its current form could probably not survive an abrupt or cataclysmic termination
of the extraordinary prolonged boom global capitalism has enjoyed since
World War II.

In the meantime, however, the prophecies, which are essentially Western
in origin, do not just respond to the possible realities in the Asia-Pacific region, they go far to shape and create them. One of the contemporary Pacific
Rim's most noteworthy cultural transactions is the spread of their practical
influence. Consider agriculture. Toffler is perhaps the Asia-Pacific region's
most popular Saint-Simonian prophet. He suggested in his book *The Third
Wave* in 1980 that economically lagging countries like China could bypass
earlier strategies of modernization by means of previously unexampled
"postindustrial" breakthroughs in education and in high technology. The

"Third Wave leads us in unconventional directions. ... Ultimately we may see the convergence of weather modification, computers, satellite monitoring, and genetics to revolutionize the world's food supply."[12] In 1983 Toffler paid what could be called a state visit to China, as the guest of Premier Zhao Ziyang and the Chinese Academy of Social Sciences, lecturing to audiences in Beijing and Shanghai who "listened to him as if he were an oracle."[13] When a Chinese language version of *The Third Wave* appeared in 1984, purged of its anti-Marxist references, it became one of China's great modern best-sellers, selling more than 13,000 copies in the city of Changsha alone in the first six months of 1985. Young Chinese research scholars publicly informed their superiors that Toffler's thought was the truth and that Marxism was moribund.[14]

The chief traces of the Toffler cult's contribution to the construction of the technocratic side of Pacific Rim thought are probably to be found in the more than 5,000 national "research and development organs" or government think tanks that proliferated in China by the end of the 1980s. The Chinese State Council's Village Development Research Center, for instance, published a massive work (almost 700,000 words) in 1985, *Zhongguo nongcun fazhan zhanlue wenti* (Strategic problems of the development of Chinese villages), which called in a Tofflerian manner for the introduction into China of intellectualized farming, or "thinking agriculture" (*sikao nongye*). Such wonders as plant genetics could be used to transcend earlier "developmental models."[15] Numerous references to, or invocations of, Toffler could be found in the hundreds of economic development journals that flourished in China in the same decade. Thus one Chinese researcher, calling in 1987 for a transfer of "surplus labor" out of Chinese agriculture, said that this transfer could not occur without a rise in the peasants' cultural and technological levels. But Toffler's enthusiasm for educational sky satellites, he added, had shown how this could be made to happen.[16]

That the times are so propitious for the reception of such optimistic futurology on the Asian side of the Pacific Rim is probably to be explained by the buoyant expectations associated with East and Southeast Asia's recent economic success. At least fourteen Asian countries or units had annual economic growth rates of 6 percent or more in 1984, a benchmark year in the transfer of the newer Saint-Simonianism across the Pacific. Moreover, optimism about the miraculous powers of science and technology is perhaps more likely in countries for which the experience of industrialization is relatively recent. It is less seductive in more middle-aged industrial societies where familiarity with the costs of science and technology is greater, and which may thus suffer from what some analysts have jokingly called "development fatigue." The Asia-Pacific region may well be riddled not merely with trade imbalances, but with psychological imbalances related to national variations in the loss of industrial innocence. But why are there so few

Chinese or Thai or Indonesian or Vietnamese Alvin Tofflers or John
Naisbitts? Why is the futurological business the reverse of the car-making
and shipbuilding businesses, with the intellectual trade deficits apparently all
occurring in Asia?

One answer to this question would point to cultural differences. People
with rich historical consciousnesses are rarely good futurologists. Left to
their own devices, most East Asians and Southeast Asians might well continue to be tempted to think of the future on the basis of more thickly historical models than would (say) Americans. Although the term "Asia-Pacific region" is current on both sides of the Pacific, the very different formula
"Pacific Rim" seems to be most fashionable in the English-speaking Pacific
democracies, with some important echoes also in Japan. Whatever its practical usefulness to physical scientists like oceanographers or seismographers,
the notion of a "rim" induces us to think of the Pacific community as a frontier. On the Western side of the Asia-Pacific region, it undoubtedly reflects
the traditionally positive view of frontiers in North America as historically
almost virgin realms where humankind could be remade. As always, John
Naisbitt marks this triumphant return of the old frontier myth with the least
subtlety and the most parochialism: "The Pacific Rim is emerging like a dynamic young America but on a much grander scale."[17]

On the Asian side, fewer people are capable of thinking of the Asia-Pacific
region as an open-ended frontier, as a sort of giant inequality-transcending
Homestead Act of the imagined future. A Chinese economist like Ma
Bohuang of Shanghai stubbornly writes about the Pacific community in
more prosaic terms, as being merely the modern world's fifth great epoch in
the exploration of the development of export-directed economies, albeit a
more culturally demanding one than the earlier four epochs, a series he sees
as beginning in Europe in the sixteenth century.[18] On the rare occasions
when Chinese do imagine the Pacific community as a frontier, they do so in
much more dialectical terms of cultural collision and confrontation. Thus in
the memorable last episode of Su Xiaokang's sensational Chinese television
series "River Elegy" in 1988, the supposedly ugly, despotism-engendering
Yellow River is urged to surrender to the beautiful great blue Pacific Ocean
beyond it that allegedly bears democracy on its waters.

A second, more simple kind of answer to this question might suggest that
although many Asian intellectuals and politicians are wishful consumers of
the products of the region's prophetic culture, actual history so far has given
far fewer of them the confidence to be extravagant creators of its more flam-
boyant visions. Ma Bohuang, the Shanghai social scientist just quoted,
stated baldly in 1988 that China was too weak to do what Japan, Taiwan, or
South Korea had done and convert other countries into being China's own
commercial goods markets or suppliers of raw materials, and use its scientific and technological superiority to "control" the "labor services" of other

countries' people.[19] Thus there could be no common Asia-Pacific region strategy based on such an ambition. Is China even properly one of the countries of the Asia-Pacific myth, with all of the advantages attributed sometimes to such countries by Western futurologists? Or is the Asia-Pacific region ideology a device for supplanting a very different earlier agenda more concerned with the tragedy of the world's "North-South divide" between haves and have-nots? The battle of agenda-defining metaphors here is hardly just academic. The older North-South divide runs right through the newer Pacific Rim, as a genuine fault line between its richer and poorer countries, if no longer the most fashionable apocalyptic symbol of the world's unperfected present. And there are still many Asian "Asia-Pacific" thinkers, like China's Ma Bohuang and others, who are driven to preserve both agenda-defining metaphors, rather like the late medieval scholars in Europe who tried to accommodate both the geocentric and heliocentric views of the universe.

The technological innovations the Pacific Rim prophetic culture celebrates are, of course, perfectly real. If ever there were a master institution of the emerging Pacific Rim community of which a Toffler or a Naisbitt might approve, with their interest in genetic engineering and the international diffusion of science, it would surely be the International Rice Research Institute in the Philippines. It is responsible for some of the Asia-Pacific region's most significant technological transfers so far. Since about 1970, for example, Vietnam, though the victim of an unrelenting U.S. trade embargo, has imported and widely planted more than fifty different fast-growing, high-yield IRRI rice strains, with the tangible result being an annual increase in Vietnam's rice productivity of about one million tons of paddy each year. The traditional Vietnamese farming world of inadequate fifth-month and tenth-month rice crops has vanished.

But the prophetic culture goes beyond the mere description of obvious economic and scientific transactions like this externally inspired agricultural revolution. Vietnamese elite thinkers now try to consolidate imaginatively this limited but real scientific internationalization of Vietnamese village life by redefining Vietnamese villages themselves in the "contemporary scientific language" of "management studies" as "open systems" (*he thong mo* in newspeak Vietnamese)—to quote from a recent study of a north Vietnamese village by two well-known Hanoi social psychologists.[20]

Within Vietnam's thousands of years of history, this is an extraordinary change in the elite conception of what a village is. A century ago, the Vietnamese elite hardly thought of villages as being "open systems." They thought of them as being religious communities, with their own tutelary deities, located inside a greater national hierarchy of religious communities. The new notion of villages as "open systems" is an elite image, borrowed from the largely U.S. storehouse of Asia-Pacific region managerial vocabulary, which still has only an imperfect capacity to summarize actual Vietnamese village life. In the 1980s, indeed, the Vietnamese army had to be used to naturalize the new definition of the village as an "open system," in the sense that most of the villagers who left their supposedly "open" villages were young men conscripted into the army: they learned scientific skills outside the village, while in the army, and then supposedly brought the skills back with them if they returned. That the minds of the villagers who must stay put and harvest the new IRRI rice crops—poorly educated, middle-aged Vietnamese females—remain quite remote from Pacific Rim "scientific language" is suggested by the fact that the Vietnamese government must recurrently round up the legions of soothsayers, fortune-tellers, and sorceresses who still exist in abundance in rural Vietnam and make them sign statements promising to give up their occupations. They must, in other words, give up their efforts to continue to define village life in the prescientific magical way. The old prophets do not mix well with the new ones.

Thus it might be useful to think of the intellectual construction of the emerging Asia-Pacific community in anthropological terms, as involving—in the long run—the imposition from above of an alien and complex new Great Tradition of thought—especially managerial and scientist as well as scientific thought—upon villages all over China and Southeast Asia. In the short run, however, the belief in an Asia-Pacific community described above amounts to less than the regional internationalization of even a single ruling-class ideology that genuinely unites diverse political elites on both sides of the Pacific in the pursuit of common goals or shared interests. What the belief does is more modest. It helps to maintain separate national elites with an identical concern for its perpetuation in very uneasy coexistence with each other, while encouraging them to think that they must take greater account of each other than they need take of the vast populations they govern. In its early stages the acceptance of the belief is more the sum of provisional elite alliances within a large region than it is the reflection of even the beginning of the unification of an "Asia-Pacific" consciousness that might weaken the region's far-flung ethnic or racial divisions.

On the surface, political leaders on the Asian if not on the North American side of the Pacific Rim have taken full account of this. As the Chinese Foreign Minister Qian Qichen told a Chinese audience at the end of 1989, the national differences within the Asia-Pacific region—uneven economic development levels; differences in "social systems" and "ideology"; dissimilarities in language, religion, and culture—make the emergence of an integrated or "organic" security system there, comparable to that of the European Community, "impossible."[21] Few politicians in power apply the language of a Toffler or a Linder to the continuingly sin-riddled landscape of international relations, which—unlike armchair economics—stubbornly resists easy utopianization. The most fashionable and superficial way of exploring the region's disharmonies is to point to the fact that its states are less similar in size and in assets than the European states. A huge and provocative dispro-portion in power or potential power is said to exist between China, Japan, India, and the United States on the one hand, and all the other countries, not excluding Indonesia, on the other.

In this context, the one enormous problem of how to coexist with Japa-nese power necessarily haunts the government-sponsored research centers and think tanks that proliferated in China and in some Southeast Asian countries in the 1980s. Discussing the advent of the "new Pacific era" in 1985, one Shanghai political economist foresaw three possible outcomes, all centered upon Japan. The first was that the future industrial successes of the region's other countries would undermine the Japanese economy, forcing it into allegedly European-style conditions of "structural stagnation" and un-employment; the second was that Japan would adapt harmoniously to her new Asian competitors and would work out a new "horizontal" division of labor with them, involving genuinely cooperative regional industrial diversi-fication; the third was that Japan would preserve the old, unequal "vertical" division of labor between itself and other Asian countries, constantly rein-vesting its profits in improving its technologies and competitive edge. He concluded that the first possibility "underestimated" the vitality of the Japa-nese; the second possibility was "ideal" but unlikely, in part because of the limited capacities of the other Asian countries; the third possibility was thus the most reasonable prediction, though it falsely assumed that relations be-tween states could be "frozen" in such unequal circumstances.[22] The barely disguised paternalism of some Japanese policymakers toward Southeast Asia, if not China, reflects their probable confidence in the third scenario. As a Japanese Ministry of International Trade and Industry official wrote in 1984, Japan's duty to Southeast Asia was similar to the European duty to Af-rica or the U.S. duty to Latin America.[23] There is a tension between the im-plicit state-transcending egalitarianism of the Asia-Pacific myth and much older reflexes for imagining regional relationships that continue in unre-formedly hierarchical ways.

But this tension is merely the symptom of larger and more treacherous ones. The pretense in the Asia-Pacific myth that it portends some regionally specific "ethos" of economic success that can belong to or be imitated by ev-eryone masks the absences of any common moral culture across the region. Back in 1944, a famous British analyst of the European colonial order in Southeast Asia, J. S. Furnivall, described Dutch-ruled Indonesia as a "plural society" in which various ethnic groups—the Dutch, the Eurasians, the Chi-nese, various kinds of Indonesians—lived side by side, interacting with each other economically, without having any discernible "common will" or com-mon social conscience. The marketplace was their only common ground. As Furnivall put it: "The fundamental character of the organization of a plural

society as a whole is indeed the structure of a factory, organized for production, rather than of a state, organized for the good life of its members." In
such a "plural society," the moral apartness of the various ethnic groups, in
outlook and in standards, meant that capitalism was freed of all restrictions
other than those imposed by written laws, which were themselves underdeveloped. There was, therefore, a concentration on materialism, and on
purely economic ends, that was far more complete and absolute in the colonized Indies than in the West European homeland of capitalism itself.[24]
What Furnivall wrote about the islands of the Indonesian archipelago in the
1940s might well be pressed into service to cover the regional Asia-Pacific
society of the 1990s. It is a factory-like "plural society" of the Furnivallian
sort writ large. The highly technocratic nature of the Asia-Pacific myth does
little to create even the rudiments of a moral "common will" that might cross
ethnic barriers.

The result is that the myth mobilizes the poor of the region without representing them. Evangelical "Pacific Century" theorists such as S. B. Linder argue that the "basic commonality" of the region that explains its prosperity is
that the Asia-Pacific economies are all "market economies"; interventionist
government policies are supposedly not one of the region's talismanic "commonalities."[25] In Southeast Asia, at least, the facts qualify if they do not con-
found this generalization. As of 1990, the Indonesian government wholly
owned at least 189 companies, ranging from Garuda Airlines to Krakatau
Steel to fertilizer maker Pupuk Kujang. In the lucrative regional cigarette industry, government tobacco monopolies reigned supreme in such countries
as Thailand and China, and high import duties, enforced licensing systems,
or limits on the foreign ownership of cigarette making otherwise controlled
the huge cigarette markets of Indonesia, the Philippines, and Malaysia.[26]
Even in Singapore, such crucial assets as shipyards were owned by govern-
ment-controlled companies. Monarchies with royal business monopolies,
not free trade traditions, shaped the precolonial economic history of the region. Even today the Thai royal family is the largest shareholder in Southeast
Asia's biggest cement producer, the Siam Cement Company.

The real key to much of the economic success on the Asian side of the Pacific Rim is the repression of the consumption rates of subaltern social
groups and classes. Here is the authentic similarity the region has with industrializing nineteenth-century Britain, although most Asia-Pacific futurologists hardly emphasize it. The region's working people still possess what
Walter Bagehot once memorably called, with reference to the nineteenth-century lower-class English, the "deferential" reflexes of incompletely
defeudalized lives. For the average Western citizen, it is probably enterprises
like the expanding Western cruise ship industry that make this situation
most obvious: it would hardly be viable without Indonesian and Filipino
sailors. The deference, of course, is a product of repression as well as of cus-

tom. Roy Hofheinz and Kent Calder, who do raise this issue of consumption control at least obliquely, are right to explain Singapore's triumphs by pointing to the Central Provident Fund. This was a compulsory savings scheme, initiated by the Singapore government in 1955, that allowed that government to impose the highest savings rate in the world upon its people, in the interests of obtaining capital for industrial expansion.[27]

It is not fashionable anywhere in the Pacific Rim these days to use the strength of labor unions as a touchstone of progress. But it is worth comparing the percentage of workers who were unionized, even in tame government-manipulated unions, on the Southeast Asian and Australasian sides of the Pacific, as of 1986: 4.8 percent of the Indonesian work force; 8.7 percent of the Malaysian work force; 1.1 percent of the Thai workforce; but 42 percent of the Australian work force and 52 percent of that of New Zealand.[28] Some Southeast Asian governments (for example, Malaysia) have guaranteed foreign investors that there will be no "union disturbances" in such countries' "free trade zones," where workers are not allowed to join unions.

The repressed popular consumption rates in Asia that Asia-Pacific rhetoricians take for granted without acknowledging as central to what reality their myth possesses will not vanish soon. These rates are linked to the continued cohesion of military governments such as the one in Indonesia that "virtually wiped out bodies which articulated the interests of less privileged groups" during the mass killings in Indonesian villages in 1965–1966.[29] But they are linked also to the region's high rate of population growth, which hardly favors lower-class bargaining positions. The "deference" of the lower classes in Southeast Asia, such as it is, is also partly cultural, just as it was in Walter Bagehot's Victorian England. The tropical Neo-Victorianism of the Pacific Rim features the same situation of technological change occurring more rapidly than cultural or political defeudalization.

Nineteenth-century Thai society, for example, was organized like a hierarchical military regiment, in which there were nine or more different status pronouns just for the word "I," and noble patrons commanded commoner clients; contemporary analysts suggest that Thailand remains an "as you please, sir" political culture, with little consciousness of individual rights that could be exercised against politically superior people.[30] The eminent journalist Mochtar Lubis charges his fellow Indonesians with preserving a timeless "feudal mentality" in which underlings submissively serve their bosses or "fathers" (*bapak*).[31] In Vietnam, neotraditional forms of state exploitation of the peasants, such as labor conscription laws that compel each adult male between the ages of eighteen and forty-five to donate ten days a year of unpaid labor to the state (as in a law of 1988) reflect the survival of premodern village expectations about corvée labor, not merely a dictatorship with Stalinist characteristics that are weakening only slowly. One remembers Matthew Arnold's comment in nineteenth-century England that railways were dealing a death blow to feudalism; it is possible that labor transfers within the contemporary Pacific Rim (more than 600,000 Filipinos were registered to work outside their country in 1990; hundreds of thousands of Vietnamese workers were sent to the Soviet Union and eastern Europe in the 1980s) may eventually have a similar effect there. But the advanced techno-logical achievements the Asia-Pacific myth celebrates, such as the genetic re-designing of Southeast Asian agriculture, occur in a far less advanced moral universe. About this fact the myth has little to say.

In its present form, the Asia-Pacific myth mobilizes the poor of the region for economic production without representing or encouraging their political and social claims. Yet it does provide one important palliative in the realm of ethnic or racial relations, which is not greatly discussed by the usual archi-tects of the myth but cannot be ignored. The myth rationalizes and gives op-timistic coloring to a formidable historical event: the de-Westernization or cultural diversification of capitalism, and the shift of its center of gravity. White Euro-American capitalism has been in relative decline, in much of Southeast Asia at least, since the 1940s and 1950s; the myth makes the gi-gantic contemporary capture by the Japanese and Asian offshore Chinese of that system seem like an inevitable stage in a common enterprise of human improvement. The moderation of the relations among the three hegemonic business cultures in the region—the Japanese one, the Chinese one, and the Western one—is not easy. Tensions exist between the two "Asian" capital-isms, as well as between Japanese or ethnic Chinese capitalism on the one hand and Western businesses on the other. One Japanese scholar recently even went so far as to accuse the ethnic Chinese business world in Southeast Asia of being "ersatz capitalism," because of its supposed cronyism and pref-erence for licensed monopolies over competition.[32] The language of the Asia-Pacific myth, with its invocation of "Third Wave" civilizations and its focus upon the "basic commonalities" of economic prosperity, rhetorically reconciles the tensely coexisting multiple rival capitalisms and usefully blurs potential battle lines among them. Its votaries on both sides of the Pacific Rim become imaginative shareholders in a common utopianized market-place.

But if the Asia-Pacific myth blurs the battle lines among competing ethnic capitalisms, it may sharpen the battle lines between regions within nation-states, and between ethnic majorities and minorities whose identities coin-cide with regional distinctions. Here the effect of the myth can be traced to places a long way away—geographically, that is—from the Pacific. Chinese administrators, for example, in the name of the doctrine that the twenty-first century will be the "century of the Pacific Ocean," inform the restless Turkic peoples in Xinjiang that the Chinese language is the "key" to entering that century and that such minorities should therefore graciously accept the bilin-gual schools they do not want.[33]

In Southeast Asia, the myth undermines the solidarity of whole nation-states that were the recent creations, in many instances, of poetic nationalists. Such nationalists were—in the words of one of them, Indonesia's Sukarno—"bound in spiritual longing by the Romanticism of Revolution," rather than by what a "Pacific century" writer like Linder calls "outward-oriented export strategy." They believed (Sukarno again) that revolutions could not "be measured by the standards of textbooks, even ones written by bald-headed professors from Oxford or Cornell University"; they saw their national future as being "like the melody of a distant *gamelan* on a moonlit night,"[34] rather than a series of sovereignty-surrendering transactions with multinational corporations and international monetary funds. The states they created were fragile, as the artificiality of their names suggests. (The term "Indonesia" was borrowed after World War I by anticolonial patriots in the Netherlands Indies from the writings of anthropologists like Adolf Bastian; Burma and Cambodia have both changed their names at least once in the past twenty years; the country between them changed its name from Siam to Thailand in 1939, after a debate over whether the new name should be spelled Tai or Thai; Malaysia, in political name and substance, came into existence only in the 1960s.) These states sometimes covered territory and people who had no overwhelming historical reasons for belonging to them.

Although a Canadian scholar in particular may have little business being surprised by such a phenomenon, it is nevertheless true that the new Pacific Rim economics stresses the maximization of regional advantages within nation-states, as part of the particularized pursuit of export earnings. This emphasis has political consequences that are yet to be measured in Asia-Pacific countries less psychologically self-contained or ethnically homogeneous as Japan or Korea or Taiwan or Singapore or Hong Kong. Painful regional differences within countries that an earlier generation of nationalists through faith and poetry (and war) had tried to overcome, threaten to reappear. One could cite many examples of regions within Asia-Pacific nation-states in which the relatively pure capitalist economic rationality of the Asia-Pacific mobilizational myth could dissolve the solidarities developed by an earlier nationalism. Aceh, for example; or northeast Thailand; or Mindanao; or Sabah.

South Vietnam might well be the most poignant example. French colonialism in Indochina strengthened an imbalance in Vietnam between a densely populated but economically backward north and a commercial capitalist economy, based far more upon French laws, in the less densely populated south. South Vietnam, because of its more generous land-to-people ratios and its weaker adherence to precapitalist village social and economic norms, then came to dominate the Indochina export trade the French promoted. The port of Saigon exported more than three-quarters of the two million tons of rice French Indochina was shipping abroad by 1907. Vietnamese nationalists attacked such structural imbalances as the legacies of Western economic colonialism. Now they are abruptly transformed into the regional economic superiorities the Pacific Rim celebrates. As one Vietnamese economist recently put it, south Vietnam is better able than north Vietnam to make a "military breakthrough" in "infiltrating" the Asia-Pacific economy with its exports.[35] The policymaking corollaries of this rhetorical militarization of regional advantages are far from trivial. They lead to proposals that all state investment in agriculture in Vietnam be concentrated in the south's Mekong delta, rather than divided evenhandedly between the Mekong delta and the Red River delta up in the north—where more people live, and where malnutrition is pervasive.[36]

Like Siva, the Asia-Pacific myth both creates and destroys. Insofar as it remains a capitalist myth, it renews an old tendency of capitalism to rationalize all behavior in the name of economic production. Despite a pretense of satisfying more general millennial human cravings that transcend economics, in practice the myth works against noneconomic faiths and spiritual concerns. For better of for worse, it contributes to the imaginative dispossession of much postwar Asian revolutionary nationalism, especially with respect to internal stability and ethnic self-assertion. The economics of the myth have a partial kinship with the more classical colonial economic arrangements of the prewar period that several generations of Asian nationalists condemned. It remains to be seen how provocative this kinship will prove to be in any major future regional trade breakdowns.

NOTES

1. John Naisbitt and Patricia Aburdene, *Megatrends 2000: Ten New Directions for the 1990's* (New York: Avon Books, 1991), pp. 184–227.

2. Ibid., pp. 336–337.

3. For an interesting Chinese discussion of the Chinese interest in the writings of such U.S. futurologists as Naisbitt, Alvin Toffler, and Daniel Bell, see the article by Shao Wenjie in *Guangming ribao,* March 18, 1984, p. 3.

4. Staffan Burenstam Linder, *The Pacific Century: Economic and Political Consequences of Asian-Pacific Dynamism* (Stanford, CA: Stanford University Press, 1986), p. 4.

5. Robert Elegant, *Pacific Destiny: Inside Asia Today* (London: Hamish Hamilton, 1990), pp. 510–511.

6. Naisbitt and Aburdene, *Megatrends 2000*, p. 217.

7. Luo Yuanzheng, *Shijie jinji yu Zhongguo* (The world economy and China) (Changsha: Hunan renmin chubanshe, 1985), pp. 157ff.

8. Arif Dirlik, "The Asia-Pacific Idea: Reality and Representation in the Invention of a Regional Structure," *Journal of World History* 3, no. 1 (Spring 1992), pp. 19, 21.

9. G. R. Searle, *The Quest for National Efficiency: A Study in British Politics and Political Thought 1899–1914* (Oxford: Basil Blackwell, 1971), pp. 57–59.

10. See the discussion in Chinese Academy of Social Sciences, comp., *Zhongguo shehuixue nianjian 1979–1989* (Chinese sociology yearbook, 1979–1989) (Beijing: Zhongguo Dabaike quanshu chubanshe, 1989), pp. 182–188. See also Raymond Bauer, ed., *Social Indicators* (Cambridge, MA, and London: MIT Press, 1966).

11. See Gao Fang, *Ping disanci langchao* (Criticizing *The Third Wave*) (Beijing: Guangming ribao chubanshe, 1986).

12. Alvin Toffler, *The Third Wave* (London: Pan Books, 1981), pp. 350–351.

13. Andrew Mendelsohn, "Alvin Toffler in China: Deng's Big Bang," *New Republic,* April 4, 1988, pp. 15–17.

14. Gao Fang, *Ping disanci langchao,* pp. 1–2 of Preface.

15. Tong Dalin, "Yige xinde 'nongye daguo' jiang chuxian zai shijie shang" (A new agricultural great power is about to appear in the world) in Guowuyuan nongcun fazhan yanjiu zhongxin, comp., *Zhongguo nongcun fazhan zhanlue wenti* (Strategic problems of the development of Chinese villages) (Beijing: Zhongguo nongye keji chubanshe, 1985), pp. 38–41.

16. Yu Mei, "Qianyi Woguo nongye laodongli yu shengyu laodonglide zhuanyi" (A simple comment on our country's agricultural labor force and the transfer of surplus labor), *Zhongguo nongcun jingji* (Chinese village economy journal) (Beijing) 12 (1987), pp. 23–28, especially pp. 27–28.

17. Naisbitt and Aburdene, *Megatrends 2000,* p. 184.

18. Ma Bohuang, "Waixiangxing jingji de jinxi guan" (Present and past conceptions of export-oriented type economies), *Shehui kexue* (Social sciences) (Shanghai) 8 (1988), pp. 32–35.

19. Ibid.

20. See the profile of An Binh village, Hai Hung province, by Nguyen Duc Uy and Bach Van Tho in *Nhan dan* (Hanoi), August 13, 1980, p. 3.

21. See Qian's interview in *Liaowang* (Outlook) (1989), p. 52; as reprinted in *Xinhua yuebao* (New China monthly report) (Beijing) 1 (1990), pp. 162–163.

22. Guo Zhaolie, "Taipingyang xin shiji de daolai he Ya-Tai diqu jidai jiejue de tike" (The advent of the new Pacific Ocean era and questions of the Asia-Pacific region that urgently wait for resolution), *Shehui kexue* (Social sciences) (Shanghai) 1 (1985), pp. 3–6.

23. See Kinju Atarashi, "Japan's Economic Cooperation Policy Towards the ASEAN Countries," *International Affairs* (London) 61, no. 1 (Winter 1984–1985), pp. 110–111.

24. J. S. Furnivall, *Netherlands India: A Study of Plural Economy* (New York: Cambridge University Press, 1944), pp. 350, 446–450.

25. Linder, *The Pacific Century,* pp. 27, 29.

26. See the special feature article by Carl Goldstein et al. in *Far Eastern Economic Review,* 29 March 1990, pp. 62–68.

27. Roy Hofheinz, Jr., and Kent Calder, *The Eastasia Edge* (New York: Basic Books, 1982), pp. 142–144.

28. See the articles by Elizabeth Cheng, Suhaini Aznam, Jose Galang, Paul Handley, Colin James, V. G. Kulkarni, Hamish McDonald, and Paisal Sricharatchanya in *Far Eastern Economic Review,* 3 April 1986, pp. 43–67.

29. Hamish McDonald, *Suharto's Indonesia* (Sydney: Fontana Books, 1981), pp. 171–172.

30. Tulyathep Suwanachinda, as quoted in J.L.S. Girling, *Thailand: Society and Politics* (Ithaca, NY: Cornell University Press, 1981), p. 148.

31. Mochtar Lubis, *The Indonesian Dilemma,* trans. Florence Lamoureux (Singapore: Graham Brash, 1983), pp. 21–23.

32. Yoshihara Kunio, *The Rise of Ersatz Capitalism in Southeast Asia* (Singapore: Oxford University Press, 1988).

33. Ding Wenlou, "Guanyu 'Shuangyu' jiaoxue de sikao" (Reflections on the pedagogy of 'bilingual' education), *Xinjiang shehui kexue* (Xinjiang journal of social sciences) (Urumqi) 6 (1990), pp. 72–75.

34. Herbert Feith and Lance Castles, eds., *Indonesian Political Thinking 1945–1965* (Ithaca, NY: Cornell University Press, 1970), pp. 32, 114, 119.

35. Le Hong Phuc, "Mien nam Viet-Nam trong phan cong lao dong quoc te" (South Vietnam in the international division of labor), *Nghien cuu kinh te* (Journal of economic research) (Hanoi) 8 (1989), pp. 9–15.

36. See the proposal by Nguyen Kien Phuoc in *Nhan dan* (Hanoi), August 22, 1989, p. 3.

Rimspeak; or, The Discourse of the "Pacific Rim"

MOST OF THE literature on the Pacific Rim is prognostic, and most of it isn't very interesting once a year or two of history flits by, disproving predictions and revealing flawed assumptions. Murray Sayle must have agreed with me when he penned this forecast for "the Pacific Rim in the 21st century":

> Britain and Ireland could respectively be Japan's Hong Kong and Macao, well placed for the European entrepot trade, the U.S. will be Japan's fabulously wealthy India, *terre des merveilles,* while Australia can be Japan's Australia, land of rugged adventure and heavy drinking, the appropriate place of exile for Japanese dissidents and remittance men. This would leave only table scraps for the others: Holland, perhaps, for the Indonesians, France for the Vietnamese.[1]

I do not wish here to contribute to this sort of literature on the Pacific Rim, since I find explaining the past or figuring out the present hard enough without moving into a different century, that is, the dawning twenty-first. I would like instead to seek an explanation of the currency of the term, Pacific Rim: where does it come from? The first answer is, currency. In the late 1970s a hue and cry suddenly emerged about the unfolding era of the Pacific, especially up and down the West Coast and particularly among academics trying to find some way to interest donors in funding Asian or international studies. "Pacific Rim" was a discourse searching out its incipient material base, targeted upon exporters with Asian markets, or importers of Asian products.

One example is the Henry Jackson School of International Studies at the University of Washington (where I taught for several years), started in 1978 (although not named for Senator Jackson until 1983), and funded by Boeing, Weyerhauser, and other corporations, in a Seattle that was otherwise sleepwalking into the Pacific century. Another is the newer School of International Relations and Pacific Studies at UC-San Diego. By now we have many other academic centers of "Rim studies."

"Pacific Rim" is not an academic subject so much as a field for academics working in the present and looking toward the future, as well as for transnational technocrats and policymakers. According to the director of the San Diego school, Peter Gourevitch, Pacific Rim inquiry is important for the "two communities who have a need to know: the community of social scientists ... and the community of policymakers."[2] That is an apt summary of one meaning of rim studies: our academic pundits and government policymakers need to know. (But to know *what?*)

Let's call this "Rimspeak," a discourse of recent origin, but one with considerable immanent power. "Pacific Rim" was a construct of the mid-1970s for revaluing East and Southeast Asia, as Westerners (mostly Americans) recognized and defined it, in ways that highlighted some parts and excluded (or occluded) others. The centerpiece of this construct was Japan, a newly risen sun among advanced industrial countries—indeed, "Number One" in Ezra Vogel's perfectly timed book,[3] published in 1979. Organized into the region were "miracle" economies in Japan, South Korea, Taiwan, Hong Kong, Malaysia, and Singapore, with honorable mention for Thailand, the Philippines, Indonesia, and post-Mao (but pre-Tiananmen) China. The miracles were "NICs" (newly industrialized countries) and their story spawned a prolific literature on Asian miracles.[4]

"Miracle" is one trope always found in the rimster's repertoire. Another is "dynamism," as in "dynamism of East Asian-North American relations" (Gourevitch again), or Linder's "Asian-Pacific dynamism."[5] The miracles of the rim, of course, do not truck with Joseph Schumpeter's notion that capitalism's dynamic is through waves of creation and destruction: it is all on the up-and-up, a whoosh of progress transforming the region.

Rimspeak is a curious discourse with a half-life of months or years, depending on the source. Situated in the dynamic present, casting one's eyes to the yet more dynamic future, all things seem possible—until something like the Tiananmen bloodletting demolishes the incorrigible optimism of this genre and sends a handful of recent books to the instant oblivion of secondhand stores. Rimspeak opens a window on the future, but it also clouds one's optic on the present: consider this statement leading off a new book entitled *Pacific Rising* (admittedly one of the more interesting and thoughtful texts in the genre): "Rarely indeed is one fortunate in being able to live through times in which a major shift in the world's history can be seen to be taking place. ... One such event ... came about when the fifty-odd countries now grouped around the Pacific Ocean seemed to take the torch of leadership from those hitherto grouped around the Atlantic. ...[6] A torch passes from Atlantic to Pacific; but into whose hands? Fifty countries including the sultanate of Brunei? The Four (or is it Five?) Tigers? A Japan that went catatonic at the mere hint that it do something significant about Iraq's invasion of Kuwait? And when exactly was that torch passed? (The answer is, of course, that the flame still burns brightly along the Atlantic Rim.)

In the subterranean text of all this palaver about "dynamism," Saint-Simon meets the theory of the Asiatic mode of production, as in: I thought they were vegetating in the teeth of time over there in Asia. But suddenly they make better cars than we do. Behold, a miracle has occurred. Tropes of dynamism and miracles also convey this: capitalist universalism is the only thing I can see; thus I discover the Pacific Rim.

The latter point is not facetious, but precise: the people of the Pacific Rim did not know they inhabited a bustling new sector of the world system until they were told, just as our "Indians" didn't know they were in America (or "West India") until Columbus told them so. "Rim" is a EuroAmerican construct, an invention just like the steam engine, incorporating the region's peoples "into a new inventory of the world"; "Pacific" is a EuroAmerican name in itself, measuring, delineating, and recognizing living space for the people who live there.[7] That these are Western social constructions does not mean that the natives think them unimportant or have self-confident definitions themselves. For example, former Chinese Premier Zhao Ziyang invited certified twenty-first-century rimster Alvin Toffler to lecture at the Academy of Sciences in 1983, to audiences who "listened to him as if he were an oracle."[8]

After the NICs come the pretenders to this throne: pre-NICs, near-NICs, would-be NICs, miracles-in-the-making if they "do the right thing." Take the Philippines, for example: bit of a basket case, not clear if those people know their comparative advantages. Digging itself out of decades of "irrationality" in the mid-1970s, China under the "enlightened" leadership of Deng Xiaoping (after his resurrection and reforms in 1978) might bid fair to make it. By 1991 the newest of the NICs was Thailand, "doing the right thing" by exporting cheaply made goods (and since the mid-1980s, allowing an ocean of Japanese capital to slosh around). Defined out of the Pacific Rim in the 1970s were North Korea, Mao's China, and Indochina—especially Vietnam, which had just won its thirty-years' war, only to find itself in the pale of the rim. OINKs, they were sometimes called: old industrialized kountries. Sometimes Rimspeak ropes in Latin American countries, too. Candidates include post-Allende Chile, *maquiladora* Mexico, even Atlantic Rim Brazil (but only in its pre-debt-crisis phase of "miracle growth").

In other words "Pacific Rim" painted the entire region differently than it had been since 1945. Paint it Red, the pundits said until 1975. Paint it black, was the post-1975 artistry. (Hollywood followed suit, with a number of films in the late 1970s and 1980s seeking "to put Vietnam behind us." This was Francis Ford Coppola's stated goal for *Apocalypse Now*. Another film that parodied the U.S. "Vietnam syndrome," Stanley Kubrick's *Full Metal Jacket*, ends with the Rolling Stones singing, "Paint it Black.") "Pacific Rim" heralded a forgetting, a hoped-for amnesia in which the decades-long but ultimately failed U.S. effort to obliterate the Vietnam revolution would enter the realm of Korea, "the forgotten war."

When East Asia was "painted Red," it held an apparent outward-moving dynamic the core of which was Beijing: "400 million Chinese armed with nuclear weapons," in Dean Rusk's 1960s scenario, threatened nations along China's rim with oblivion: South Korea, South Vietnam, Taiwan, Indonesia, Thailand, and the big enchilada, Japan. Thus another secretary of state, Dean Acheson, drew a "defense perimeter" through island Asia in 1950. China and North Korea were among the most rapidly growing industrial economies in the world in the 1950s and early 1960s, "success stories" sadly to be contrasted with basket case South Korea (as AID people always named it up through the mid-1960s), running sore Indonesia (with a formidable internal Communist "threat" until 1965), incompetent South Vietnam, mendicant Philippines, and Lucian Pye's hopelessly obtuse and retarded Burma.

"Pacific Rim" revalued all that. Suddenly the rim was the locus of dynamism, bringing pressure on the mainland of Asia. The basket cases were any countries still foolish enough to remain committed to self-reliance or socialist development (from Burma to North Korea), the success stories were any countries that sought export-led capitalist development. The new discourse was deeply solicitous of the benighted and laggard socialist economies, however, and therefore sought a formal end of ideology: "Pacific Rim" invoked a newborn "community" that anyone, socialist or not, could join ... as long as they were capitalist. Rimspeakers of course continued to look with curiousity if not disdain upon anyone who did not privilege the market. (But only *sotto voce*.)

With hindsight the decade 1961–1971 was the critical turning point toward Rimspeak. In 1961 Soviet Chairman Nikita Khrushchev fashioned a voluntarist programmatic ideological vision that anticipated the overcoming of capitalism on a world scale within a few decades. At about the same time Mao's "East is Red" theme placed socialist Asia in the van and the Great Leap Forward sought to overtake Great Britain in fifteen years. At Bucharest in 1961 the socialist camp openly split, however, and Mao's private writings laid the cause of the failure of world socialism at Khrushchev's feet: his revisionism consisted of replacing two world systems within a single planet with one world system, which the Soviets wished to join (symbolized by Camp David in 1959), and through which it would exploit other socialist bloc nations in an international division of labor. State capitalism in Moscow prefigured Russia in the capitalist world system, according to Mao.[9]

W. W. Rostow joined the Kennedy administration in 1961, with his "non-Communist manifesto" of capitalist growth by stages, a view deeply influenced by technological determinism. One of his first projects was to get

South Korea and Taiwan moving toward export-led policies and to reintegrate them with the booming Japanese economy. Facing the first U.S. trade deficits, the Kennedy administration sought to move away from the expensive, draining security programs of the Eisenhower years toward regional pump priming that would bring an end to the bulk grant aid of the 1950s and make allies like Korea and Taiwan more self-sufficient. The economism of the Kennedy years inaugurated the phase of export-led development, but was short-circuited by Vietnam. Richard Nixon later revived these ideas through his Guam Doctrine and opened relations with Red China: policies that were in place by 1971 and that thereby completed the Kennedy agenda. "Pacific Rim" was now incipient, as Nixon hinted in an influential 1967 article: "The U.S. is a Pacific power. ... Europe has been withdrawing the remnants of empire, but the U.S., with its coast reaching in an arc from Mexico to the Bering Straits, is one anchor of a vast Pacific community. Both our interests and our ideals propel us westward across the Pacific, not as conquerers but as partners. ..."[10]

The many working-class and antisystemic movements of the region in the past decades suddenly became poxes, irrationalities that bespeak immature "political development" in the rim. Standing above all else was the nearly instantaneous revaluation of China. The very real slaughters of Mao's failed Cultural Revolution—many directed against the intellectual class—became for U.S. intellectuals the signifier to rename and parenthesize the entire history of the Chinese Revolution, not to mention occasioning a vast rewriting throughout the scholarly apparatus of the China field. But the same thing has happened throughout the rim: when South Korean students protested the pipe-beating murder of an activist by police in the spring of 1991, many U.S. editorials greeted this with exclamations of sheer amazement, that students or workers should be "radical" in a world in which—as all agreed— the role model was the democratic and market-driven United States, led by George Bush and Dan Quayle. The logic seems to be this: Stalinism has palpably failed, therefore why should we have day care centers?

"Pacific Rim" has a class-based definition of Asia. The "community" is a capitalist archipelago, based on indigenous labor power and purchasing power—although mainly labor power until recently. It has thus been the "workshop of the world," using cheap and efficient labor to manufacture exports for other regions with consumer buying power; the vast U.S. market has been and is its mainstay. The archipelago runs through, but also divides, the Pacific and Asian region.

Capitalist classes, obviously, are organized into the archipelago. Peasant Asia (Vietnam; Kampuchea; much of India, Indonesia, and China) is out. Dense, developed, highly differentiated urban nodes are in; the two most im-

portant are Tokyo and Los Angeles, but city-state nodes like Hong Kong and
Singapore are also critical. China's old Treaty Ports and new Special Export
Zones like Shenzhen are in; vast reaches of interior China are out. South Korea is in, North Korea is out (unless Kim Il Sung "does the right thing"). In
other words the majority of the populations in Asia are either out or participate only as unskilled or semiskilled laborers.

This class-based archipelago is also an hierarchy: not just the core urban
nodes, the peripheral peasantries and the intermediate zone of strivers (NICs
and OINKs), but a virtual pyramid of power on C. Wright Mills's model (in
The Power Elite): at the top, a transnational power elite, intertwined in various networks and educated at top-rated U.S. or British universities; then an
echelon of urban middle and working classes; and finally a vast mass below.
The echelon connoted by terms like democracy and pluralism encompasses
at best a decile or two of the stratification, but legitimates the whole. In *The
German Ideology* Marx said that the bourgeoisie views the world as if in a
camera obscura, that is, upside-down; a narrow echelon claims its particular
view to be universal and thus paints the whole in its hue.

This hierarchy reproduces itself throughout the region. Los Angeles is the
perfect example: first, in its contemporaneous polyglot Hispanic, black, and
Asian masses, its putatively universal Yuppie life-style, and its world-class
elite drawn from financial, industrial, and mass culture industries; second, in
its sanitized history that paints black a homegrown Asiatic mode of production and paints white an elite liberalism.

That is, Los Angeles was created through hydraulic engineering that
brought water to the arid coast, and the city to the water through vast sub-
urbanization,[11] by Anglo-Saxon despots who corruptly utilized privileged
public position to make vast private fortunes in real estate, a history collapsed but not violated in the film called *Chinatown.* The interior history of
Los Angeles capitalism until the 1940s was of a "private sector" distant
from the central state and taking upon itself innumerable works of irriga-
tion, transportation, port building, and the like (infrastructure and "social
overhead") that places it at opposite poles from the "state-dominant" capitalism of Japan, and that energizes a free market myth that deeply influenced (among other things) Ronald Reagan and his furious 1980s deregula-
tion.

In the film *Chinatown,* John Huston plays Noah Cross, a man who owned
the city water system and then gave it up to "public" control by
nepotistically inserting his son-in-law as head of Water and Power; it is Oriental despotism in our own backyard. The film ends with the knowing detective being led away from a scene of incestuous murder by his friend: "Forget
it, Jake, it's Chinatown." This might be the perfect metaphor for the history
of Anglo-Saxons in the Pacific Rim.

MANIFEST DENSITY:
"PACIFIC RIM" AS ANGLO-SAXON LAKE

Roland Barthes used Japan as a system of difference[12] to develop a radical critique of the West and its assumptions, instead of a mirror to reflect back to the West what is good and true here, and sadly lacking there. Barthes developed an optic that offers a parallax view, or a salutary boomerang, to question ourselves. As he said, Japan afforded him "a situation of writing ... in which a certain disturbance of the person occurs, a subversion of earlier readings, a shock of meaning." And later, "Someday we must write the history of our own obscurity [or provincialism]—manifest the density of our narcissism."[13]

Nietzsche used the term "emergence," *entstehung,* to mean "the principle and the singular law of an apparition." Emergence does not mean "the final term of a historical development"; "culminations" are "merely the current episodes in a series of subjugations," and so, "Emergence is thus the entry of forces; it is their eruption, *the leap from the wings to the center stage ...* emergence designates a place of confrontation. [emphasis added]" An event (or an emergence) is not a decision, a treaty, a war, but "the reversal of a relationship of forces, the usurpation of power, the appropriation of a vocabulary turned against those who had once used it." And thus his conclusion: "The body [or history, or the descent, or the present] is molded by a great many distinct regimes."[14]

Barthes and Nietzsche help us to ask the question, Where do tropes come from? Whence come the dynamics and miracles of far-off Asia? They help us understand our own density and a history in which "Pacific Rim" and "Japan" seem to emerge suddenly and mysteriously not just in the 1970s, but at several points throughout the past 150 years. They also underline a central point in my argument: we have had "emergence," but we have not had "the reversal of a relationship of forces." The torch has not been passed. Throughout the Pacific industrial era, Japan has been junior to Anglo-American hegemony save for six years or so, from 1939–1945. But we know what happened then ... and it doesn't go under the title "Pacific Rim Community."

"Pacific Rim" was there from the beginning, soon after Commodore Perry's "Black Ships" arrived in Tokugawa port. A famous secretary of state, William Seward, found in world history a movement of empire making its way "constantly westward, and ... it must continue to move on westward, until the tides of the renewed and the decaying civilizations of the world meet on the shores of the Pacific Ocean."[15]

The high-tech conveyance of that era was the steamship, so much less expensive than the ongoing building of continental railroads that it rendered the Pacific as a vast plane traders could skate across, toward the putative

China market. These longings brought U.S. ships to Hawaii, where more Noah Crosses subdued the natives and gave the islands over to pineapple and sugar production, and to Manila Bay in 1898, seen as the first important colonial waystation to the treasures of the rim itself.

Somehow, then as today, Japan was thought to be separate from the rest of the rim—honorary Westerner, pearl of the Orient, good pupil, or as Dean Acheson put it in the 1940s, "the West's obstreperous offspring"; earlier, in 1852, the *Edinburgh Review* reported: "They are Asiatics, it is true, and therefore deficient in that principle of development which is the leading characteristic of those ingenious and persevering European races ... but amidst Asiatics the Japanese stand supreme."[16]

The steamships skated toward Asian markets, but also toward a presumed earthly paradise offering occult knowledge unavailable to the rational Westerner. That the second theme persists today is evident in the pages of the *Economist:* a recent article on the "Pacific Idea" is subtitled, "There Is a Better World." The Pacific idea, the article alerts us, "is important for the mental well-being of the world," because it stands for "belief in the survival of innocence." The accompanying map centers the globe on various tropical islands in the middle and south of the Pacific (described in the article as "a village pond for the Seventh Fleet"), unwittingly placing Bikini at the epicenter—an island the United States made uninhabitable with H-bomb tests in the 1950s. The British did better, destroying by the same means an island called Christmas. The French still test nuclear weapons in the region, and the United States uses Johnston Island for the destruction of chemical weapons. Meanwhile the *Economist* speaks wistfully of Gauguin's women, Melville's lorylory, Marlon Brando's Tahiti and places the burden of rim exclusion on the natives: "The places that people call Eden and Paradise can really become so, if only the Pacific islanders will heave themselves to their feet [translation: get dynamic]."[17]

The Pacific Rim in the nineteenth century was a realm of formal empire for the European powers, and so the United States enunciated the "open door" in 1900 to deal with other empires and made its effective if informal alliance with Great Britain in search of Anglo-Saxon condominium. Japan was the junior partner, in formal alliance with Great Britain from 1902 onward, in informal alliance with Teddy Roosevelt's United States.

Japan was also a junior partner in a hierarchical, product cycle driven regime of technology (the productivist aspect of U.S.-British hegemony). Viewed temporally, Japan has been a "late" industrializer, just as South Korea and other NICs have been "late-late" (to use Albert Hirschman's term for mid-twentieth century industrialization), benefiting from the adaptation of core technologies. Japan maximized its economic power in the one region not claimed by other imperial powers (except for Tsarist Russia)—Taiwan,

Korea, Manchuria—creating a closely linked regional political economy that has promoted and skewed the development of East Asia ever since.[18]

In Japan's first wave of industrialization in the 1880s, we find fish canneries in Hokkaido, the pioneer Kashima Cotton mill, the huge Kobe Paper Factory, the first cigarette company, tanning and leather firms, the Osaka Watch Company, the Tokyo Electric Company with its own brand of light bulbs, even tasty Kirin Beer: and every last one based on U.S. technological start-ups or U.S. expertise. And we would find that Japan's favorite economist in the 1880s was an American, Henry Carey. Marx thought Carey was the only original U.S. economist, inveighing against "English economics" (see his wonderful essay "Bastiat and Carey," in the *Grundrisse*); actually Carey was a protectionist who learned much from Friedrich List, whose theories were also favored in Japan.

General Electric was dominant in the delivery of electricity, and by the 1890s Standard Oil had placed both Japan and China well within the world oil regime, which was increasingly dominated by U.S. firms. Standard's comparative advantage was financial and technical, but also resided in innovative marketing schemes: monopoly on a world scale, combined with creative ways to sell "oil for the lamps of China."[19] The joint British-U.S. condominium is perhaps best symbolized by the British-American Tobacco Company, a subsidiary of the Duke tobacco interests in North Carolina, which got Japan and China hooked on something else, a cigarette habit so deep that "non-smoking sections" can hardly be found anywhere in either country today.[20]

Japanese textile firms, leading sector in Japan's first phase of industrialization, for decades bought their machines from the famous Pratt Brothers of Great Britain—until about 1930 when they came up with their own "high-tech" equipment and quickly became the most efficient textile producer in the world, becoming Great Britain's bête noire of industrial dumping, market stealing, and general villainy. A few years later Japan's obsolescent machines were stoking Korea's first textile conglomerate, courtesy of "technology transfer."[21]

During the halcyon days of the British-Japanese alliance, however, Japan was a model of industrial efficiency for Great Britain in incipient decline. As Phillip Lyttleton Gell put it in 1904: "I shall turn Japanese for they at least can think, and be reticent! [Witness] their organization, their strategy, their virile qualities, their devotion and self-control. Above all, their national capacity for self-reliance, self-sacrifice, and their silence!"[22] Or as a Fabian put it in 1907: "Witness the magnificent spectacle of Japan today; the State above the individual; common good above personal good; sacrifice of self and devotion to the community. ... "[23] By the 1930s matters had descended from that sublime point, however, as British business publications vented their rage at "The wily Jap [who is] determined to stop at nothing in his ef-

forts to bamboozle shoppers in this country [and is] STEALING OUR
MARKETS![sic]"[24]

JAPAN AS NUMBER TWO

What about today: Is Japan the core power of the Pacific Rim? I do not know
what the future will hold, but today the answer is: not yet. However close Japan may be to hegemonic emergence, in "concrete reality" for this entire century it has been a subordinate part of either bilateral U.S. hegemony or trilateral U.S.-British hegemony. Here is our metaphor for 1900–1991: Japan as
Number Two.

An archaeology of Japan in the twentieth century world system unearths
the following time lines:

1. 1900–1922: Japan in British-U.S. hegemony
2. 1922–1939: Japan in U.S.-British hegemony
3. 1939–1945: Japan hegemonic in East Asia
4. 1945–1970: Japan in U.S. hegemony
5. 1970–1990: Japan in U.S.-European hegemony

Three of the periods (1, 2, and 5) are trilateral, and none are colonial or necessarily imperial. A bilateral regime is predictable in the temporary phase of
comprehensive hegemony (1945–1970 for the United States), a trilateral regime in the rising and falling phases of transitional hegemonies.

Shortly after World War I ended, in 1922 to be exact, the United States
came to be the major partner in the trilateral hegemony. This was the period
when U.S. banks became dominant in the world economy;[25] in general, the
British-Japanese alliance had become tattered, and the United States became
more important than Great Britain in Japanese diplomacy. The Washington
Conference was the occasion for this transfer of the baton, a "locking in"
with the critical element of global military reach, the U.S. navy.[26]

Japan accommodated to these trends with a very low posture diplomacy
throughout the 1920s. Meanwhile it girded its loins at home for trade competition, inaugurating tendencies in its political economy that remain prominent today. Here was an early version of NIC-style "export-led development." Both Johnson and Fletcher date Japan's national industrial strategy
and "administrative guidance" from the 1920s, and both the Americans and
the British were receptive to Japan's outward-turning political economy.[27]
We can note that it has only been in 1931–1945 and the 1980s and 1990s
that this strategy has been perceived as a problem for the United States.

The Export Association Law of 1925 was an important turning point,
stimulating industrial reorganization, cartels, and various state subsidies to

exporters; Japan was careful to direct these exports to the noncolonial semiperiphery and not to the core markets of the United States and Great Btitain.[28] The 1920s also inaugurated a period of import-substitution industrialization[29] that went hand in hand with the exporting program, although it was more pronounced in the 1930s, when Japan accomplished its heavy-industrial spurt and its virtuoso mastery of the industrial product cycle.

Japan's "old" empire in Northeast Asia was, from 1910 to 1931, the empire the United States and Great Britain *wanted it to have,* and even when Manchuria was colonized in 1931, the United States and Great Britain chose to do little about it, save for a lot of rhetoric about the "open door." The reason they did little was that Japan preserved a modified open door in Manchuria until 1941 and encouraged U.S. and British investment—of which there was much more than generally thought. And in the postwar period, from 1947 to the present, U.S. planners have urged a modified restoration of Japan's position in Northeast Asia.

Dean Acheson and George Kennan masterminded this repositioning of Japan in the world system, by deciding in 1947 to place Japan as an engine of the world economy, a U.S.-defined "economic animal," shorn of its prewar military and political clout. Meanwhile the United States kept Japan on a defense dependency and shaped the flow of essential resources to it, thus to accumulate a diffuse leverage over all its policies and to retain an outer limit veto on Japan's global orientation. This strategy was articulated precisely at the time of the formal onset of the cold war, in the spring of 1947. The postwar U.S. empire has not rested upon territorial exclusivity like the old European colonies. It has been an "open door" empire, policed by a far-flung naval and military basing system and penetration of allied defense organizations (e.g., the prohibition on the use of military force in the Japanese constitution; U.S. command of West German and Korean militaries).[30]

Japan would also need an economic region "to its south," in Kennan's words, and Acheson came up with an elegant rim metaphor to capture this restoration: a "great crescent" from Tokyo to Alexandria linked Japan with island Asia, around Singapore and through the Indian Ocean to the oil of the Persian Gulf. It was this crescent that lay behind Acheson's famed "defense perimeter" speech in January 1950.[31] This definition was hammered out coterminous with the emergence of the cold war and deepened as Japan benefited from U.S. wars to lock in an Asian hinterland, in Korea and Vietnam.

Here we intuit a truth that Rimspeak would rather forget: the "Pacific Rim community" has been a region fashioned in warfare. The United States was "at war with Asia" from 1941 to 1975, to use Noam Chomsky's term. If Pearl Harbor functions as original sin for Americans, Hiroshima and Nagasaki connote a cataclysmic rendering of "Japan as Number Two." The Korean War drew the Northeast Asian boundaries of Pacific capitalism until the 1980s, being also "Japan's Marshall Plan" (Chalmers Johnson's term)—war

procurements propelled Japan along its world-beating industrial path. In
Korea, too, original sin came on a Sunday morning, when Kim Il Sung's
forces invaded, seeking to overturn a Korean original sin: the U.S. decision
to divide Korea, carried out by Dean Rusk at John J. McCloy's request in
August 1945. Original sin was harder to determine in Vietnam; Ho Chi
Minh resembled neither Tojo nor Kim. For some Americans it was the Ton-
kin Gulf incident; for the Vietnamese perhaps it was Acheson's decision to
link Indochina to the revival of Japanese industry, bringing the United States
in on the side of French imperialism.[32]

In this era, which ran from Truman through Johnson, Japan was a dutiful
U.S. partner and the partner was tickled pink at Japan's economic success.
As the U.S. capacity unilaterally to manage the global system declined in the
1960s, however, a new duality afflicted the U.S.-Japan relationship: Japan
should do well, yes ... but not so well that it hurt U.S. interests. Richard
Nixon was again the agent of change, with his neomercantilist "New Economic Policy," announced on V-J Day in 1971. U.S. thinking about Japan remains firmly within that duality today, symbolized by the inability of elites to
do more than oscillate between free trade and protectionism, between admiration for Japan's success and alarm at its new prowess.

In short, Japan has been thriving within the hegemonic net for ninety
years, but nonetheless "emerges" in the Western mind—leaps from the wings
to the center stage—at three critical and incommensurable points: at the turn
of the century when it was a British wunderkind (but a "yellow peril" to the
Germans); in the world depression of the 1930s, when it was an industrial
monster to the British (but a wunderkind to the Germans and the Italians);
and in the 1980s, when it was a wunderkind to U.S. internationalists and a
monster to U.S. protectionists. The Four Tigers, Three or Four Tiger Cubs,
and all the others tread the same path: do well, please, but not so well that
you threaten us (whereupon the tropes all reverse, and you move from miracle to menace, from market-driven dynamo to crypto-fascist upstart).[33] The
main point is that there has been no fundamental reversal of relationships;
no torches have been passed, nor are likely to be passed for "the near term."

THE NEAR TERM: TRILATERAL FUTURES

As I said earlier, I am not good at prognosis: I find it hard enough to predict
the past. In the near term of the next couple of decades, however, I would
hazard the guess that the world system will have three nodal, central points,
symbolized by New York, Tokyo, and Berlin, and a core point of hegemony,
headquartered in Washington. New York will have a tendency to connect
with Europe, Los Angeles with East Asia, and Washington will seek to manage a trilateral condominium. In other words, we are not on the eve of a re-

gionalization of the world economy, but a period of prolonged North-North cooperation propelled by an historic "peace interest," to use Karl Polanyi's term, on the part of high finance and the modal capitalist organization of our era, the transnational corporation.[34]

The Pacific Rim is neither a self-contained region nor a community, but just that: a rim—peripheral and semiperipheral societies oriented toward Tokyo and the U.S. market. Consumer purchasing power is still lower than in Western Europe or the United States, and labor cost advantage still orients the region toward assembly and finishing work using Japanese or U.S. technology. It is still a region under dual economic hegemony, held by a unilateral U.S. security network. No common culture unites the region: Japanese do not interact culturally with Koreans, Koreans have little noneconomic intercourse with Filipinos, Indonesians do not interact with Thais.

Instead the lineaments of "culture" run through Los Angeles and New York: Hollywood and the global center of television, purveying U.S. mass culture throughout the region. South Korea has three networks, of which one is the Armed Forces Korea Network, broadcasting in English. The other two run dubbed versions of "Dallas" and "Miami Vice," and Korean shows on similar themes. Most Americans have never seen a single Korean movie. Japanese films play in U.S. art houses, if at all; U.S. films play throughout the region. The unrelenting seductions of Hollywood's vision of a universal bourgeois life-style are apparent ultimately in two scions of the antisystem being unable to resist it: Mao's wife, Jiang Qing, watched *Gone With the Wind* in the Forbidden City, and Kim Il Sung's heir-apparent son, Kim Jong Il, reportedly has a personal library of 20,000 films, most of them American. Travelers even to remote Nepal report street urchins tug at their sleeves yelling "Michael Jackson, Michael Jackson." Japanese investors' recognition of the epicenter of late twentieth century culture led, of course, to their purchase of Columbia Pictures and MCA.

Since the mid-1980s, it is true, Japan has deepened its regional influence in Asia, with much higher levels of direct investment in Northeast and Southeast Asia. Its direct investment in the region has grown sixfold since 1985, its trade with Taiwan tripled in the same period, and its manufactured imports from the Asian region as a whole more than doubled from 1985 to 1988 (contrary to pundits who argue that its economy is basically closed). Japanese investors have been especially active in Thailand: on the average one new Japanese factory opened every working day in 1989.[35] The Pacific region inclusive of Northeast Asia, the ASEAN countries, and Australia will have a GNP of $7.2 trillion by the year 2000, according to current projections, which will be bigger than that of the European Community (EC); the number of effective consumers will be about 330 million, as large as the EC, but not as affluent.[36]

Japan has also been assiduous in breaking barriers to trade with the Asian socialist countries: it is North Korea's biggest capitalist trading partner (which is not to say much), and may normalize relations with P'yongyang soon; it went back into China much more quickly than other investors in the wake of the Tiananmen bloodletting in June 1989. As the Asian "Berlin walls" crumble, Japan will be poised to pursue a "German" option, that is, to deepen its market position in socialist China, Korea, and Vietnam as Germany has been doing in the old semiperiphery of East Europe. Indeed, Japanese experts have been asked to come back and renovate industrial technology in Manchuria, and even to revive big gold mines in North Korea formerly owned by Japanese and U.S. firms.

All this regional activity is grist for the mill of those who find a developing tendency toward regional economic blocs. But this is unlikely short of a major world depression; a trilateral regime of cooperation and free trade linking Europe with East Asia and the Americas is much more likely, with the three great markets of each region underpinning and stabilizing intercapitalist rivalry in the world system, and encouraging interdependence rather than go-it-alone strategies that would be deleterious to all. Japan's regional investment hedges against exclusion from the European Community after 1992, but it has other hedges in the form of direct investment in manufacturing in Great Britain and East Europe. The United States is strongly pressuring its European allies not to exclude Japan from the post-1992 arrangements, in favor of trilateral cooperation.

Japan is also constrained regionally, in that "actually existing socialism" persists, above all in "the East." There is no break yet in Asian communism, with the predictable exception of Soviet-aligned Mongolia. China has thus announced that "the center of socialism has moved East." With the demise of the "people's democracies" in Europe, predictably, the *Wall Street Journal* ran an article under the title, "The Coming Collapse of North Korea."[37] Strange, therefore, that the most recalcitrant outpost of communism today is in North Korea, which seems almost a museum of 1950s–1960s revolutionary socialism. Today it is the most interesting Communist nation, because it is the last unadulterated redoubt of what all the others used to be: the last Communist. Furthermore for forty years it has been a state organized as an anti-Japanese entity, an apotheosis of the resistance to Japanese penetration that exists throughout the Asian rim.

The simplest answer for the seeming anomaly of persisting Asian communism in "Pacific Rim community" is precisely the Chinese claim that "the center of socialism has moved East." It's just that they are off by a few decades: it moved there after World War II, or perhaps in the 1930s, when formidable revolutionary nationalist movements emerged in China, Korea, and Vietnam. Today octogenarians in China and septuagenarians in North Korea and Vietnam are guardians of that deep-running anti-imperialist tradition. In China, of course, "Marxism–Leninism–Mao Zedong Thought" remains today little more than a justification for one-party rule. The post-1978, rim-joining economic reforms hang in a balance, or along a spectrum, from a young urban and coastal crowd that is following the capitalist road blazed by the Four Tigers, an old crowd whose preferred Marxism is the Stalinist variety (central planning; heavy industry first), and the still-vast peasantry for whom nobody but Mao had a policy—other than that they should disappear as a class, by becoming workers, urbanites, or the latest slogan, "getting rich." (In forty years of industrialization perhaps half a billion of them have done none of the above.)

Centrist national security elites in the United States have frankly promoted a reviving trilateralism. Internationalists are sure they know which direction the U.S.-Japan relationship should take: deepened collaboration, pointing toward a joint condominium, in which Japan will continue to play second fiddle.[38] The trilateral logic also expressed itself at the dawn of German reunification in the fall of 1989. Henry Kissinger and David Rockefeller both journeyed to Berlin and Tokyo in September; Kissinger was second only to U.S. Ambassador Vernon Walters in announcing his support for German unity. By not opposing what soon became a fait accompli, U.S. leaders succeeded in keeping Germany within the postwar settlement, and "containment" continues apace: not of the old enemy, the USSR, but of the old ally, Germany, just as U.S. bases still dot Japan in spite of the end of the cold war.

How long this will last is anybody's guess, but it makes of the enormous U.S. commitment to the Persian Gulf in 1990–1991 something less than the "first post–cold war crisis." U.S. forces are there to shape the flow of resources to Japan, Germany, and the other industrial economies, thus to maintain "outer limit" hegemonic lines that were central parts of the postwar settlement. (Imagine the reverse: a German or Japanese airlift of 500,000 troops to Saudi Arabia!)

The ultimate logic of trilateralism for the near term resides in Japan being for the United States today what the United States was for Great Britain in the 1920s: the emergent financial and technological center, but a long way from assuming hegemonic responsibilities. As the recent Gulf War demonstrated, Japan (and Germany) will be content to "let George do it" for some time, there being no interest in taking on an expensive security role when the United States is willing to do so, and in the absence of major security threats from the USSR or any place else.

North-North cooperation, including the Soviet Union (or whatever Russia and its allied republics will come to call themselves), is thus the order of the day in what is perhaps the most bourgeois era in world history. It is the Third World in our midst, another archipelago running from Los Angeles through Seoul and Manila to the hinterland masses of China and Indonesia, that will find no exit in the "Pacific Rim community," save hard work at low pay. The Third World is dominated by the advanced countries in a way un-precedented since the colonial era, with no convincing antisystemic model to follow. It is outside the loop of the prosperity of recent years, and therefore is the prime source of war, instability, and class conflict.

CONCLUSION:
THE SIGNIFICANCE OF THE RIM

Is there a way of constructing "Pacific Rim" other than that which I have given you in this chapter? Is there an indigenous path toward reconstituting Western Rimspeak? The people of the rim have tried two ways before: the imperial pan-Asianism of Japan in the late 1930s and early 1940s, never very successful in gaining non-Japanese adherents; and the Communist pan-Asianism of the 1950s, when Mao's China deeply influenced Korea, Viet-nam, and various socialist movements in Asia. It has a brief heyday after North Korea and China fought the United States and its allies to a standstill in Korea, with the high point at Bandung in 1954. It is as dead as dead can be today, when China courts the NICs, and like Russia, tries to wash its hands of North Korea and Vietnam.

Perhaps capitalism Chinese-style will provide an alternative model. South-east Asia is not Northeast Asia, but both are part of the rim. It was an his-toric trading area for another world economy, the Chinese, and it was the centerpiece of Great Britain's "Pacific Rim" empire. It has been shaped re-cently by a number of anticolonial independence movements (Vietnamese socialism, Indonesian nationalism, Malayan and Philippine guerrillas, Bur-man autarky, etc.) that make it less open to U.S. and Japanese ministrations than Northeast Asia. Today Southeast Asia has an alternative organization of capitalism, the long-standing interstitial commerce of "island China," the Chinese diaspora. Some pundits think this might provide a different way of organizing rim capitalism, with Hong Kong and Vancouver being principal nodes, patrimonialism and family-based entrepreneurship the means, and Chinese the lingua franca. A reorganization of the region under Chinese aus-pices seems remote, however, until the mainland itself is so organized; other-wise Chinese commerce will continue to operate in the pores of the system.

So we are left, I think, with but one grand event symbolized by "Pacific Rim," and that is the rise to power of Japan. It is the only true entrant in the past century to the ranks of the advanced industrial core, with the possible exception of the (now-deindustrializing) Soviet Union. It is the only non-Western entrant. If it does not wish to be, and cannot today be, the lodestone for an autonomous non-Western reorganization of the region, one day it will be. When that happens, an old soldier and charter Pacific rimster, General Douglas MacArthur, Japan's benign U.S. emperor, will have been right: in an address in Seattle back in 1951, MacArthur opined that "Our economic frontier now embraces the trade potentialities of Asia itself; for with the gradual rotation of the epicenter of world trade back to the Far East whence it started many centuries ago, the next thousand years will find the main problem the raising of the sub-normal standards of life of its more than a billion people."[39]

It is a classic piece of Rimspeak.

NOTES

This chapter is a revision of my keynote address to the 15th Annual Conference on the Political Economy of the World-System, Honolulu, Hawaii, March 28, 1991.

1. Murray Sayle, "Bowing to the Inevitable," *Times Literary Supplement,* April 28, 1989. I am grateful to Gavan McCormack for drawing my attention to this statement.

2. Peter Gourevitch, "The Pacific Rim: Current Debates," *Annals of the American Academy of Political and Social Science* 505 (September 1989), pp. 8–23.

3. Ezra F. Vogel, *Japan as Number One: Lessons for America* (Cambridge, MA: Harvard University Press, 1979).

4. Chalmers Johnson, *MITI and the Japanese Miracle* (Berkeley: University of California Press, 1982); see also Thomas Gold, *State and Society* in *The Taiwan Miracle* (Armonk, NY: M.E. Sharpe, 1986); Gary Gereffi, ed., *Manufacturing Miracles* (Princeton, NJ: Princeton University Press, 1991). According to Gereffi, he wanted to title his book *Manufactured Miracles,* but the publisher changed it (to go along with the trope).

5. Gourevitch, "The Pacific Rim," p. 19; Staffan Burenstam Linder, *The Pacific Century: Economic and Political Consequences of Asian-Pacific Dynamism* (Stanford, CA: Stanford University Press, 1986).

6. Simon Winchester, *Pacific Rising: The Emergence of a New World Culture* (New York: Prentice-Hall, 1991), p. xiii. Sociologists will be happy to know, even if East Asianists will drop to their knees in mortification to find out, that in Winchester's view, Max Weber offered "the most complete, if not the most readable, account of Confucius" (in his *Religion of China*—see p. 487). Weber famously sought the source of East Asia's failure to develop capitalism in the absence of the Protestant ethic, or its equivalent; generations of graduate students got this as an explanation for why the West was dynamic and the East was not. But at least it *was* readable, especially compared to the East Asianist texts.

7. See Arif Dirlik, "The Asia-Pacific Idea: Reality and Representation in the Invention of a Regional Structure," *Journal of World History* 3, no. 1 (Spring 1992).

8. Andrew Mendelsohn, "Alvin Toffler in China: Deng's Big Bang," *The New Republic,* April 4, 1988, quoted in Alexander Woodside, "The Asia-Pacific Idea as a Mobilization Myth" (Chapter 2, this volume). Woodside notes that there are no Chinese, or Indonesian, or Vietnamese Alvin Tofflers.

9. I have argued this point at length in "The Political Economy of Chinese Foreign Policy," *Modern China* (October 1979), pp. 411–461.

10. Richard M. Nixon, "Asia After Vietnam," *Foreign Affairs*, 46, no. 1 (1967), pp. 111–125.

11. See Mike Davis, *City of Quartz* (London: Verso, 1990).

12. Barthes, *Empire of Signs* (New York: Hill and Wang, 1982).

13. Ibid.

14. Friedrich Nietzsche, *On the Genealogy of Morals,* ed. and trans. by Walter Kaufmann (New York: Vintage Books, 1969), pp. 15–23, 77–78.

15. Quoted in Richard Drinnon, *Facing West: The Metaphysics of Indian-Hating and Empire-Building* (New York: New American Library, 1980), p. 271. This book is a wonderful antidote to Rimspeak.

16. Quoted in Jean-Pierre Lehmann, *The Image of Japan: From Feudal Isolation to World Power, 1850–1905* (London: George Allen & Unwin, 1978), p. 46.

17. "The Pacific Idea," *Economist*, March 16, 1991.

18. For more elaboration see Bruce Cumings, "The Origins and Development of the Northeast Asian Political Economy," *International Organization* (Winter 1984), pp. 1–40.

19. By 1894, U.S. kerosene exports to Japan had reached 887,000 barrels of 42 gallons each. Standard entered the production field in Japan with its International Oil Company, 1900–1906. See Harold F. Williamson and Arnold R. Daum, *The American Petroleum Industry, 1859–1899: The Age of Illumination* (Evanston: Northwestern University Press, 1959), p. 675; *Sōritsu shichijù-shùnen kinen Nihon sekiyu shi* [seventieth anniversary history of Japanese petroleum] (Tokyo: Nihon Sekiyu K.K., 1958).

20. James B. Duke formed BAT in 1902, in league with a chief rival, the Imperial Tobacco Company; Duke held 2/3 of the stock. By 1915, BAT had almost $17 million in investments in China and was one of its two largest employers. (Michael H. Hunt, *The Making of a Special Relationship: The United States and China to 1914* [New York: Columbia University Press, 1983], pp. 282–283.)

21. Carter Eckert, *The Origins of Korean Capitalism* (Seattle: University of Washington Press, 1991).

22. Quoted in Colin Holmes and A. H. Ion, "Bushido and the Samurai: Images in British Public Opinion, 1894–1914," *Modern Asian Studies,* 14, no. 2 (1980), pp. 304–329.

23. Sir Oliver Lodge, quoted in Holmes and Iron, "Bushio and the Samurai," p. 321.

24. Quoted in Isohi Asahi, *The Economic Strength of Japan* (Tokyo: Hokuseido Press, 1939), pp. 207–209.

25. See Harry N. Schreiber, "World War I as Entrepreneurial Opportunity: Willard Straight and the American International Corporation," *Political Science Quarterly,* 84 (September 1969), pp. 486–511; more generally see Carl P. Parrini, *Heir to Empire: The United States Economic Diplomacy, 1916–1923* (Pittsburgh, PA: University of Pittsburgh Press, 1969).

26. Akira Iriye, *After Imperialism* (Cambridge, MA: Harvard University Press, 1965). Although Iriye's analysis is different from mine, he demonstrates more the failure than the success of the "Washington system," and underlines the upper hand that the United States now had in East Asian diplomacy.

27. Johnson, *MITI*; William Miles Fletcher III, *The Japanese Business Community and National Trade Policy, 1920–1942* (Chapel Hill: University of North Carolina Press, 1989).

28. Gö Seinosuke, formerly head of the huge Oji Paper Company and director of the Tokyo Stock Exchange for 12 years, drafted a report in 1929 recommending, among other things, "a new national committee ... to rationalize industrial production in order to 'aid industrial development'"; "Go endorsed the principle of export planning—selecting products that might sell well abroad and fostering their growth." The plan led to the Export Compensation Act of May 1930, and other measures to aid export industries; the plan was to help exports to Central America, Africa, the Balkans, "central Asia Minor," and the USSR, and it later expanded to include "the whole world except for Europe, the U.S., India, and the Dutch East Indies" (Fletcher, *The Japanese Business Community*, pp. 59, 61–62).

29. Ibid., p. 28.

30. See Robin Luckham, "American Militarism and the Third World: The End of the Cold War?" (Working paper no. 94, Peace Research Center, Australian National University, October 1990), p. 2.

31. See Bruce Cumings, *Origins of the Korean War*, vol. 2 (Princeton, NJ: Princeton University Press, 1990), Chapter 2.

32. See Andrew Rotter, *The Path to Vietnam* (Ithaca, NY: Cornell University Press, 1986).

33. By the 1990s pundits have already begun to suggest that Japan and South Korea may represent a different, "third" kind of political economy—"what we used to call fascism," in Jude Wanniskie's words ("Some Lines on the Rest of the Millennium," *New York Times*, December 24, 1989). Karel von Wolferen, in an important book called *The Enigma of Japanese Power* (New York: Knopf, 1989), hints at a similar perspective with his discussion of the mysterious "system" at the core of Japan's political economy.

34. For an elaboration, see Bruce Cumings, "The Seventy Years' Crisis and the Logic of Trilateralism in the 'New World Order,'" *World Policy Journal* (Spring 1991). For Polanyi's explanation of *haute finance* and the 100 years' peace (1815–1914), see *The Great Transformation* (Boston: Beacon, 1944).

35. *Far Eastern Economic Review*, July 21, 1990, and August 30, 1990.

36. *Far Eastern Economic Review*, August 9, 1990.

37. *Wall Street Journal*, June 26, 1990.

38. See for example Zbigniew Brzezinski, who advocated a U.S.-Japan condominium called "Amerippon" in "America's New Geostrategy," *Foreign Affairs* 66, no. 4 (Spring 1988), pp. 680–699.

39. Speech in Seattle, 1951. Quoted in Michael W. Miles, *The Odyssey of the American Right* (Oxford: Oxford University Press, 1980), p. 170.

PART TWO

Constructing a Region:
The Political Economy
of the Asia-Pacific

GARY GEREFFI

Global Sourcing and Regional Divisions of Labor in the Pacific Rim

MOST EFFORTS to define the region variously known as Pacific Rim, Pacific Basin, Asian-Pacific, and so on, have been quite unsatisfactory. There is an inherent geographical bias in all these definitions, since they tend to view the region as a geographical given despite the difficulties of "delineating the boundaries of the region, determining its center(s), and deciding whom of all the people who inhabit the region to include within it as serious participants in its activities."[1] "Pacific Rim," one of the most commonly used terms, has the drawback of focusing too exclusively on the edges of the region, leaving out of the picture all that is inside the region. "Pacific Basin" has the opposite problem, since it suggests that the center of the region is somewhere in the ocean. "Asia-Pacific" has the advantage of referring not just to the region's location but also to one of its principal human components although the Asian peoples are so diverse that the term loses any social specificity. Finally, the term "Asian-American Pacific" might be preferred as descriptively more comprehensive, including the peoples on both sides of the Pacific, but this apparent egalitarian inclusiveness is misleading because it glosses over the historical problem of changes in the scope and structure of competing interests in the constitution of Asia and the Americas.

This chapter has not been written to defend any of these definitions of the region, nor to add a new one. The Pacific Rim is not just a geographical region nor is it solely the by-product of elite-centered, EuroAmerican "hegemonic ideologies" of expansion into the Pacific hinterland, although geopolitical factors undoubtedly have been important in shaping the internal dynamics of the region as well as its insertion into the world economy. Rather, I prefer to take a more inductive or grounded approach and look at the Pacific Rim as a geographical arena tied together by a variety of economic and social networks. My empirical focus will be a comparison of

51

three global industries: garments, automobiles, and personal computers. During the post–World War II period, the trade, investment, and migration patterns associated with these industries have linked East Asian and Latin American nations with the United States in ways that have both consolidated and reshaped the Asian-American Pacific region. Furthermore, one of the important consequences of these transnational production networks has been a weakening of the role of individual governments in the formulation of national development policies, and in determining how these regions will be linked to the global political economy.

Evidence from the garment, automobile, and personal computer industries indicates the evolution of a pattern of global sourcing whereby the "national segmentation" that characterized the import-substituting industries of the past is being replaced by a new logic of "transnational integration" based on geographical specialization and tightly linked international supply networks. In other words, the shift from import-substituting industrialization (ISI) to export-oriented industrialization (EOI) in many Pacific Rim nations has ushered in a new international division of labor in the world economy.[2] The flows of goods, capital, and people within East Asia and North America serve to consolidate each region, as well as the trans-Pacific connections that link the regions on either side of the Pacific Basin, creating similar regional divisions of labor in East Asia and North America.[3] In addition, the trans-Pacific trade, investment, and migration flows are leading to a multilateralization of these regional blocs, with important consequences not only for the development strategies of the East Asian and Latin American nations involved, but also for the process of industrialization being carried out in the United States.

GLOBAL SOURCING: DIVERSE PATTERNS IN THREE INDUSTRIES

Industrialization today is the result of an integrated system of global production and trade, buttressed by new forms of investment and financing, promoted by specific government policies, and entailing distinctive patterns of spatial and social organization. International trade has allowed nations to specialize in different branches of manufacturing and even in different stages of production within a specific industry, leading to the emergence of a global manufacturing system in which production capacity dispersed to an unprecedented number of developing as well as industrialized countries.[4]

In the contemporary global manufacturing system, production of a single good commonly spans several countries and regions, with each nation performing tasks in which it has a cost advantage. This is true for traditional manufactures, such as garments, as well as for modern products, like automobiles and computers. In order to understand the implications of this worldwide division of labor for specific sets of newly industrializing countries (NICs) in East Asia and Latin America, it is helpful to analyze the distinct patterns of global sourcing that characterize each of these industries.

Three kinds of international subcontracting are used to promote global sourcing, but their relative importance varies across industries. *Export processing* production involves the labor-intensive assembly of manufactured goods, often in officially designated industrial zones that offer special incentives to foreign investors. This form of global sourcing has been significant in certain phases of all three of the industries considered below, since garments, certain auto parts (e.g., wiring harnesses), and the manufacture of semiconductors for use in personal computers all have assembly-intensive phases in the production process enabling major savings in low-wage countries. *Component supply subcontracting* refers to the manufacture of technologically sophisticated component parts for export to original-equipment manufacturers in the developed countries. This is an increasingly important feature of the automobile, computer, and household appliance industries. *Commercial subcontracting* of finished goods is based on specification buying by large-volume retailers who market the goods under private labels or in their own retail outlets. This is particularly common in the garment industry, but it also is of growing significance in the personal computer, replacement auto parts, and footwear industries.[5] Finally, there are *independent exporters* who do not utilize subcontracting relationships to sell their goods abroad. They assume the responsibility not only for production but also for overseas marketing utilizing their own brand names, as exemplified by auto producers in South Korea (Hyundai) and personal computer companies in Taiwan (Acer) and South Korea (Leading Edge).

These various types of global sourcing entail different sets of preconditions for the exporting countries. Export processing production is based on abundant cheap labor, political stability, and often a battery of official investment incentives. This is the easiest of the export roles for a developing country to adopt, but it also is inherently unstable as wage levels and political conditions change.

The component supplier role requires more highly skilled labor and investors willing to set up capital- and technology-intensive plants in the NICs. A nation's proximity to core country markets is an advantage for both the export-processing and component supplier forms of global sourcing, decreasing transport costs and increasing the speed of delivery for seasonal industries like garments and footwear.

Commercial subcontracting requires a local entrepreneurial class that has the capital and technological ability to supply large-volume, original-equipment manufacturer (OEM) contracts for developed country markets. Size of

TABLE 4.1   U.S. Imports of Textile and Clothing Products, 1980 and 1985–1988 (millions of U.S. dollars, customs value)

		Total	Latin America[a]		East Asia	
				% of U.S. Imports		% of U.S. Imports
1980	Textiles	$2,676	$239	8.9	$929	34.7
	Clothing	6,848	586	8.6	5,035	73.5
1985	Textiles	5,274	389	7.4	1,985	37.6
	Clothing	16,056	1,070	6.7	10,727	66.8
1986	Textiles	5,768	446	7.7	2,177	37.7
	Clothing	17,288	1,216	7.0	10,814	62.5
1987	Textiles	6,511	543	8.3	2,268	34.8
	Clothing	20,490	1,627	7.9	12,606	61.5
1988	Textiles	6,748	567	8.4	2,225	33.0
	Clothing	22,877	2,231	9.8	13,642	59.6

[a]Excluding Central America and the Caribbean.
SOURCE: U.S. Department of Commerce, *Highlights of U.S. Export and Import Trade*, various years.

firms is not as important as the ability to flexibly shift output in response to the buyers' needs.

Finally, the successful independent exporters must control export and distribution networks in global commodity chains, in addition to attaining a high degree of productive efficiency. Large vertically integrated firms have a major advantage here, as do those with distinctive or technologically innovative products. So far, South Korea is the NIC that has made the biggest strides in this direction because the *chaebols* have the financial, technological and marketing resources needed to become fully internationalized.

Garments

The garment industry was one of the first sectors in which developing nations achieved a rapid growth of manufactured exports to the industrialized economies. The Third World share in international trade in this sector nearly doubled from 22 percent to 41 percent between 1970 and 1981. In the mid-1980s, clothing accounted for 21 percent of all Third World manufactured exports, with Hong Kong, South Korea, and Taiwan being by far the largest clothes exporters.[6] Together, the East Asian NICs produced 60 percent of all clothing imports to the United States in 1988 ($13.6 billion), whereas the total share for Latin American nations was just under 10 percent ($2.2 billion). As we can see in Table 4.1, although the East Asian share of U.S. clothing imports declined by 14 percentage points (from 73.5 percent to 59.6 percent) between 1980 and 1988, the Latin American nations (excluding Central America and the Caribbean) only increased their share of the U.S. market by 1 percentage point (from 8.6 percent to 9.8 percent) during this same period.

The manufacture of apparel traditionally has been a highly labor intensive activity with low capital and technology requirements. The industry relies on a combination of dextrous, low-paid, and predominantly female workers, and sturdy, flexible, and relatively inexpensive sewing machines as the basic unit of production. Clothing manufacturing is a sequential, multistage activity that can be divided into three phases: (a) preassembly (the inspection, grading, marking, and cutting of the cloth); (b) assembly, which involves up to 100 sequential sewing operations; and (c) finishing, which basically entails pressing and packaging the completed garment.[7] Since the assembly of clothes from soft, limp fabrics requires considerable manual manipulation of the materials by machine operators at all stages of production, the industry has been highly resistant to automation.

The international organization of garment production basically is a response to three kinds of factors: (a) manufacturing costs, (b) national protective barriers, and (c) industrial flexibility. Materials and labor are the two primary manufacturing costs in garment production. Material costs are roughly the same for all producers. Labor costs, however, vary considerably from region to region and thus are the main determinant of international competitive advantage in the apparel industry. The hourly wage for textile workers in 1982, for example, was $5.20 in the United States, $1.80 in Hong Kong, $1.50 in Taiwan, $1.00 in South Korea, $0.40 in the Philippines, and $0.20 in mainland China.[8] Since labor costs are at least four times greater in the United States than in the Asian NICs and China, firms operating in the United States are at a considerable cost disadvantage. The large savings in labor costs thus has led U.S. apparel producers to invest heavily in offshore production.

Protective trade legislation (voluntary and involuntary export quotas, import tariffs, and other trade restrictions) continues to have a dramatic effect upon global sourcing in the garment industry. The consequences of tariffs generally are more straightforward than quotas because they directly increase the overall cost of imported products. Price sensitive retailers tend to source their garments from firms in nations with low tariffs because it lowers total costs. The effect of the U.S. export quota system on international sourcing is much more convoluted than that of tariffs, largely because the U.S. system itself is so complex. For example, the United States uses seventy-five narrow product categories for garment quotas, with many U.S. quotas based upon the quantity (or number) rather than the value of exports. To evade these quotas, exporting nations commonly switch their production to items or materials not yet subject to quotas. In the late 1970s, Hong Kong apparel producers began to export garments largely composed of ramie, a rough linenlike fiber that was not included in U.S. quotas at the time, and in the early 1980s some Hong Kong manufacturers started making jackets with zip-on sleeves since the quota on jackets was tight, but there were no quotas on vests or sleeves.[9]

Industrial flexibility refers to the ability of the industry to produce what buyers demand. In recent years, U.S. firms have started to become more responsive to retailers' demands in order to meet the challenge from foreign companies in a wide range of industries ranging from apparel to autos. Liz Claiborne, a major U.S. fashion company, began to source abroad less as a matter of price than because of the difficulty of finding capable domestic suppliers who were willing to give Claiborne the variety of fabrics and the careful tailoring she wanted.[10]

Technological innovations in the garment industry have begun to change the logic of global sourcing, however. Sophisticated computer-aided design (CAD) and computer-aided manufacturing (CAM) systems are now available to carry out the design, grader, and marking activities in the preassembly stage of production. In the assembly and finishing stages as well, numerical control and microcomputer-based sewing machines, robotic handling devices, and automated transfer systems are becoming more commonplace.[11] Garment producers in the United States thus can keep tariff duties to a minimum by performing the technology-intensive and high-value-added preassembly stage of apparel production in the United States; the more labor intensive assembly stage is still sourced offshore to low-wage nations. In addition, U.S. quotas based on quantity (rather than value) of exports have led some of the major East Asian garment-producing nations to make higher value-added clothes in order to increase the profitability of their fixed supply of exports. This strategy of climbing the value-added ladder has been hindered by the marked currency appreciations that have affected East Asian nations like Taiwan and South Korea.

Automobiles

The international motor vehicle industry underwent a profound change in the 1970s and 1980s. The oil price rises of 1973 and 1979, coupled with the rapid growth of the Japanese automotive industry since the 1960s and the decline in demand for motor vehicles in the main producing countries, significantly advanced the internationalization of capital and fostered the creation of a truly global industry. The three regional blocs of North America, Europe, and East Asia are becoming much more closely linked in trade, cross-investments, and joint production arrangements.[12]

The leading automotive transnational corporations (TNCs) have transformed their global sourcing arrangements in two novel ways. First, the industry is integrating its production process on a global scale by the international sourcing of standard parts and engineering resources needed to design and build "world cars." In this way, certain countries have emerged as the key suppliers for basic components or even entire vehicles. Second, automotive TNCs are producing more complex components with advanced technologies in developing countries. This "world component supply strategy" entails a higher degree of technological sophistication and country specialization than the complementary "world car strategy," which emphasizes broadly based, and sometimes regional, production schemes of a more labor intensive nature.

The trend toward regional integration within the global strategies of car makers is well illustrated by Toyota's recent agreement with members of the Association of Southeast Asian Nations (ASEAN) to begin a component-parts exchange program.[13] Diesel engines from Thailand, gasoline engines from Indonesia, steering gears from Malaysia, and transmissions from the Philippines are to be shipped among the participating countries for assembly of cars that eventually will be sent back to Japan for export to overseas markets. Such an arrangement will help Japan minimize tariffs within the ASEAN bloc and also avoid U.S. export quotas, since component supplies from the other Asian nations would not be counted as Japanese domestic content.

Mexico provides a good example of specialized component assembly for the U.S. market. Lured by low wages, a favorable currency exchange rate, close proximity to the United States, and favorable Mexican legislation, world automakers and parts suppliers have increased their exports from plants in Mexico.[14] Automobile engines are being manufactured by U.S.-based TNCs in high volume for incorporation into cars built in their U.S. plants. Mexican engine production is the epitome of global integration, combining "U.S. managers, European technology, Japanese manufacturing systems, and Mexican workers."[15]

The common pressures toward internationalization in both production and trade have produced distinct results in the Latin American and East Asian NICs.[16] Although South Korea and Brazil both have stressed exports of *finished vehicles,* these results stem from different kinds of corporate strategies and structures. The large integrated domestic auto companies in South Korea have been able to fund both long-term investment and product development at home and overseas, leading to the establishment of Korean automobile subsidiaries in major external markets like the United States and Canada. Brazil's exports of finished vehicles, however, reflect the desire of the U.S., Japanese, and European TNCs to use Brazil as a regional base to serve their customers in neighboring Latin American and other Third World countries.

Taiwan and Mexico have tended to emphasize the production of *auto parts* in the global motor vehicle industry, with close ties to the U.S. market. Whereas Mexico has implemented this component supplier strategy through the intrafirm networks of automotive TNCs, Taiwan has relied heavily on the efforts of 2,000 domestic auto parts companies, the majority of which are family businesses that are able to respond quickly to shifting consumer demand, but less able to invest in the research and expensive production machinery needed to improve their design capability and technological sophistication. Taiwan's auto assembly industry provided around 10,000 jobs in the mid-1980s; its parts industry employed 50,000 people. Nearly 60 percent of Taiwan's auto exports are sent to the United States. They are add-on accessories or spare parts sold in the after market; relatively few of Taiwan's auto parts exporters have major OEM contracts.[17]

In summary, these differences in the mode of incorporation of each of the NICs into the global motor vehicle industry are caused by national variations in industrial structure, the competitive strategies of the leading auto manufacturers worldwide, and the distinctive role of automobiles in advanced phases of ISI and EOI.

Personal Computers

The production of personal computers consists of four different stages that can be separated in time and space: knowledge-based research and design, advanced manufacturing, unskilled assembly work, and final product testing.[18] Each stage has distinct labor requirements, which has led to the spatial segmentation of the global industry. Research and design activities require ready access to highly trained scientists and engineers, which is facilitated by proximity to universities and research institutes such as those found in the innovative centers of the United States, Europe, and Japan. Advanced manufacturing and testing functions require skilled manual workers, technicians, and quality control supervision. This phase of production has been dispersed to semiperipheral locations in East Asia and Latin America in recent years containing at a minimum isolated pools of skilled labor and an adequate industrial infrastructure. Increased automation in the advanced manufacturing and testing areas of production, however, has led to a gradual return of some of these jobs to the more developed countries. Finally, assembly activities continue to draw mainly on unskilled labor, and they overwhelmingly are located in the low-wage areas of East Asia, Latin America, and the Caribbean.

Three primary patterns of global sourcing are evident within the personal computer industry.[19] First, much like the garment and footwear industries, the personal computer industry depends to a considerable degree on the sourcing of semiskilled, labor-intensive production operations from low-wage locations offshore. Second, the global sourcing of components and "peripherals" is common in the personal computer industry because developing nations are able to manufacture components without necessarily having the technological capability to make complete computer systems. South

Korean and Taiwanese producers have specialized in producing computer hardware on an OEM basis for computer TNCs.[20] Third, the sourcing of finished personal computers from the Third World into the United States is a relatively limited phenomenon since most developing nations lack the internal market needed to allow them to become efficient broad-line producers of completed personal computers. Mexico has an arrangement with IBM, however, to export finished computers to the U.S. market, and similar arrangements are being considered in other NICs.

REGIONAL DYNAMICS AND THE RESHAPING OF THE PACIFIC RIM

The trend toward global sourcing arrangements and international subcontracting in the world economy has profoundly affected the regional dynamics in East Asia and North America. Even as the internal division of labor *within* each region has become more complex, the economic and social linkages *between* the two regions have increased. This has produced a simultaneous consolidation and multilateralization of these regional blocs. Changes in the flows of goods (international trade), capital (direct foreign investment), and people (international migration) that link nations within the Pacific Rim illustrate these changes.

Industrial Upgrading and the Consolidation of Regional Divisions of Labor

Manufactured exports from Japan and the East Asian NICs (Hong Kong, Taiwan, South Korea, and Singapore) have been a central feature of the so-called East Asian economic miracle of the past three decades. The level of these exports has skyrocketed throughout the 1970s and 1980s, as the East Asian NICs clearly established themselves as the Third World's premier exporters. Hong Kong topped the list in 1988 with U.S.$63.2 billion in exports, followed closely by South Korea and Taiwan with export totals of just over U.S.$60 billion each; Singapore had U.S.$39.2 billion in exports. Although quite successful by their own historical and regional standards, the Latin American NICs trailed their East Asian counterparts by a considerable margin. Brazil was the leading Latin American exporter at U.S.$33.7 billion, followed by Mexico with an export total of U.S.$20.7 billion.[21]

The East Asian and Latin American NICs' export promotion efforts have been centered on the U.S. market since their onset in the 1960s. Nonetheless, the degree of export reliance on the United States varies considerably among the NICs. In 1987, Mexico's dependence on the U.S. market was the greatest, at 65 percent, followed by Taiwan at 44 percent; South Korea, 39 percent; Hong Kong and Brazil, around 28 percent; and Singapore, 25 percent.[22] The United States was the leading export market for each of these nations.

The willingness and ability of the United States to continue to fuel the NICs' export growth in the future is very doubtful, however. The United States has had world-record trade deficits in the late 1980s. With the exception of Germany, most of the other West European nations are running trade deficits as well. The political pressures for protectionism in the developed countries are well documented and likely to grow. How the NICs respond to this challenge rests to a large degree on their ability to diversify their export markets, both geographically and through product specialization.

One way this diversification has occurred is through the process of industrial upgrading that has characterized many of the export-oriented industries in the NICs. Although the first significant wave of exports from the East Asian NICs in the late 1950s and the 1960s came from traditional, labor-intensive industries like textiles, apparel, and footwear that relied on low wages and an unskilled work force, there has been a very pronounced shift in the 1980s toward an upgraded, skill-intensive version of EOI. These new export industries include higher value-added items that employ sophisticated technology and require a more extensively developed, tightly integrated local industrial base. Products range from computers and semiconductors to numerically controlled machine tools, televisions, videocassette recorders, and sporting goods. This export dynamism in East Asia does not derive solely from introducing new products, but also from continuously upgrading traditional ones (such as garments).

The Latin American NICs also have developed a sophisticated array of exports on the basis of their earlier import-substituting industries. U.S. automobile companies are setting up world-class engine plants in Mexico, for example, partly to cope with Japanese competition.[23] Brazil too has developed state-of-the-art, technologically advanced, and increasingly export-oriented industries from an ISI base in fields like automobiles, computers, armaments, and assorted capital goods.

There are a variety of causes associated with this shift from labor-intensive to technology- and capital-intensive exports. One of the most obvious factors in the consumer goods industries is *U.S. protectionism*, which includes a battery of measures such as tariffs, quotas, and voluntary export restraints intended to protect U.S. firms from Third World manufactured exports. Ironically, these policies frequently have been counterproductive since they have encouraged overseas manufacturers (especially in East Asia) to develop more sophisticated exports to escape the protectionist barriers. Industrial upgrading also has resulted from the *rising wage rates* and recent *currency appreciations* within the East Asian NICs, which pushed them toward exports that were technology intensive and utilized better paid, skilled workers. This latter factor is coupled with the strong competition that has come from *relatively low wage neighboring Asian economies,* such as Malaysia, Thailand, the Philippines, Indonesia, and China.

From a regional perspective, one of the most important consequences of this industrial upgrading has been the emergence of a rather complex internal division of labor within the East Asian political economy. Japan is the technologically advanced core country of the East Asian region, with the East Asian NICs (South Korea, Taiwan, Hong Kong, and Singapore) playing the role of a semiperiphery with continuous industrial upgrading pushing them toward more technology intensive, higher value added exports. Taiwan and South Korea also have taken in some of the energy-intensive and heavily polluting industries no longer encouraged to remain in Japan (such as chemicals, fertilizers, and mineral smelting operations). The periphery in East Asia is the resource-rich, lower wage countries such as the Philippines, Malaysia, Thailand, Indonesia, and China, that not only supply the region with raw material exports but also specialize in the labor-intensive manufacturing industries that were the export success stories of the East Asian NICs in the first stage of their EOI in the 1960s.[24]

A very similar regional division of labor is emerging in North America. Obviously, the United States is the core country in North America, both as a production center and a market. It has established tight transnational linkages with Canada and now also Mexico in a range of capital-intensive, high-technology industries such as automobiles, and electrical and nonelectrical machinery. Unlike the East Asian situation, however, all three of the main economies in North America also are rich in natural resources. Although Mexico traditionally has been the site for labor-intensive exports from its "old" *maquiladora* plants, many of these same export-oriented assembly operations are now springing up in a number of Caribbean nations, which may become the favored locales for these peripheral economic activities. One additional element in the North American situation is the growing importance of Asian investments in the region, with Japanese firms concentrating on the "new" technology-intensive export industries and Korean and Taiwanese companies investing in the "old" labor-intensive assembly operations.[25]

This latter feature moves us beyond the vertical integration of the regional political economies in East Asia and North America to the trans-Pacific linkages between the two regions. This can be seen most clearly if we focus on the growth of garment exports to the United States from countries in the Caribbean Basin.

The Multilateralization of Regional Blocs

This cross-penetration of regional blocs in the world economy is fast making nations in the Caribbean Basin a preferred source of manufactured exports destined for the U.S. market. This is most readily apparent in the garment in-

TABLE 4.2   Textiles, Apparel, and Footwear: Duty-Free Value of U.S. Imports for Consumption Under Harmonized Tariff Schedule (HTS) Subheading 9802.00.80, by Principal Sources, 1985–1988 (millions of U.S. dollars)

Source	1985	1986	1987	1988
Mexico	282	363	380	406
Dominican Republic	143	190	234	318
Costa Rica	62	84	92	131
Haiti	80	78	97	102
Jamaica	28	49	84	96
Colombia	22	26	30	50
Honduras	17	20	27	39
Guatemala	6	9	20	30
South Korea	4	4	7	27
El Salvador	6	6	13	17
All other	74	76	81	94
Total	723	906	1,065	1,312

NOTE: Because of rounding, figures may not add to the totals shown.

SOURCE: U.S. International Trade Commission, *Production Sharing* (USITC Publication No. 2243, 1989), p. 6-3.

dustry. Caribbean apparel exports to the United States more than quadrupled to nearly U.S.$1 billion in the four years following the passage of President Reagan's Caribbean Basin Initiative (CBI) in 1983, creating upwards of 100,000 jobs in the Caribbean.[26] The CBI allows U.S. apparel manufacturers to ship fabric for sewing to low-wage factories in the islands and reimport the finished goods with substantial tax breaks. The *maquiladora* factories in Mexico have a similar preferred status.

If we look more generally at garment exports into the United States that enjoy duty-free content under the Harmonized Tariff Schedule (HTS) subheading 9802.00.80 (formerly item 807 under the tariff schedules of the United States in effect prior to January 1, 1989), most of the foreign sewing operations are located in Mexico and four Caribbean countries: the Dominican Republic, Jamaica, Costa Rica, and Haiti (see Table 4.2). These nations have an abundant supply of low-cost labor, and their proximity to the United States provides U.S. and other foreign firms with greater control over production and shorter delivery lead times than goods shipped from East Asia. In addition, Section 936 of the U.S. Internal Revenue Code provides a tax break to U.S. companies operating "twin" or complementary plants in Puerto Rico and CBI beneficiary nations.[27]

Table 4.3 shows the cost of producing four typical garments in the United States, in the Caribbean Basin under HTS subheading 9802.00.80, and in Hong Kong, the major source of U.S. imported apparel. The figures show that assembly costs in the Caribbean are only one-third of U.S. assembly costs and three-fourths of Hong Kong's costs. Even after subtracting the duties and other expenses associated with importing, the use of Caribbean assembled products still results in cost savings of between 15 and 30 percent.

TABLE 4.3   Cost Comparison of Producing Selected Apparel Products Among the United States, the Caribbean Basin, and Hong Kong Under Harmonized Tariff Schedule (HTS) Subheading 9802.00.80, 1987

	Materials		Labor and Overhead		Freight, Duty and Related Costs	Total Costs
	Fabric	Total	Cutting	Assembly		
	Women's Blouses[a]					
Domestic	$2.91	$13.33	$0.29	$4.75	$0.04	$8.41
Caribbean	2.90	13.33	.29	1.66	.77	6.05
Hong Kong	2.10	12.53	.09	2.20	1.41	6.23
	Men's Sport Coats[b]					
Domestic	$9.00	$14.90	$3.84	$15.66	$0.08	$34.48
Caribbean	9.00	14.90	3.84	5.44	3.49	27.67
Hong Kong	7.20	11.63	1.26	7.24	8.12	28.25
	Brassieres[c]					
Domestic	$0.55	$2.19	$0.18	$1.79	$0.01	$4.17
Caribbean	.55	2.19	.18	.73	.45	3.55
Hong Kong	.43	1.65	.07	.83	.87	3.42
	Men's Casual Slacks[d]					
Domestic	$3.03	$3.59	$0.16	$4.46	$0.02	$8.23
Caribbean	3.03	3.59	.16	1.50	6.57	5.88
Hong Kong	2.51	2.93	.06	2.08	1.26	6.33

[a]Long-sleeved blouses, not ornamented, of 55 percent cotton and 45 percent polyester.
[b]Men's sport coats, not ornamented, of 100 percent polyester.
[c]Artificial-fiber underwire brassieres. The 9802.00.80 cost assumes finishing in the United States. The Hong Kong cost is for a finished package.
[d]Men's casual slacks, not ornamented, of 100 percent cotton canvas fabric.

SOURCE: U.S. International Trade Commission, *Production Sharing* (USITC Publication No. 2243, 1989), p. 6-4.

East Asian garment makers, who are facing labor shortages and rising wages at home, are beginning to flock into the Caribbean Basin to circumvent quota problems and take advantage of lower production costs and faster reaction times.[28] The Dominican Republic provides a good example of this "reverse investment" by the East Asian NICs in the Caribbean. Although the majority of the 225 firms in the Dominican Republic's "Industrial Free Zone" are of U.S. origin, there already are fifteen South Korean companies, employing 6,000 workers, and nine firms from Taiwan.[29] Furthermore, East Asian projects usually contribute higher value added, more jobs, higher levels of investment, and a greater utilization of skilled labor than the 9802.00.80 sewing operations by other foreign firms.[30]

Despite these gains, one should be skeptical of the longer term role that labor-intensive EOI can play in the development of these Caribbean nations. Although export processing activities such as those that have grown so rapidly in Mexico and the Caribbean Basin in recent years have undeniable benefits in job creation, foreign exchange earnings, and the fostering of industrial experience, they do not constitute an appropriate basis for a long-term development strategy. Export processing industries may be a starting point for industrialization, but they are not a permanent solution for the countries of the region. They are best seen as a transitional phenomenon: the first stage in a process of moving to a higher level of industrial development when other, more secure jobs will be available.[31]

The major problems of labor-intensive export industries are that they typically have very shallow roots in the local economy and they contribute little to the technological progress of a nation. Mexico's *maquiladora* plants, for example, used only about 3 to 6 percent domestic content in the mid-1980s; well over 90 percent of the materials employed by the manufacturers were imported. This is one of the reasons why Taiwan and South Korea moved very quickly to increase the levels of local integration by export industries in their economies by allowing "bonded factories" to be established anywhere in the country as long as the majority of their output was destined for export.[32] In addition, even very small exporting firms in the East Asian NICs have been encouraged to use modern technology in their factories to enhance their industrial competitiveness.

Although it usually takes a generation for a country's skill base to advance from garment work to electronics, both U.S. and East Asian electronics companies are beginning to establish new plants in the Caribbean to export electronics goods duty free into the United States.[33] A favorable geographical location thus is a major positive factor that can help the Caribbean Basin nations spur their industrial development if accompanied by the right domestic priorities.

The proposed free trade agreement between the United States and Mexico, or a broader North American Free Trade Agreement (NAFTA) that would include Canada and perhaps the Caribbean as well, is unlikely to diminish the substantial transnational integration that already has been established in the region. Although NAFTA explicitly focuses on trade, the ongoing globalization of production in the world economy has produced a "silent integration" in North America that makes the strategic investment decisions by TNCs the prime determinant of new intraregional and interregional trading patterns.

In a formal sense, *maquiladora* industries will cease to exist in Mexico as a legal category if a zero-tariff NAFTA is put into place. Historically the main reason *maquiladoras* were set up was to take advantage of the U.S. tariff provisions (806/807) that allowed participating firms to receive duty-free inputs from the United States and thereby to pay tax only on the value added in Mexico. With no tariffs, *maquiladora* plants are an anachronism.

In reality, however, labor-intensive assembly industries tend to be established wherever low wages, adequate infrastructure, and political stability are to be found. Mexico remains a very attractive site for these investments, although there also is likely to be a sharp growth of "old"-style *maquiladoras* in the Caribbean and Central America where labor costs are as low as in Mexico and the "rules of origin" restrictions of a NAFTA may not apply. If Mexico follows the example of the East Asian NICs, it will try to promote the "new" *maquiladoras* because of their added contributions to national development objectives and allow many of the "old" *maquiladoras* to migrate to other sites in the region.[34]

Global Capitalism and Urban Restructuring in the United States

The dynamics of global sourcing and international subcontracting within and between East Asia and North America involve not only the flow of manufactured products and investment capital, but also of people. Migrant labor flows are significantly changing the spatial organization of production in global industries as core capitalist economies are becoming ever more dependent upon young migrant workers from the Third World. This is reflected in the urban restructuring that currently is under way in the United States. There has been a proliferation of turn-of-the-century-type sweatshops in the garment and electronics industries in large North American cities, especially Los Angeles, Miami, and New York City, that draw on vast pools of low-wage and in many cases undocumented immigrant workers from Mexico, Central America, the Caribbean, and Asia. Many of these U.S. plants have been set up by East Asian entrepreneurs to avoid U.S. trade barriers and to exploit low-cost labor, with the added advantage of direct access to the design and marketing centers in the United States.

Los Angeles County, for example, has become the largest manufacturing metropolitan area in the United States in the 1980s, and its heavy influx of Latin American and East Asian (especially South Korean) migrants has played a major role in this process.[35] Like New York City and Miami, whose resurgence is tied to diverse immigrant flows, Los Angeles combines manufacturing of the highest technical level and the lowest. For instance, garment manufacture in Los Angeles expanded by nearly 60 percent in the past fifteen years, while at the same time the industry contracted by 20 percent in the United States as a whole.[36] Over half of the 3,500 garment factories in Los Angeles County are owned by Asians, the three main groups being Korean, Vietnamese, and Chinese; another third of the factory owners are Latinos, primarily from Mexico.

If one takes a closer look at the bustling garment district near downtown Los Angeles, one finds a predominance of Korean subcontractors making clothes for manufacturers located all around the United States. The local subcontracting networks are exceptionally dense. A single Los Angeles–based manufacturer of blue jeans sold under the brand name "Yes" employs 500 different ethnic subcontractors in Los Angeles alone.[37] It is not uncommon for Korean garment contractors to employ a mix of Asian and Latino workers, who battle many ethnic antagonisms as they struggle to make ends meet with several members of the family working in the area's needle trades. The most skilled and enterprising may save enough money to set up their own shops, using ethnic networks to entice their Mexican, Guatemalan, or Chinese compatriots to provide the labor and services needed to survive under conditions of cutthroat competition.

The garment industry in Los Angeles is but one example of the resurgence of domestic subcontracting in the United States, using local pools of immigrant workers and entrepreneurs to compete with the "runaway shops" that went to East Asia and Latin America in search of cheap and reliable labor. It draws the U.S. economy tightly into the Pacific Rim, not only as the world's largest market but also as a site for labor-intensive manufacturing in the tenement sweatshops of major U.S. metropolitan areas. And since many of these workers have come to the United States with the intention of staying as permanent immigrants, these new ethnically dominated industrial districts are likely to be stable domestic production alternatives to the overseas export platforms.

If development theory is to be relevant for the 1990s, it will have to be flexible enough to incorporate increased specialization at the product and geographical levels along with new forms of integration that link the core, semiperipheral, and peripheral nations of the Pacific Rim in novel ways.[38] The production and export networks of the garment, automobile, and personal computer industries illustrate the various modes of incorporation of the NICs in the world economy and the continuing geographical realignment of the location of core and peripheral economic activities in today's global commodity chains.

NOTES

A related version of this paper appears in Ravi Arvind Palat, ed., *Pacific-Asia and the Future of the World-System,* Westport, CT: Greenwood Press, 1992.

1. Arif Dirlik, "The Asia-Pacific Idea: Reality and Representation in the Invention of a Regional Structure," *Journal of World History* 3, no. 1 (Spring 1992).

2. See Gary Gereffi and Donald Wyman, eds., *Manufacturing Miracles: Paths of Industrialization in Latin America and East Asia* (Princeton, NJ: Princeton University Press, 1990); Gary Gereffi, "International Economics and Domestic Policies," in Neil J. Smelser and Alberto Martinelli, eds., *Economy and Society: Overviews in Economic Sociology* (Newbury Park, CA: Sage, 1990), pp. 231–258.

3. "North America" includes the United States, Canada, Mexico, and the Caribbean.

4. Gary Gereffi, "Development Strategies and the Global Factory," *Annals of the American Academy of Political and Social Science* 505 (1989): 92–104.

5. Regarding footwear, see Gary Gereffi and Miguel Korzeniewicz, "Commodity Chains and Footwear Exports in the Semiperiphery," in William Martin, ed., *Semiperipheral States in the World-Economy* (Westport, CT: Greenwood Press, 1990), pp. 45–68.

6. Kurt Hoffman, "Clothing, Chips and Competitive Advantage: The Impact of Microelectronics on Trade and Production in the Garment Industry," *World Development* 13, no. 3 (1985): 371.

7. Hoffman, "Clothing, Chips and Competitive Advantage," pp. 375–376.

8. Ashoka Mody and David Wheeler, "Towards a Vanishing Middle: Competition in the World Garment Industry," *World Development* 15, no. 10/11 (1987): 1,281.

9. Michael L. Dertouzos, Richard K. Lester, and Robert M. Solow, *Made in America: Regaining the Productive Edge* (Cambridge, MA: MIT Press, 1989), p. 292; James Lardner, "The Sweater Trade," part 1, *New Yorker*, January 11, 1988, pp. 60, 62–65.

10. Lardner, "The Sweater Trade."

11. Hoffman, "Clothing, Chips and Competitive Advantage."

12. Rhys Jenkins, *Transnational Corporations and the Latin American Automobile Industry* (Pittsburgh, PA: University of Pittsburgh Press, 1987).

13. Charles Smith, "Parts Exchange," *Far Eastern Economic Review,* September 21, 1989, p. 73.

14. Gary Gereffi, "Big Business and the State," in Gereffi and Wyman, *Manufacturing Miracles,* pp. 90–109.

15. Harley Shaiken, with Stephen Herzenberg, *Automation and Global Production: Automobile Engine Production in Mexico, the United States, and Canada* (La Jolla, CA: Center for U.S. Mexican Studies, University of California, San Diego, Monograph Series No. 26, 1987), p. 2.

16. Gereffi, "Big Business and the State," p. 106.

17. Andrew Tank, "Made in Taiwan: Will Taiwan Be Asia's Next Automotive Powerhouse?" *Automotive News,* September 29, 1986, pp. 29–31.

18. Jeffrey Henderson, *The Globalisation of High Technology Production: Society, Space and Semiconductors in the Restructuring of the Modern World* (London: Routledge, 1989); Manuel Castells, "The New Industrial Space: Information-Technology Manufacturing and Spatial Structure in the United States," in George Sternlieb and James W. Hughes, eds., *America's New Market Geography* (New Brunswick, NJ: Center for Urban Policy Research, Rutgers University, 1989), pp. 43–99.

19. See David C. O'Connor, "The Computer Industry in the Third World: Policy Options and Constraints," *World Development* 13, no. 3 (1985): 311–332; Henderson, *The Globalisation of High Technology Production.*

20. Peter B. Evans, and Paulo Bastos Tigre, "Paths to Participation in 'High-Tech' Industry: A Comparative Analysis of Computers in Brazil and Korea," *Asian Perspective* 13, no. 1 (1989): 5–35.

21. World Bank, *World Development Report 1990* (New York: Oxford University Press, 1990), pp. 204–205.

22. United Nations, *1987 International Trade Statistics Yearbook,* vol. 1 (New York: United Nations, 1989); Council for Economic Planning and Development, *Taiwan Statistical Data Book, 1988* (Taipei: CEPD, 1988), p. 222.

23. Shaiken, *Automation and Global Production.*

24. Bruce Cumings, "The Origins and Development of the Northeast Asian Political Economy: Industrial Sectors, Product Cycles, and Political Consequences," *International Organization* 38, no. 1 (Winter 1984): 1–40; Henderson, *The Globalisation of High Technology Production.*

25. Gary Gereffi, "Mexico's Maquiladora Industries and North American Integration" (Paper presented at a conference titled "Facing North/Facing South: Canadian–United States–Mexican Relations," University of Calgary, Alberta, Canada, May 2–4, 1991).

26. Edward A. Finn, Jr., "Who Made Your Underwear?" *Forbes,* July 25, 1988, p. 56.

27. U.S. International Trade Commission, *Production Sharing: U.S. Imports Under Harmonized Tariff Schedule Subheadings 9802.00.60 and 9802.00.80, 1985–1988* (USITC Publication No. 2243, 1989), p. 6–5; Guillermo Hillcoat and Carlos Quenan, "Restructuración internacional y re-especialización productiva en el Caribe" (Paper presented at the Second Conference of Caribbean Economists, Bridgetown, Barbados, May 28–30, 1989).

28. Transit time by sea for U.S. clothing imports coming from East Asia is at least four weeks, compared to a matter of hours for goods flown to the United States from the Caribbean.

29. Hillcoat and Quenan, "Restructuración internacional y re-especialización productiva en el Caribe," p. 32.

30. U.S. International Trade Commission, *Production Sharing,* p. 6-5.

31. Sidney Weintraub, "The Maquiladora Industry in Mexico: Its Transitional Role," in Commission for the Study of International Migration and Cooperative Economic Development, ed., *Unauthorized Migration: Addressing the Root Causes,* vol. 2 (Washington, DC: U.S. Government Printing Office, 1990), pp. 1,143–1,155.

32. Gereffi, "Mexico's Maquiladora Industries and North American Integration."

33. Finn, "Who Made Your Underwear?" p. 58.

34. Gereffi, "Mexico's Maquiladora Industries and North American Integration."

35. Ivan Light and Edna Bonacich, *Immigrant Entrepreneurs: Koreans in Los Angeles, 1965–1982* (Berkeley: University of California Press, 1988).

36. Kevin F. McCarthy and R. Burciaga Valdez, *Current and Future Effects of Mexican Immigration in California* (Santa Monica: California Roundtable, Rand-R-3365-CR, 1986).

37. Author's interview with a Guatemalan garment subcontractor in Los Angeles, December 1, 1990.

38. Gary Gereffi, "Rethinking Development Theory: Insights from East Asia and Latin America," *Sociological Forum* 4, no. 4 (December 1989): 505–533.

Restructuring Manufacturing: Mexican *Maquiladoras* and East Asian EPZs in the Presence of the North American Free Trade Agreement

*I*N THE DISCUSSION below, we examine the Mexican *maquiladora* program (MMP) within an Asia-Pacific perspective. In this perspective, two aspects of the *maquiladora* program are especially important. First is the resemblance between *maquiladoras* and the export processing zones (EPZs) of Asia-Pacific economies. Although EPZs today are not restricted to the Asia-Pacific region, the classic examples are to be found in this region. The EPZs, we argue, played a significant part in the economic development of Asia-Pacific societies such as Taiwan and South Korea, and are emblematic of an Asia-Pacific, or more precisely, Japanese model of development. To the extent that the *maquiladora* program bears resemblances to Asia-Pacific EPZs, it may be viewed as part of a regionally shaped pattern of development, if not in its origins at least in the shape it has assumed in response to Asia-Pacific development. Two successful examples of Asia-Pacific EPZs, Masan in South Korea and Kaohsiung in Taiwan, provide a base for comparison between Mexican and Asia-Pacific development. The experience of these EPZs may also have much to tell us about the future of the *maquiladora* program in Mexico.

The second aspect points to a more direct relationship between the *maquiladora* program and the Asia-Pacific region. In recent years, Asia-Pacific involvement in Mexican *maquiladoras* has intensified; especially prominent are Japanese investments in the *maquiladoras*. The question is no longer one of parallels between Mexican and Asia-Pacific development, but the incorporation of the *maquiladoras* in the Asia-Pacific regional economy, which means that the Asia-Pacific or Japanese model of development now directly shapes the dynamics of Mexican development.

This development at the same time points to problems (or even contradictions) in the conceptualization of an Asia-Pacific region that rather than being a region unto itself, is merely one region in the global economy and subject to its tensions. The Mexican *maquiladoras* developed initially on the U.S.-Mexican border as part of an economic relationship between those two countries. Although the new *maquiladoras* are significantly different from the initial ones both in location and in structure, important forces are at work to sustain their original status as primarily U.S.-Mexican economic enclaves. We are referring here to the North American Free Trade Agreement (NAFTA), which is intended to establish a distinct economic region in North America, standing in a problematic relationship to the Asia-Pacific region with which it overlaps spatially as well as in terms of economic structure. Asia-Pacific involvement in the *maquiladoras* implies, in other words, that the *maquiladoras* may serve not just as a site of interaction between two regional economies, but also as a site of contradiction and conflict. How to reconcile these two dimensions of the *maquiladoras* is, we will try to demonstrate, a central concern of NAFTA. The contradictions also lend insights into contradictions within the contemporary global economy, both in terms of the relationship between national economies and intranational economic enclaves (which are *inter*national in structure and character), and in terms of overlapping regional formations in the global economy. These contradictions render uncertain the future of national economies as well as of regional economic organizations; but in the short run, we argue, they may prove to be beneficial to countries such as Mexico that are located, in a manner of speaking, on the frontiers of regional economies.

EPZS AND THE JAPANESE MODEL

For obvious reasons EPZs are most effective within the context of global trade and production of which they are in some ways the product. The success of EPZ nations such as Taiwan and Korea coincided with a shift in national development strategies from import substitution to export orientation. Without the presence of foreign investment, in this case Japan, however, these strategies would have yielded little results.

Some scholars have argued that without the Japanese model of Foreign Direct Investment (FDI), the industrial "miracle" of East Asian countries might not have been possible.[1] Hill and Johns's[2] research suggests that essential to the Japanese model of FDI were the macroeconomic policies toward exports of Japanese multinational companies, which differed significantly from U.S. and European models with regard to the recipient economies. Compared to the latter, Japanese FDI evolved in a way more integrated in the recipient countries, making more likely the development of the local economy through the process of subcontracting and the creation of satellite industries.

A significant aspect of Japan's emergence as a world economic power has been its overseas investments in neighboring regions, especially in Korea, Taiwan, Hong Kong, and Singapore. Having exhausted domestic productive possibilities at the lowest labor cost and accumulated substantial financial assets, the Japanese turned to exporting funds in the form of donations, credits, technical cooperation, and foreign investment, increasing from U.S.\$486 million in 1965 to U.S.\$12.2 billion by 1981.[3] East Asian countries, with an excess of cheap labor and in dire need of foreign capital, welcomed such foreign investment to develop the production of manufactured goods for export. The developmental model represented by free export processing zones, enclave economies established in specific geographic sites outside of national customs borders, served this purpose well and flourished with the flow of Japanese funds. The principal characteristics of EPZs are exemption of manufactured goods from duty taxes together with a variety of incentives offered to foreign investors. In theory at least, the purpose of the EPZs was to benefit the whole national economy by serving as nodes for the diffusion of industrial development, generating employment, technology transfer, and revenues. The EPZs were to catalyze a domestic industrial network through subcontracting for the international industrial production within the zones.[4]

The experience of the EPZs shows that the Japanese subcontracting system has worked only under certain conditions of assimilation and technological adaptation by small- and medium-sized firms. East Asian countries, recipients of the first phase of technology transfer, had to put forth a great deal of effort and extend support to Japanese companies to modernize local scientific and technological research and development. Where they have been able to do so, local firms in the EPZs as well as outside of them have formed a unique symbiotic relationship with Japanese companies through subcontracting. A national economic policy that incorporates the EPZs into an overall strategy of national development, in other words, would seem to be indispensable to transforming the development of enclaves within the nation into the development of the national economy as a whole.

The port city of Masan is an outstanding example of a successful industrial enclave policy; with the aid of massive Japanese investments and through international industrial subcontracting, South Korea was transformed within two decades from an importing country to an exporting nation. Peter G. Warr[5] (see Table 5.1) indicates that over a thirteen-year period, South Korean industries of the Masan EPZ were rapidly integrated, increas-

TABLE 5.1 Masan EPZ: Aggregate Economic Performance, 1970–1982

	1970	1971	1972	1973	1974	1975	1976	1977	1978	1979	1980	1981	1982
Number of firms	4	22	70	115	110	105	99	99	97	94	88	89	83
	(0)	(6)	(24)	(71)	(98)	(101)	(96)	(97)	(95)	(86)	(85)	(81)	(80)
Employment	0	1,248	7,072	21,240	20,822	22,248	29,615	28,401	30,960	31,153	28,532	28,016	26,012
Average wage per employee (U.S.$ per month)	n.a.	66.0	69.3	70.2	75.5	86.8	101.9	121.5	127.8	137.7	144.3	175.6	191.0
Exports (U.S.$ million)	0	2.4	23.9	145.5	298.0	257.1	441.0	496.5	579.2	621.7	577.3	664.4	601.3
Local sales (U.S.$ million)	0	0	0	0	6.2	7.9	25.2	28.1	81.7	90.7	82.5	99.0	92.1
Imports (U.S.$ million)	0	1.9	16.5	91.7	176.7	137.8	216.7	239.3	270.7	293.0	266.2	295.9	281.7
Local raw material (U.S.$ million)	0	0	1.0	23.1	48.6	44.6	92.7	120.0	130.0	149.4	131.3	144.0	142.7
New investment (U.S.$ million)	4.8	9.1	77.8	94.8	10.0	0.1	13.1	8.0	9.6	3.3	–1.9	4.2	–1.0
Value added (U.S.$ million)	n.a.	0.5	6.4	30.7	78.9	82.6	156.8	165.3	260.2	270.0	262.3	323.5	269.0
Value added per worker (U.S.$ 1,000 per annum)	n.a.	0.40	0.90	1.45	3.79	3.71	5.29	5.82	8.40	8.67	9.19	11.55	10.34

NOTE: Calculated from data obtained from Administration Office, Masan Free Export Zone, and International Monetary Fund, *International Financial Statistics*, various issues, at constant 1982 prices. Figures in parentheses indicate the number of operating firms.

SOURCE: Peter G. Warr, "Korea's Masan Free Export Zone: Benefits and Costs," *Developing Economies*, 22(2), June 1984, p. 171.

ing their share of local sales of inputs to the foreign companies for the first decade and then registering a stable pattern during the subsequent years. Healey suggests that EPZs undergo four stages in their life cycle: formation, expansion, maturity, and decline.[6] This view is confirmed by the International Labour Organisation (ILO) model that suggested a distinguishable number of common patterns in a typical life cycle of an EPZ (see Figure 5.1).[7] During the formative stage, approximately the first five years, foreign investment decisions are based mostly on the availability of cheap labor; during an expansion stage in the sixth to the tenth year domestic manufacturers begin to supply goods to the foreign companies and technology is transferred to domestic industries to make them more efficient; maturity generally begins after the tenth year and is characterized by strong linkages to the national economy[8] and investments in urban infrastructure. At this point, incremental increases in the share of national exports and the rapid decline of the share of foreign industry in total employment are common. Finally, between the fifteenth and twentieth years the decline stage is characterized by stability or decline in foreign investment into EPZs and the beginning of international subcontracting by domestic firms.[9] For example, in the maturity stage of Masan, from 1977 to 1979, the increment of joint ventures with domestic Korean firms and foreign companies increased from 21 percent to 28 percent of total domestic and foreign investment.[10] Moreover, Warr shows this percentage had increased to 34.9 percent by 1983.[11] Consequently, South Korea as well as Taiwan and Singapore have taken an active role in foreign investment in less developed neighboring countries. Today, South Korea products and technology compete advantageously in international markets. Thus, history repeats itself as countries that formerly received foreign investment are transformed into providers of the same, reinforcing Japanese foreign investment strategies in the Pacific Rim in a process referred to as investment feedback.

Japanese presence through direct investment in South Korean EPZs like Masan has been very significant. For Masan, the statistics show that in 1986 Japanese investment in the electronics industry accounted for 94.2 percent of the total, compared to 3.7 percent from the United States. In other industrial sectors there are similar patterns. In the production of machinery the relation was 85.1 percent by Japan to 4.2 percent by the United States, and in the production of precision products 84.7 percent and 0.1 percent, respectively.[12] The influence of high-tech Japanese firms through DFI for assembly and export has been crucial in the Masan EPZ and therefore in the industrial and technological development of South Korea.

Another important example of growth outside EPZs being generated by the implementation of the "Japanese model" can be seen in the Kaohsiung EPZ in the Republic of China (Taiwan). In 1973, during the expansion stage eight years after establishment, 25.8 percent of foreign direct investment in

74

FIGURE 5.1   The Typical Life Cycle of an East Asian EPZ

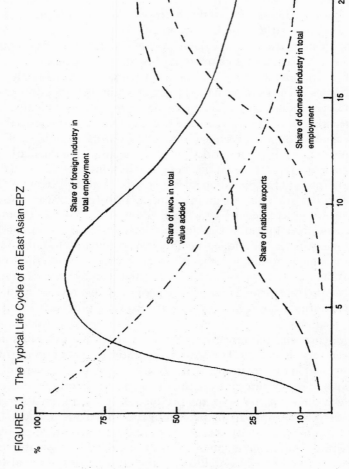

Source: Adapted by author from International Labour Organisation (ILO) and United Nations Centre on Transnational Corporations (UNCTC), *Economic and Social Effects of Multinational Enterprises in Export Processing Zones* (Monograph Series, Geneva, Switzerland, 1988), p. 151.

TABLE 5.2   Kaohsiung EPZ's Integration Performance: A Ratio of Imports from Custom Territory, 1967–1975 (in thousands of U.S. dollars)

	(A) Total Import		(B) Import from Custom Territory		
	Amount	Increase Rate	Amount	Increase Rate	B/A
1967	13,607	—	290	—	2.1%
1968	29,598	121%	1,464	405%	4.9%
1969	54,308	84%	4,145	183%	7.6%
1970	87,916	62%	7,161	73%	8.1%
1971	98,669	12%	13,330	86%	13.5%
1972	139,616	41%	20,852	56%	14.9%
1973	207,083	48%	34,965	68%	17.5%
1974	197,680	−5%	32,340	−8%	16.4%
1975	158,120	−20%	31,019	−4%	19.6%
Total	986,597		145,566		14.8%

SOURCE: W. Wang, *The Establishment and Development of Kaohsiung Export Processing Zone (KEPZ), 1965–1975: A Study of Economic Decision-Making in Taiwan, R.O.C.* (Taipei: Asia and World Institute, 1981), p. 73. Calculated from EPZs' "Essential Statistics" in EPZ Concentrates.

Kaohsiung was of Japanese origin. During the same year 17.6 percent of total joint venture investment was by foreign and Taiwanese companies; of this percentage 12 percent was by Japanese and Taiwanese companies.[13] From this fact it can be established that the integration between the industrial activities of the enclave economy and foreign companies through subcontracting occurs usually in the first ten years of operation. Kaohsiung also offers an example of how companies oriented toward export increasingly require local inputs. In Kaohsiung in 1967 the level of integration characterized by the percentage of national inputs of the total imports to Kaohsiung EPZ represented only 2.1 percent, but by 1975, with the expansion stage under way, had increased to 19.6 percent[14] (see Table 5.2). For the maturity stage, the 1985 subcontracting data for Kaohsiung EPZ show the established companies subcontracting with more than 1,200 local firms outside the EPZ.[15]

All evidence points to EPZs as having played a significant role in the development of newly industrialized countries (NICs) such as Taiwan and Korea, which has led to their incorporation into development strategies around the world. EPZs are to be found today in ASEAN countries and along the Pacific Rim as the trigger for industrialization. Among noteworthy ones are the Darwin EPZ in Australia and Papua New Guinea in the South Pacific;[16] several zones in India, among which the Kadla EPZ is especially prominent;[17] and those in Communist states like the People's Republic of China. In the early part of the 1980s, countries such as South Korea, Taiwan, and Hong Kong, in order to become more competitive internationally, expanded outside of their political boundaries to neighboring territories that not long before had been considered enemy territory. The end of the cold war and the deepening crisis of socialist countries have made it possible to open up new forms of regional integration in which the enclave EPZ model has been used as the predominant strategy. South Korea and North Korea have entered a negotiation process aiming toward economic integration, in which the capital and advanced technology of the former is to be combined with the inexpensive land and labor costs of the letter. The Chinese province of Guangdong is increasingly integrated with the Hong Kong economy, and Fujian southeastern China is on its way to becoming a new enclave for Taiwan. The future special economic zone in Pyongyang, North Korea, is expected to encourage joint venture projects with South Korea.[18] Other such possible zones in Vietnam and the Pacific provinces of the former USSR are in the offing. Because of their flexibility in operating in an open global economy, EPZs are enjoying a boom as global producers seek to liberate themselves from the constraints imposed by nation-states. This, however, also intensifies competition for foreign investments. Some of the new EPZs, such as those in India, have recently increased incentives to attract foreign capital.[19]

In this framework the development of the East Asian EPZs in the last twenty-five years, of which the most outstanding examples are those from Taiwan and South Korea, provides a rich source of policies and strategies that can inform the Mexican experience in the 1990s. Similarities will not be exact in direction or intensity; Mexico's current economic, cultural, political, and social conditions differ from those prevailing in 1966 in Taiwan. But the experience of the East Asian EPZs may offer parameters for forecasting the likely course of the *maquiladora* industry during the 1990s with the emergence of a new *maquiladora* industry and NAFTA. What we see in North America along with NAFTA is a global economic process similar to that earlier experienced in Asia. The inclusion of Mexico in a free trade agreement with the United States and Canada demonstrates the need not only for expanded markets but also for a regional constituency that remains competitive in a new international economy. The question that arises is: Can the infusion of Asian investments in Mexico replicate the model of domestic growth and development observed in East Asia?

THE MEXICAN "MAQUILADORA" PROGRAM

The Mexican *maquiladora* program (MMP) was initiated in the mid-1960s, about the same time as the EPZs in Eastern Asia. An EPZ-like program, Mexican *maquiladoras* represented an experiment in developing the northern border region by inviting U.S. capital investment. This restricted goal, failing to tie the *maquiladoras* to the rest of the national economy, led to the stifling of the *maquiladoras* as well.

For most international development economists, the 1980s began a new era favoring the neoclassical paradigm of development over Keynesianism and state socialism. The neoclassical school integrated a wide spectrum of policies that could be applied similarly in all countries facing economic crisis. One of the countries to implement these policies is Mexico.

Following the economic crisis of 1982, Mexico agreed to abandon the protectionism and state intervention that characterized the period of import substitution and oil dependency in favor of a model of development consistent with the general trend toward building up an industrial sector to solve the problem of inflation, increase production, and reduce the external deficit of the country. At the time, the Mexican economy was characterized by an inefficient industrial production system that was technologically backward, suffered from high sectoral and regional concentration, and could manage at best a fragile coordination of the productive sector; all of which resulted in limited competitiveness at the international level.

As Mexico enters the 1990s, the country has consolidated a productive sector that may prove to be of strategic importance in its short-term economic growth plans, the *maquiladora* industry. Because it differs significantly from the *maquiladoras* of the 1960s, the new *maquiladora* industry (NMI), as it has been aptly described, represents a new departure (see Figure 5.2). The new *maquiladora* industry, in the liberalization of foreign investment strategies and the "opening" of Mexico's economy, is very much in line with the neoclassical economic trends of the 1980s. Its emergence also represents an internal transformation of the *maquiladora* program, comparable to the transformation of the Asian EPZs in the 1970s.[20] The question that remains is whether the lessons that have been learned from the analysis of East Asian EPZ subcontracting experiences are applicable to the Mexican *maquiladora* program.

Available statistics show that by the end of 1991, there were more than 2,000 *maquiladora* plants, employing close to 500,000 workers and occupying second place as the major source of revenue for Mexico, with an approximate annual rate of growth of 20 percent surpassed only by the oil industry. According to 1989 estimates of the total number of *maquiladora* plants in Mexico, 80 percent were totally foreign owned subsidiaries of multinational companies. This implies that the remaining percentage represents joint ventures between Mexican and foreign investors, or firms that are solely Mexican owned. As there is no internationally competitive productive sector in Mexico, the *maquiladora* industry will continue to be the most important option supported by the federal government in Mexico's future national industrial programs.[21]

FIGURE 5.2 The New *Maquiladora* Industry (NMI) of the Mexican *Maquiladora* Program (MMP) and the Masan EPZ of South Korea in 1990

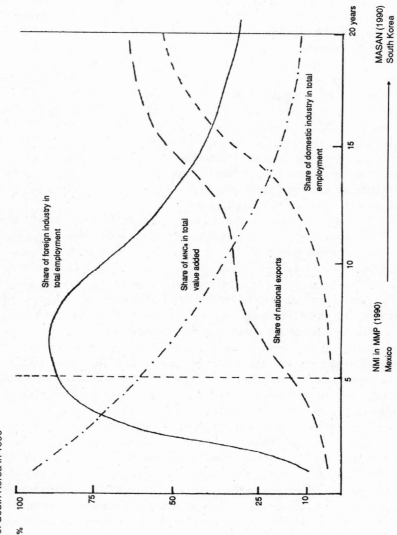

Share of foreign industry in total employment

Share of MNCs in total value added

Share of national exports

Share of domestic industry in total employment

NMI in MMP (1990)
Mexico

MASAN (1990)
South Korea

Source: Adapted by author from International Labour Organisation (ILO) and United Nations Centre on Transnational Corporations (UNCTC), *Economic and Social Effects of Multinational Enterprises in Export Processing Zones* (Monograph Series, Geneva, Switzerland, 1988), p. 151.

Despite extensive work in recent years on the effects of the *maquiladora* industry in Mexico, and particularly in the northern border area, there are still many questions remaining about the development of the *maquiladora* industry and its interaction with the economic structure of the country. In addition to the revenue brought to the country (quantitative factors), there are also indirect benefits, or spillover effects, including infrastructure, transfer and generation of technology, and the development of satellite industries complementary in the use of inputs and subcontracting. These are the qualitative factors of the process. The new *maquiladora* industry (NMI) should be understood in this context as the unfolding of the subsidiaries of the multinational corporations (MNCs) in the Mexican *maquiladora* program (MMP), along with total direct foreign investment (DFI) or majority foreign investment.[22]

Can subcontracting like that in the Asian EPZs discussed above be repeated in the northern border of Mexico, and what lessons from the Asian experience could be useful for the MMP? The answers to these questions must be phrased in the context of the new *maquiladora* industry, a different industry from the one started twenty-five years ago and one that has the potential for expansion under the new model of economic liberalization Mexico has begun to pursue. This process undoubtedly will have spillover effects in the Mexican domestic economy through the increase in the level of integration and subcontracting.

Table 5.3, which shows the contrast between old and new *maquiladora* industries, suggests that both in their geographic location and in the structure of production, the NMIs are more closely integrated into the national economy than the earlier border economy and are more likely to trigger developments within national economy through subcontracting and the creation of satellite industries. Although some of this development may be ascribed to the maturation of the *maquiladoras* as economic enclaves, the entry into the *maquiladora* industries of Asian, in particular Japanese, enterprises is also a factor not to be ignored, and makes comparison with East Asian EPZ experience more relevant than before.

In the northern border states of Mexico, the MMP has been quite successful. The case of Baja California is a good example. At the end of 1991, 41 percent of the *maquiladora* plants in Mexico were concentrated in Baja California, and almost 30 percent of these were to be found in Tijuana. It is not possible to speak of the *maquiladora* industry today without explicit reference to the "Asian *maquiladoras*"; their influence is spread over the entire electronics industry and recently has begun to diversify to other sectors such as the heavy-industrial sector. The Asian *maquiladoras* have followed a very interesting dynamic (see Table 5.4). Japanese *maquiladoras* in particular are on the increase in the number of plants. At the end of 1991 there were fifty-three *maquiladora* plants between Tijuana and Mexicali; of these, forty were

TABLE 5.3   Functional Structure of the New and Old *Maquiladora* Industry in Mexico

Characteristics	New Maquiladora Industry	Old Maquiladora Industry
Economic Model	Neoclassic.	Keynesian.
Economic Policy	The trend is toward privatization based on market forces and orientation toward the exterior.	Based on a strong participation of the state in the economy with a very protective influence over the economy.
Regional Policy	The Mexican *maquiladora* program (MMP) is a substantial element in the national development plan of its spatial development policy.	The MMP is seen as a regional drawback in the national development plans.
Industrial Policy	Wide fiscal incentive policy and facilities for its development.	Moderate and marginal fiscal incentive policy.
Externalities	Important indirect spillover effects in technology, integration (local content), subcontracting, administration, and urban infrastructure.	Creation of employment, value added, and taxes.
Technology	It has completed the first phase of transfer of technology and is in the preliminary stage of local adaptation.	Technology transfer only in few and traditional industrial sectors.
Integration	Firms located in the most mature industrialized regions starting to be supplied with significant national inputs.	Very low level of local inputs (raw materials), not greater than 2 percent.
Subcontracting	Linkage with local firms for the elaboration of some productive processes.	Few linkages with local firms but much subcontracting among themselves.
Administration	Starting of administrative and entrepreneurial changes with an intense hybridization process.	Direct administration by foreign personnel.
Urban Infrastructure	The widening of operations implies the need for considerable urban infrastructure investment by the government and foreign investors willing to cooperate in its development.	Does not force the growth of urban infrastructure, usually takes advantage of the existing one.
Size	High level of investments in companies that usually surpass 1,000 employees.	Generally small and medium companies.
Origin	Diversified, with growing East Asian investment.	Basically from the United States.
Establishment and Operation	Emerged at the end of the 1980s; fairly new in its participation in the economy.	Established in 1965; contribution remains stable after 20 years.

TABLE 5.4 *Maquiladora* Plants in Mexico, Baja California, Tijuana, and Mexicali, and Asian *Maquiladoras* in Tijuana and Mexicali, 1980–1991

	1980	1981	1982	1983	1984	1985	1986	1987	1988	1989	1990	1991
Mexico	620	605	585	600	672	760	890	1,125	1,396	1,660	1,886	2,103
Baja California	230	215	200	211	248	307	366	458	626	649	770	932
Tijuana	123	127	124	131	147	192	238	296	348	427	530	656
Asian *Maquiladoras* in Tijuana	1	1	3	3	3	5	9	14	20	25	39	45
Japan	1	1	3	3	3	5	9	13	16	20	33	36
South Korea								1	3	4	4	5
Taiwan									1	1	2	4
Mexicali	79					77		109	141	144	154	122
Asian *Maquiladoras* in Mexicali					1				4	5	6	8
Japan					1				2	2	3	4
South Korea										1	1	1
Taiwan									2	2	2	3

SOURCES: Secretaría de Comercio y Fomento Industrial, (SECOFI), *Relación de Empresas Maquiladoras de Exportación Orientales Instaladas* (Tijuana, 1989); Instituto Nacional de Estadística, Geografía e Informática (INEGI), *Estadísticas de la Industria Maquiladora de Exportación* (México: D.F. Secretaría de Programación y Presupuesto, 1989); "Monthly Scoreboard", *Twin Plant News* (December 1990 and September 1991).

Japanese, and were characterized as being the largest *maquiladoras* with the largest numbers of employees.

During the last few years the *maquiladora* industry has sought new locations in Mexico. The state of Jalisco has emerged as one of the most favored for industrial location, with thirty *maquiladoras* in Guadalajara in September 1991. These *maquiladoras* are subsidiaries of multinational corporations such as IBM, Hewlett-Packard, Siemens, Unysis, Wang, NEC, and so on, mostly in the electronic sector, another example of how Asian corporations are moving ahead of their counterparts.[23] The same process is being repeated in the cities of Monterrey and Merida, with eighty and twenty-eight *maquiladoras*, respectively, as of September 1991.[24]

These *maquiladora* companies can be grouped as the NMIs, having a stronger potential for integration with the local companies through the absorption of local inputs and subcontracting. This is visible in their decision to locate in geographic regions of Mexico where there is a greater degree of industrialization and consequently a greater supply of components and experience in the industrialization process of intermediate components, with quality often at approved international levels, and the highest potential to engage in dynamic processes of subcontracting.

NAFTA AND THE "MAQUILADORA" INDUSTRY

In the implementation of the North American Free Trade Agreement (NAFTA), the future of the *maquiladora* industry in Mexico has been at the center of speculation and debate. At the heart of the problem is the question of rules of origin, which is a technical question of eligibility, but includes in its concerns the relationship of North American societies to other economic regions (non-NAFTA countries), in particular the Asia-Pacific region. The direct involvement of Asian countries in *maquiladoras* raises the question of the integrity of NAFTA as an economic region. The question is further complicated by the emergence of a new global production system over the last two decades in which international subcontracting is an integral component, and which makes it nearly impossible on occasion to determine the exact origin of any one product.[25] The *maquiladoras*, like the EPZs in their freedom from direct national control, represent ideal sites for a global production process that is no longer containable within the boundaries of nations or even of regions. The efforts of nations or regional organizations to contain production bring them into contradiction with the process of production. Seemingly technical conflicts over rules of origin have their roots in this more fundamental contradiction—a contradiction that ironically may help the development of a country such as Mexico by encouraging subcontracting to meet the demands of the rules. A basic goal of the rules of origin is to limit the entry of third countries that wish to take advantage of nontariff privileges in a free trade zone by using a country in the agreement that offers advantages in the cost of production as a point of entry and a platform from which to export commodities to other countries in the trade zone.

In the free trade agreement, rules of origin will make certificates of origin mandatory. For example, an Asian or European company can locate in Mexico with the double benefit of a low-cost labor force and low or no tariffs, incorporate foreign materials and components in the product manufactured or assembled, and sell this product within NAFTA. This is why the countries participating in the agreement will agree on the origin requirement of the product based on one of four methods: a percentage of regional originality, the change in the tariff classification, substantial transformation, and the determination of the specific productive processes. In the first case, product "originality" (Mexico), a product that originates in the territory of that NAFTA country is determined to be wholly produced or obtained in that country if the value of the components added (Japanese) is not greater than the percentage level previously defined by the member countries of the agreement. The second method requires that the nonoriginated components (Japanese) be established by a different tariff classification for entry and interregional reexport (from Mexico to the United States). In the third method, nonoriginated components (Japanese) acquire during the productive process in the region (Mexico) different names, characteristics, and use for reexport purposes (from Mexico to the United States). The fourth method defines the manufacturing process of the nonoriginated components (Japanese) with the purpose of establishing substantial modifications for regional transformation (Mexico).

The experience in the application of the rules of origin based on the change of tariff classification supported by the percentage of local content in the free trade agreement between the United States and Canada of 1988 has been in general satisfactory.[26] In the case of the Asian *maquiladoras* in Mexico that export to the United States, the change of tariff classification in NAFTA could be inadequate for clearly defining the origin of a product due to the wide variety of materials and components used in the process. The spillover effects, such as the absorption of Mexican inputs and components, would also be few. The method that would bring the greatest benefits to Mexico would be to determine the percentage of local content. Under this method, the Asian *maquiladoras* would be obligated to integrate, with high percentages of participation, in the national economic activity.

Since the inception of NAFTA in the 1980s by the U.S. government, and continuing through the phase of renegotiations and approval of the fast track in 1991, there has existed a fear in Mexico about the negative effects of the rules in several industrial sectors. This is also the case with the future development of the *maquiladora* industry, particularly Asian investment in this sector. Some questions have risen from these issues, and they will persist until the agreement is ratified. What will be the effects in the *maquiladora* industry? What will be the most important transformations that the Asian *maquiladora* industry in Mexico would experience in relation to the rules of origin? And more precisely, what kind of effects would the subcontracting process experience?

There is a widespread fear in Mexico of the Japanese companies establishing there, because these companies (mostly in the electronics industry) still use foreign materials and components extensively and then ship to the United States.[27] A recent unpublished survey by the University of Baja California of thirty Asian *maquiladoras* found that in the case of twenty of them more than 40 percent of the components that went into production come from outside North America. For Asian companies NAFTA can easily become a counterproductive protectionist measure that will in the long run deeply effect trade and investment flows.

The fact that strict rules of origin can be applied in NAFTA has important implications. For example, an Asian *maquiladora* that basically uses Mexican, U.S., or Canadian components will not have any problems; but if it requires components from Japan or other countries, the rules of origin will represent an extraordinary obstacle, prohibiting access to the U.S. market. For this reason the Asian *maquiladoras* might go into one of two alternative phases if they wish to continue their activities in Mexico. They may begin to produce previously imported components locally, which will require important capital investments and the transfer of advanced technology from the United States, or they may use the subcontracting process in Mexico. Real competition could arise among Mexican, U.S., and Canadian companies to supply the additional demand created by the Asian *maquiladoras* in Mexico. For the Mexican industries a plus would be the low cost of the labor force; for its competitors this will be a disadvantage.

The chances that the Asian *maquiladoras* can start a dynamic process of subcontracting in Mexico are high. The University of Baja California survey also found that fifteen of the thirty companies already subcontract, 50 percent to Mexican companies. Moreover, of those subcontracting, 72 percent gave technical support and financial assistance, 83 percent expressed the need to widen their range of subcontracting, and 40 percent promised an expansion in the use of Mexican components. Consequently, Asian *maquiladoras* in Tijuana, with particularly greater intensity in the industrially mature regions, can be expected to expand the scope of subcontracting, which should assure additional inputs in accordance with rules of origin.

In NAFTA negotiations, "strict" rules of origin require more than 50 percent integration of original content, supported by nonflexible mechanisms in terms of substantial transformation and tariff classification. This will force important changes in the *maquiladora* industry in Mexico, namely substantial transformations in its operating system. The production, availability, and supply of components will have to be generated entirely in North America. The *maquiladora* companies from countries outside the agreement that want to operate under this system will be required to make large investments either in the United States, Mexico, or Canada in a process of relocation of industrial relationships much more complex than that experienced in Mexico by the MMP. The question that arises is: If Mexico does achieve the general conditions of transportation, public administration, quality of the components, efficiency of national industry, and supply of trained labor, would it be in accordance with the new requirements?

"Flexible" rules of origin offer better circumstances for the development of the *maquiladora* industry, although without the transformations, such as the process of integration with the Mexican national industry through joint venture projects for supplying the industry. Within this environment the nonmember countries will invest in Mexico to meet the requirement of the rules of origin through subcontracting or acquiring more local components. This seems to be the better alternative for Mexico in the context of a national strategy of diversification and commercial relations at the international level.

CONCLUDING REMARKS

North America, consisting geographically of Mexico, the United States and Canada, is rapidly restructuring its economic relations through closer interaction and cooperation under these new international conditions with an inevitable policy leading to economic integration, with the first step being NAFTA. Gradually, barriers to the economic integration of North America will be eliminated, although there are some external factors present that are not subject to the control of negotiation. We refer specifically to the influence of Japan and East Asia in this process.

What will be the common denominator that will enable us to understand this complex process? It is our belief that this common denominator is the flow of investment from East Asia to Mexico, specifically to the *maquiladora* industry. Similar strategies were employed by Japan in the export processing zones of its neighboring countries (Taiwan, South Korea, Hong Kong, and Singapore). Japanese investment was diffused into the economies of these countries with variable intensity through the process of industrial subcontracting, and this is what is happening today in the Mexican northern border region. These recipient economies soon absorbed Japanese technology and capital and rapidly transformed into NICs, successfully competing in world markets with leading industrial countries at the same level. This, we believe, can be repeated by Mexico.

In this context, the empirical evidence concerning the regions of Masan in South Korea and Kaohsiung in Taiwan shows that foreign investment in the EPZs was fundamentally Japanese and suggests an interesting process that resulted in strong linkages to the national economies. The development of these linkages began with the absorption of the labor force, followed by the formation of a national industrial network through the process of industrial subcontracting with local companies. The natural outcome was the development of the subcontracted country's own national products and technology, which were later to compete effectively in international markets.

It is important to note that not all the EPZs in Asia had the same success. In some the process was slower and more modest, in others faster, with a more profound relationship to the national economy. The key seems to be that the EPZs must form part of an overall, countrywide, export-oriented development strategy. For this to be successful the appropriate macroeconomic policies must be in place for the economy as a whole, policies that are designed to stimulate exports. Where there were poor results, usually EPZs were not considered a strategic element of a general program and remained isolated in the establishment of national economic policy. This is an important lesson for other countries undergoing similar processes, such as Mexico.

A quarter of a century after South Korea and Taiwan, Mexico started an export-oriented development strategy with many characteristics similar to the export-oriented industrialization model of East Asia. It is in this new national global scenario that the *maquiladora* industry is developing and becoming a fundamental and leading industry for Mexico.

This new scenario of an export-oriented development program in Mexico, together with the *maquiladora* program with similar characteristics to the EPZs established in East Asian countries at the end of the 1960s, repeats the pattern of investment in which the principal protagonist is Japan. Along the northern border of Mexico, when one spoke of the *maquiladora* industry before 1985, it was understood that the investment was of U.S. origin. In contrast, it is not possible to speak today of the *maquiladora* industry without referring to Japanese investment, particularly in electronics. This perspective implies the rise of a new *maquiladora* industry in which the Asian *maquiladora* is the leader.

The EPZ model in the past played a significant role in triggering national industrial development. EPZs as a form of restructuring manufacturing in the global economy still have a role to play and can be remarkably potent for the national economies. Recent cases in Asia and the new forms of economic integration implicit in the NAFTA rules of origin suggest that the new *maquiladora* industry may well emerge as one of the most successful instances of the EPZ model of economic development.

NOTES

1. Kiyoshi Kojima, *Direct Foreign Investment: A Japanese Model of Multinational Business Operations* (London: Croom Helm, 1978).

2. Hal Hill and Brian Johns, "The Role of Direct Foreign Investment in Developing East Asian Countries," *Wiltwirtschaftliches Archiv,* 121 (2), 1985, pp. 355–381.

3. Shibagaki Kazuo, "Japan's Development Aid Policy as a Motor for the Asia-Pacific Cooperation," in *East Asia: International Review of Economic, Political and Social Development,* vol. 4 (Boulder, CO: Westview Press, 1987).

4. Chris Milner (ed.), *Export Promotion Strategies: Theory and Evidence from Developing Countries* (New York: New York University Press, 1990).

5. Peter G. Warr, "Korea's Masan Free Export Zone: Benefits and Costs," *Developing Economies,* 22 (2), June 1984, pp. 169–184.

6. Derek T. Healey, "The Underlying Conditions for the Successful Generation of EPZ-Local Linkages: The Experience of the Republic of Korea," *Journal of the Flagstaff Institute,* 14 (1), 1990.

7. International Labour Organisation and United Nations Centre on Transnational Corporations, *Economic and Social Effects of Multinational Enterprises in Export Processing Zones* (Monograph Series, Geneva, Switzerland, 1988).

8. Asian Productivity Organization, *Linkage Effects and Small Industry Development: Symposium on Linkage Between Large and Small Industries* (Monograph Series, Tokyo, Japan, 1986).

9. International Labour Organisation, *Economic and Social Effects,* p. 151.

10. Rudy Maex, *Employment and Multinationals in Asian Export Processing Zones* (Multinational Enterprises Programme, Working Paper No. 26, International Labour Office, Geneva, Switzerland, 1983).

11. "Korea's Masan Free Export Zone," p. 174.

12. Kim Mun-Hwan, "Export Processing Zones in the Republic of Korea," *Export Processing Zones and Science Parks in Asia* (Symposium Report on Export Processing Zones, Asian Productivity Organization, 1987), pp. 44–45.

13. Wei-ming Wang, *The Establishment and Development of Kaohsiung Export Processing Zone (KEPZ), 1965–1975. A Study of Economic Decision Making in Taiwan, R.O.C.* (Asian and World Institute, Asia and World Monographs, No. 22, 1991), p. 62.

14. Ibid., p. 73.

15. Kuei-Sheng Wang, "Export Processing Zones in the Republic of China," *Export Processing Zones and Science Parks in Asia* (Symposium Report on Export Processing Zones, Asian Productivity Organization, 1987), p. 24.

16. Singapore International Chamber of Commerce, "Darwin's Export Processing Zone Woos Singapore Companies," *Economic Bulletin,* March 1991.

17. Rajiv Kumar, *India's Export Processing Zones* (Delhi, Bombay, Calcutta, Madras, Karachi: Oxford University Press, 1989).

18. *Korea Update,* "South to Participate in Special Economic Zone in the North," 2 (16), August 19, 1991.

19. N. Vasuki Rao, "India Eases Export Zone Rules; Trims Two State-Run Monopolies," *Journal of Commerce,* August 15, 1991.

20. Victor M. Castillo and Ramón de Jesús Ramírez Acosta, "East Asian Export Processing Zones and the Mexican Maquiladora Program: Comparisons and Lessons in Subcontracting and the Transfer of Technology" (Paper presented at the International Symposium: The Impact of the Maquiladora Export Processing Industry: Economic Transformation and Human Settlement in the U.S.-Mexico Border Region, College of Architecture and Environmental Design, Arizona State University, 1991).

21. Leobardo F. Estrada and Victor M. Castillo, "Asian Export Industries in the Northern Mexico Border: Implications for the Integration of Mexico-United States" (UC MEXUS Critical Issues Program, in press).

22. Rene Villareal and Rocio R. de Villareal, "The Supply Side Case for Free Trade with Mexico," *Economic Insights,* March/April 1991, pp. 17–19.

23. Allyn Hunt, "Asian Assembly Plants Moving to Mexico," *El Financiero International,* September 9, 1991.

24. *Twin Plant News,* "Monthly Scoreboard," September 1991, p. 68.

25. Robert B. Reich, "Multinational Corporations and the Myth of National Origin," *Harvard International Review,* Summer 1991, pp. 15–17.

26. *El Mercado de Valores,* "Reglas de Origen: El Estimulo a la Inversion Productiva," 19, October 1991.

27. *El Financiero,* "Temen Maquiladoras Japonesas Cambios en las Normas de Origen," June 24, 1991.

6

China's Growing Integration with the Asia-Pacific Economy

The great enigma in the Pacific area today is the future policy of China. The Korea War of 1950 showed that China was prepared to come to the rescue of a neighboring communist government threatened with military defeat. ... Subsequent developments—notably the frontier disputes with India, Burma and Pakistan—showed that China has a long arm and a formidable punch. But for China, by tradition a land power, to challenge the American ascendancy in the Pacific would be more difficult than it was for Japan. It would run counter to her history. But history does not show what is possible in the future, only what has happened in the past.[1]

This prophecy by Morrell, a British historian writing about the great powers in the Pacific three decades ago, is partially borne out by the developments in the Asia-Pacific region since the early 1960s. It was Japan, not China, that rose as an economic superpower to challenge the United States both globally and regionally. What was not foreseen, however, was that the newly industrializing countries (NICs) of South Korea, Taiwan, Singapore, and Hong Kong would emerge as economic powers in both regional and global economies. The onset of the 1980s saw not only the rapid growth of the ASEAN nations, especially Malaysia and Thailand, into new NICs, but China's growing presence and new role in the Asia-Pacific region.

China's new role in the Asia-Pacific region differs qualitatively from its past one of exporting the Communist ideology and practice by either confronting the United States in Indochina or supporting indigenous Communist insurgencies in the ASEAN countries. China also shifted from settling its border territorial disputes with neighboring India, Vietnam, and the former Soviet Union through military means to engaging in cross-border trade with those countries. Most important, China has focused development along its long eastern seaboard to maximize economic cooperation with the dynamic Western Pacific nations—Japan, the four NICs, and the ASEAN bloc.

89

THE SUBREGIONAL DIVERSITY
OF PACIFIC-ASIA AND CHINA

The recent literature on the Asia-Pacific ranges from stressing the similarities and coherence within the region[2] to emphasizing its internal differences and diversity.[3] Between the extremes are some excellent development studies[4] that integrate East Asian regional and country-specific analyses in a broader comparative framework. The numerous case studies of individual Asia-Pacific countries have also contributed to our cumulative knowledge of the region. Despite the wide range of focuses in the literature, the primary unit of analysis tends to be either the entire region or an individual country in the region. But there are exceptions where the subnational systems (e.g., industrial sector) of Pacific countries are analyzed in regional and global contexts.[5]

Given China's immense size and geographical location, a study of China's economic integration in the Asia-Pacific region involves different units of analysis based on a meaningful definition of the regional, subregional, and local boundaries and contexts. China's vast land mass borders a number of countries in the north, west, and south, which are either landlocked (Afghanistan, Laos, Mongolia) or face a different ocean (Burma, India). The geographical focus of this study implies excluding these countries from the analysis. This still leaves the relational construct of China and the Asia-Pacific region to be further defined. Even if Pacific Asia is taken to comprise the two major sociogeographical subsets of *East Asia* and *Southeast Asia,* East Asia may be subdivided into different parts. China and Inner Asia (i.e., Mongolia, Tibet) form one part; Japan, the two Koreas, and East Siberia constitute another.[6] Segal used "Fringe East Asia" to include Japan, Taiwan, Hong Kong, and the two Koreas, grouping China and the eastern portion of the former Soviet Union into a separate part of the Pacific.[7] Lardy's broader category of Northeast Asia included China with Japan, Mongolia, the former Soviet Union, Hong Kong, Taiwan, and the two Koreas.[8] Using the substantially overlapped parts of East Asia and the unambiguous designation of Southeast Asia (the ASEAN), I focus on China's economic links with Japan, the Soviet Far East, the ASEAN nations, Hong Kong, Taiwan, North Korea, and South Korea. The significance of the United States as an economic superpower in the Pacific Basin makes it necessary to include Sino-U.S. economic ties in the analysis.

Given the subregional diversity of Pacific Asia and China, I have designed a two-tiered comparative case analysis. The primary comparison features a pair of economic subregions—the Greater South China Economic Zone (GSCEZ) and the Yellow Sea Economic Zone (YSEZ). The secondary analysis focuses on the Shanghai-Pudong Economic Zone (SPEZ) and China's open border areas involving the Soviet Far East. Within these Asia-Pacific subregions, I also examine the role of major cities, Chinese and foreign, in anchoring and channeling the economic activities that shape the subregions. Three substantive and theoretical criteria guide this analytical design. First, the analysis is intended to cover China's economic links with all major Western Pacific countries and the United States at various areal levels. Second, there are relatively distinctive spatial boundaries that encircle and envelope parts of China and neighboring or geographically proximate countries into economic subregions, especially the GSCEZ and YSEZ. Most important, it is assumed that these geographically delimited subregions and areas not only contain internal flows of trade and investment, but constitute a division of labor reflecting economic dynamics at the global and Asia-Pacific regional levels. Ideally, this analysis will combine the advantages of *individualizing* comparison (contrasting specific instances of a given phenomenon as a means of grasping the peculiarities of each case) and of *encompassing* comparison (placing different instances at various locations to explain their characteristics as a function of their varying relationships to the system as a whole.[9]

CHINA'S GROWING LINKS WITH MAJOR ASIA-PACIFIC ECONOMIES

China's links with Asia-Pacific countries have been shaped by historical antecedents. Although China long had a dominating presence in the Pacific because of its size, rich civilization, and heavily populated eastern seaboard, its role in the region was largely confined to cultural influence on Japan, the Korean peninsula, and Vietnam and outward migration of people to the Southeast Asian countries.[10] For several dynasties after the Tang (circa A.D. 600), China conducted most of its trade with West and Central Asian and European countries along the famous Silk Road. It was only in the mid-1800s that the commercial penetration of China's ports by Western powers brought about a major eastward shift to the Pacific Ocean. Even then China's primary trading partners at such key ports as Canton were European countries or South Asian countries like India. With the Communist government that came to power in 1949 implementing a self-reliant and closed economic policy through the mid-1970s, China remained disconnected from the rapidly growing export-oriented Asia-Pacific economies, especially South Korea and Taiwan.

That China began an "open door" economic policy in 1977–1978 has been a familiar story and much commented upon. The phrase "open door" does not simply mean trade liberalization in the conventional economic sense. The key elements of the policy instead were to be discriminate in imports (not importing items that China could make), to promote speedy entry

TABLE 6.1   China's Trade with Major Asia-Pacific Nations, 1976–1991 (millions of U.S. dollars in current price)

	Hong Kong[a]	Japan	United States	Soviet Union	ASEAN Six[b]	North Korea	South Korea		Taiwan
1976	1,787	3,039	317	415	390	395	NE[c]		40
1977	1,913	3,465	294	329	478	374	NE		30
1978	2,533	4,824	992	437	569	454	NE		47
1979	3,328	6,708	2,452	493	762	647	19	100	77
1980	4,353	9,201	4,811	492	1,035	678	188	200	321
1981	5,174	9,978	5,888	225	1,592	480	353	400	467
1982	4,977	8,761	5,336	276	2,153	545	129	300	298
1983	5,382	9,077	4,024	674	1,807	493	134	260	265
1984	8,954	12,728	5,960	1,183	2,243	500	462	550	553
1985	10,844	16,434	7,020	1,881	3,964	473	1,100		1,104
1986	15,395	17,217	7,349	2,640	3,350	509	1,282		925
1987	22,215	16,472	7,868	2,519	3,433	513	1,679		1,516
1988	30,242	19,429	10,011	3,258	5,854	579	3,100		2,717
1989	34,458	18,897	12,254	3,997	6,650	563	3,200		3,483
1990	41,540	16,550	11,640	4,370	6,692	483	3,800		4,040
1991	39,170	15,170	10,690	2,980	7,959	610	4,500		5,800

[a]Data for 1990 and 1991 also include Macao.

[b]Brunei, Indonesia, Malaysia, the Philippines, Singapore, Thailand. Data for 1976–1980 include only Malaysia and Singapore. Since Brunei did not join the ASEAN until 1984, the figures for 1982 and 1983 include only five nations.

[c]Negligible. The left column of figures for South Korea for 1979–1984 is from Chung, the right column from Lardy. Both are presented due to the differentials in the two estimates. As both estimates converged from 1985, only data from Lardy are presented.

SOURCES: Adapted from Jae Ho Chung, "Sino–South Korean Economic Cooperation: An Analysis of Domestic and Foreign Entanglements," *Journal of Northeast Asian Studies,* 9, p. 61; Qingguo Jia, "Changing Relations Across the Taiwan Strait," *Asian Survey,* 32, p. 280; Won Bae Kim, "Yellow Sea Economic Zone: Vision or Reality?" *Journal of Northeast Asian Studies,* 10, p. 38; Nicholas R. Lardy, *China's Entry into the World Economy: Implications for Northeast Asia and the United States* (Lanham, MD: University Press of America, 1987), p. 7; State Statistical Bureau, *Zongguo Tongji Nianjian 1981* [China Statistical Annual 1981] (Beijing: China Statistical Press, 1981), p. 358, *Zongguo Tongji Nianjian 1983* (1983), pp. 496–97, *Zongguo Tongji Nianjian 1990* (1990), pp. 644–46, *China Trade and Price Statistics 1989,* pp. 144–49; *China Statistics Monthly* (University of Illinois at Chicago), February 1991, p. 59, December 1991, p. 58; Ken Yun, "Crossing the Yellow Sea," *China Business Review,* January-February 1989, p. 40.

of Chinese products into the world market, and to adopt the world's advanced technologies and equipment through attracting foreign investment.[11] Nevertheless, the policy led to unprecedented growth in China's foreign trade, which has been documented sufficiently[12] to warrant no repeat here. Instead, I have compiled only data[13] on China's trade with the Asia-Pacific nations whose economic ties with China at the subregional and local levels will be examined later (see Table 6.1).

Although China's trade with all these nations grew in 1976–1991, the rate of increase varied considerably from case to case. China's trade with Hong

Kong expanded very rapidly, surpassing Sino-Japanese trade in 1988. The fastest growth of Sino-U.S. trade occurred in the late 1970s and again from 1987 to 1991, whereas trade between China and the former Soviet Union soared in 1982–1984, and thereafter experienced a more gradual climb. China's trade with the ASEAN nations grew most rapidly in 1979–1982 and surged again toward the end of the 1980s. Although China's trade with North Korea stayed at basically the same level, its trade with South Korea and Taiwan grew astronomically, from very small initial bases. In 1979–1989 China's trade with South Korea and Taiwan rose 32-fold and 45-fold, respectively, compared with the third fastest rise of 10-fold for China–Hong Kong trade. As some of the China–South Korea trade and almost all of the China-Taiwan trade have been conducted via Hong Kong, the huge volume of China–Hong Kong trade in the second half of the 1980s is overstated. (The increasing entrepôt role of Hong Kong in channeling South Korea and Taiwan's trade and investment flows into China will be further analyzed at the subregional and local levels.)

The dynamic differential growth of China's trade with these countries has reshaped the patterns of trade within the Asia-Pacific region. In 1976 Japan was China's largest trading partner, with Sino-Japanese trade accounting for 22.6 percent of China's total trade. Hong Kong ranked as China's second largest trading partner, with 13.3 percent of China's total trade. No trade between China and any other country exceeded 3.5 percent of China's overall trade. In 1983 Japan and Hong Kong held their respective rankings of trading partners and share of China's total trade. The more striking change was that U.S.-China trade rose to 9.2 percent of China's total trade, making the United States China's third largest trading partner. By 1989 Hong Kong surpassed Japan to become China's top trading partner, accounting for 36.6 percent of China's overall trade in 1991, while Japan's share dropped to 14.9 percent. Trade between the ASEAN countries and China increased to 6 percent of China's total trade, trailing behind only Hong Kong, Japan, and the United States. Trade with South Korea and Taiwan as a share of China's total trade rose to approximately 3 percent for each, making Taiwan and South Korea China's sixth and seventh largest trading partners after fifth-place West Germany.

China's rapid trade expansion also improved its status in the international economic relations of these Asia-Pacific countries. In 1976 China was Japan's eighth largest trading partner. In 1985 China became Japan's second largest trading partner, behind only the United States. By 1985 China also became the fourth largest trading partner with both South Korea and Taiwan. China's role in the overall Pacific trade also grew steadily. By 1987 China contributed 6.4 percent of Pacific exports and received 5.9 percent of the region's imports, the fifth largest country in Pacific trade. Only one other socialist country (the former Soviet Union) in the region had over one (1.7) percent of Pacific trade.[14] China's growing trade with major Asia-Pacific countries also helped promote greater intraregional trade, which increased from 54 percent in 1977 to more than 60 percent of the total trade of the Asia-Pacific region in 1985.[15]

China's increasingly closer economic integration with major Asia-Pacific countries can also be measured by their direct capital investment in China. Official Chinese government data show that Hong Kong has been the dominating overseas investor in China.[16] Hong Kong and Macao (the latter with an insignificant share of the sum of the two) accounted for 49.0 percent of the total direct foreign investment (DFI) in China in 1985 and 54.9 percent in 1990. (Data by investing country prior to 1985 are not available.) In 1985–1990 Japan's direct investment as a proportion of China's total DFI averaged 13.1 percent, ranking a distant second behind Hong Kong. Although the United States provided 18.3 percent of China's total DFI in 1985, slightly ahead of Japan, 1990 saw the U.S. share drop to 13.1 percent, still higher than the 9.5 percent for the "others," which rose from 5.0 percent in 1985. "Others" includes investment from South Korea and Taiwan, which China had chosen not to identify until 1990 for political reasons. South Korean sources, however, revealed that as of September 1990, twenty-six Sino–South Korean joint ventures were operating in China, with South Korean equity contribution amounting to U.S.$26 million.[17] Another Korean estimate put the amount of South Korean investment at U.S.$55 million as of December 1989.[18] Having made greater investment in China than South Korea, Taiwan's investment in China by the end of the 1980s was estimated as high as U.S.$3 billion. In 1991 Taiwan surpassed the United States to become the third largest supplier of China's DFI, behind only Hong Kong and Japan.[19] The ASEAN countries' investment in China rose from 1.2 percent of the total in 1985 to 1.7 percent in 1990, ranking fifth collectively on the list of foreign investors. Of the ASEAN countries, Singapore stood out as the largest single investor.[20]

The data thus far have shown growing economic links between China and major Asia-Pacific countries through trade and investment. The aggregate statistics, however, mask the differential subregional and local dimensions of China's Asia-Pacific economic links, which will be closely examined below.

THE SPATIAL DIMENSIONS OF CHINA'S ASIA-PACIFIC ECONOMIC LINKS

China's economic integration with the Asia-Pacific has been strongly conditioned by its spatially targeted open door policy since the late 1970s. As there have been numerous accounts and assessments of this policy,[21] only a brief chronological recount is in order as a backdrop for the subregional and local analysis.

In 1979 China began an open and coast-oriented development strategy by granting special favorable policies to Guangdong and Fujian provinces. Of the four Special Economic Zones (SEZs)—China's first and most open areas to DFI, three (Shenzhen, Zhuhai, Shantou) are along Guangdong's coast and one (Xiamen) is a port city in Fujian. In 1984 China designated fourteen coastal "open cities" to further attract DFI. SEZ status was also conferred on Guangdong's Hainan Island. In 1985 China opened three river deltas in its coastal region to DFI. In 1988 China extended the coastal development strategy to all coastal provinces, including the Shandong and Liaoning peninsulas, and upgraded the Hainan SEZ to a province.

The geographical distribution of DFI in China constitutes an indicator of the open policy's broad spatial consequences, as trade data at the subnational levels have not been reported. Table 6.2 shows DFI in China by province and region in 1985–1991.[22] (Again, earlier data are not available.) At the provincial level, Guangdong received a disproportionately large share of China's total DFI. Besides Guangdong, only Beijing and Shanghai (central government municipalities with provincial status) took an average of 10 percent of China's total DFI in 1985–1991. Fujian, Tianjin, Hainan, Jiangsu, Liaoning, Shandong, and Tianjin formed the third tier in attracting a large proportion of DFI. DFI by China's six administrative regions confirms its uneven spatial distribution. The Central-South, East, and North ranked consistently first, second, and third as regions in which the bulk of DFI was concentrated. It is clear that these regional averages are heavily influenced by the provinces with an extremely large amount of DFI, such as Guangdong for the Central-South. The data also show the overwhelming concentration (over 90 percent) of DFI in China's coastal provinces. In fact, eleven of the twelve coastal provinces and municipalities (except for Hebei province) ranked among the top twelve in attracting DFI in 1985–1991. The inland province that sneaked into the tenth spot, Shaanxi (see Table 6.2), hosted heavily capitalized resource extractive ventures.

The uneven geographical distribution of DFI in China, coupled with the state policy of encouraging some areas and localities to become more integrated with the world economy than others, have either reinforced existing regional and subregional economic differences or shaped distinctively new economic subregions.

THE GREATER SOUTH CHINA ECONOMIC ZONE (GSCEZ)

Origin and Definition

The origin of the GSCEZ may be traced to mid-1980s ideas about economic cooperation among South China, Hong Kong, and Taiwan, based on their

TABLE 6.2 Percent Direct Foreign Investment (DFI) in China by Receiving Province and Region, 1985–1991 (ranks in parentheses)

Province and Region	1985[a]	1986[a]	1987[a]	1988	1989	1990	1991	1985–1991 Average
Beijing[b]	6.80 (4)	8.60 (2)	6.58 (4)	19.20 (2)	10.42 (4)	8.74 (3)	5.93 (4)	9.47 (2)
Shanghai[b]	8.23 (3)	8.55 (3)	14.74 (2)	8.91 (3)	16.12 (2)	5.49 (5)	3.52 (8)	9.37 (3)
Tianjin[b]	4.28 (5)	2.95 (6)	8.79 (3)	1.22 (12)	0.92 (13)	1.10 (12)	3.20 (9)	3.21 (9)
Anhui	0.99 (14)	2.02 (10)	0.10 (21)	0.44 (18)	0.16 (22)	0.30 (21)	0.23 (20)	0.61 (19)
Fujian	9.08 (2)	3.59 (5)	3.54 (7)	4.97 (4)	10.76 (3)	9.15 (2)	11.30 (2)	7.48 (4)
Gansu	0.04 (23)	0.07 (25)	0.01 (23)	0.08 (28)	0.04 (24)	0.03 (27)	0.02 (26)	0.04 (28)
Guangdong	49.84 (1)	49.53 (1)	41.60 (1)	36.58 (1)	37.84 (1)	46.08 (1)	44.18 (1)	43.66 (1)
Guangxi	2.35 (8)	2.83 (7)	2.60 (9)	0.79 (16)	1.50 (11)	0.90 (14)	0.61 (15)	1.65 (12)
Guizhou	0.75 (16)	0.70 (18)	–	0.17 (24)	0.24 (19)	0.15 (24)	0.18 (22)	0.37 (23)
Hainan[c]	–	–	–	4.36 (6)	3.11 (8)	3.25 (8)	4.27 (7)	3.75 (6)
Hebei	0.63 (17)	0.65 (19)	0.51 (16)	0.64 (17)	0.88 (14)	1.24 (11)	1.08 (12)	0.80 (17)
Heilongjiang	0.30 (20)	1.41 (14)	0.78 (15)	1.53 (11)	0.73 (16)	0.77 (15)	0.23 (20)	0.82 (16)
Henan	0.63 (17)	0.61 (20)	0.31 (18)	2.45 (9)	1.40 (12)	0.33 (20)	0.92 (13)	0.95 (14)
Hubei	0.61 (18)	0.71 (17)	0.82 (14)	0.85 (15)	0.75 (15)	0.92 (13)	1.13 (11)	0.83 (15)
Hunan	2.09 (10)	0.56 (21)	0.16 (20)	0.39 (19)	0.21 (20)	0.35 (18)	0.55 (17)	0.62 (18)
Jiangsu	2.56 (7)	1.94 (11)	3.21 (8)	3.93 (8)	3.06 (9)	3.92 (7)	5.15 (5)	3.40 (7)
Jiangxi	0.80 (15)	0.52 (22)	0.27 (19)	0.20 (22)	0.19 (21)	0.20 (22)	0.47 (18)	0.38 (22)
Jilin	0.37 (19)	1.39 (15)	0.01 (23)	0.24 (21)	0.11 (23)	0.56 (16)	0.44 (19)	0.44 (20)
Liaoning	1.12 (13)	2.77 (8)	4.45 (6)	4.40 (5)	3.88 (6)	7.69 (4)	8.46 (3)	4.68 (5)
Nei Mongol	0.20 (21)	0.43 (23)	0.08 (22)	0.13 (25)	0.01 (26)	0.34 (19)	0.03 (25)	0.17 (24)
Ningxia	–	0.003 (27)	0.002 (24)	0.01 (29)	–	0.01 (28)	0.004 (28)	0.006 (29)
Qinghai	–	–	–	0.10 (27)	–	–	–	0.10 (27)
Shaanxi	1.19 (12)	2.13 (9)	5.02 (5)	4.27 (7)	3.18 (7)	1.32 (10)	0.77 (14)	2.55 (10)
Shandong	2.73 (6)	3.77 (4)	1.64 (10)	1.65 (10)	4.30 (5)	4.76 (6)	4.35 (6)	3.31 (8)
Shanxi	0.04 (23)	0.01 (26)	0.16 (20)	0.25 (20)	0.29 (17)	0.11 (25)	0.09 (23)	0.14 (26)
Sichuan	2.20 (9)	1.83 (12)	1.46 (12)	0.90 (14)	0.26 (18)	0.51 (17)	0.59 (16)	1.11 (13)
Tibet	–	–	–	0.001 (30)	–	–	–	0.001 (30)
Xinjiang	–	0.80 (16)	1.21 (13)	0.19 (23)	0.03 (25)	0.17 (23)	0.005 (27)	0.40 (21)
Yunan	0.12 (22)	0.22 (24)	0.33 (17)	0.12 (26)	0.24 (19)	0.08 (26)	0.07 (24)	0.17 (24)

TABLE 6.2 (continued)

Province and Region	1985[a]	1986[a]	1987[a]	1988	1989	1990	1991	1985–1991 Average
Zhejiang	2.04 (11)	1.42 (13)	1.61 (11)	1.13 (13)	1.70 (10)	1.53 (9)	2.22 (10)	1.66 (11)
Total	100.00	100.00	100.00	100.00	100.00	100.00	100.00	–
Central-South[d]	55.53 (1)	54.25 (1)	45.49 (1)	45.33 (1)	44.80 (1)	51.83 (1)	51.66 (1)	49.84 (1)
East	25.67 (2)	21.80 (2)	25.11 (2)	21.22 (3)	33.97 (2)	25.35 (2)	27.24 (2)	25.77 (2)
North	11.94 (3)	12.63 (3)	16.11 (3)	21.44 (2)	12.51 (3)	11.53 (3)	10.33 (3)	13.78 (3)
Northeast	2.56 (5)	5.56 (4)	5.24 (5)	6.17 (4)	4.72 (4)	9.02 (4)	9.12 (4)	6.06 (4)
Northwest	1.23 (6)	3.01 (5)	6.24 (4)	4.65 (5)	3.24 (5)	1.53 (5)	0.80 (6)	2.96 (5)
Southwest	3.07 (4)	2.74 (6)	1.80 (6)	1.19 (6)	0.75 (6)	0.74 (6)	0.84 (5)	1.59 (6)
Total	100.00	100.00	100.00	100.00	100.00	100.00	100.00	–
Coastal[e]	90.41 (1)	86.59 (1)	89.27 (1)	87.78 (1)	92.16 (1)	94.96 (1)	94.28 (1)	90.78 (1)
Inland	9.59 (2)	13.41 (2)	9.73 (2)	12.22 (2)	7.84 (2)	5.04 (2)	5.72 (2)	9.08 (2)
Total	100.00	100.00	100.00	100.00	100.00	100.00	100.00	–

[a]The figures for 1985, 1986 and 1987 include both DFI and other forms of foreign investment.

[b]Central government municipalities with provincial status.

[c]Hainan, formerly part of Guangdong province, did not become a province until 1988.

[d]Central-South (Guangdong, Guangxi, Hainan, Henan, Hubei, Hunan); East (Anhui, Fujian, Jiangsu, Jiangxi, Shandong, Shanghai, Zhejiang); North (Beijing, Hebei, Nei Mongol, Shanxi, Tianjin); Northeast (Heilongjiang, Jilin, Liaoning); Northwest (Gansu, Ningxia, Qinghai, Shaanxi, Xinjiang); Southwest (Guizhou, Sichuan, Tibet, Yunan).

[e]The coastal area includes Beijing, Fujian, Guangdong, Guangxi, Hainan, Hebei, Jiangsu, Liaoning, Shandong, Shanghai, Tianjin and Zhejiang (see Figure 6.1); the inland area encompasses the rest of China.

SOURCES: State Statistical Bureau, Zongguo Tongji Nianjian 1986 [China Statistical Annual 1986] [Beijing: China Statistical Press, 1986), p. 583, Zongguo Tongji Nianjian 1987 (1987), p. 605, Zongguo Tongji Nianjian 1988 (1988), p. 657, Zongguo Tongji Nianjian 1990 (1990), p. 655, Zongguo Tongji Nianjian 1991 (1991), p. 631.

comparative advantages: China's land, raw materials, and labor; Hong Kong's international financial services and transport hub; and Taiwan's capital and manufacturing technology. Scholars in China, Hong Kong, Taiwan, and the United States proposed such concepts as the "Greater China Common Market" (presumably after the model of European Common Market) and the "Greater Chinese Economic Bloc" (implying the inclusion of the Chinese business communities in the ASEAN countries).[23] A recent *Business Week* article clearly identified Greater China (referring to China's Guangdong and Fujian provinces, Hong Kong, and Taiwan) as a dynamic growth zone.[24]

Following the basic consensus, I define the GSCEZ as an Asia-Pacific subregion that involves China's Guangdong and Fujian provinces, Hong Kong, and Taiwan (see Figure 6.1). Distinctive as it is, the GSCEZ should not be regarded as a closed system. Besides the triangular ties among Guangdong and Fujian provinces, Hong Kong, and Taiwan, the GSCEZ also involves DFI from the ASEAN countries, especially Singapore. The permeable boundary of the GSCEZ is also reflected in Hong Kong's entrepôt role in relaying and channeling trade and investment flows from other Asia-Pacific countries (e.g., South Korea) into China.

The Nodes and Nexuses of Trade and Investment Flows

The city-state of Hong Kong is the dominating node in this subregional network of commercial and industrial activities. South China, especially Guangdong, has had larger, stronger, and closer economic connections with Hong Kong than with Taiwan. South China was Hong Kong's primary hinterland until the 1920s, when the north-south railroad reached Guangzhou (Canton) and improved Hong Kong's access to central and north China. Although Hong Kong lost its vast hinterland as a result of the embargo against China during the Korean War in the early 1950s, the opening of Guangdong in the late 1970s allowed Hong Kong to reassert its key economic role in linking China with the global and regional economies.

Although China–Hong Kong trade grew rapidly during the 1980s (see Table 6.1), the volume of entrepôt (indirect) trade passing through Hong Kong to and from China increased five times faster than direct trade in 1980–1987.[25] China-Taiwan trade would not have been possible or grown so rapidly without Hong Kong linking the flow of goods between the mainland and the island. Of China's U.S.$4.5 billion imports from Hong Kong in the first half of 1988, U.S.$890 million (20 percent) came from Taiwan, second only to Japan (U.S.$1.6 billion) and ahead of the United States (U.S.$540 million), and South Korea (U.S.$470 million).[26] Measured by the volume and form of trade flows, economic integration of China, Hong Kong, and Taiwan tightened in the 1980s.

FIGURE 6.1 China's Open Coastal and Border Cities and Areas, Subregional Economic Zones Along the Western Pacific Rim

Compared with trade, DFI is a stronger mechanism for integrating South China, Hong Kong, and Taiwan. Of the heavy concentration of DFI in Guangdong province (see Table 6.1), approximately 90 percent of the cases and 70 percent of the capital came from Hong Kong. In Fujian province about 60 percent of the DFI are from Hong Kong.[27] Given the government ban on direct investment on mainland China, Taiwan's companies, mostly small, have made a huge amount of investment in China through Hong Kong. It is estimated that more than one-third of Taiwan's investment in China is located in Fujian province.[28]

Below Hong Kong, a pair of cities in Guangdong and Fujian provinces serve as second-tier nodes for drawing DFI and spreading economic influence. For Guangdong, they are Shenzhen and Guangzhou; Fujian has Xiamen and Fuzhou. Shenzhen, China's largest SEZ, established in 1979, is on the border with Hong Kong (see Figure 6.1). In 1979–1985, Hong Kong and Macao (predominately the former) accounted for 98 percent of the DFI cases and 88 percent of contracted capital in Shenzhen. (Taiwanese investment in Shenzhen was either not reported or buried in the "others" category.) Japan, the United States, and the ASEAN group ranked a distant second, third, and fourth behind Hong Kong in DFI cases, whereas contracted capital was in the descending order of the ASEAN countries, the United States, and Japan. Singapore contributed 76 percent of the ASEAN DFI cases and 30 percent of contracted capital in Shenzhen. In 1989, when official reporting of Taiwan's investment in Shenzhen began, Taiwan emerged as the second largest investor to Hong Kong in terms of DFI cases, even though its average case was less capitalized than Hong Kong, Japan, and the United States. In 1990 Taiwan was ahead of Japan and the United States in DFI cases, contracted capital, and average capital intensity. In 1990 the ASEAN countries ranked third after Hong Kong and Taiwan in contracted capital.[29]

Ghangzhou, named one of the fourteen open cities in 1984, is located at the northern end of the Pearl River Delta (see Figure 6.1). It is the largest port in South China and the country's third largest industrial city behind Shanghai and Tianjin. Guangzhou has also been the site for China's national spring and fall trade fairs since 1957. Guangzhou attracted 15.6 percent of the total DFI in Guangdong in 1979–1984 and 18.3 percent in 1987.[30] Although there are no DFI data by nationality, the dominance of Hong Kong DFI in Guangdong, especially in the Pearl River Delta, suggests that the bulk of DFI in Guangzhou has also been from Hong Kong.

Xiamen, one of the four SEZs created in 1979–1980, has long been an important seaport, located as it is across the water from Taiwan (see Figure 6.1). By 1988 Hong Kong ranked first in both DFI cases and contracted capital. Taiwan, which began investing in Xiamen later than Hong Kong, was the second largest investor in both DFI cases and contracted capital. Singapore was third in both categories, followed closely by the United States, Japan, and the Philippines.[31] Of Guangdong and Fujian's cities, Xiamen has remained the primary site for Taiwan's investment. As of October 1991, Taiwan provided 42.4 percent of Xiamen's DFI cases and 42.1 percent of its contracted capital.[32] The evidence suggests that Taiwan is already surpassing Hong Kong to become the largest overseas investor in Xiamen.

Fuzhou, Fujian's capital and one of the fourteen open cities designated in 1984, is an important seaport for foreign trade and a transport hub for distributing goods in southeastern China (see Figure 6.1). Fuzhou is also Fujian's largest industrial center. Although detailed data are lacking, Fuzhou has attracted DFI from a number of countries such as Japan, the United States, the ASEAN, and South Korea. Since the mid-1980s, Fuzhou has become a favorable site for Taiwan's investment. As of May 1990, Fuzhou set up over one hundred projects involving Taiwan capital, trailing behind only Xiamen and Shenzhen.[33]

Despite their dominant roles, these four cities appear to have lost some appeal to Hong Kong and Taiwan companies, as the latter began to invest in other, often smaller inland cities in Guangdong and Fujian where labor costs are lower. As an indicator of this shift, the share of DFI in Guangdong and Fujian provinces accounted for by these four cities declined from 64 percent in 1987 to 51 percent in 1990.[34]

Division of Labor in the GSCEZ

The spatial concentration of Hong Kong and Taiwan's investment in Guangdong and Fujian reflects a deeper economic transformation that can be characterized as a new subregional division of labor. It is shaped by the realigned niches of the Asia-Pacific countries as they have experienced mobility in the global and regional economic systems. As the East Asian NICs follow Japan's footsteps in moving up the industrial technology ladder, they began to shift their labor-intensive industries down to low-wage countries like China. The small and medium-sized companies in Taiwan's most labor-intensive industries (e.g., textiles, footwear), which have been squeezed most severely by internal industrial upgrading and external competition, have taken the lead in relocating operations to nearby mainland provinces.

The shoemaking industry provides an illustrative case of the division of labor that is simultaneously subregional, regional, and global. Fujian province is known for its history and skill in making shoes. The city of Putian, located between Xiamen and Fuzhou, has become China's major production site for athletic shoes. Recently, three China-Taiwan athletic joint ventures, through which Nike places a lot of orders, moved from their original locations in Beijing and Shanghai to Fujian and Guangdong—the provinces closest to sourcing and marketing. Most of the raw materials come from Taiwan through Hong Kong to South China. At each shoe factory Nike keeps several

Taiwanese resident managers who have been in the shoe business for years and speak the local dialects. Nike's Hong Kong staff deal with designs, make sure the sample and raw materials reach the factory on time, and ship the finished Nike shoes out of China through Hong Kong to their destined markets, mainly the United States. This division of labor takes the form of a commodity chain that stretches across the Pacific Ocean through the United States, Taiwan, Hong Kong, and China.[35]

The first major factor leading to economic integration among South China, Hong Kong, and Taiwan is the changing comparative advantages in the Asia-Pacific regional economies. High labor costs in Hong Kong—about five times those in Shenzhen (already the highest in Guangdong)—coupled with the continued shift toward a high-service economy, have driven Hong Kong's labor-intensive manufacturing industries into Guangdong. It is estimated that Hong Kong companies now employ more than two million workers in Guangdong's Pearl River Delta, and the figure doubles to four million if jobs generated indirectly by Hong Kong investment are included. For Taiwan, the end of the 1980s saw rapidly rising labor costs and increasing labor shortages, the latter being caused by the smaller birth cohorts of the 1960s entering the work force. Pay raises averaged 12.2 percent annually in 1987–1990, faster than productivity gains of 8.3 percent per year. Taiwan's labor force shrank slightly in 1990 for the first time, and the labor force participation rate dropped to 58.2 percent, the lowest in five years.[36] And there is talk about importing workers from Thailand and even mainland China.

The growing economic integration between Taiwan and Guangdong and Fujian is also a result of new state policies on both sides. A series of reciprocal policy moves starting in the mid-1980s created a favorable atmosphere for bilateral trade to grow, even though trade still has to go through Hong Kong due to the absence of formal political relations. The concentration of Hong Kong and Taiwan's investment in selected cities in Guangdong and Fujian also reflects the effect of location-specific policies implemented by China. In addition to such incentives as lower taxes associated with the status of SEZs and open cities, Shenzhen, Guangzhou, Xiamen, and Fuzhou offered competing preferential treatments specifically tailored to Taiwan businesses in the late 1980s.

Guangdong and Fujian's extensive kinship ties with Hong Kong and Taiwan provide convenient and encouraging opportunities for their companies to invest in South China. For example, an estimated 230,000 Hong Kong Chinese have family ties with Shenzhen residents. The proportion of Taiwan's population with ancestral roots in southern Fujian is estimated to be around 70 percent. Many residents in Fuzhou have kinship relations with overseas Chinese living in Malaysia, the Philippines, and Singapore.[37] The fusion of kinship ties and shared subregional culture fosters close economic links among South China, Hong Kong, Taiwan, and the ASEAN countries.

Geographical proximity is the last but certainly not the least contributing factor, best exemplified by the closely integrated and increasingly open border between Hong Kong and Shenzhen. This phenomenon approximates what Herzog calls the "transfrontier metropolis," which is created by the frequent movement of population, industry, and capital across an increasingly porous international border.[38] Hong Kong businesspersons now commute freely across the border to supervise production in Shenzhen and other Guangdong cities daily or weekly. Guangzhou is only three hours from Shenzhen by rail and a recently completed highway. The cities clustered in the Pearl River Delta are reasonably accessible to Hong Kong and Taiwan investors through rail and roads. Physical distance, however, does not seem to inhibit the concentration of Taiwan's investment in Xiamen and Fuzhou, which are much farther away from the entry point of Hong Kong. A statistical analysis showed a consistently negative relationship between DFI in Guangdong and Fujian's cities and their distance to Hong Kong for 1984, 1987, and 1990, even though this association attenuates over time.[39] This suggests that with rare exceptions, Hong Kong and Taiwan's investment may continue to locate in cities closer to Hong Kong for some time to come.

THE YELLOW SEA ECONOMIC ZONE (YSEZ)

Origin and Definition

The initial idea of an entity approximating the YSEZ was embedded in the broad discussion of potential economic cooperation among some Western Pacific countries (Japan, South Korea) on the one hand and in the specific reference to China's Bohai Bay (the sea within China's territorial waters) on the other. As early as May 1986, the mayors and commissioners of China's cities and prefectures around the Bohai Bay held a conference to discuss ways of coordinating regional economic activities. But it was only in 1989–1990 that China's scholars and policy analysts began to explicitly propose developing the YSEZ in order to maximize economic cooperation with Japan and South Korea.[40] China's posture, coupled with the rapidly growing Sino–South Korea trade in the late 1980s (see Table 6.1), helped sharpen the attention of overseas analysts on economic integration among China, Japan, and South Korea across, around, and beyond the Yellow Sea.[41] For this analysis, I define the YSEZ to include China's Liaoning and Shandong provinces, South Korea, and Japan (see Figure 6.1).

Like the "triple alliance" among Hong Kong, Taiwan, and China's Guangdong and Fujian provinces in the GSCEZ, the YSEZ comprises triangular economic ties among Japan, South Korea, and China's Liaoning and Shandong provinces, which on average between 1985 and 1991 ranked fifth and eighth in attracting China's DFI (Table 6.2). Of the fifty-four Sino–South Korean joint ventures either in operation or under contract as of January 1990, thirty (55.6 percent) were sited in Shandong, Liaoning, Beijing, Tianjin, and Hebei in that descending order. Shandong and Liaoning provinces were first and second in drawing South Korean capital into China, combining for 42.7 percent of all South Korean–invested projects in China in 1990–1991. The number of South Korean–invested ventures in Shandong province grew more rapidly, from ten in 1990 to thirty-four in 1991, than in any other coastal province.[42] Of the twenty-six China–South Korean joint ventures in operation as of October 1990, fifteen (57.7 percent) were located in the major Chinese cities (e.g., Beijing, Dalian, Qingdao, Tianjin, Yingkou) rimming the Bohai Bay.[43] The Chinese press has reported Japanese companies prefer to invest in Liaoning, especially in the city of Dalian. From 1984 to October 1988, Japan set up fifty-five direct investment projects in Dalian, capitalized at U.S.$230 million.[44] Dalian also became a major Chinese seaport for trade with South Korea. In 1988 the volume of Sino–South Korean trade (all indirect) through Dalian amounted to U.S.$27.9 million, U.S.$21.4 million of which were exports to South Korea; U.S.$6.5 million were imports. In January–August 1989, indirect and direct Sino–South Korean trade passing through Dalian rose to U.S.$63.6 million, U.S.$55.5 million for China's exports and U.S.$8.1 million for China's imports.[45] Dalian also plays a crucial role in Sino-Japanese trade. Of the total volume of trade leaving Dalian, 48 percent went to Japan.[46]

Dalian is not the only key Chinese port city with strong economic links to South Korea and Japan. With Dalian, the city of Qingdao on the Shandong peninsular and Tianjin midway along the Bohai Bay constitute a triangle of coastal nodes that anchor the investment and trade flows into that part of China. Dalian is China's second largest port, behind only Shanghai in total tonnage, but it ranks ahead of Shanghai in total foreign trade and in total exports. Tianjin and Qingdao are China's third and fourth largest ports in both freight and passenger traffic, with trade connections to over one hundred countries and regions. By February 1992, South Korea and Japan ranked second and third (behind only Hong Kong) in investing in Qingdao, accounting for 13.8 and 10.8 percent of the ventures and 12.6 and 11.3 percent of the capital, respectively. In 1991 Qingdao's trade with Japan and South Korea made up 23.0 and 8.1 percent of its total foreign trade.[47] While data on DFI in Tianjin by all investing countries are not available, 7 percent of South Korean–invested ventures in China by 1991 were located in Tianjin.[48]

The concentration of DFI in these cities makes them key economic nodes, capable of spreading development benefits into hinterlands of varying sizes. For example, Dalian's hinterland covers China's three northeastern provinces (see Figure 6.1). In 1986 these provinces contained 8.9 percent of China's population, but accounted for 14.6 percent of China's gross industrial output.[49] Constituting China's major heavy-industrial region, in 1986, the three northeastern provinces produced 51.8 percent of China's petroleum, 30.3 percent of China's automobiles, and 23.6 percent of China's steel.[50] This vast and productive hinterland is easily accessible through an extensive network of railroads and highways. A newly constructed highway between Dalian and Shenyang, the capital city of Liaoning province, allows the movement of people and goods within four hours, faster than train transport. Dalian's favorable transport system facilitated economic links with its hinterland and beyond. By the end of 1986 Dalian had signed over 1,600 economic and technology agreements with interior cities and regions. The number of Dalian-interior joint ventures and wholly interior owned firms in Dalian amounted to four hundred and were capitalized at U.S.$22 million.[51] A recently completed highway between Qingdao and Yantai has cut the travel time from about five hours to a little over three. Construction is already under way to extend the highway to Jinan, the capital city of Shandong province, thus improving the transportation link between Shandong's coastal nodes and interior cities.

Facing China's coastal nodes across the Yellow Sea are several South Korean coastal cities that are emerging as key points for economic interaction with China. The South Korean government has recently unveiled a spatially targeted plan for developing its southwestern Chollar province. The plan included: (a) attracting capital investment for new industrial complexes to be located at Asan Bay and Kunsan Port; (b) building a 505-km highway from Inchon to Sunchon to link all major west coast cities; (c) giving Kunsan Port the key role in handling Sino–South Korean trade; and (d) upgrading other western ports, such as Inchon, Asan, and Mokpo (see Figure 6.1).[52] South Korea's initiation of its "west coast development strategy" was quickly reported by China's regional analysts[53] as a stimulus to further internationalize cities like Dalian for closer economic cooperation with South Korea.

Division of Labor in the YSEZ

The emerging subregionalized division of labor in the YSEZ differs somewhat from that in the GSCEZ because of the different industrial structures of the national and regional economies involved in the two zones. On the one hand, South Korea has been imitating Hong Kong and Taiwan's strategy by setting up heavily labor intensive projects in Liaoning and Shandong province. The fifteen Sino–South Korean joint ventures in Chinese cities around the Bohai Bay as of 1990 were labor-intensive operations, such as toys, sporting goods (e.g., ski gloves), restaurants, and daily consumer projects (e.g., lamps, brushes, souvenirs).[54] On the other hand, two South Korean companies (Korea Steel Pipe Company and Pohang Iron and Steel Company) have established in Shandong capital-intensive ventures to make steel pipes and other steel products. In addition, Kia Industrial Company has agreed with a Chinese state enterprise in Yantai to manufacture passenger cars, microbuses, and trucks.[55]

The most "natural" division of labor in the YSEZ, however, still occurs in typical labor-intensive industries like toys. A Sino-foreign joint venture with multinational capital in Dalian has been making stuffed animals, especially Disney characters. The raw materials (e.g., flannel) were brought in from South Korea, and sewn and pressed by cheap Chinese labor into finished products, which are then sent to the U.S. market. Because these Chinese-made products are not as good as similar stuffed animals made with South Korea's own materials and labor, they are sold only at the middle rung of the overseas market.[56] Nevertheless, the sourcing, manufacturing, and marketing sections of this toy chain link the subregional division of labor in the YSEZ to the global economy.

Explaining Economic Integration in the YSEZ

The first explanation for the close economic links between China, particularly Liaoning and Shandong provinces, and South Korea is their complementary economies. Three specific economic factors contribute to close Sino–South Korean economic cooperation through trade and investment. First, some of South Korea's mid-level production and processing technologies may be more needed in and suited to China than Japanese or Western technologies. This is especially true of Liaoning and Shandong provinces, with heavy industries like chemicals, steel, and shipbuilding that are compatible with the same industries in South Korea. Second, China's lack of hard currency, coupled with the rising price of Japanese products and technologies due to the sharp appreciation of the yen, make the cheaper manufactured goods from South Korea more appealing to China.[57] Third, with domestic labor costs especially manufacturing wages, rising rapidly, South Korea is eager to relocate its labor-intensive industries to nearby Chinese locales. With an average wage lower than that of China's Guangdong and Fujian provinces,[58] Shandong province is a logical target for South Korea's labor-intensive investment.

Economic complementarity is a necessary but not sufficient condition for close Sino–South Korean economic cooperation, which could not be established and strengthened without changes in state policies in both China and South Korea at the national and regional levels. China's adoption of the open door policy and domestic reform in the late 1970s provided an initial opportunity for Sino–South Korean (indirect) trade to develop quietly. From 1983 both China and South Korea relaxed restrictions on travel in both directions, leading to reciprocal visits of athletes, businesspersons, economic officials, scholars, and sailors. These policies facilitated more bilateral trade and South Korea's DFI in China. Between 1988 and 1991, 3,580 South Korean business groups with 8,600 people visited Shandong province, with 3,510 groups coming in the first half of 1992 alone.[59] The establishment of former diplomatic relations between China and South Korea in August 1992 would further promote and expand their business ties.

China's regional and location-specific policies, intended and unintended, helped create favorable conditions for the emergence and growth of Sino–South Korean economic ties across the Yellow Sea. Although also consistent with its reform of decentralizing economic management, China's policy of "provincial contact only" with South Korea helps to avoid angering North Korea. Both Liaoning and Shandong, taking advantage of the policy, established a provincial trade and liaison office in South Korea. Six major coastal citites in Shandong have recently been allowed to set up special trading companies for dealing with South Korean businesses.[60] In return, South Korea opened promotional missions in Qingdao and Beijing. Although not intended specifically as a policy toward South Korea, China's designation of fourteen open cities in 1984, including Tianjin, Dalian, Qingdao, and Yantai, made the greater autonomy and lower taxes in these locations very attractive to South Korean investors.

Similar to the kinship ties that seal many business bonds between Taiwan and China, there is an ethnic component to Sino–South Korean economic integration in the YSEZ. It is estimated that South Korea has approximately 100,000 Chinese-Koreans of Shandong descent, many of whom became successful in business and desire to invest in their place of ancestry.[61] Some of the Chinese Koreans originally emigrated from Dalian and other parts of Liaoning, and are interested in promoting business relationships between South Korea and Liaoning.[62] Kinship ties between Shandong and Liaoning and South Korea, less extensive and deep as they may be than those connecting Guangdong, Fujian, Hong Kong, and Taiwan, are a contributing factor in Sino–South Korean economic cooperation in the YSEZ.

The last explanatory factor is geographical proximity. South Korea and Japan happen to be the two countries closest to China's coastal provinces around the Bohai Bay. Dalian is only two hundred nautical miles from Inchon, with a one-way shipping trip taking a maximum of thirteen hours. After direct air service to Tokyo began in early 1985, a jet flight from Dalian took less than four hours. Although direct air services linking the key Chinese and South Korean cities across the Yellow Sea are currently under discussion, direct shipping between China and South Korea's ports around the Yellow Sea is still constrained. Although South Korean ships are allowed to carry goods directly to China, they have to register with a third country and often conclude the paperwork in a third country. It is estimated that direct shipping can save up to 20 percent on transport costs.[63] In September 1990 a shipping route was opened between Inchon and Weihai, an industrial port city on the Shandong peninsula closest to South Korea's west coast (see Figure 6.1). A South Korean ocean ship makes one round trip each week, carrying both passengers and cargo, and covers the 230 nautical miles in less than seventeen hours. Other suggested direct shipping links are between Yantai, Mokpo, and Nagasaki; between Kunsan and Qingdao; and between Dalian, Tianjin, Inchon, and Nampo, the North Korean port closest to its southern neighbor.[64]

In spite of the continued transport barriers across the Yellow Sea, the relatively short physical distance between China and South Korea and between China and Japan provides a favorable spatial environment within which economic, political, and sociocultural factors interact to bring about close economic integration.

CHINA'S OTHER COASTAL AND BORDER ECONOMIC ZONES

China's long coastline and inland border, coupled with decentralized, spatially targeted, and location-specific open policies, have created other distinctive subregions that have developed strong economic ties with Pacific Rim countries. In this section I briefly examine two different cases.

The Shanghai-Pudong Economic Zone (SPEZ)

The Shanghai-Pudong Economic Zone (SPEZ) began in 1985, when China designated the Changjiang (Yangtze River) Delta as an open coastal region for DFI and international economic cooperation. More recently, scholars proposed a broader coast-oriented region—the East China Sea Economic Zone—that involves Shanghai, Jiangsu, Zhejiang, and Fujian provinces.[65] The East China Sea Economic Zone (with Fujian) overlaps with the GSCEZ discussed earlier. For this analysis, the Shanghai-Pudong Economic Zone is defined as the area covered by the Yangtze River Delta (see Figure 6.1). In April 1990 China's central government announced a grand plan for developing Pudong, a large suburban district of Shanghai municipality. Pudong, literally meaning "the east of Huangpu," refers to the large area east of the Huangpu River. It abuts Hangzhou Bay to the south, is closed in by the mouth of the Yangtze River to the northeast, and borders on the Huangpu River to the west. Pudong covers two thousand square kilometers, about one-third of Shanghai's total land, and has about 1.4 million people, close to 10 percent of Shanghai's total population.[66]

The development of Pudong strengthens Shanghai's functions as the central node in linking the global, Asia-Pacific, and domestic subregional economies. Shanghai is China's largest port, carrying 30 percent of the country's international cargo. Shanghai's customs processes and channels 20 percent of China's consumer goods.[67] With only 1 percent of China's population, Shanghai accounted for 10.6 percent of China's gross industrial output in 1984.[68] Although this figure dropped to 6.8 percent in 1990, Shanghai's industrial weight was chipped away only by Jiangsu province (the city's immediate hinterland), Guangdong province (the core segment of the GSCEZ), and Shandong province (a major part of the YSEZ), which ranked first, second, and third in provincial shares of China's total industrial output in 1990.[69]

Shanghai ranked third (behind Ghangdong and Beijing) in receiving the proportion of China's total DFI in 1985–1991 (see Table 6.2). With regard to the nationality of investors in Shanghai, Hong Kong leads all countries. Of Shanghai's 160 foreign-invested ventures by the end of 1985, 92 (57.5 percent) had Hong Kong partners. With involvement in twenty-six of these ventures, the United States was a distant second, ahead of Japan (twenty), the European Community (ten), Thailand (four), and Singapore (three).[70] Shanghai, however, was the most favorable site for U.S. DFI in China. By the end of 1986 Shanghai had signed thirty-four investment agreements with the United States involving U.S.$600 million in U.S. capital. Beijing and Tianjin were the second and third choices for U.S. DFI, attracting thirty-six projects (U.S.$250 million) and twenty-two projects (U.S.$53 million), respectively.[71] Foreign companies have begun to invest in Pudong, especially after the latter was declared an open zone in 1990. By the end of 1990 Pudong approved eighty foreign-invested enterprises, including seventy Sino-foreign equity joint ventures, five Sino-foreign cooperative ventures, and five wholly foreign owned firms. The capitalization of these ventures ranged between U.S.$3 and U.S.$6 million,[72] high by the average size of DFI projects in China.

The emergence and growth of the SPEZ result from the meshing of economic, political, and locational factors. Economically, Shanghai remains China's most dominant industrial center, and its labor force is among the country's best educated and most productive. An estimate shows that labor productivity in Shanghai was second only to Shenzhen in 1985.[73] These comparative advantages help overcome Shanghai's disadvantage of higher (than Liaoning and Shandong's) wages in attracting more capital intensive DFI projects. Politically, Shanghai benefited from being named one of the fourteen open cities in 1984 and being given the right to approve DFI projects of up to U.S.$30 million, compared with the caps of U.S.$10 million for Guangzhou and Dalian, and U.S.$5 million for Qingdao. The SPEZ also includes the open cities of Nantong and Ningpo (see Figure 6.1), which can function as secondary growth centers for stimulating development of the surrounding areas. Geographically, located midway along China's eastern seaboard, Shanghai is more accessible to all foreign investors, which may account for the fact that Shanghai has more evenly distributed nationalities of foreign investors than key cities in the GSCEZ and YSEZ.

Subregional and Border Economic Areas
Involving the Soviet Far East

China's growing economic integration with Asia-Pacific nations is not restricted to market economies. The rapid growth of Sino-Soviet trade in the 1980s (see Table 6.1) indicates that both socialist states have tried to improve their bilateral economic relations. Like economic links with the Western Pacific countries, China's trade with the former Soviet Union has distinctive subregional and local dimensions. Although a number of Chinese cities along the northeastern and northwestern Sino-Soviet border have been opened to trade, my analysis focuses on the border cities and areas in China's Heilongjiang province and the former Soviet Far East. This analysis will also be extended to the characteristics and conditions of broader economic integration involving Japan and the two Koreas around the Yellow Sea and the Sea of Japan (see Figure 6.1).

Sino-Soviet border trade in the Far East is mostly conducted through the two Heilongjiang cities of Suifenhe and Heihe (see Figure 6.1). Suifenhe is an inland port city sitting on Heilongjiang's southeastern border with the Soviet Far East. Opened to border trade in 1983, Suifenhe is linked by rail to the Soviet Pacific cities of Art'om, Vladivostok (the largest Soviet Pacific port), and Nakhodka (another major Soviet port city). Suifenhe is only twenty-six kilometers from the highway system connecting the Soviet cities. Internally, Suifenhe is a border terminal of a rail network that links all major cities in Heilongjiang, Jilin, and Liaoning provinces. Boosted by growing border trade, Suifenhe's revenue income rose from about U.S.$600,000 in 1987 to U.S.$5.2 million in 1991.[74] From the Soviet side, the state decided to set up a special economic zone at Nakhodka to attract Japanese and South Korean investment. This was only a small component of a larger development strategy for turning the resource-rich Far East into a strong economic subregion in the Pacific. The plan included modernizing and expanding the port facilities at Vladivostok, Nakhodka, and Ol'ga (see Figure 6.1).

To the north along the same border is the city of Heihe, which has emerged since 1985 as a competing center for Sino-Soviet border trade. With 145,000 people in 1990, Heihe is 5.4 times larger than Suifenhe.[75] Facing Heihe on the Soviet side is Blagoveshchensk, the third largest city in the Soviet Far East with 230,000 people. The two cities are separated by only 0.75 km across the Heilong (Amur) River. The distance can be covered by a five-minute truck ride over the frozen river half of the year. In 1989 Heihe's border trade accounted for 25 percent of Heilongjiang's total trade with the Soviet Far

East and 41 percent of the combined border trade passing through Heihe, Suifenhe, and Tongjiang,[76] another border-port city midway between Heihe and Suifenhe (see Figure 6.1).

Sino-Soviet border trade in Suifenhe and Heihe are only one dimension of growing economic integration in the Northeastern Pacific. Guided by economic complementarity, geographical proximity, and pragmatic policies, countries based on either market or command economies and at different levels of development have begun to seek mutually beneficial opportunities in a regional context. The Soviets have already obtained loans and DFI from Japan and South Korea to harness such rich natural resources as petroleum and natural gas.[77] As China and the former Soviet Union have come closer to South Korea economically, North Korea has had no choice but to reach south for capital investment and other economic assistance. Neff and Nakarmi reported that South Korean companies planned to start joint ventures in North Korea in 1992, including a proposal to set up a ship repair dock at the city of Wonsan on North Korea's east coast (see Figure 6.1).[78] On the border with China and the Soviet Far East, North Korea was planning to open an economic development zone to lure Japanese investors. As early as 1986, China and the Soviet Union (at the time) negotiated to allow China to supply labor for Siberian projects in exchange for raw materials such as timber.[79] The South Korean press reported that Korean companies and some Chinese provincial governments discussed the use of Chinese labor, Korean-Chinese labor in particular, in third country construction projects.[80] These multilateral economic ties suggest the potential formation of a sprawling regional economy that extends southward to overlap with the YSEZ.

CHINA'S INTEGRATION WITH THE ASIA-PACIFIC ECONOMY: IMPLICATIONS

The preceding comparative analysis of four cases, two primary and two secondary, suggests that there has emerged increasingly distinct subregionalized and localized economic integration across the national boundaries within the Asia-Pacific region. This new reality strongly challenges the repeated multilateral efforts to create and promote regionally based cooperative organizations and bodies since the early 1980s, such as the Pacific Economic Cooperation Conference (PECC) and the Asia-Pacific Economic Cooperation (APEC).[81] The primary implication of this study is that the Asia-Pacific region should be reconceptualized as a network of multiple subregions connected and mediated by a complex division of labor and commodity chains. That the Asia-Pacific is a homogeneous regional structure comprising politically defined and economically autonomous nation-states may be a rapidly fading perspective.

These Asia-Pacific subregions, as this chapter shows, are shaped by a multitude of factors. They have different combinations of effects on the formation of different subregions. Sociocultural similarity and kinship ties, for example, play a stronger role in integrating the economies of South China, Taiwan, and Hong Kong than in fostering economic integration among northeast China, Japan, and South Korea. The dominating factor in the growth of trade and economic cooperation along the Sino-Russian border in the Far East is geographical proximity. On the one hand, the comparison has revealed the peculiar characteristics of each subregion. On the other hand, the integration in the subregions is driven by the same basic economic determining conditions because they are all embedded in the global system of contemporary capitalism. The prevalent logic of global capitalism implies that the Asia-Pacific subregions are not self-contained. Just as South Korea's investment has flown into Fujian and Guangdong provinces in the GSCEZ, Taiwan's investment has penetrated Liaoning and Shandong provinces in the YSEZ. Both zones have commodity chains stretching out to such distant markets as the United States.

By analytical design, China's various coastal parts and partial inland border form the spatial cores of the various Western Pacific subregions. The differential incorporation of a large socialist state into the capitalist world economy in the Asia-Pacific context carries many implications for China's national development and for the other countries in the region. As the cooperative aspects of China's integration with major Asia-Pacific countries have already been examined at length, I devote the concluding remarks to discussing contradictions with regard to China itself and the countries that have different economic ties with China in the Asia-Pacific region.

Within China at the intranational level, the most favorable economic policies granted to Guangdong and Fujian provinces, especially to their SEZs, through the 1980s, and their effect on rapid growth in South China have created some economic gaps and policy conflicts with the northern portions of the coastal region. These were often subject to new interventions by the central government, which tended to reshape and realign the already differentiated regional and local interests. The Pudong development plan was intended to shift the policy focus away from the favored south to the central and northern parts of China. This new spatial orientation to Shanghai and surrounding areas was also interpreted as a victory by one party faction over another at the central level.[82] In 1989–1990 the central state also withdrew some export subsidies from Guangdong to curb that province's growing power and privileges. Although the purposes of these policies were to rebalance regional disparities and to recentralize some lost power, they may have strengthened the SPEZ as another regional competitor against other regions and the central government.

At a broader intranational level, the rapid development of the entire coastal region in the 1980s widened existing spatial inequalities with China's vast interior. From 1981 to 1988, the initial differential in gross industrial output between China's coastal provinces and its nine western provinces grew 2.7 times.[83] The rapid development of similar export-oriented processing industries in both the coastal and inland regions, especially the former, also generated fierce competition for raw materials, which tend to come from the western provinces. The shortage of domestic raw materials, coupled with double competition from labor-intensive processing industries in the interior and other low-wage countries (e.g., Indonesia, the Philippines), constrain the traditional export sectors of the coastal provinces while giving them little time to diversify their industrial structure.

The increasing differentiation within the coastal region and across the coastal-interior divide constitutes a frontal assault on socialist China, which has historically taken some measure of national political unity, economic autonomy, and social integration as its premise for existence. The argument against uneven development between the coastal and inland regions in Chinese socialism goes back further than Mao's post-1949 ideology and practice to the 1920s.[84] One serious social consequence of China's spatially uneven insertion into global capitalism is growing class differentiation. Sklair identified three new social "strata": the officials (many of them former Communists) who deal with foreign capitalists as representatives of state agencies or managers of industrial enterprises; private enterpreneurs, many of whom do business with foreigners; and the so-called red capitalists—a growing number of PRC Chinese who live and work in Hong Kong and abroad.[85] With the first and third groups developing into a global managerial elite with extensive international ties, the crucial question to be asked is whose interests will they represent: Chinese national, Chinese regional or local, or multinational across political and geographical boundaries.

Contradictions and conflicts have also emerged among the Asia-Pacific countries that compete for shares of China's national, regional, and local markets. In the GSCEZ, the recent surge of Sino-Taiwan trade and Taiwan's DFI in South China threatens to weaken the existing stronghold and influence of Hong Kong in that part of China. Taiwan also resents improved economic relations between China and South Korea, fearing loss of its legitimate ideology against communism and some of the China market. Japan was reported to have obstructed Sino–South Korean business ties by disclosing a joint venture between Fujian province and the Daewoo Group in 1985. The subsequent objection by North Korea caused a delay in that project. Japan also encouraged South Korea to export cheap goods toward China and away from itself, thus driving China and South Korea to compete against each other, not with Japan. The suspicion of Japan's economic motive to dominate the region, coupled with economically integrated East Asia markets, prompt the United States to challenge Japan by facilitating Sino–South Korean economic cooperation.[86]

How do these contradictory and divisive forces affect the future shape of the Asia-Pacific region? The answer to this question lies in the present reality, as documented by this chapter. The fusion of economic comparative advantages, geographical proximity, sociocultural affiliation, and practical state policies has considerably weakened ideological barriers and territorial boundaries that defined and separated the nation-states in the Asia-Pacific region. The consequent emergence of subregional economic networks have already reshaped the entire Asia-Pacific region. The complex and intertwined division of labor within and between the subregions presents both cooperative opportunities and contradictory outcomes for the nations involved. The future welfare of each nation and of the region as a whole hinges on how these opportunities are maximized and the contradictions minimized.

NOTES

This research was supported in part by a grant from the Campus Research Board of the University of Illinois at Chicago. I am grateful to Arif Dirlik, Xiaoyan Hua, James Norr, and William Parish for suggestions and comments on an earlier draft and to Raymond Brod for his skilled production of the map.

1. W. P. Morrell, *The Great Powers in the Pacific* (London: Routledge and Kegan Paul, 1963), p. 34.

2. See David Aikman, *Pacific Rim: Area of Change, Area of Opportunity* (Boston: Little, Brown, 1986); Roy Hofheinz, Jr. and Kent E. Calder, *The Eastasia Edge* (New York: Basic Books, 1982); Staffan Burenstam Linder, *The Pacific Century: Economic and Political Consequences of Asian-Pacific Dynamism* (Stanford, CA: Stanford University Press, 1986).

3. See Gerald Segal, *Rethinking the Pacific* (New York: Clarendon Press, 1990).

4. See Frederic C. Deyo, ed., *The Political Economy of the New Asian Industrialism* (Ithaca, NY: Cornell University Press, 1987); Gary Gereffi and Donald Wyman, eds., *Manufacturing Miracles: Paths of Industrialization in Latin America and East Asia* (Princeton, NJ: Princeton University Press, 1990).

5. Gary Gereffi, "Global Sourcing and Regional Division of Labor in the Pacific Rim," this volume.

6. Mark Borthwick, *Pacific Century: The Emergence of Modern Pacific Asia* (Boulder, CO: Westview Press, 1992), p. 4.

7. Segal, *Rethinking the Pacific*, p. 10.

8. Nicholas R. Lardy, *China's Entry into the World Economy: Implications for Northeast Asia and the United States* (Lanham, MD: University Press of America, 1987).

9. See Charles Tilly, *Big Structures, Large Processes, Huge Comparisons* (New York: Russell Sage Foundation, 1984), pp. 81–83.

10. Borthwick, *Pacific Century*.

11. Samuel P. S. Ho and Ralph W. Huenemann, *China's Open Door Policy: The Quest for Foreign Technology and Capital* (Vancouver: University of British Columbia Press, 1984), p. 21.

12. See State Statistical Bureau, *China Trade and Price Statistics 1989* (New York: Praeger, 1991), various tables.

13. Data in Table 6.1 are adapted from Jao Ho Chung, "Sino–South Korean Economic Cooperation: An Analysis of Domestic and Foreign Entanglements," *Journal of Northeast Asian Studies*, 9, p. 61; Qingguo Jia, "Changing Relations Across the Taiwan Strait," *Asian Survey*, 32, p. 280; Won Bae Kim, "Yellow Sea Economic Zone: Vision or Reality?" *Journal of Northeast Asian Studies*, 10, p. 38; Lardy, *China's Entry into the World Economy*, p. 7; State Statistical Bureau, *Zhongguo Tongii Nianjian 1981* [China Statistical Annual 1981] (Beijing: China Statistical Press, 1981), p. 358, *Zhongguo Tongji Nianjian 1983* (1983), pp. 496–497, *Zhongguo Tongji Nianjian 1990* (1990), pp. 644–646, *China Trade and Price Statistics, 1989*, pp. 144–149; *China Statistics Monthly* (University of Illinois at Chicago), February 1991, p. 59, December 1991, p. 58; Ken Yun, "Crossing the Yellow Sea," *China Business Review*, January-February 1989, p. 40.

14. Segal, *Rethinking the Pacific*, p. 334.

15. Robert F. Dernberger, "Economic Cooperation in the Asia-Pacific Region and the Role of the P.R.C." *Journal of Northeast Asian Studies*, 7 (1988), p. 6.

16. State Statistical Bureau, *Zhongguo Tongji Nianjian 1986* (1986), p. 582, *Zhongguo Tongji Nianjian 1987* (1987), p. 604, *Zhongguo Tongji Nianjian 1988* (1988), p. 656, *Zhongguo Tongji Nianjian 1990* (1990), p. 654, *Zhongguo Tongji Nianjian 1991* (1991), p. 630.

17. Kim, "Yellow Sea Economic Zone," p. 40.

18. Chung, "Sino–South Korean Economic Cooperation," p. 63.

19. Xiangming Chen, "The New Spatial Division of Labor and Commodity Chains in the Greater South China Economic Region," in Gary Gereffi and Miquel Korzeniewicz, eds., *Commodity Chains and Global Capitalism* (Westport, CT: Greenwood Press, 1993); State Statistical Bureau, (1992), p. 642.

20. Same as note 16 above.

21. Xiangming Chen, "China's City Hierarchy, Urban Policy, and Spatial Development in the 1980s," *Urban Studies*, 38 (June 1991), pp. 341–367.

22. State Statistical Bureau, *Zhongguo Tongji Nianjian 1986* [China Statistical Annual 1986] (Beijing: China Statistical Press, 1986), p. 583, *Zhongguo Tongji Nianjian 1987* (1987), p. 605, *Zhongguo Tongji Nianjian 1988* (1988), p. 657, *Zhongguo Tongji Nianjian 1990* (1990), p. 655, *Zhongguo Tongji Nianjian 1991* (1991), p. 631, and *Zhongguo Tongji Nianjian 1992* (1992), p. 643.

23. See Chaoming Lu and Tianxiang Zheng, "Yianhai Fazhan Zhanlue Xin Jianyi" (New Proposals for the Coastal Development Strategy), *Tegu Yu Kiafang Chengshi Jingji* (Special Zone and Open City Economy), 5 (1990), pp. 45–48.

24. Dinah Lee, "Asia: The Next Era of Growth," *Business Week*, November 11, 1991, pp. 56–59.

25. Ezra F. Vogel, *One Step Ahead in China: Guangdong Under Reform* (Cambridge, MA: Harvard University Press, 1989), p. 67.

26. Kimiaki Taira, "Hong Kong—Ever Entrepôt," *China Newsletter,* Japan Export Trading Corporation (JETRO), 77 (November-December 1988), p. 1.

27. Chen, "The New Spatial Division of Labor."

28. Hui Luo and Ming Chen, "Qiantan Xiamen Tequ Yinjin Taizi de Tezheng yu Qianjing" (A Preliminary Analysis of the Characteristics and Prospect of Taiwan's Capital Investment in Xiamen), *Tequ Yu Kaifang Chengshi Jingji* (Special Zone and Open City Economy), 10 (1989), pp. 31–34.

29. State Statistical Bureau, *Shenzhen Tongji Nianjian 1991* [Shenzhen Statistical Annual 1991] (Beijing: China Statistical Press, 1991), pp. 284–294.

30. Computed from State Statistical Bureau, *China Urban Statistics 1985* (London: Longman, 1985), p. 549, *Zhongguo Chengshi Tongji Nianjian 1988* [China Urban Statistical Annual 1988] (Beijing: China Statistical Press, 1988), p. 443.

31. Fengqing Zhang, "Shixi Xiamen Tequ Waizi Laiyuan de Diqu Fenbu Wenti" (A Preliminary Analysis of Xiamen's Foreign Investment by Nationality), *Tequ Yu Kaifang Chengshi Jingji* (Special Zone and Open City Economy), 7 (1990), pp. 59–62.

32. "Taishang Chengwei Xiamen Jingji Tequ Fazhan de Zhongyao Liliang" (Taiwan Businesses Have Become An Important Force in Xiamen's Economic Development), *Tequ Yu Kaifang Chengshi Jingji,* 2 (1992), p. 41.

33. Mitchell A. Silk, "Silent Partners," *China Business Review,* September-October 1990, p. 37.

34. Computed from State Statistical Bureau, *Zhongguo Chengshi 1988*, pp. 440, 443, *Zhongguo Chengshi Tongji Nianjian 1991*, pp. 509, 512.

35. See David Chang, "Speaking the Same Language," *China Business Review,* September-October 1990, p. 39; Chen, "The New Spatial Division of Labor."

36. Julian Baum, "Taiwan's Building Block," *Far Eastern Economic Review,* May 2, 1991, pp. 36–37.

37. David K. Y. Chu and Xun-zhong Zheng, "Fuzhou: Capital of a Frontier Province," in Yue-man Yeung and Xu-wei Hu, eds., *China's Coastal Cities: Catalysts for Modernization* (Honolulu: University of Hawaii Press, 1992).

38. Lawrence A. Herzog, *Where North Meets South: Cities, Space, and Politics on the U.S.-Mexico Border* (Austin: Center for Mexican Studies, University of Texas Press, 1990).

39. Chen, "The New Spatial Division of Labor."

40. Lu and Zheng, "Yianhai Fazhan Zhanlue Xin Jianyi."

41. A group of researchers at the East-West Center in Hawaii has been studying economic cooperation and regional development issues in the Yellow Sea Rim and northeast China. Recently, the East-West Center launched a new program for the Center on Northeast Asia Economic Development. The program would focus on the evolving relations among North and South Korea, the Russian Far East, Mongolia, northeast China, Japan, and the United States. See *East-West Center Views,* 2, no. 3 (May-June 1992), p. 2.

42. Chung, "Sino–South Korean Economic Cooperation," p. 68; South Korean Trade Association, *The Current Status of the Chinese Economy and China–South Korean Business Ties* (in Korean), March 1992, p. 18.

43. Kim, "Yellow Sea Economic Zone," p. 40.

44. Yongle Fang, "Dalian Shi zai Dongbeiya Diqu Jingji Hezuo Zhongde Diwei Jiqi Fazhan Zhanlue Chutan" (A Preliminary Examination of Dalian's Position in Northeast Asian Economic Cooperation and Its Development Strategy), *Tequ Yu Kaifang Chengshi Jingji* (Special Zone and Open City Economy), 8 (1990), pp. 46–48.

45. Qian Tang, "Dalian Kouan dui Taiwan he Nanchaoxian Maoyi Jiankuang" (A Brief Summary of Trade Between Dalian Port and Taiwan and South Korea), *Tequ Yu Kaifang Chengshi Jingji* (Special Zone and Open City Economy), 3 (1990), p. 58.

46. Hiroshi Tanimura, "Dalian Jingji Kaifa de Xianzhuang yu Wenti" (The Current Situation and Problems of Economic Development in Dalian), *Tequ Yu Kaifang Chengshi Jingji* (Special Zone and Open City Economy), 4 (1987), pp. 33–36.

47. Xingdi Li, "Jingji Quyu Jituanhua Chaoliu he Huanghai Jingjiqu" (The Trend of Regional Economic Conglomeration and the Yellow Sea Economic Zone), unpublished manuscript, 1992, tables 2 and 5.

48. South Korean Trade Association, *The Current Status of the Chinese Economy,* p. 18.

49. Computed from State Statistical Bureau, *Zhongguo Chengshi 1987*, pp. 91, 268.

50. Tanimura, "Dalian Jingji Kaifa de Xianzhuang yu Wenti."

51. Xiangming Chen, *Some Social Aspects of China's Special Economic Zones as a Development Strategy: A Capitalist Means to Socialism* (Unpublished Ph.D. Dissertation, Department of Sociology, Duke University, Durham, North Carolina, 1988).

52. Yun, "Crossing the Yellow Sea."

53. Fangshuo Liu, "Shehui Zhuyi Zhidu Nei Zhengfu Hongguan Guanli Xiade Xinxing Kuaguo Jingji" (The New Cross-National Economy Macromanaged by Government Under Socialism), *Tequ Yu Kaifang Chengshi Jingji* (Special Zone and Open City Economy), 1 (1991), pp. 54–63.

54. Kim, "Yellow Sea Economic Zone," p. 40.

55. Pam Baldinger, "Deals Involving China and South Korea," *China Business Review,* January-February 1989, p. 41.

56. Personal interview with a Chinese national who is involved in buying toys made by Sino-foreign joint ventures in China and selling them to U.S. wholesalers, April 1992.

57. Borthwick, *Pacific Century;* Kim, "Yellow Sea Economic Zone"; Yun, "Crossing the Yellow Sea."

58. Xingdi Li, "Wuoguo Yianhai Fazhan Zhanlue he Shandong de Cilue Tantao" (Exploring China's Coastal Development Strategy and Shandong's Options), *Tequ Yu Kaifang Chengshi Jingji* (Special Zone and Open City Economy), 11 (1989), pp. 49–52.

59. Ralph N. Clough, "Political Implications of Sino–South Korean Trade," *China Business Review,* January-February 1989, pp. 42–45; personal interview with a high-ranking official of Shandong province, September 4, 1992.

60. Chung, "Sino–South Korean Economic Cooperation"; same interview cited in note 59 above.

61. Li, "Wuoguo Yianhai Fazhan Zhanlue he Shandong de Cilue Tantao."

62. Fang, "Dalian Shi zai Dongbeiya Diqu Jingji Hezuo Zhongde Diwei Jiqi Fazhan Zhanlue Chutan."

63. From the Chinese side, China National Foreign Trade Transportation Corp. has chartered a Panamanian-registered container ship to go between Shanghai and Pusan via Japan. From the Korean side, Chungyung Shipping Co. Ltd., using a Hong Kong shipping company, began direct semicontainer shipping service between Pusan, Inchon, Shanghai, and Tianjin in July 1988. See Baldinger, "Deals Involving China and South Korea"; Yun, "Crossing the Yellow Sea."

64. It was reported that Dongnama Shipping and Hyundai Merchant Marine Co. Ltd. negotiated with China to launch direct shipping services between South Korea and China. See Baldinger, "Deals Involving China and South Korea"; Kim, "Yellow Sea Economic Zone."

65. Lu and Zheng, "Yianhai Fazhan Zhanlue Xingjianyi."

66. Zunwei Yan, "Pudong Xinqu 'Sanzi' Qiyi Fazhan Xianzhuang ji Jingrong Duice" (The Development of Foreign-Invested Enterprises and Its Fiscal Policy in the Pudong New Zone), *Tequ Yu Kaifang Chengshi Jingji* (Special Zone and Open City Economy), 9 (1991), pp. 44–46.

67. Chen, *Some Social Aspects of China's Special Economic Zones as a Development Strategy.*

68. State Statistical Bureau, p. 327.

69. State Statistical Bureau, *Zhongguo Tongji Zhaiyao 1991* [China Statistical Abstract 1991] (Beijing: China Statistical Press, 1991), p. 11.

70. Richard Pomfret, *Investing in China: Ten Years of the 'Open Door' Policy* (New York: Harvester Wheatsheaf, 1991), p. 86.

71. Baosen Chen, "Zhongguo Yianhai Diqu Jingji Fazhan Zhanlue he Meiguo Duihua Touzi" (The Economic Development Strategy of China's Coastal Region and the U.S. Investment in China), *Tequ Yu Kaifang Chengshi Jingji* (Special Zone and Open City Economy), 10 (1988), pp. 45–57.

72. Yan, "Pudong Xinqu 'Sanzi' Qiyi Fazhan Xianzhuang ji Jingrong Duice."

73. Pomfret, *Investing in China*, p. 88.

74. "Heilongjiang Bianjing Diqu Jingji Xunsu Fazhan" (The Economy of Heilongjiang's Border Areas Has Been Developing Rapidly), *People's Daily*, May 7, 1992, p. 2.

75. State Statistical Bureau, *Zhongguo Tongji Zhaiyao 1991*, p. 47.

76. Yan Zheng, "Guanyu Hehei Jingji Tequ de Yanjiu Baogao" (A Research Report on the Establishment of the Heihe Economic Zone), *Tequ Yu Kaifang Chengshi Jingji* (Special Zone and Open City Economy), 3 (1990), pp. 12–22.

77. The former Soviet Far East has half of the country's oil reserve, 70 percent of its coal and coke reserve, 75 percent of its timber, and 70 percent of its natural gas, as well as over 70 different mineral resources. See Qiang Du, "Zhongguo Canyu Dongbeiya Quyu Jingji Hezuo de Qiaotoubao" (The Outpost of China's Participation in the Regional Economic Cooperation of Northeast Asia), *Tequ Yu Kaifang Chengshi Jingji* (Special Zone and Open City Economy), 12 (1989), p. 63.

78. Robert Neff and Laxmi Nakarmi, "Asia's Next Powerhouse: An All-But-United Korea?" *Business Week*, October 14, 1991, p. 63.

79. Lardy, *China's Entry into the World Economy.*

80. Kim, "Yellow Sea Economic Zone."

81. In 1980 the prime ministers of Australia and Japan advocated the formation of a government-supported private body, the Pacific Economic Cooperation Conference (PECC), based in Singapore. The PECC currently includes the ASEAN, Australia, New Zealand, the former Soviet Union, Japan, South Korea, China, Taiwan, Hong Kong, the Pacific Islands, Canada, the United States, Mexico, Peru, and Chile. There were already existing academic regional groups such as the Pacific Trade and Development Conference (PAFTAD) and the Pacific Trade and Development Conference (PBEC), but neither had government financial support and participation. In early 1989 the Australian prime minister proposed the creation of an intergovernmental forum called Asia-Pacific Economic Cooperation (APEC), which originally comprised twelve nations—the six ASEAN countries, Australia, New Zealand, Japan, South Korea, Japan, and the United States. In 1991 the APEC was enlarged to include China, Hong Kong, and Taiwan. See Borthwick, *Pacific Century,* pp. 526–528.

82. Elizabeth Cheng, "The East Is Ready," *Far Eastern Economic Review,* May 13, 1990, pp. 57–58.

83. Bing Sheng and Lun Feng, eds., *Zhongguo Guoqing Baogao* [China's State of Union Report] (Shenyang, Liaoning: Liaoning People's Press, 1991), p. 676.

84. See Arif Dirlik, "National Development and Social Revolution in Early Chinese Marxist Thought," *China Quarterly,* 58 (1974).

85. Leslie Sklair, "Problems of Socialist Development: The Significance of Shenzhen Special Economic Zone for China's Open Door Development Strategy," *International Journal of Urban and Regional Research,* 15 (1991), pp. 208–213.

86. See Chung, "Sino–South Korean Economic Cooperation"; K.A. Namkung, "The US Role in Sino–South Korean Trade," *China Business Review,* January-February, 1989, pp. 45–46.

7

Adjusting to the Rim: Japanese Corporate Social Responsibility in the United States

DURING THE Persian Gulf War the affiliates of Japanese corporations in the United States showed their solidarity with the U.S. troops in the battlefields through monetary and material contributions as well as blood donations. Such corporate behavior may be seen as a response to U.S. public opinion, which was accusatory against the "indecisive" policy toward the war taken by the Japanese government. Despite Japan's U.S.$13 billion financial contribution (the largest amount among the allies), the U.S. perception that Japan did not contribute to the war remained. Because of this, the Japanese government strongly advised Japanese corporations not to get involved in lucrative reconstruction projects in Kuwait—to avoid their being seen as merely "economic animals."[1] Japanese corporations were thus vulnerable to the geopolitical order in which the United States maintains dominant influence over Japan.

On the other hand, as Choate and the Tolchins have illustrated, Japan's lobbying activities in the United States have been very conspicuous in influencing U.S. national politics.[2] This has led to congressional debates on preventing "foreign agents" from lobbying. Similarly, many individual states have competed for Japanese investments by offering huge amounts of incentives. Due to incentive issues, gubernatorial races in Indiana and Kentucky States became controversial and resulted in victories for Democratic candidates opposing incentives.[3]

These cases indicate how vulnerable U.S. politics are to Japanese corporations. Japanese corporate behavior is influenced by and influences both international (U.S.-Japan) and national (U.S.) politics.

In this chapter, I will present pivotal issues related to the corporate social responsibility of Japanese corporations in the United States toward key stakeholders: internal constituencies (workers) and external environments (surrounding communities). These issues have become contentious in the media and for governments, the public, and Japanese corporations both in the United States and Japan as Japanese investments have increased. How can Japanese corporations, with growing transnational, political, and economic power, be socially accountable to the welfare of their own work force and surrounding communities? In this exploratory chapter, I intend to illuminate new research and community action approaches to what the problem is and how it can be resolved.

AT THE CORPORATE LEVEL

Japanese Management

At the corporate level, Japanese management practices have been praised by academics such as Vogel and Ouchi for their efficiency and harmonious operations.[4] The characteristics praised include lifetime employment, participatory management, team work style, flexible job classification, enterprise-based unions, seniority wage systems, and worker loyalty. Akio Morita, chairman of the Sony Corporation, asserted that Japanese corporations consider workers' welfare more seriously than their U.S. counterparts do.[5] Such behavior has been partially implanted in U.S. soil in recent years as Japanese corporations set up offices and plants with growing confidence.[6]

The employees of Japanese corporations seemingly welcome "Japanese" ways. Kujawa and Bob compared the opinions of U.S. employees of Japanese companies, community leaders, and the general public in the states of California, Michigan, and Tennessee, where Japanese investments are sizable.[7] According to the survey, the employees of Japanese companies generally believe that Japanese-affiliated companies provide more training, attention, and job security to their employees than U.S. companies. Nissan workers in Tennessee also exhibited their satisfaction with the Japanese management by opposing the unionization efforts of the United Auto Workers.

The "success" of Japanese companies' inroads into the United States while maintaining "Japanese" management practices will decisively affect the lives of many U.S. workers positively and negatively. Even U.S. corporations such as General Motors have begun to implement "Japanese ways" as a model in their operations. The problem, however, lies with what we mean by "Japanese ways." Japanese corporate practices are often attributed to some esoteric element in Japanese culture, which distorts understanding. Less a product of some mysterious Japanese culture, Japanese corporate culture derives from historically concrete economic and political structures and conflicts.[8] An understanding of these structures and conflicts are essential to resolving the problems this corporate culture presents in its transplantation to a U.S. context by Japanese or by U.S. companies.

The scope of relevance of this corporate culture presents another problem. It has been noted that "four-fifths of researchers' energy has been put into investigating the careers of one-fifth of the labour force."[9] This fifth consists mainly of male, college-graudate, full-time employees who are guaranteed lifetime employment. There is an acute need to study the impact of the management practices upon the lives of the four-fifths (majority) of workers in Japan if we are to gauge the full possible impact of "Japanese" management practices in the United States. The majority of workers include women, minorities, the elderly, foreign workers, and those in subcontracting and medium to small-sized companies.[10] An overwhelming majority of women in Japan, for instance, are not recipients of the benefits of "success." They are expected to lose their job upon marriage and to start all over again when they come back into the work force after childrearing. Thus, the research to date has resulted in a skewed perception of the issues involved.

Because of this significant gap in knowledge, it is difficult to assess the quality of "Japanese" management practices in real terms. It is reasonable to assume that imported "Japanese" management practices in the United States cannot be provided unless the four-fifths of the labor force are included. Is it coincidental, then, that many Japanese corporations have been accused of violating equal employment opportunities for women and minorities in the United States?

Equal Employment Opportunity

Japanese corporations have been compelled to adjust to U.S. practices that may be "foreign" to them. These include equal employment opportunity and affirmative action.[11] Because of this unfamiliarity, Japanese corporations in the United States are faced with the challenges of foreign regulations. Major Japanese corporations have experienced employment discrimination complaints and litigation based on race, sex, age, and national origin, which they have not been forced to deal with in Japan.

Women employees at Sumitomo Shoji America in New York sued the company because the company treated them as second-class employees by not giving them promotional opportunities. Sumitomo defended its policy by saying that the Japanese company should be exempt from U.S. laws under the Friendship, Commerce and Navigation Treaty between Japan and the United States. The U.S. Supreme Court ruled that the company violated U.S. law prohibiting employment discrimination. Since then, Japanese companies operating in the United States have been considered U.S. companies.

Honda of America Manufacturing, which had experienced an age discrimination suit earlier, was accused by 370 African American and women job applicants of unfair practices. The U.S. Equal Employment Opportunity Commission intervened to make Honda settle the case for U.S.$6 million. This settlement with African Americans was later followed by a series of accusations by African Americans against the racial attitudes of Japanese corporations and politicians toward them.

Finally, it was not only women and minorities who criticized Japanese corporations but also EuroAmerican men as well. A former manager of Ricoh, U.S.A., charged that the preference the company gave to Japanese managers sent from Japan in promotion repeatedly deprived him of opportunities and therefore violated equal employment opportunity based on national origin. This case, covered at length by the *New York Times,* June 3, 1991, prompted Congressional hearings by the House Subcommittee on Employment and Housing in summer 1991. When Tom Lantos, chair of the subcommittee, called for an investigation by the General Accounting Office, employment discrimination by Japanese corporations became politicized.[12]

Japanese corporate leaders, in response, insisted on their "ignorance" of these employment practices. For example, Maruyama, having served as chair of the Committee on Investment Environments of the Japanese Business Association (a Los Angeles–based group), told a reporter that Japanese companies could not catch up with U.S. companies in a few years regarding Japanese–African American relations.[13]

Employment discrimination against women and minorities in Japan has a long history. It was only in the mid-1970s that major Japanese corporations were accused of purchasing *Buraku* ("social outcasts") district directories showing *Buraku* districts in Japan. The directories were meant to be used by corporations to find out whether job applicants were of *Buraku* origin so that they could reject *Buraku* applicants. The Equal Employment Opportunity Act of 1985 to protect women from employment discrimination was a victory for management because it relaxed statutory protections for women employees and lacked sanctions against employer violations. Thus, an implicit and explicit policy to exclude women and minorities, rather than ignorance of equal employment opportunity laws, may be at the core of Japanese corporations' behavior in the United States.[14]

Due to forceful outcries in the United States, some major Japanese corporations, such as Toyota Motors Sale and Bank of California, were quick to implement equal employment opportunity and affirmative action policies. Internationalists[15] in Japan, such as the Ministry of Foreign Affairs, Japan External Trade Organization (JETRO), Keidanren, and the national media, have also advocated equal employment opportunities for women and minorities in the United States.[16] However, despite their emphasis, individual politicians and businesspeople in Japan with nationalistic inclinations do not find the issue of equal employment very pressing. Statements racially discriminatory against African Americans continue to prevail in Japan.[17] There is no structure in Japan to facilitate the understanding of civil rights issues and policies.

It is possible that the more enlightened among the Japanese leadership, who have an internationalist perspective, have advocated equal employment opportunity in the United States simply because they do not wish to further damage the already deteriorating U.S.-Japan ties. A higher priority may have been placed on this bilateral concern than on civil rights principles.

However, numerous civil rights advocates in Japan, such as women and *Buraku* groups, now express their interest in implanting "American" civil rights practices in Japanese corporations in Japan. Japanese corporations are now challenged by both the U.S. and Japanese civil rights groups. This is particularly significant given that a large number of foreign workers are arriving in Japan to work, and calls for "internationalization" have become more audible in Japan.

AT THE COMMUNITY LEVEL

Philanthropy

At the community level, Japanese corporations in Japan have made little contribution. It is said that the government, rather than corporations, are mainly responsible for the welfare of communities.[18]

A number of Japanese corporations were accused by community residents in the early 1970s for ignoring environmental pollution generated by the companies. With strong political pressure, the Japanese government was forced to legislate antipollution laws that are among the toughest in the world. Also, when U.S.-Japan trade frictions began to occur, and former Prime Minister Kakuei Tanaka's visit to Southeast Asia in 1974 generated anti-Japan feelings and demonstrations, Japanese corporations realized the importance of keeping good relations with communities abroad. Does this indicate that the concept of better community relations in Japan can only evolve through political pressures?[19]

The concept of "good corporate citizenship" was a corporate response to public outcries by U.S. consumers, environmentalists, and local residents against unethical corporate behavior. U.S. corporations were compelled to establish good community relations, considering it risk management to combine public image with marketing interests. Programs include establishing foundations, corporate donations, and volunteerism. However, for many Japanese corporations, the concept of "good corporate citizenship" was so "foreign" that they were slow to implement programs to build positive community-corporate relations. Certainly, it involves overcoming cultural and language barriers on the part of Japanese corporations.

U.S. affiliates of Japanese automobile and consumer electronics companies, such as Hitachi, Toyota, and Matsushita, are probably the most advanced in these areas and provide funds to minority scholarships, educational improvement, and so forth.[20] This trend accelerated after Sony was severely bashed by the U.S. public for its purchase of Columbia Pictures in 1989.

Keidanren and the Japan Center for International Exchange sponsored a study mission in 1988 to learn more about good corporate citizenship in the United States. The delegates visited U.S. foundations, such as the Ford Foundation, United Way of America, and Levi Strauss Foundation. Most recently, the Council for Better Corporate Citizenship (CBCC), set up by Keidanren, has attempted to serve as a broker of corporate philanthropy in the United States. The idea was for the Japanese government to provide tax exemptions to Japanese corporations making contributions, through the CBCC, to nonprofit organizations in the United States. The Japanese government has responded favorably to this request. This "Americanization" was necessary since U.S. corporations are allowed to deduct contributions to nonprofit groups, whereas Japanese are not.

The fever of Japanese corporate philanthropy also spread in Japan in 1990 and 1991 as seen in business organizations' recommendations, abundant literature, and educational seminars concerning philanthropy. Concepts, such as "beautiful company," "gentle company," "CI" (corporate identity), philanthropy, "1 Percent Club" (corporations that donate 1 percent corporate profits are eligible for memberships), and "mécénat" (a French word meaning to support culture and art) have become fashionable.[21] However, nonprofit groups in Japan have not yet become interested in this issue and remain skeptical, with the exception of a small number of consumer and environmental groups.

Social Responsibility

To address issues of corporate responsibility, the terms philanthropy and social responsibility must be clarified. The former relies upon corporate initiatives to show good will through charitable donations and volunteerism. The latter assumes that corporations, as powerful and resourceful organizations, are critical members of society and must be socially accountable. Corporations may be accused of violating laws and lacking ethics and morals. Thus, the implementation of social responsibility may come only through public pressures against corporations.

A consumer activist, Ralph Nader, pointed out that the money power of foreign capital in Washington, D.C., (including Japanese) threatens U.S. local community residents and small businesses (including nonprofit groups) due to an increase in rents and land prices, which squeeze out local nonprofit groups and many low-income residents. The following exemplifies Nader's point vividly, also showing that the responsibility does not lie solely with Japanese corporations.

Many Japanese-American community residents in Los Angeles and San Francisco were evicted from homes and small businesses when the two cities invited Japanese investors to "redevelop" the Japanese-American communities so that the cities, eroded by U.S. fiscal crisis, could secure needed revenues.[22] The cities bought up sizable parcels of land in order to sell them to Japanese investors. The community residents organized anti-eviction campaigns and clashed with city police forces. As a result, Japanese investors, although invited by the cities, faced fierce opposition in the communities.[23]

In the end, the Japanese investors entered the communities, but antagonism involving Japanese Americans, city officials, and Japanese investors remained. Today, the communities have become tourist sites with commercial enterprises, expensive houses, and condominiums. However, we can still see a few remnants of the city-community conflicts in the presence of Japanese-American community centers and housing for senior citizens.

The San Francisco Bay Area–based Greenlining Coalition,[24] a coalition of minority and low-income groups, successfully challenged some Japan-based banks, including California First Bank (later named Union Bank, taking the name of a British-owned bank bought out by California First Bank) and Mitsui Manufacturers Bank, a U.S. subsidiary of Mitsui Bank that merged with Taiyo-Kobe Bank.[25] The coalition criticized the banks for "redlining," for not having women and minorities in management positions, and for failing to provide loans to assist low-income and minority communities. The coalition asked the Federal Deposit Insurance Corporation and the Federal Reserve Board, which examine the social responsibility of financial institutions, to prohibit mergers of these banks with other banks. This oversight by federal institutions is mandated by the Community Reinvestment Act of 1977, which requires financial institutions to demonstrate sound contributions to communities when they merge with or acquire other financial institutions.

The Greenlining Coalition obtained an agreement from California First Bank to invest in low-income communities. The agreement now serves as a model for low-income and minority communities, and the coalition uses this model in confronting other financial institutions, both U.S. and Japanese owned. Despite well-publicized demonstrations against Mitsui Manufacturers Bank, and public testimony before the Federal Reserve Board showing the bank's poor record in social responsibility, however, the merger of Taiyo-Kobe and Mitsui banks in the United States was permitted. Nevertheless, aware of the possibility that the application by a subsidiary of Taiyo-Kobe-Mitsui Bank in New York to obtain a commercial bank permit might be rejected on the grounds of poor corporate social responsibility, the bank withdrew its application.

The third example is the case of Toyota Motors Manufacturing in Kentucky, one of the largest Japanese investors in the United States. It experienced a number of political conflicts, as documented by Gelsanliter in his detailed account of the problems the Japanese company faced at the early stage of investment.[26]

It was obvious that a number of community groups and individuals were concerned about Toyota's entry due to its sheer size. The hiring of nonunion construction workers by Ohbayashi, a Japan-based construction company, for the construction of the Toyota plant was fervently opposed by union workers affiliated with the AFL-CIO, who organized a boycott of Toyota products, as well as picketing at the Japanese Embassy. An environmental group as well as local landowners opposed Toyota for the environmental destruction (water and air pollution, as well as sewage generation) that they anticipated the company might bring into surrounding communities. The city of Georgetown was concerned with the social consequences of Toyota's entry, including the cost of providing for the social needs of workers' families, such as education and traffic problems. Finally, the local Urban League chapter organized a press conference to denounce Japan's former prime minister's racial remarks against African Americans and warn Toyota to hire African Americans.

Kentucky residents were concerned with the state incentive package to Toyota. The U.S.$125 million incentive included tax exemption, financial assistance in land acquisition, and technical assistance in screening job applicants. This resulted in court litigation to examine whether incentives (public money) to Toyota (private company) were constitutional. The incentives issue also became an issue in the gubernatorial race: the Democratic candidate won by attacking the incumbent administration over the incentive package.

In response, Toyota maintained a modest and accommodating style in relating to the community. It accommodated African-American demands by working with local African Americans in the recruiting and hiring of African Americans. Toyota also asked Ohbayashi to hire union workers and encouraged studies by the University of Kentucky to assess the environmental and social impacts of the plant. It donated U.S.$1 million to build a local community center and built a day care center for Toyota employees. Toyota's response was greeted in Japan as an example of good corporate citizenship.[27]

AT THE MACROSTRUCTURAL LEVEL

On a broader, macrostructural level, we need to examine the economic impact of Japanese direct investments in the community at large, as they affect the lives of U.S. workers and communities. Many scholars have listed U.S. trade and budget deficits, the yen's evaluation, "deindustrialization," and "protectionist" demands as the causes of Japanese direct investments in the United States. The United States badly needs capital revenues and jobs to replace those lost in the late 1970s and after. Japanese direct investments, indeed, brought in capital to supplement U.S. deficits, generated tax revenues to the public sector, and created jobs. Thus, they have been praised by many who believe in free trade and investment.[28]

Despite the apparent benefits generated by Japanese direct investments, an increasing number of scholars have begun to scrutinize Japanese direct investments critically, as they threaten U.S. "national security" in economic and military arenas; do not provide sufficient jobs comparable to those lost by "deindustrialization" and global competition; and tend to locate their operations in high-growth areas where minorities do not reside, contributing little to revitalizing economically depressed areas.[29]

Japanese automobile companies have been criticized for adding more imports because the U.S. local content of their products is limited and they tend to bring in subcontractors from Japan (importation of a *keiretsu* system), to the detriment of U.S. "national" businesses.[30] U.S. parts suppliers are now compelled to choose between becoming loyal subcontractors to Japanese automobile companies or calling for "protectionist" policies to prevent them from being wiped out.[31]

For the purpose of this chapter, a case in point is that of communities and workers disproportionately affected by the "deindustrialization" process: inner-city residents, Midwestern blue-collar workers, and African Americans rarely benefit from new Japanese direct investments, which tend to locate operations away from depressed areas. The quantity and quality of jobs as well as rapid demographic changes, followed by new racial tensions, are some pressing issues faced by workers, communities, policymakers, and business communities. As U.S. corporations have been criticized for closing numerous plants, Japanese corporations will also become targets of criticism both in the United States and in Japan for decisions to relocate operations elsewhere. The question, whether Japanese direct investments are "good" or "bad" does not touch upon the core of the problem. Instead, we need to examine how Japanese direct investments, which are a part of a drastic economic transformation in the United States, can be rendered socially accountable to workers and communities.

Current reality is huge flows and transactions of goods, money, information, services, and technology by Japanese corporations between Japan and the United States. There should certainly be inquiry as to their quantity and quality. However, such inquiries do not lead to understanding macrolevel problems. As the phrase "think globally, act locally" properly points out, human interations between corporate entities and workers and communities become crucial in analyzing new issues and finding solutions to the problems.

PROBLEM SOLVING

Japan Bashing

The most prevalent approach to the problems discussed above has been to blame Japan as a whole, or "Japan bashing." Because of the emotional and political implications, attacks on Japan or Japanese corporations as a whole have largely attracted members of Congress, the media, labor, and nationally oriented U.S. corporations. Japan-bashing tactics with their political thrust at times have clarified problems and forced Japanese corporations to change their behavior; but these same tactics have made solutions problematic because of oversimplification and chauvinism.

Although problems faced by U.S. workers and communities may be to some extent due to "Japanese" political or economic practices, such as *keiretsu*, as "revisionists" may point out, many problem areas can be neither analyzed nor resolved by solely identifying Japan as a "bad guy." In addition, the growth of anti-Japanese sentiment and activity in the United States has conspicuously detrimental consequences, as in the infamous murder of Vincent Chin in Detroit and a recent racial attack against Japanese students by KKK-connected youths in Denver.

At the same time, we see the emergence of anti-American sentiments in Japan, as expressed by noted politician Shintaro Ishihara.[32] Japan and America bashing, since they attract the media and the public by resorting to nationalistic chauvinism, are not only irresponsible in misleading the public, but also dangerous in creating a political atmosphere in which serious analysis and community organizing become impossible.[33]

Elitist Approach

Problems facing Japanese corporations in the United States have been addressed in various ways by groups in power or in control of resources. In the case of Toyota in Kentucky, the state government was responsible for setting up conditions for Toyota to invest. Japanese investors were also welcomed to invest in the Japanese-American communities by the city administrations of Los Angeles and San Francisco. Both cases indicate that there exist alliances between Japanese investors and local government officials, particularly executive and economic development officials.

To correct the image of Japanese corporate practices as racially discriminatory, Japanese corporate leaders have begun to work with leaders of minority communities, including the National Association for the Advancement of Colored People (NAACP), the United Negro College Fund, the Black Business Council.[34] However, these organizations represent neither grass roots African-American communities nor inner-city ghettos, about which Japanese politicians continue to hold negative stereotypes. Tensions between grass roots African Americans and Japanese corporations are not likely to be resolved by an elitist approach.

Such an elitist linkage became more apparent and ultimately controversial once Japanese investors entered the United States. With the serious criticisms at all levels of the society against Japanese investments, Japanese corporate communities have learned an important lesson: issues of diversity must be addressed not only in terms of cultures and races but also classes and regions. The elitist linkages became vulnerable targets of grass roots opposition. This leads to the need to examine Japanese direct investments more dynamically, looking into both their relationships with diverse groups at different levels (federal, state, grass roots, etc.) and the interactions between distinct levels.

A New Framework for Inquiry and Action: The Comparative and Global Approach

Studies of an action on the social responsibility of Japanese corporations in the United States must start by investigating interactions between and among Japanese corporations, and workers and communities in Japan, since they are mirror images for the United States. A comparative analysis of these interactions in the United States and Japan, also examining the roles of diverse actors (i.e., governments, the middle class, etc.) is decisive.

However, it is imperative to avoid separating these two nation-state units. These two units interact with each other. Interactions between Japanese corporations and U.S. workers and communities do affect similar interactions in Japan and vice versa. Often workers and communities on both sides of the Pacific work together in solidarity. This I call a "common ground" approach, as it brings in transnational inquiries. By looking into relationships between corporations and workers and communities in the United States and Japan dynamically, we may be able to advance both analysis and action.

We must raise questions about how relationships in Japan affect those in the United States through the interactions of governments, corporations, and workers and communities across the Pacific. Research questions include how these relations change in an international context, what the nature of the political economy of Japanese direct investments in the United States might be in the Pacific Era, and how successful international solidarity on the part of workers and communities has been.

Japanese corporations, as transnational actors, have carried their business activities across national boundaries and created a global network of corporations. In light of these corporate strategies, the question of Japanese corporate social responsibility in the United States presents challenges and opportunities for academic research and community action that compel our imagination beyond a national framework.

NOTES

This chapter owes much to the members of the Japan Pacific Resource Network, particularly Gina Hotta, Hiroshi Kashiwagi, and Martha Matsuoka for their critical comments and editing. Also, I am thankful to Keiko Higuchi and Frances Lee for their proofreading. I am indebted to Arif Dirlik, the editor of this book, who encouraged me to write this paper, and helped edit it.

1. See Tomoji Ishi, "Wangan Senso to Zaibei Nihonjin Shakai" [Gulf War and Japanese in the United States] *Keizai Seminar,* April 1991.

2. Pat Choate, *Agents of Influence* (New York: Alfred A. Knopf, 1990); and Martin Tolchin and Susan Tolchin, *Buying into America* (New York: Times Books, 1988).

3. Ernest J. Yanarella and William C. Green, eds., *The Politics of Industrial Recruitment: Japanese Automobile Investment and Economic Development in the American States* (New York: Greenwood Press, 1990).

4. Ezra Vogel, *Japan as Number One* (Cambridge, MA: Harvard University Press, 1979); and William G. Ouchi, *Theory Z: How American Business Can Meet the Japanese Challenge* (New York: Avon Books, 1981).

5. Akio Morita and Shintaro Ishihara, *No to Ieru Nippon* [The Japan That Can Say "No"] (Tokyo: Kobunsha, 1989).

6. Tetsuo Abo, ed., *Nihon Kigyo no Amerika Genchi Seisan* [Local Production in the United States by Japanese Corporations] (Tokyo: Toyo Keizai Shimposha, 1988).

7. Duane Kujawa and Daniel Bob, *American Public Opinion on Japanese Direct Investment* (New York: Japan Society, 1988).

8. For example, Taira refuted the argument that the seemingly paternalistic Japanese management originated in the feudal society by showing how Japanese employers rationally designed the labor-management system in modern industrial development. See Koji Taira, *Economic Development and the Labor Market in Japan* (New York: Columbia University Press, 1970); and Taishiro Shirai, ed., *Contemporary Industrial Relations in Japan* (Madison: University of Wisconsin Press, 1983) on industrial relations in Japan.

9. David W. Plath, *Work and Life Course in Japan* (Albany: State University of New York Press, 1983), p. 31.

10. See Anthony Burick, comp., *Work in Japan: A Reader* (Berkeley, CA: Japan Pacific Resource Network, 1991).

11. It should be noted, however, that the U.S. concept of civil rights is also the political product of the civil rights movements rather than something "American."

12. For details see Hiroshi Kashiwagi, "Mo Hitotsu no Rikuruto Jiken" [Another Recruit Scandal], *Asahi Journal,* September 22, 1989; Hiroshi Kashiwagi, "Japan-bashing Yobu Zaibei Nikkei Kigyo no Koyo Sabetsu" [Employment Discrimination by Japanese Corporations in America, which leads Japan-Bashing], *Asahi Journal,* September 20, 1991; and Takeshi Yabe, *Nihon Kigyo wa Sabetsusuru!* [Japanese Companies Discriminate] (Tokyo: Diamond Sha, 1991).

13. *Japan News Magazine,* December 10, 1988.

14. See *Koria Shushoku Joho,* September 30, 1986; Michihiko Noguchi, "Discrimination and the Buraku," in David Coates, ed., *Shattering the Myth of the Homogeneous Society: Minority Issues and Movements in Japan* (Berkeley, CA: Japan Pacific Resource Network, 1990); and Frank K. Upham, *Law and Social Change in Postwar Japan* (Cambridge, MA: Harvard University Press, 1987) on equal employment opportunity violations in Japan.

15. Internationalists are those who try to maintain international political and economic relationships rather than to protect domestic interests.

16. See *Taibei Toshikyo Nyusu,* August 21, 1989 and *JETRO Sensa,* February 2, 1989.

17. Tomoji Ishi, "Racism, Politics, and Markets: Japanese Corporations and African Americans" (Working Paper, Japan Pacific Resource Network, Berkeley, CA, 1991).

18. See Edwin M. Epstein, "The Enigma of Japanese Business Ethics" (Paper presented at the 1989 Annual Summer Conference of the Society for Business Ethics, Washington, D.C., August 11, 1989); Hitachi Sogo Keikaku Kenkyusho, *Kaigai Genchi Seisan Jidai ni Okeru Kigyo no Shakaiteki Sekinin* [Corporate Social Responsibility at the Era of Overseas Production] (Tokyo: 1988); Japan Center for International Exchange, *The Role of Philanthropy in International Cooperation* (Report on the JCIE 15th Anniversary International Symposium, Tokyo, December 1985); and Hiroshi Kashiwagi, *Amerika ni Okeru Kigyo no Shakaiteki Sekinin: Firansoropi to Nikkei Kigyo no Taio* [Corporate Social Responsibility in America: Philanthropy and Responses of Japanese Corporations] (Berkeley, CA: Japan Pacific Resource Network, 1991).

19. See discussions in T. J. Pempel, *Policy and Politics in Japan* (Philadelphia: Temple University Press, 1982); and Upham, *Law and Social Change.*

20. Hiroshi Kashiwagi, *Amerika ni Okeru.*

21. For literature on this feverish atmosphere in Japan, see Toshiaki Fujiwara, Hiroyuki Tamura, and Hiroshi Kashiwagi, *Kigyo no Shakai Koken to Jinken* [Contributions to Society and Human Rights of Corporations] (Osaka: Buraku Kaiho Kenkyusho, 1991) and Yabe, *Nihon Kigyo.*

22. Japanese Americans are defined as U.S. people of Japanese descent. They are mainly comprised of children and grandchildren of Japanese immigrants who came to the United States before World War II.

23. Little Tokyo Anti-Eviction Task Force, "Los Angeles' Little Tokyo," in Emma Gee, ed., *Counterpoint: Perspectives on Asian America* (Los Angeles, University of California at Los Angeles, Asian American Studies Center, 1976).

24. The term "greenlining" is used to counter practice of financial institutions circumscribing low-income and minority communities for investment by encircling such communities by red lines on maps.

25. See Hiroshi Kashiwagi, "Chiiki Shakai Saitoshiho to Hogin" [Community Re-investment Act and Japanese Banks] *Keizai Seminar,* June 1991; and Hiroshi Kashiwagi, "Beigin no Choraku to Hogin e no Kisei Kyoka" [Demise of U.S. Banks and Restrictions on Japanese Banks] *Keizai Seminar,* October 1991, on Japan-based banks and community groups regarding social responsible investments.

26. David Gelsanliter, *Jump Start* (New York: Farrar Straus Giroux, 1990).

27. Nihon Hoso Kyokai, "Kigyo wa Shakai ni Nani ga Dekiru ka?" [What Can Corporations Do to Society?], *Gendai Journal,* 1991.

28. See Edward M. Graham and Paul R. Krugman, *Foreign Direct Investment in the United States* (Washington, D.C.: Institute for International Economics, 1989); and Kozo Yamamura. "The Significance of Japanese Investment in the United States: How Should We React?" in Kozo Yamamura, ed. *Japanese Investment in the United States: Should We Be Concerned?* (Seattle, WA: Society for Japanese Studies, 1989) on debates on foreign direct investments in general and Japanese in particular.

29. See Robert Cole, "Racial Factors in the Employment Patterns of Japanese Auto Firms in America," *California Management Review* 31(1), Fall 1988; Douglas Frantz and Catherine Collins, *Selling Out: How We Are Letting Japan Buy Our Land, Our Industries, Our Financial Institutions, and Our Future* (Chicago: Contemporary Books, 1989); Norman Glickman and Douglas Woodward, *The New Competitors* (New York: Basic Books, 1989); Tomoji Ishi, *Japanese Automobile and Television Assembly Plants and Local Communities: County Demographic Profile* (Berkeley, CA: Japan Pacific Resource Network, 1988); and Tolchin and Tolchin, *Buying into America.*

30. See U.S. General Accounting Office, *Foreign Investment: Growing Japanese Presence in the U.S. Auto Industry,* March 1988; and U.S. International Trade Commission, *U.S. Global Competitiveness: the U.S. Automotive Parts Industry,* December 1987.

31. If they become subcontractors, a Japanese "just-in-time" relationship between manufacturers and subcontractors may be created within the United States. The former require the latter to bring in parts and supplies at the right moments of production. The former's cost in inventory is thus transferred to the latter. This may transform industrial structure in the United States very significantly.

32. See Morita and Ishihara, *No to Ieru.*

33. Many scholars may become afraid of criticizing Japan lest they jeopardize chances to receive grants derived from Japan.

34. See Ishi, "Racism."

Market Dependency in U.S.–East Asian Relations

*T*HE ARGUMENT of this chapter is that U.S.–East Asian relations are afflicted not just by trade tensions that have grown since the early 1970s, to which we have become accustomed, but also by a new cultural and rhetorical divide that increases friction at the same time that it obscures the continuing realities of the relationship. This divide in turn derives from asymmetries of power that have been consistent in U.S.–East Asian relations for decades. Whereas the United States increasingly looks toward East Asia with apprehension, Asians look to the United States much as they have since 1945, as a bigger, stronger, even dominating nation that is nonetheless essential to their continuing growth.

I will argue that certain aspects of this relationship are changing, like the single-market dependency that has characterized Japan, Korea, and Taiwan and the security situation, which is considerably relaxed from the troubled years of the cold war. East Asian moves toward diversifying markets—primarily in Europe—signal a growing departure from the previous structure (going back to the World War II settlement) whereby the United States interacted bilaterally with Western Europe and Japan, and Japan and Europe had little interaction. Additionally, the deepening of economic relations between Northeast and Southeast Asia heralds an interregional reorganization that will carve out more autonomy for all the Asian nations, and perhaps lead to changes in the security structure.

I will also argue that this attenuation of bilateral relations across the Pacific—perhaps we can call it constructive disengagement—is not necessarily bad, and that it will afford the United States greater flexibility in its conduct of foreign economic policy.

While these changes occur, the deeper problem is the absence of an intellectual framework within which to understand the ongoing transition. I will suggest that Japanese and East Asian economic success has provoked both admiration and deep worry in the United States, giving rise to a "new Orientalism" that both honors and shames Asians too much; quick to find fault and exaggerate difference, this tendency is also quick to patronize and praise, the excessiveness in both directions being the index of the failure of the one to understand the alien Other.

In this chapter I will switch the optic to adopt the perspective of the "Other," to see how it all looks from a different shore—what we might call East Asia's America Problem. I will argue that the cultural constructs and contradictions by which Americans confront East Asian industrial prowess reflect not just an inability to apprehend a still-alien Other, but also the antagonistic currents in U.S. politics between protectionism and free trade, and deep conflicts in the U.S. orientation to the world between expansionism and imperialism, or between what used to be called Asia-firsters and Europe-firsters.[1]

If East Asia has an America problem, of course it is by no means only Americans who partake of it. Indeed, the United States has been more tolerant and open than several European countries, particularly Italy and France. These days it is the French above all whose well-known nationalism increasingly becomes the handmaiden of an appalling racism. The former Prime Minister Edith Cresson referred to "little yellow men" who stay up nights thinking about how to "screw" Europe. Japan is "another universe which wants to conquer," basing itself on a "hermetically sealed" system. "That's the way they are," she announced knowingly.[2]

THE NEW ORIENTALISM

"Orientalism" is a term used by Edward Said and others to connote a Western discourse about Asia that both projects Western hopes and fears onto Asia and fails to uncover the reality of Asia itself.[3] It is a species of prejudice, but one so deeply rooted that its practitioners are generally unaware of it. U.S. Orientalism in regard to East Asia today is Janus faced and given to dramatic exaggeration: one face looks anxiously back, to find in the past a prelude to a new yellow peril shaking the edifice of Western civilization or even to find analogues in the decade of fascist political economy in the 1930s, whereas another looks forward euphorically to a Pacific Rim golden age in the next century, of "miracle" economies and budding East Asian post-modernity.

If Mark Twain's "innocents abroad" were non-Americans visiting the United States, one of the oddest cultural traits they might encounter would be the mysterious liberal probity of the United States: public utterance and private thoughts seem remarkably divorced, and voicing private thoughts is verboten. Yet racism appears to be on the rise on college campuses, on the far right, and elsewhere. We have heard much lately about a "politically correct" liberal United States in which ethnic jokes and racial stereotypes are forbidden in public discourse and uttering them can quickly get a college student expelled or a prominent person fired. Except in one's living room, or except with regard to one ethnic group: the Japanese in particular, Asians in general.

Some aspects of the problem are quite visible. It is still common on television, for example, to see crude stereotypes of rotund samurai made to masquerade as Japan's everyman, with concomitant bellowing and swordplay. Even the stalward critic of U.S. education and popular culture Allan Bloom feels free to refer to Asians as "yellows" in his recent best-seller.[4] The business of "making strange" in regard to the Japanese and other "Asiatics" like them is still visible in spite of liberal probity and it sells goods in the marketplace. Perhaps such stereotyping even acquires a patriotic halo in this age of perpetual trade deficits. But this realm of the visible is merely the tip of an iceberg.

If caricatures of East Asia in France are one aspect of inveterate French nationalism, we can argue that similar expressions in the United States are animated by the protectionist impulse of "Middle America" (or what Richard Nixon characterized as "mainstream," or "Newark factory gate").[5] Historically this current has been the repository of U.S. nationalism and has conceived East Asia as a frontier for the United States, to be conquered, organized, and civilized. Today the East Asian countries are perceived to be in but not of the world, free riders in "defense" and predatory in economics—thus sapping U.S. strength such that it fast becomes, in Joseph Chamberlain's words, "a weary Titan staggering under the too vast orb of its fate," or just an amicable fool, taken advantage of at every turn. The contemporary rancor of representatives of this view (Lee Iacocca, for example) indicates a frustration about Asians getting off the reservation and "doing their own thing," so to speak.

The most influential book in the recent and growing genre of "Japan-bashing" literature is by Karel van Wolferen, a Dutch journalist stationed in Tokyo, who recently catapulted into the intellectual limelight in the United States when his book got rave reviews across the spectrum. *The Enigma of Japanese Power* both presents to us a cogent account of Japan's industrial growth and partakes of the new Orientalism. Van Wolferen shows how a long pattern of state-led "developmentalism," combined with a typical pattern of followership in industrial development (copying more advanced technology, adapting previously successful management skills), lies behind Japan's successes. But he also indulges in harmful stereotyping by explaining Japanese success to Americans in terms that only multiply misunderstanding by measuring Japanese deviance from what Westerners hold dear: the Japanese have no regard for "transcendental truths," are "less free than they should be," and are at odds with "one single command that has reverberated throughout Western intellectual development ever since the Greeks: [sic] 'Thou shalt not cherish contradictions.'"

The Japanese, the implication is, are not individuals, are not rational, not logical, and perhaps not "enlightened"; there seems to be no Eastern equivalent of the great Western caesura termed the Enlightenment. Some Japanese, of course, cherish rationality and individualism—van Wolferen has even "met quite a few who want to be taken for distinct persons." But the Japanese remain by and large indistinct to him. In any case his generalizations are so blanketed and opaque that they make refutation difficult: that a people are "less free than they should be" can probably be said about any society in the world, the assertion rests on an unstated conception of freedom and morality.

When van Wolferen peered into the heart of the Japanese system of political economy, moreover, like Conrad he saw a horror staring back at him: not liberal pluralism, but an all-encompassing and mysterious "System" with no exit, one as "inescapable as the political system of the Soviet Union," only worse because it was more pervasive, and culturally legitimate.[6]

To see Japan as enigmatic, impenetrable, not individualistic, and run by a mysterious system of course recalls stereotypes that go back to the first Western encounters with Asians. What is more irresponsible, however, about the new Orientalism provoked by Japanese economic success is its dramatic exaggeration: not just indictment of Japan and its East Asian facsimiles—South Korea and Taiwan—as illiberal, run by subterranean "systems," and substituting strong states for the presumed natural workings of the market, but also hints that this might really be a kind of fascism.

Van Wolferen thus exhorts Americans to deal harshly with "the Japan Problem," as Europe had to in the past with "the German Problem,"[7] and Ian Buruma, the peripatetic observer for all of Asia for the *New York Review of Books,* compared the impressive Korean show during the opening ceremony of the Seoul Olympics to Hitler's Nuremburg extravaganza in 1936.[8] More recently Buruma has predicted a "Pax Axis" between Japan and unified Germany, pacifist and quiescent in the wake of the Persian Gulf War, but who knows what to expect from this "axis" in the future.[9] And now, perhaps, the inevitable title has appeared: *The Coming War with Japan.*[10]

Ishihara and Morita do little more than reflect back to and play upon these dark fears in *The Japan That Can Say No.* In their idiosyncratic Japanese way they also proffer a postwar replay of the prewar repertoire. Their ethnocentric view asserts Yamato superiority in empire building (as evidenced in the postcolonial performance of South Korea and Taiwan), over a slovenly Yankee imperialism (as seen in the mess in the Philippines). They indulge in a kind of epithet one-upmanship, seeing who can do best in previewing the contestation of the Pacific as a Japanese, and not a U.S. lake.[11] Perhaps Ishihara and Morita reveal more than they wish, however, because their book reads like the battered schoolboy finding a way to get back at the playground bully; it reeks of insecurity.

The new Orientalism thus has counterparts on both sides of the Pacific, and is contradictory and unsettled. For every dark worry about who the Japanese "really are," another U.S. genre looks happily forward to a budding Pacific Rim century in the offing. An admixture of Saint-Simonism and genteel Darwinism, this prophetic culture—and its gurus, such as Alvin Toffler and John Naisbett—privileges the denizens of the Pacific Rim as the mainstay of international capitalist utopia in the next century.[12]

To these prophets the Confucian culture incapable of "transcendental truths" is swell, even if it is non-Western, and indeed constitutes what Hofheinz and Calder call the "East Asia Edge," traditional culture being the background and driving ethic of the "miracle" economies. The old shibboleth that Confucianism stifled the entrepreneurial spirit, so prevalent in the "modernization" literature of the 1950s, is now replaced by a new shibboleth that equates capitalist spirit with hyphenated Confucianism: Post-Confucianism, Aggressive-Confucianism, and even Samurai-Confucianism.[13] In other words, Confucianism is an all-purpose grab bag for both faulting and praising East Asia—but "as Confucius say," you can't have it both ways.

The cheerleaders for the Asia-Pacific capitalist utopia tout the internationalist line that nationalism is less important (or inconsequential) in an age of mobile capital and mobile labor. Pacific Asia is a manufacturing basin for consumer goods, and its wealthy class consumes Pacific America's high technology and agriculture: Cray supercomputers for the workaday world, California's mangoes for the dinner table. Meanwhile its poor labors for—anybody. The competitive edge of the United States, so this argument goes, likewise is bolstered through free trade, including free movement of capital, commodities, and people—especially fresh infusions of skilled labor and brains that the new immigration law promises: 600,000 Koreans in the Los Angeles area show that in the Pacific Rim era, you can bring the mountain to the prophet.

This is liberal imperialism at its finest, assuming that all are equal in the empyrean of free trade and ignoring the disparate power relations between the United States, now the only superpower, and Japan, South Korea, and Taiwan. From an objective point of view, Japan is an economic titan and a military wimp; South Korea is a rising economy, but still just half of a divided country with a semisovereign polity, its army still controlled by a U.S. general; Taiwan is a rising economy, a political midget, and a diplomatic nonentity.

The futurologists and the Japan bashers come together, however, in two ways: first, they both have difficulty grasping an East Asia that is neither a miracle nor a menace, but rather some hundreds of millions of people working hard to better their lot, coming along "late" to the task of industrial development and trying to make the best of it with a quite ordinary mixture of good and bad human traits. Second, they both tend to soft-pedal the remaining power asymmetries between the United States and East Asia, which severely constrain either the best or the worst outcome, and which predict that for the next several decades we will have neither fascist political economy nor capitalist valhalla, but a persisting structure in which East Asia will continue to play second fiddle. Thus both they and the periodic outbursts of Japan's leaders conceal more than they reveal about the reality of power across the Pacific.

One would never know from the rhetoric of the new Orientalism that the Pacific is still a U.S. lake, where a dominant United States holds sway not just with the Seventh Fleet, myriad military bases, and a panoply of high-tech and nuclear weapons, but also with a U.S. presence that in all its forms—cultural, political, economic—remains pervasive. One would not know that Japan and the East Asian newly industrializing countries (NICs) largely retain a single-market dependency that has influenced their political economies for several decades and that this market is the U.S. one. Nor would one know that Japan and its East Asian neighbors still tend to interact with each other and with the rest of the world through a trilateral structure mediated by Washington.

The U.S. lake has opened, of course, especially in the postwar years, a realm of opportunity for East Asia. But it has also been an albatross, denying the countries of the region their national agency and purpose. The U.S. market has been both a realm of vast opportunity and a drag on the flexibility of East Asian economic policy. Both of these aspects of the relationship, however, are mostly concealed in the U.S. discourse on East Asia, so that we end up either with the specter of authoritarian behemoth states chewing up U.S. industries or the international capitalist utopia.

These fundamental limitations, however, are rarely voiced. The East Asian counterparts of the United States tend to maintain silence on these points except for an occasional and predictably bigoted belch from the conservatives who rule Japan, people too often taken for all of Japan in the United States. The reason for this silence is that Japan, Korea, island China, and (increasingly) mainland China are "rule takers," and not "rule makers" in the international system. Perhaps more important, liberal free market discourse is *the* hegemonic discourse, with no challengers in the international realm.

No one stands for East Asia today and voices a distinctive regional perspective; rather its leaders tend to prefer a weak posture. (The last East Asian theorist of international politics was the now repudiated Mao Zedong.) The East Asian response is reactive, usually a mark of insecurity: an occasional riposte that often partakes of the same, visceral bias with which some Americans view newly risen Asian prowess.

Thus Japanese conservative leaders charge that the U.S. problem is indolence, selfishness, greed, or racial diversity, almost always in the burplike manner that reveals "what they really think," apart from surface politeness and displomatic legerdemain. The liberals and internationalists of East Asia, on the other hand, plead that their politics is no different from that in the West: democratic and open, a pluralist mirror image (after all, the ruling party is called Liberal Democratic in Japan and Democratic Liberal in South Korea.) Their economies, too, are said to be open, with vast and impressive statistics on trade and investment deployed for the argument—and whatever trade barriers remain are on their way down, nothing more than a matter of time. This is a view of East Asia getting along and going along in the interstices of the international system, molding itself and being molded in the image of the Western creator.

Conservative response and liberal apologetics alike tend to obscure "private thoughts" that are increasingly strong, a growing nationalism in East Asia that lies behind a Japan trying to find a way to say No and a rising tide of self-assertion uniting right and left in South Korea, uniformly interpreted as anti-American by pundits and policymakers. The private thoughts cannot, however, gainsay the reality that the capitalist states of Northeast Asia are semisovereign in their politics and defense, and barely sovereign in their mass culture—the epicenter of the latter still being firmly in Hollywood and New York. They are regionally bereft of anything akin to the European Economic Community, let alone a sense of Europeanness, or common adherence to the legitimacy of social democratic ideals. Japanese, Koreans, and Chinese barely talk to each other, if truth be known.

For all the talk about Japan as Number One, Japan remains utterly unable to fashion an alternative hegemonic discourse, one that can leap across civilizational boundaries to create a universal appeal and turn Japan's solipsism into everyone else's universalism. There is little indigenous weight to offset overwhelming U.S. influence, save the increasingly slim reed of "the East Asian tradition." Money can buy culture and ideology, as did Sony and Matsushita Columbia and MCA, but it has not—as yet—created any; as one literary critic put it, Japan can produce "the signifiers, but not the signified."[14]

This poverty of philosophy, I will argue, stems from the reality of postwar U.S. hegemony in East Asia, which has been overwhelming and unilateral, much more so than in Western Europe, and the reality of relations today, with the U.S. market remaining the engine of the world economy and the talisman of East Asian export success. Starting with MacArthur's suzerainty during the occupation of Japan, the United States has had mostly unilateral sway in the region, symbolized by its frequent apologetics for forgetting to "consult" with its East Asian allies—about opening relations with China, withdrawing troops from Korea, or forgiving debts to the Poles (a recent brouhaha with Japan). And however penetrated its market may be by Asian imports, that market remains the lifeline of East Asian economic success, giving the United States a reverse influence that it rarely acknowledges.

THE POLITICAL ECONOMY OF
U.S. EAST ASIA

Given all the heated rhetoric of recent years, it is useful to look at the basic structure of the East Asian region. In the postwar years, the United States has prevailed over the capitalist countries of East Asia through two historical compacts. One might be thought of as an international Brumairean compact[15] between the victor in the last world war on the one hand and the defeated and its colonial possessions on the other. Just as the bourgeoisie of Louis Bonaparte's France, prostrate before the rifle butt, traded its political rights for the right to make money, so did Japan—and in a curious working of the dialectic, its newly liberated colonies.

Through the "San Francisco framework" of postwar peacemaking, Japan essentially gave up its military power and its autonomy in foreign-policy making. South Korea did the same at the time of the Korean War. Elemental sovereignty over defense and security matters was and is mortgaged to the structure of U.S. defense policy in Japan and Korea, and the state's role in mediating the relationship between the domestic and the international spheres is decidedly weak, at least where the United States is concerned.

National defense, which would ordinarily be a primary task of any state, the Japanese included, was passed on to Washington, and to the U.S. bases in Japan and Korea. In the aftermath of the Korean War, moreover, Washington created under its nuclear umbrella a modified apparition of Japan's prewar military empire, with South Korea's massive military as a regional gendarme, not just to protect the Republic of Korea but to fight Communist insurgents in Vietnam in the 1960s. Vietnam's seventeenth parallel was to have been another cordon sanitaire. Thus former colonies and dependencies, not to mention the GIs in the bases in the Pacific, were to do their bit in protecting the big enchilada, the Japanese archipelago. This was not a bad deal for Japan, of course, and the compact was justified by a weird formula that reverberates today: the Japanese really had to be protected from themselves.

The result of this Brumairean compact was to place South Korea on the geopolitical fault line, with the Korean military as a backstop to Japan's defense—a political disaster for the Korean people. Korea's civil society came under the tight grip of the state, which was in turn thoroughly penetrated by the United States. Its formidable military force is one of the biggest and best in the world, but under the operational control of the United States: South Korea is a semisovereign state. It has a vast military establishment it does not fully control and a foreign policy that is essentially dictated from without. This was a great deal for the Korean military, which became the dominant force in political life, but it wasn't much of a deal for the South Korean people (not to mention the North Koreans). Even after the war, the Korean peninsula continued to be an armed-to-the-teeth tinderbox.

From 1948 to 1978 Taiwan had a similar "deal," with the Guomindang mainlanders dealt the best hand, native Taiwanese excluded from power, another huge military organization devastating democracy, but all the islanders free to make money. In 1978, of course, the United States demonstrated its ultimate trump hand by switching this China for the other one, leaving Taiwan to make the best of its very bad deal—the saving grace being that they were still free to make money, which they have done with a vengeance.

A virtual monopoly on the means of violence and the whip hand in important foreign policy decisions is one aspect of U.S. hegemonic politics in East Asia. The other compact shaping the region is economic, and this was the maintenance of a U.S. market open to the capitalist upstarts in East Asia. The history and the workings of this compact are complicated, but the upshot, I will argue, was to deny the states of the region national agency in the conduct of domestic politics and economics. We can call this the compact of *single-market dependence* and seek to understand its political logic.

In 1988 the United States absorbed more than a third of all of Japan's exports, about 40 percent of South Korea's, and 44 percent of Taiwan's exports. Even when Japan is excluded, U.S. imports from the four East Asian NICs, ASEAN, and China totaled U.S.$90 billion in 1989. The three Northeast Asian capitalist economies are thus remarkably dependent on the U.S. market. Canada and Mexico are the only other countries more singularly dependent on the U.S. market; no other West European, African, or Middle Eastern nation shows any comparable level of single-market dependence for its exports. It is a sobering thought that the only area in the world that is comparable in its trade pattern was the former Eastern European bloc, with its single-market dependence on the Soviet Union.[16]

The political side of this economic coin is obvious. As Albert O. Hirschman once argued, a large economy that can accommodate a great portion of the exports of a small economy, with the latter having a relatively small fraction of import share, determines the relations of trade *and* political dependence for its trading partner. Germany, for instance, cultivated this pattern vis-à-vis smaller Eastern European nations in the interwar years.[17] Hirschman's argument, one of the first to articulate the logic of international dependence, gave grist to the mill of Latin American *dependencia* school, but has been mostly overlooked by students of East Asia.

This is quite a reversal from the turn-of-the-century open door policy toward East Asia; in fact, one might with some license characterize the situation today as a reverse open door. The open door was a modal foreign policy for a rising power like the United States, say, from the 1870s to World War I, seeking to penetrate markets in East Asia and Latin America that were held or influenced by European powers. Once hegemony was achieved, however, in the postwar period, the door also opened on the home turf, threatening weak domestic industries.

This did not happen without a struggle, of course. Some U.S. protectionist interests, mostly in declining industries, as well as big business that wished to invest behind the tariff barriers in the Third World, fought to encourage import-substitution industrialization as the strategy for foreign economic development in the 1950s and not export-led growth as economic pundits would have us believe.[18] Even the economic reconstruction of Japan, which was deemed necessary for closing the postwar dollar gap, had been predicated on restoring for Japan its colonial markets, not on opening the U.S. market.

Things worked out differently, however, in part because Japan's former colonies threw a monkey wrench into the plan for regional recovery. North Korea and China had their doors shut tight by 1949, recalcitrant South Korea all throughout the 1950s sabotaged U.S. attempts to recycle aid money by getting Koreans to procure goods from Japan, and even the Southeast market was difficult to penetrate because of competition from China and overseas Chinese. The only exception was Taiwan, which did welcome Japanese investment, but Japan did not want to touch it, looking nervously over its shoulders at China.[19] The major boost to the Japanese economy from the East Asian market—in fact, allowing Japan to "take off"—was the three years of the Korean War, "a gift of the gods," according to Prime Minister Yoshida Shigeru.[20]

With that boost Japan was able to sell in the U.S. market, and the United States opened its market to Japanese products in a big way. In the 1950s, however, this was no problem. As Dulles put it to Yoshida, "The Japanese [did] not make the things [the United States] likes." Taiwan and South Korea followed Japan into the U.S. market, which remained open as an essential component of U.S.-sponsored models of "export-led growth" in the 1960s, and as a trade-off to South Korea for its contribution to the U.S. war effort in Vietnam. The U.S. market was also necessary to Korea and Taiwan because Japan remained mercantilist, closing its market to its former colonies. Even as of 1988, Japan, although the second largest export market after the United States for South Korea and Taiwan, takes in only 18 percent of Korea's total exports, and 13 percent of Taiwan's.

The deluge of commodities from East Asia to the United States since the 1960s did not occur without conflicts between the protectionist and internationalist camps, leading to periodic lifting and closing of the U.S. gate. Japan and South Korea, for instance, are comparable in the speed and structure of industrial development, but are by no means at the same level, with Korea remaining "behind" Japan by about fifteen years.[21] This has actually worked against the protectionists, enabling the United States to play one East Asian ally off against another (and U.S. protectionists and internationalists off against each other). That is, to appease its protectionists, the United States has often stiff-armed Japanese firms after they flood the U.S. market in a given commodity, only to have the Koreans supply the same goods even more cheaply, thus satisfying consumers but still doing harm to domestic industries. There has ordinarily been an interval of about fifteen years between the entry of a Japanese commodity and protectionist measures directed against it, followed by the entry of Korean goods into the space where the Japanese goods had been. This process has occurred in textiles, color television, steel, automobiles, VCRs, and now computers and semiconductor chips.

Thus the United States has accommodated East Asian imports differentially and discriminately. But for all the East Asian economies, big and small, from the opposing shore the United States still looks like the only game in town, and this is where the United States has wielded a unilateral influence, making and breaking the essential fabric of political economy in the region. The logic of these exchanges is rarely articulated, however, beyond lots of rhetoric about supporting free trade. In fact the logic has often been solipsistically American and not without contradictions governed by shifting U.S. interests.

All throughout the 1950s, for instance, Americans urged the Japanese to reduce their trade barriers to conform to the General Agreement on Trade and Tariffs (GATT), only to turn around by the end of the decade and in violation of the spirit of GATT, pressure Japan to curb its increasing exports of textiles. Japan, to be sure, remained mercantilist despite the U.S. urging. But this was acceptable because to United States came to see Japan as a designated defender, so to speak, of the dollar: mercantilist Japan safely absorbed an immense quantity of exported U.S. dollars, and by supporting the dollar, helped to maintain the Bretton Woods order. In that sense, it is possible to argue that Japanese neomercantilist practice happened in part because the United States specifically *allowed* it to happen.[22]

By 1971, all that changed. Throughout the 1960s, the United States had supported a regime of fixed exchange rates and convertible currencies. But with inflation on the rise and the dollar heading for a fall, Richard Nixon resorted to the "New Economic Policy," a mercantilist revolution that suspended indefinitely the dollar's official convertibility into either gold or foreign currencies, leaving the Japanese and the Europeans holding the bag. Nixon also slapped a discriminatory 10 percent duty on Japanese imports. The hell with you, said Nixon and Connally; and Europe and Japan took it because they had nowhere else to go.

The Japanese commitment to GATT was slow in coming, but it has grown systematically over time; the problem is that at the same time, the U.S. commitment to the same GATT system, although still strongly defended by free traders and the administration in power, has gotten more capricious as protectionists make inroads on U.S. trade policy.

What we might call "hegemonic irresponsibility" continued through the 1980s, to the extent that the U.S. Treasury bill market came to be financed by Japan. The United States now combines selective closing of the U.S. market ("voluntary restrictions,") with mysterious codes—MOSS (Market-Oriented, Sector-Specific), SII (Structural Impediment Initiative), and Super 301—to restructure the way domestic politics and markets are organized in Japan. It has had more success than many observers realize.

Much the same can be said about U.S. pressure on the smaller East Asian countries. But these countries lack reciprocal leverage even more than Japan. Besides, their politics are much too brittle and their societies much too fragile to accommodate U.S. demands for liberalization, open markets, and democratized states without tidal waves of change. South Korea is one such country. With all its visceral animosity toward Japan, it nonetheless fashioned its political economy after Japan's—in part as a legacy of four decades of colonialism, but mostly because Japanese neomercantilist alchemy had industrialized the country rapidly and was there to be emulated. But the essential difference between South Korea and its much envied "mirror of the future" (that is, Japan) was that South Korea was a bulwark of containment; thus, instead of the "soft authoritarianism" of Japan, Korea ended up with hard-core military authoritarianism.

Another difference was that South Korea industrialized even later than the "late" developing Japan and thus was allowed—by the United States—a greater insularity in its conduct of political economy, so long as it occupied an innocuous place in the pores of the international market. The result was neomercantilism with vengeance, a developmental economy that was more tightly sealed and orchestrated from above even than Japan's.

In the 1980s when the United States began a frontal assault on South Korea to liberalize its commodity and financial markets, leading from the U.S. comparative advantage in agribusiness, high technology, and service industries, the authoritarian state went into a tailspin. Its power had been predicated on its ubiquitous ability to control developmental resources, to mold the investment pattern by selectively allocating credit, and to supplant and supplement the market and thus create and control a huge constellation of entrepreneurial forces. U.S. demands for economic liberalization helped to shift power from the state to the society and from the domestic to the international sphere. The military regime collapsed like a house of cards in 1987, as Korea's *haute bourgeoisie* sat on the side, silent spectators to a massive revolt begun by students and workers but swelled by members of the middle class. This was an unexpected outcome for a regime that had been so tightly embraced by the Reagan administration; it became a victim of the antinomies in U.S. foreign policy.[23]

The point here is not to argue the merits of this outcome, nor to say that the Koreans were mere puppets of the United States, but merely to point out the structural logic. The regime's demise came mainly because of widespread popular dissatisfaction, but U.S. pressure was a factor that helped shape the outcome. Hounding out a military dictator like Chun Doo Hwan may be a good thing in itself, but a situation whereby a hegemonic power undermines and compromises the political economy underpinning another society is profoundly problematic. This is a dilemma for the East Asian semisovereign states as they grapple with the U.S. hegemony in the region that still structures much of the political discourse by which we understand Asian politics.

The U.S. policy of restructuring East Asian economies is generally viewed as valid and enlightened, whereas Asian—especially Japanese—obstruction is seen as devious and self-interested. From the East Asian perspective, however, it looks very different. Why this is so requires some discussion of how Asians think about the question of national agency and purpose, and the role of the state in society. At bottom, as we will see, is a disparity over the purpose of politics and its agency, government.

THE STATE IN WEST AND EAST

Liberal political theory has always seen state power as problematic, if not dangerous. The state in the United States is an imagined vacuity, a space in which interest groups contend and conflict. According to pluralist theory, the state is merely a referee that maintains rules and the political order and thus lubricates market and society. To the extent that the state is perceived to be autonomous of society, it has a negative image: a brooding presence that as it grows, threatens to expropriate the market and civil society. These assumptions are so strong that it is often difficult even to discuss alternatives to the U.S. political pattern; state intervention or state autonomy conjures in the liberal mind the European 1930s, and there discussion ceases and the shouting begins.

Alternative views of the state exist, however, apart from the extremes of fascism and Stalinism. The state, for instance, can be benevolent, protective, exemplary; it can be bountiful and generous, and it can be harsh and disciplinarian. Catholic cultures believed that and so did Confucian cultures. State and society do not compete in an adversarial relation or expropriate each other. Instead the state was an exemplary and meritocratic order that guided and educated the society. The Anglo-Saxon tradition of the minimal state is the exception, not the rule (rather than the other way around, as the Orientalist discourse would have you believe).

It would be fair to say that the peoples of China, North Korea, South Korea, Japan, and other Confucian cultures deeply believe that the state ought to provide not only material wherewithal for its people but moral guidance, and in that sense, the distinction between state and society is not one that is sharply drawn. By and large Westerners have no way to understand this point except to assert a series of absences: no individual rights, no civil society, no enlightenment, and thus a weak or absent liberalism. In so doing they are saying little more than that northern Europe and North America had a different historical pattern than did other parts of the world. But too often this particular pattern presents itself as universal.

The state conceived by the East Asian Other is, furthermore, a practical necessity of development. Karl Polanyi, who was a Catholic socialist of a sort, thought of the modern state (however tragically flawed it was at times) as a prophylactic to protect society against the ravages of the world market. The resulting protected economy may have its inefficiencies—antique rice farmers and family store owners in East Asia, as well as the consumers who have to pay more for this "moral economy"—but who is to say, except the hegemonic power that believes in mammon and Adam Smith, that efficiency ought to reign as the only acceptable doctrine of political economy? And is it not true that the U.S. state might have done *more* in recent years to protect its people—especially blue-collar workers—against the vicissitudes of international competition?

Japan's habits of mercantilism are of long standing, of course. But from Japan's point of view this is a tried-and-true system that protected its domestic society from the ravages of the world market as Japan pursued "late" development, catch-up ball with the West. Viewed as narrow and irrational by liberal economists, this system has virtues that are rarely voiced in the United States.

For example, Japan is littered with small mom-and-pop stores of all types, with laws against major corporations absorbing them. Small business was a nineteenth-century ideal in the United States, too, but has suffered dramatically as national and international franchises, fast-food chains, K-Marts, and superstores have replaced family enterprises—late capitalism demolishing what some have called "moral economy." Japan's much-criticized protectionism also protects this valuable kind of business, and it now perceives that the United States will not be satisfied unless the whole world is turned into its mirror image of superstores and transnational economies of scale.

Simply to make this argument opens one to attack in the current climate in the United States, but U.S. pressure on the Japanese domestic market is a counterpart to the interior desires of U.S. Orientalists, who find the Japanese soul insular and unempathetic to the rest of the world and want to turn it inside out, into a gleaming reflection of the U.S. liberal Self: another triumph for "the end of history," the vanquishing of one more perceived nonliberal polity, after the demise of Stalinist systems in Eastern Europe.

EAST ASIAN SOLUTIONS FOR THE 1990S

If this analysis of growing tensions and misunderstanding in the East Asian–U.S. relationship is correct, what ought to be done about it? It is important to call attention to the gross bias and exaggeration in recent U.S. accounts of East Asia, but there is too much money and fame in Asia bashing to think that it will go away soon. Similarly, the more deeply rooted and contrary ways that Americans and East Asians think about the state and politics are likely to persist. It does appear, however, that the East Asian states are moving slowly to attenuate the economic Gordian knot that ties the region to the U.S. market, something that has been well known to policymakers in the region, but about which they have done little until the last few years.

The single-market dependency that characterized previous economic relationships now seems to have reached an impasse, partly because of U.S. protectionism, but also because, as I have argued, it leads to unwonted reciprocal pressures by the United States on Japan and Korea—in the first instance, to "open markets," but in the last instance to give up domestic sovereignty and no longer protect the moral economy of small producers, that is, to give up national autonomy. Single-market dependency is something that policymakers can change, however, and they have recently begun to do so.

Recent figures suggest that Japanese dependence on the U.S. market dropped from 33 percent of its total worldwide trade in 1986 to 27 percent in 1990 and an estimated 25 percent in 1992. Trade with Western and Eastern Europe is a particular target and has grown rapidly. Japan's imports from the United States climbed by 76 percent from 1986 to 1990, but they increased by 300 percent from France, and 133 percent from the EC countries in general. South Korea and Taiwan have followed suit, actively reducing their shares of exports to the United States and aggressively cultivating markets elsewhere.[24]

To the extent that this pattern continues, it means a move away from the previous structure whereby the United States interacted bilaterally with Western Europe and Japan, with Japan and Europe having little interaction, toward a triangular structure, the base of which would be created through growing investment and commodity trade between Europe and Japan. East Asia's position in the world system continues to move toward a multiplicity of markets, away from "trilateralism" and toward a kind of triangulation and interregional reorganization. This implies also that Japan will have more direct relations with the other East Asian economies, rather than relations mediated by and through the United States, and that the smaller East Asian economies will also have stronger ties with Europe.

This revised North-North articulation is likely to be accompanied by a reorganization of North-South relations within the region. This would be achieved by greater cohesion among the region's more prosperous Northeast Asian economies, looking eventually toward something like the EC in East Asia, and deepened links with Southeast Asia, a region that is increasingly a good bet for the next round of rapid industrialization.

Trilateralism, Bruce Cumings argues, has characterized U.S. global policy since the late 1940s. Western Europe and Japan were the legs of the triangle, with the United States spending Marshall Plan and AID money to get war-torn economies going in the 1940s while maintaining for itself ultimate veto power over allied behavior—especially that of Japan and Germany, maintained on a U.S. defense dependency.[25] The lineaments of the triangle, however, ran through Washington back to Tokyo or Bonn, with little contact on the East Asian–European "axis" (I use the term gingerly). Communication was frequently mediated by Washington, especially on issues of critical importance, like the conflict with the Soviets or crises in Korea, Vietnam, or the Persian Gulf.

Richard Nixon was the best symbol of this, somehow forgetting to consult Japan's leaders about dramatic departures like the New Economic Policy and dealing with Brezhnev over the heads of European leaders. It was all too apparent that communication flowed through Washington, on its terms. During the heyday of "formal" trilateralism in the Carter administration, however, everyone still assumed that the initiative remained in Washington's hands, and there was little Japanese-European bilateral contact. This is a structure of one hegemonic power, reigning over regional associates.

A shift toward triangulation in the 1990s is likely to entail increased Japanese investment in Europe (as a way to break into post-1992 fortress Europe), as well as the beginning of such investment by the East Asian NICs. The United States seeks to do the same thing, so it is likely to support such Asian initiatives. European firms may welcome such investments, as a quid pro quo for technology transfer and for infiltrating into East and Southeast Asia, where returns on investment remain high. The announced collaboration of Daimler-Benz and Mitsubishi, and Kloeckner Werke and C. Itoh are moves in that direction.

To be sure, Japanese investment in Europe is still picayune in comparison to that by the United States: in 1990, Japanese direct investment in Germany remained, for instance, a paltry U.S.$1.1 billion against U.S.$32.5 billion made by the United States. Yet, the Japanese figure for that year was double what it was a year before, and the trend is on the rise, as it has been for Taiwan and South Korea.

Japanese interaction with the territories of its former empire has been tightly controlled by the United States, more so than the trilateral structure discussed above. This is widely misunderstood and thus requires some explanation. Despite much talk about the atavistic return of the "Greater East Asian Co-Prosperity Sphere," the only area in which ties were thick and thus easier to revive was in Northeast Asia. But even that took two decades and a war in Vietnam to make it into a reality; and when it happened it did so under U.S. auspices. Furthermore, the interaction between Japanese, Koreans, and Chinese was almost exclusively economic, rather than cultural or political, and it remains so today, nearly a half century after the "Co-Prosperity Sphere" met its demise.

Containment of communism in the mid-1960s required, among other things, placing East Asian and Southeast Asian nations on a sound economic footing. Japan was thus reintroduced to the region in the 1960s, as a U.S. partner and surrogate in developmental efforts. A critical year, 1965, saw the linking of the economies in the region, as the United States escalated its war efforts in Vietnam, in the normalization of the Japan-Korea relationship, which was with its big package of loans and credits, in part responsible for the Korean economic takeoff. Also inaugurated was the Asian Development Bank, which in addition to U.S. and Japanese aid, transferred vast amounts of loans, with priority going to Taiwan and South Korea and secondarily to the Philippines, Thailand, and Malaysia.

This task of linking Japan to other Northeast Asian capitalist economies in the 1960s is slowly coming to fruition. If we accept the forecast that by the year 2000 Japan's living standards will rise by 50 percent and that of the East Asian NICs will almost double—and this is not so unrealistic—the gap between Japanese living standards and the other East Asian economies will have narrowed from 4.3 times to 3.3 times. That is comparable to the gap in living standards between the richest member of the EC (Germany) and the poorest (Portugal), which is currently about five times. Should North and South Korea, and Taiwan and China reunify, that would expedite the process of reginal interpenetration in Northeast Asia and help to offset Japan's dominance in the region.

Southeast Asia is a different story. Japan left no colonial imprint from which the region could create a political economy resembling Japan's. Southeast Asia was really a classic wartime occupation territory, existing only to "contribute resources to Japan," as Tojo put it. Before Pearl Harbor there was no blueprint for administration and development of Southeast Asia, and Japan's information on the region derived from existing "enemy" sources, usually meaning British sources; often Japan simply reestablished the former colonial government, relying on local personnel who had worked for colonial regimes. Thus, social systems in Southeast Asia remained by and large untouched.[26] Since the war, Japan and the Southeast Asian countries have

had a less intense and more distant interaction than that between Japan and
Northeast Asia, and again, the interaction is mostly economic.

Change is under way, however, and we might think of it in terms of the
East Asian product cycle extending to Southeast Asia. Whereas the Northeast Asian economies represented an economic hierarchy created through
transfer or labor-intensive industries from Japan to Taiwan and South Korea
through the 1980s,[27] now the same process is being reproduced vis-à-vis
ASEAN, with Japan and the NICs busily bequeathing their obsolete industries. Combined investment in ASEAN, for instance, by four NICs—South
Korea, Taiwan, Hong Kong, and Singapore—exceeded Japanese investment
in the area in 1988.

Thus we have the creation of a more lateral economic structure between
Japan and the NICs, with a hierarchical structure stretching down from
north to south in East Asia, from rich to poor countries. Economic activity
within this dual structure has been bustling. Intraregional trade west of the
Pacific is growing by more than 40 percent annually, amounting to U.S.$256
billion in 1989, representing a whopping 40 percent of the Pacific region's
total worldwide trade. This ratio is anticipated to rise to 55 percent in ten
years. Japan now invests upwards of US$10 billion a year in Asia, engages in
U.S.$126 billion worth of trade, and has dispensed a total of U.S.$4.4 billion in aid to the area, overtaking the United States in the mid-1980s as the
largest aid donor in the area. More important, however, a high proportion of
Japanese investment in Asia is in manufacturing and thus is less sensitive to
short-term factors. Whereas Japanese investment in the United States and
Latin America is done primarily to defuse trade friction and thus tends to
rise and fall with protectionist pressures, its investments in Asia tend to be
driven by much longer term objectives.

Another force propelling change in the area is geopolitical. Anticommu-
nism and containment was the rationale for organizing Pacific Asia after
1947, but that began to come apart with Nixon's overtures to China and the
fall of Saigon. Since the early 1970s economic development replaced anti-
communism as the defining trait in East Asia, with a sudden surge of euphoria around 1978 when the Chinese normalized relations with the United
States and embarked on market-oriented reforms. Japan has moved into
China in a big way, maintaining an embassy in Beijing that is second in size
to its Washington delegation. During the 1979–1989 decade of economic reform, Japan invested some U.S.$2.2 billion in China, compared to U.S.$1.8
billion invested by the United States. The Chinese government, for its part,
insists that Japan invest and manufacture in China, so as not to repeat the
all-too-familiar agony of a nation hooked on perpetual trade deficits vis-à-
vis Japan. Thus, whereas China recorded U.S.$6 billion in trade deficit
against Japan (36 percent of total Chinese imports) in 1985, it garnered
U.S.$6 billion in trade surpluses from Japan, and imports from Japan were

only a 15 percent share of the total Chinese imports in 1990.[28] Taiwan, South Korea, Hong Kong, Singapore, and others have also been investing in China with great alacrity.

The late 1980s, moreover, saw a number of socialist countries linking up with the capitalist orbit in the region, and agencies of Japanese expansion abroad, the so-called general trading companies, have lost little time in opening offices in Mongolia, Laos, and Vietnam. They came armed with tried-and-true methods successfully tested elsewhere: feasibility studies, followed by enunciation of Japanese "strategic interest," then signing of official aid to pay for infrastructure development, which leads to a tapping of inexpensive labor supply. Japan has been particularly quick to link Vietnam to its economy: Japan is now Vietnam's biggest oil customer and its second biggest trading partner after the Soviet Union, and business has been on the rise.

The East Asian NICs are also getting in on the act with alacrity. In the case of South Korea, there is more than a little triumphalism in its desire to push the North Koreans up against the wall: South Korea has normalized relations with the Soviet Union amid much talk about billions of dollars in aid to the Soviet Union and developing Siberia with South Korea's know-how in construction (and maybe North Korean labor). Meanwhile South Korea's *chaebôl* have been busily supplying Russia with consumer goods, computers, and other high-technology equipment, helping Boris Yeltsin to shore up his shaky rule. Taiwan's smaller firms have begun doing the same.

These trends harbinger an East Asia that wants to set itself free from the asymmetric and often smothering relations across the Pacific and wrest greater autonomy from the world system. This should be welcomed by the United States as it attempts to forge a "new world order," because it also affords the United States an opportunity for disengagement from hegemonic burdens.

CONCLUSION

It would appear from our evidence that Japan and the East Asian NICs have made considerable progress in reducing their single-market dependence on the United States, and that they increasingly find ways of interacting economically that are different from the rules of the game since 1945. Growing economic integration and interregional trade will establish more latitude for East Asians in determining their own fate, not necessarily separate from the United States, but without the palpable U.S. pressures of past years. Substantial changes in the economic realm, then, are slowly dissolving the Gordian knot that has created both economic opportunities and a political albatross for the nations in East Asia.

The security situation is likely also to continue relaxing, thus diminishing U.S. leverage over the East Asian states. Tensions in East Asia have been significantly relaxed since 1985, the Soviets having withdrawn 200,000 troops from the Sino-Soviet border, and the Chinese having demobilized 25 percent of their total military strength. And the preponderance of U.S. and Japanese conventional air and naval power over Soviet military power in the North Pacific—as part of global strategy linked to the European situation—is an anachronism now that the Soviet Union does not even exist.

A relaxation of tensions, then, is clearly going on in East Asia. But unlike the economic realm, these changes have not begun to touch the basic security structure. As a result it is much harder to project what will happen to the international Brumairean compact—what will be the role of the United States in Asian regional security in the future? The United States is slow to let go in East Asia and vice versa. Japan has thus far been content to keep the postwar security arrangement, and Japan's neighbors feel safer with U.S. troops, certainly, than with Japanese.

As one Chinese strategist noted, Japan has 300,000 troops, of whom 70 percent are officers and noncommissioned officers, and is thus capable of quickly increasing the number of troops. Japan also possesses economic and technological potential to leap over several generations of weapons technology and develop intelligent or "smart" weapons as it pleases—a choice it has not yet made and is unlikely to make in the near future.[29] For the neighbors of Japan, this is not a proposition that they want to test. Regional security, then, is likely to remain in U.S. hands for some time to come. It is likely that the United States will seek to hold onto the levers of security as a way of continuing its influence in the region.

The change that will be the slowest in coming (if it comes at all) will be in regard to what one might call the hegemonic psychology in East Asia. The United States is still the world's greatest and most vibrant center of cultural and ideological production. Japan may slowly replace the U.S. lead in finance, manufacturing, and technology, but it does not begin to articulate a posthegemonic ideology, nor does its culture have a regional, let alone universal, appeal: at most it exports nintendo hardware (the signifier without the signified), maudlin songs, *karaoke* bars (where drunken males mimic pop hits), and the culture of sex tourism to East Asia.

Thus East Asia remains an area without an identity, a region incapable of imagining itself as a community, to borrow Benedict Anderson's conception. Former victims of Japanese aggression like Korea and China also partake of the either/or absolutes of the new Orientalism, projecting for the future either a dreaded neo-Co-Prosperity Sphere or the capitalist utopia of the Pacific Rim. That Alvin Toffler is listened to as a prophet throughout the region, including the PRC, is merely a token of the utter absence of any regional self-definition.

East Asia lacks the language and psychology for self-assertion, which is an artifact of its long domination by the West. This palpable absence is also testimony to the terrible difficulty of hegemonic transfer across a civilizational divide, something that has never before occurred. When Great Britain passed the hegemonic baton to the United States in the 1940s, it could do so in partnership with an ally sharing much of its culture and tradition. With Japan's meteoric rise, another such transition perhaps beckons on the horizon, but all too many pundits can only greet it with thoughts of conflict, eternal difference, the dire absence of (our) "transcendental truths," and even "the coming war with Japan." Surely our imaginations ought to do more than merely project into the future a past everyone—the Japanese included—would rather forget.

Japan's neighbors can hardly bear to watch Japan again assert itself as a superior, homogeneous nation uniquely fit among Asians to the tasks of the modern world. But then it isn't particularly comforting, either, to see Americans also "going nationalist" over the past decade, with huge displays of flag-waving that perhaps began at the Los Angeles Olympics in 1984 and certainly continued through the national celebration of the humiliation of Iraq. The first display—Japan's—is thought to be pathological, and the second—that of the United States—is accepted as normal. Yet both bespeak the attenuation of internationalism that occurred in the 1980s, caused by both Japan's competitiveness and the unilateralism of Reagan's foreign policy.

Orientalism coupled with East Asian aphasia does not make for happy prognostication on the future U.S.–East Asian relation. In the absence of a full airing of the issues that separate Americans and Japanese, public utterance becomes euphemistic, private thoughts run rampant, and slips of the tongue welling up from the viscera taint the relationship and poison the atmosphere.

It would be far better if we exclude antique conceptions of race and of Orient and Occident entirely from the ongoing debate and focus instead on what divides East and West—almost always some predictable and intelligible conflict of interest—and what unites East and West in a common endeavor of development.

Policies of "constructive disengagement" from the asymmetrical relations of the past can not only leave more room for Asian autonomy but also aid the United States by reducing security burdens and promoting a salutary period of "looking inward" that could help domestic U.S. industries revive and flourish—which after all is the best way to meet "the Asian challenge."

We need to think about a positive disengagement that prepares for truly equal and mutually beneficial relations in the future. We need to talk openly, if not "politically correctly," about what ties us together and what pushes us apart, what we really think about each other, how to build bridges of mutual understanding, and what American East Asia has truly been about.

NOTES

This chapter is a revised version of my article (under the name Jung-en Woo) "East Asia's America Problem" in *World Policy Journal* (Summer 1991), published by the World Policy Institute, New York.

1. Franz Schurmann, *The Logic of World Power* (New York: Pantheon, 1978).

2. *Newsweek,* May 20, 1991; *New York Times,* May 20, 1991.

3. Edward Said, *Orientalism* (New York: Random House, 1978).

4. Allan Bloom, *The Closing of the American Mind* (New York: Simon & Schuster, 1988), p. 34.

5. *New York Times,* April 4, 1991.

6. Karel van Wolferen, *The Enigma of Japanese Power: People and Politics in a Stateless Nation* (New York: Alfred A. Knopf, 1989), pp. 8, 10, 20, 23.

7. Karel van Wolferen, "The Japan Problem Revisited," *Foreign Affairs,* 69, no. 4 (Fall 1990), pp. 42–55.

8. Ian Buruma, "Jingo Olympics," *New York Review of Books,* November 10, 1988.

9. Ian Buruma, "The Pax Axis," *New York Review of Books,* May 22, 1991.

10. George Friedman and Meredith Lebard, *The Coming War with Japan* (New York: St. Martin's Press, 1991). Readers who want a sincere and thoughtful appraisal of racism in the last war with Japan ought to read John W. Dower's *War Without Mercy: Race and Power in the Pacific War* (New York: Pantheon Books, 1986).

11. Akio Morita and Shintaro Ishihara, *The Japan That Can Say No* (Washington, D.C.: Bootleg Edition, 1989).

12. See Alexander Woodside, "The Asia-Pacific Idea as a Mobilization Myth," Chapter 2, this volume.

13. Kent Calder and Roy Hofheinz, *The East Asia Edge* (New York: Basic Books, 1983); Michio Morishima, *Why Japan Has Succeeded: Western Technology and the Japanese Ethos* (New York: Cambridge University Press, 1982); Lucien Pye, *Asian Power and Politics: The Cultural Dimension of Authority* (Cambridge, MA: Belknap Press, 1982).

14. Remarks made by Masao Miyoshi at the Conference on the Asia-Pacific, Duke University, March 22–24, 1991.

15. The reference is to Marx's *Eighteenth Brumaire of Napoleon Bonaparte.*

16. T. J. Pempel, "The Developmental Regime in a Changing World Economy" (Paper presented at the meeting of American Political Science Association in San Francisco, August 1990).

17. Albert O. Hirschman, *National Power and the Structure of Foreign Trade* (Berkeley: University of California Press, 1945).

18. Sylvia Maxfield and James Nolt, "Protectionism and the Internationalization of Capital: United States Sponsorship of Import Substitution Industrialization in the Philippines, Turkey, and Argentina," *International Studies Quarterly,* Winter 1989.

19. Jung-en Woo, *Race to the Swift: State and Finance in Korean Industrialization* (New York: Columbia University Press, 1991), p. 56.

20. John Dower, *Empire and Aftermath: Yoshida Shigeru and the Japanese Experience, 1878–1954* (Cambridge, MA: Harvard University Press, 1979), p. 316.

21. For discussion of Japanese and Korean industrial structures, see Peter A. Petri, "Korea's Export Niche: Origins and Prospects," *World Development,* January 1988, pp. 47–68.

22. David Calleo, *The Imperious Economy* (Cambridge, MA: Harvard University Press, 1982), p. 66.

23. Jung-en Woo, *Race to the Swift,* Chapter 7.

24. *Fortune,* May 6, 1991.

25. Bruce Cumings, "The Seventy Years' Crisis and the Logic of Trilateralism in the 'New World Order,'" *World Policy Journal,* 8, no. 2 (Spring 1991).

26. Akira Iriye, *Power and Culture: The Japanese-American War, 1941–1945* (Cambridge, MA: Harvard University Press, 1981), Chapter 2.

27. Bruce Cumings, "The Origins and Development of the Northeast Asian Political Economy: Industrial Sectors, Product Cycles and Political Consequences," *International Organization,* Winter 1984, pp. 1–40.

28. *Wall Street Journal,* December 13, 1990.

29. *Far Eastern Economic Review,* December 13, 1990, p. 28.

PART THREE

Down and Out in the
Realm of Miracles:
Class and Gender
Perspectives on the
Asia-Pacific

DONALD M. NONINI

9

On the Outs on the Rim:
An Ethnographic Grounding of the
"Asia-Pacific" Imaginary

*T*HE NOTION of "Asia-Pacific," or the "Pacific Rim," poses an analytical problem on one hand, but on the other, it is a concept that theoretically at least, is difficult to take seriously. A focus on the regions of the world central to strategic military and economic interests of the United States, its allies, and its ruling elites led to the emergence and codification of "area studies" in the social sciences in the 1950s and 1960s (see, e.g., Horowitz 1971; and Roberts 1971), with much definitional controversy about what constituted an "area."[1] There is presently a similar haphazard and hazy appearance on our disciplinary horizons of something called the "Asia-Pacific," or "Pacific Rim," quite clearly again tied to these interests, with its correlative forms of institutionalization and discursive inscription.[2] Can the whole thing be considered with a straight face, without irony? My skepticism is of particular relevance to the topic I intend to address here: labor, gender, and ethnicity—within the area, however we end up defining it, under discussion.

As an anthropologist, I have certain implacable disciplinary loyalties toward locale and place—toward the understanding of how people lead their lives, in all their specificities, in certain "small" spaces: in their households, neighborhoods, communities, towns, and villages. My emphasis is therefore on the everyday, the pedestrian, the local. From the perspective of those people I have studied and done research among, something so grand as the "Asia-Pacific" or "Pacific Rim" has no meaning; it does not even exist as illusion. Yet, as Henri Lefebvre reminds us, "The *unrecognized*, that is, the everyday, still has some surprises in store for us"—and this arises, above all, from the fact that the "everyday," *la quotidienne*, has a history as a "modality for extending the capitalist mode of production" (Lefebvre 1988: 78–80) with all the intrinsic dynamism this implies. This is as true for the societies of those countries referred to as being part of the "Asia-Pacific" as elsewhere in

161

the capitalist world order. All this must be conceded and, more than that, conceptualized.[3]

What I have observed from ethnography as part of the everyday has been persons and groups implicated in various ways with something that I recognize on other, theoretical grounds as being the "Asia-Pacific," or to be more precise, implicated in *processes of relation* with something identified closely with the "Asia-Pacific"/"Pacific Rim" neologisms. Thus, I have seen the factory buses circulating through the outlying neighborhoods of a Malaysian market town, picking up throngs of young Malay and Indian women who are employed in the foreign- and state-owned electronics and textile factories of the industrial estates and free trade zones of the Penang area; I have witnessed Chinese men, women, and children in Malaysia engaged frenetically in the piecework of home labor—sewing, shoemaking, packaging, and the like—to produce commodities for the international market; I have talked with Chinese men who aspire to work as illegal laborers in Japan or Taiwan, then return to Malaysia with money saved to open their own businesses.

I thus find it incumbent on me to make some sense of this "Asia-Pacific" that links these disparate experiences together. But not as such. Rather, I reject the notion of "Asia-Pacific" as unitary, as a thing. At worst, it is an intellectual construction that serves those who serve state and corporate power—as in the case of "area studies" in the immediate postwar period. At best, it refers to a set of economic, political, and cultural processes creating relationships within an area—perhaps one could call it a "supraregion"—that link up different regions each with their own social and cultural integrity: regions with households, neighborhoods, towns, centers, hinterlands, cores, and peripheries.

Because the "Asia-Pacific" imaginary appears to presuppose, even if it is not coextensive with, such linkages—flows of people, capital, commodities, ideas and information, microbes, sources of energy—there have been many groups, in the United States as elsewhere, who will be able to construct histories—*their* histories or autobiographies—from memories of experiences of earlier migrations traced across this supraregion. This is as it should be. Thus, for instance, there are the memories carried by an author such as Maxine Hong Kingston of her parents come from China to the American mainland (Kingston 1980); there are the life stories created by the Japanese sugar plantation laborers and studied by Ronald Takaki (1983) of early years in Japan and the ordeal of working in Hawaii; there are the accounts of Mexican-American migrants laboring in the food-crop plantations of California (Galarza 1971). But these histories, centrally important as they are to the identities of Asian Americans and Mexican Americans, do not as such validate or privilege the "Asia-Pacific" imaginary, for they like all experiences on a human scale, are lived through in small spaces step by step: in itineraries, paths, voyages, passages from one small space through others, arriving at yet others as sojourners, migrants, or pilgrims. Memory and experience cannot constitute either a past or present "Asia-Pacific": such a grand conception can only arise through the act of theoretical construction. In what follows, I first set out some theoretical propositions about the recent social and material history underlying the new "Asia-Pacific." I then turn to the theme of the place of labor, gender, and ethnicity within this history. My focus tends to be on those countries within the Southeast Asia "edge" of the "Pacific Rim," and especially on Malaysia, which I know best in terms of an ethnography of the everyday. I believe that the generalizations I advance will, however, have broader application to other regions bounded by the imaginary. Throughout, I attempt to consider the dialectic between those whose structures of power ground the imaginary and those subaltern groups "on the outs" that are ruled and regulated on the edges of the "rim."

THE ''ASIA-PACIFIC'' IMAGINARY AND THE GEOPOLITICS OF CAPITAL

At the risk of being identified with a "totalizing" intellectual position, I would argue that the "Asia-Pacific" or "Pacific Rim" can best be understood as the trope for a set of economic, political, and cultural processes creating relationships within a supraregion of Asia and the United States that have been under way since approximately the mid-1970s—processes arising from what the Marxist geographer David Harvey has called the "spatial displacements" or "spatial fixes" of contemporary capitalism (Harvey 1985, 1989). Harvey discerns that within the capitalist mode of production there exist processes that generate surpluses of capital and labor power. These processes—internal to the accumulation dynamic of capitalism—will lead, if unchecked, to crises of "overaccumulation," the incapacity of capitalism to absorb simultaneously the surpluses of capital and labor power, which in turn brings about the precipitous and calamitous devaluation or destruction of both (Harvey 1985: 133–36). Two principal means of confronting these processes and avoiding the crises they otherwise entail are temporal and spatial "displacements."

Temporal displacements absorb surplus capital and labor power in the form of investments in physical and social infrastructure with a long-term return. Railroads, roads, universities, research laboratories, airports, hospitals are examples (Harvey 1985: 135–36). Yet temporal displacements by themselves only postpone the day of reckoning, of crisis, since their "fictitious capital" represents a claim on future labor, and the heavy debt it generates must eventually be paid, and when this proves impossible, as is often the case, then devaluation of invested capital and labor power sets in with catastrophic results (Harvey 1985: 136–40).

According to Harvey, it is the combination of temporal displacements with "spatial displacements" or "spatial fixes" that has allowed postwar world capitalism to forestall the advent of profound crisis, at least until recently (Harvey 1985: 156; Harvey 1989). Spatial displacements occur when the surplus capital or labor power or both that are generated in one region are exported across (what are generally) international boundaries and invested in another region. These spatial "fixes," however, must accord with the internal dynamic of capitalism, which constrains all capitalist enterprises not to exceed the socially necessary turnover time required to realize profits. Under these time constraints, what—paradoxically—makes such spatial displacements possible are the temporal displacements. These are of two kinds: direct displacements that embody transformations in transport and communications technologies, and indirect displacements that represent investments in productive technology and organization that free capitalists from place-specific constraints, such as localized labor skills and commodity markets and immobile fixed capital and productive materials (Harvey 1985: 135–36; Harvey 1989: Part 3).

These displacements and their associated technologies, taken ensemble, have over the last 150 years drastically reduced the time and cost of moving liquid capital, commodities, raw materials, and productive facilities and machinery for the capitalist, and they increasingly allow the flexible integration of production, exchange, and consumption markets. And it is over the last two to three decades, Harvey argues, that a quantum leap in the reduction of the friction of distance has taken place: space has now "imploded" with innovations in satellite telecommunications, air travel, miniaturization, containerization, and so on. This is but the most recent episode of "time-space compression," the recurrent transformation of the meanings of time and space in the direction of speeding economic processes and progressively overcoming spatial barriers that has been fundamental to the history of capitalism (Harvey 1985: 147–48; Harvey 1989: 240, 284–91).

Such temporal displacements make spatial fixes *possible*. But what makes spatial fixes *necessary*, or at least probable, is the condition of class struggle within an already developed region and its associated state. Both capital and labor within a region are caught in an endless dilemma: whether to "cut and run" to regions of higher profits or more favorable wages and working conditions, or to remain in more or less stable contest with each other within a region in which both capital and labor power have already been substantially invested in order to recoup embodied value (Harvey 1985: 150–53). What has occurred with the emergence of the "Asia-Pacific," one could argue, is a shift in the balance of regional class struggles such that capitalists specifically have sought recently to cut and run to peripheral regions and states with lower wages, more tractable labor, and higher profits, away from core regions and states where the prevailing strength of laboring classes and their supporters has been relatively great. Labor in these regions, being comparatively immobile, in contrast has remained behind and has begun to suffer catastrophic devaluation. Thus, for example, since about 1965 in the United States deindustrialization has proceeded apace, with an estimated net loss of about 15 million industrial jobs due to plant closures from 1968 to 1976 (Nash 1983a: ix; see also Bluestone and Harrison 1982); industrialization in our "Asia-Pacific" accelerated its increase in the same period (Snow 1979) and subsequently. On this account, the two trends are not merely connected, but are in fact different manifestations of the same process at work (Arrighi 1990). It is just such a process, together with its ramifications on a variety of fronts, that has been reified as the "Asia-Pacific"/"Pacific Rim" imaginary.

Applied to the spatial imaginary before us, capital transfers by transnational corporations and international lenders (e.g., the World Bank) to productive sites throughout the "Asia-Pacific" represent precisely such spatial displacements, which have proliferated since the mid-1970s. U.S. national and transnational corporations have shifted capital (and a small number of skilled laborers and managers) from the previously industrialized Northeast and Central United States to the South and Southwest and southern California, and to Mexico and Southeast Asia (Thailand, Malaysia, Singapore, Philippines); Japanese corporations have exported capital to Southeast Asia (Malaysia, Singapore, etc.), as have Korean and (most recently) Taiwanese corporations. It is equally important, however, to note that it was the existence of *prior* spatial displacements of surplus U.S. and European capital during the late 1940s, the 1950s, and the 1960s as an element of postwar "reconstruction" and the cold war that allowed Japanese, Korean, and Taiwanese capitalist enterprises, under strong state direction and encouragement, to develop their economies to become competitors with U.S. capital to begin with (Hamilton 1983; Haggard and Cheng 1987; Nolan 1990). This is not to deny that prior to World War II, Japan, Korea, and Taiwan already manifested (to various degrees depending on colonialism) "structured coherence" as regions internally dominated and organized by industrial and agrarian capitalist production.[4]

By invoking Harvey's analysis I mean neither to be economistic nor to make claims to comprehensiveness, but rather to point to underlying tendencies within transnational capitalism *that are both embodied in but are also constrained by* the economic, political, and cultural features of the regions and states defined as being within our "Asia-Pacific." In this vein, I want to discuss briefly some of the sequelae of *and* blockages to these spatial displacements as they bear on the theme of labor, gender, and ethnicity.

LABOR, PATRIARCHAL POWER, AND
THE NEW INDUSTRIALISM

Capital flight to the regions of the "Asia-Pacific" has, I suggested, been prompted by successful struggles by labor in preexisting core regions such as the United States to force capitalists to subsidize in part the social costs of economic growth in these regions—notably through high wages and taxes to support the welfare state. Such was the historic compromise between capital and labor prevailing from the end of World War II up to the 1970s that became known as Fordism (Harvey 1989; also see O'Connor 1984: 2–9). It is no surprise, then, that such capital export has been marked by the aggressive seeking out of sources of new inexpensive and tractable labor in order that the capitalist process of exploitation might continue through the production of commodities, but with the realization of higher profits. What this has led to has been the emergence and crystallization of what are called "segmented labor markets," with certain socially disadvantaged or stigmatized populations in Asia and the Americas—especially women and international labor migrants—channeled into "secondary labor markets" for poorly paid and relatively unskilled labor and excluded from "primary" labor markets for skilled laborers, technicians, and managers (Gordon, Edwards, and Reich 1982: 200–2; Green 1983).

Above all, these laborers have been the young unmarried women of Asia and increasingly the Americas, such as in the U.S.-Mexican border area. Thus we find the thousands of young Malaysian, Taiwanese, Hong Kong, Filipino, Mexican, and other young women working in export-oriented industries—in electronics assembly plants, textile mills, and garment factories owned and managed by transnational, indigenous, and state capitalists, working for extremely low wages, often under physically hazardous and stressful conditions (Nash 1983a, 1983b; Snow 1983; Southeast Asia Chronicle/Pacific Research 1978–79). In 1980, there were more than 600,000 workers in export processing zones in Asia alone (Pineda-Ofreneo 1987: 95), the vast majority young women—specific examples suggesting between 80 and 90 percent. The number has increased greatly since then. In some regions these women either reside in or are recent migrants from rural areas—such as those who work in the export processing zones and industrial estates of Malaysia, Indonesia, Thailand, Taiwan, and the Philippines (Ong 1983, 1987; Ackerman 1984; Jamilah 1984; Mather 1983; Charoenloet 1988, 1991; Bello, Kinley, and Elinson 1982: 127–64; Enloe 1983: 415); in other regions, such as in northern Mexico, they are migrants from highly urbanized areas elsewhere (Fernandez-Kelly 1983a, 1983b). Neither their physical distance nor nominal economic independence from their natal family and household necessarily means that these young women are socially cut off from them. To the contrary: the very physical and social infrastructures (roads, railways, telephone systems, etc.) that attracted transnational capital to these regions also facilitate workers' frequent communication and interaction with families, which in turn both allow and require these women to contribute to their natal household economy by direct payments or remittances (for examples, see Stivens 1986; Huang 1984; Strauch 1984). They are thus simultaneously "good daughters" and "good workers." One consequence, of course, is that whatever patterns of patriarchal power are in effect within these households—which generally hierarchically subordinate those who are female and young—reinforce the economic power of the new employers. Within such dual patriarchal regimes, the enhanced monetized contributions of these young women to their natal household budget may give them some personal leverage vis-à-vis their father and brothers in terms of new "freedom" and "independence" in making certain minor decisions (for this argument, see Lim 1983); however, the money these women earn can bind them even more closely, as in the case of Hong Kong parents who pressure their daughters to delay marriage so as to ensure that they will continue working in factories and maintain their financial support to their natal household (Grossman 1978–79).

Complementary to such rationalized factory production and also subject to patriarchal control, women's and children's waged labor has been employed "in the home" through extensive putting-out arrangements. Such contracted-out piecework to be done "at home" has preceded the advent of the new transnational factories, previously being common in such lines of production for the domestic market as garment manufacturing (for one example, see Nonini 1983: 173–75), but in some areas recently has become integrated with export-oriented factory production. Thus, for instance, on a visit one evening in 1990 to the home of a Chinese informant in Penang state in Malaysia, I witnessed his wife, mother, and three small children working energetically filling boxes with sports garments manufactured in a factory at a nearby industrial estate—a domestic assembly line in which women and children labored to earn a few cents per box on a piecework basis while my informant, his grown younger brother, and I all watched idly. Such "homework" has a definite place in the new "regime of flexible accumulation" (Harvey 1989), which is characterized by such innovations as subcontracting and "just-in-time" production (with concomitant "just-in-time" hirings and layoffs) as employers take advantage of the putting-out system to avoid paying pensions and other legally mandated benefits.[5] Too little is known about such women's (and children's) home labor—probably just because it is informal, its importance in the production trail is belittled, and it easily escapes official statistical attention—and there is a pressing research need to study it and its implications for working-class households in the "rim."

The placement of young women in these secondary labor markets of course is by no means merely an economic phenomenon. Indeed, the work tasks are themselves gendered, and in this sense these women's employment is surrounded by discourses, practices, and ideologies of "femininity" and by conditions of patriarchal social control. That the elements of the labor process are in some deep cultural sense gendered as well as classed is an important insight coming out of recent feminist theory (Weston 1990). Thus, there is the common mythic notion held fervently by factory managers—apparently widespread throughout our supraregion (e.g., from the U.S.-Mexico border region to the Philippines and Malaysia)—that it is young factory women in particular who show the "utmost patience and high dexterity for the delicate assembly job of fine connection" (Pineda-Ofreneo 1987: 96; see also Elson and Pearson 1981).[6]

Forms of patriarchal power that reinforce the employers' economic control within the workplace are common and take such forms as male factory managers and supervisors adopting the metaphorical roles of male family relatives (as "fathers," "brothers"); inciting rivalry between workers for their attention or affection (often linked to performance evaluations); organizing diversions such as athletic events, raffles, parties, and even "beauty contests" among women operatives; and exhorting workers to show such supposed "traditional" Asian female values as loyalty (to the corporation), hard work, honesty, deference to men, self-denial, and even piety. More punitive practices include sexual harassment of women workers; shaming of workers seen as recalcitrant or performing poorly through dressings-down before their peers; the making of invidious comparisons between the performance of the workers at a specific factory and of operatives in other offshore factories of the corporation, with the implicit threat of plant closures and "retrenchment" if quotas are not met; and petty Taylorist monitoring of workers' time use (Grossman 1978–79; Bello, Kinley, and Elinson 1982: 127–64; Mather 1983; Ong 1987; Pineda-Ofreneo 1987; Lin 1984; Arrigo 1984).

These forms of patriarchal power reinforce the constant pressures placed on these women workers by managers to intensify their labor and to meet continually increasing production quotas (see e.g., Lin 1984). Such pressures, Harvey (1989: 229) argues, are a basic feature of the industrial labor process given individual capitalists' efforts to reduce "the turnover time of capital"—but have accelerated during the latest episode of time-space compression throughout our supraregion, with such innovations as "just-in-time" processing (Rajah 1981).[7] Despite the prevalent image of female passivity held by managers and government officials, women workers have resisted these pressures, at times with great militance, by overt means such as strikes (Pineda-Ofrenco and del Rosario 1988; Bello, Kinley, and Elinson 1982: 157–59), by more covert means such as work slowdowns and "mass hysteria" (Ong 1987), and by job hopping (Huang 1984; Deyo 1989).

Another stigmatized and socially disadvantaged population in the "Asia-Pacific" that is actively sought out and employed by offshore and indigenous capitalists in secondary labor markets is the "new helots" (Cohen 1987)— the various illegal and quasi-legal immigrant workers, *gastarbeiter,* or "guest workers." Here are included "undocumented aliens" from Mexico and Central America in the factories and sweatshop industries of southern California and the U.S. Southwest (Cohen 1987: 33–72; Davis 1989); Southeast Asian Chinese working in Taiwan and Japan, Indonesian laborers in Malaysia, Chinese and Malay Malaysians in Singapore (Rodan 1989), and many other groups. What distinguishes these groups is their distinctive ethnic and national identity, although their success in remaining in employment often depends upon their abilities to "pass" as citizens of the host regions. It is precisely their disadvantaged status as illegal or quasi-legal migrant laborers and their willingness to accept lower wages than local residents that permit employers within these regions to intensify their exploitation relative to local regimes of accumulation. The threat of deportation acts as a compelling form of industrial discipline. The conditions under which guest workers labor may in some instances approach involuntary servitude, as in the extreme case of one major Korean corporate contractor who imported Korean convict labor to work on the construction of a bridge in Malaysia. The presence of guest workers—and the requisites of capital accumulation that lead capitalists to seek them out and employ them—have as yet unexplored implications for the definitions of "nationality" and "citizen" within these regions, particularly in times of recession when these people are seen as threatening the jobs of indigenous workers.

It is worthwhile to consider how gender relations, patriarchal power, and the new forms of labor migration interact. Culturally specific local regimes of patriarchal power, reinforced by state regulation of women's bodies and actions, vary within and across the regions of the supraregion. These regimes constrain the geographic mobility of young women far more than that of young men. Young working-class women tend to remain at or near their place of natal residence under a regime of combined family and factory control—though highly modernized transport and communications infrastructure and technology in these regions, as noted above, allow social proximity to persist over long physical distances. Where young women do migrate over considerable distances to find work, it is often to live with kinfolk who have previously migrated (see e.g., Strauch 1984 for a Malaysian example). With some major exceptions, it is young working-class men who have become international labor migrants, working as illegal or quasi-legal laborers in countries where wages are higher, but whose indigenous laboring populations disdain to perform certain work because of its low pay (in local terms), "danger," and "dirtiness." Therefore working-class males far more than working-class females are able to respond to the differentiation in wealth and industrial technologies between countries within the supraregion; the specific exploitation of women workers in large numbers within their own country allows the differential generation of surplus-value that in turn over time provides an impetus that accelerates this international diversification. For example, young single working-class Chinese Malaysian males "jump from airplanes," (*tiao feiji*), "parachute in," that is, migrate to work illegally at factory, construction, and other relatively low-paid work in Japan and Taiwan. Their unmarried sisters remain in Malaysia to labor in petty self-employed enterprises, in their natal households in putting-out piecework, and in small-scale sweatshop industries in or near the cities or towns where their parents live. And at the same time young Javanese and other Indonesians, mostly men, migrate illegally into Malaysia to work in the housing construction and plantation sectors. Returning to Harvey's argument discussed above that both capital and labor within a region are caught in an unending dilemma whether to "cut and run" to other regions with higher profits and wages or to remain within a region, it should be pointed out that the dilemma is almost always a gendered one. In Southeast Asia, working-class men, like capitalists, are far more often allowed to cut and run, whereas working-class women tend to confront destabilization "at home" due to the class conflicts centered on their exploitation, created by the installation of new "offsource" capital imported from elsewhere in the supraregion.

There are, as stated, exceptions to this tendency. Thus, the recent histories of migration in both the Philippines and Thailand show trends in which women have migrated in greater numbers than men to the primate cities, respectively, Manila and Bangkok (Eviota and Smith 1984; Singhanetra-Renard 1987; Arnold and Piampiti 1984; Piampiti 1984). This also suggests that patriarchal regulation of these women migrants, to the extent that it exists, must take some form other than restraints on their geographic mobility. In some instances, the history of such experience for female migrants within a country may predispose them to become international labor migrants, as with rural-born Filipino women, who have a tradition of migrating to Manila to engage in domestic labor (Eviota and Smith 1984), but have also entered international labor circuits both across the cities of the supraregion and indeed beyond it, as the presence in large numbers of Filipino domestic workers trapped in Kuwait during the recent Persian Gulf War tragically illustrated. And on the eastern edge of the "rim," in contrast, a different tendency altogether appears to prevail, in which women migrate over long distances from central and southern Mexico to labor in the *maquiladora* factories of the U.S.-Mexico border region, whereas the men who accompany them remain largely unemployed and economically dependent on them (Fernandez-Kelly 1983b).

The fundamental points to be made are that instead of reifying "patriarchy," critical scholars must investigate the great variety of patriarchal controls within the supraregion in all their cultural and historical specificities; but that even then the working out of gender relations and the effects of patriarchal power must be accorded some autonomy in the making and the history of our supraregion. Similar points apply, as the discussion of guest workers suggests, to the variety of forms of state power that make persons "citizens" or not and members of one ethnic group or another, and confer or hold back rights of "nationality"—thus acting as a device to sort and classify workers throughout our supraregion as appropriate human materials for primary or secondary labor markets and the conditions of labor exploitation associated with them.

LABOR, HEGEMONY, AND DOMINATION

What makes the regions of the "Asia-Pacific" so attractive to the new transnational investors is not only the low cost of women's and guest workers' labor in these regions, but also its tractability; hence its articulation with patriarchal and state-nationalist forms of power. These forms of power represent the exercise of "hegemony," which on the cultural fronts of "civil society" conduces to consent on the part of working populations to the rule of national elites throughout the countries of the supraregion and to their arrangements with transnational and local capitalists (see Gramsci 1971).[8] Another hegemonic process provides an additional line of defense against the mobilization of the new workers against the new order: the romance of commodities, or what has been called "commodity aesthetics." As the highly transient transnational corporations penetrate the economies of the regions of the "Asia-Pacific," they also initiate new consumption markets—made possible again by representations in the media of television, videotapes, radio, and film—directed toward specific consumer populations, especially young adults and children. Commodities are offered that carry the cachet of certain "life-styles," supposedly defining the good life in the preexisting core areas (especially the United States and Europe); thus we find McDonald's, Kentucky Fried Chicken, Levi-Strauss and Lee jeans, Rolex watches, Louis Vuitton luggage, Guinness stout, the music of the Beegees, and so forth. The inducement of desires for these commodities reinforces the emerging structured coherence of these new regional economies. The affirmation of such desires by the new industrial workers at whatever petty level they can afford to satisfy them also reconciles them to some extent to the oppressive conditions of their work (McGee 1987).

But if the gendering of production and the romance of commodities represent specific sites for the exercise of hegemony in regional class struggles,[9] then certainly hegemony's alter—"domination" (Gramsci 1971)—also makes its appearance, in its most extreme form of overwhelmingly repressive state power. Of course, outright resort to state coercion against recalcitrant laborers is a crude advertisement of weakness and creates friction between transnational capitalists and host states in the supraregion and therefore is resorted to only at times of perceived extreme crisis. Instead, there are a variety of intermediate stratagems that have been employed by transnational capitalists and their host states to regulate labor and ensure its pliability within the supraregion. The promotion of divisions between workers along ethnic lines within the same factories (Boulanger 1991; Wad 1989); the creation of house unions, as in Malaysia and the Philippines (Boulanger 1991; Pineda-Ofreneo 1987); the state incorporation of labor unions and their demands, as in Singapore (Rosa 1990) and the Philippines (Bello, Kinley, and Elinson 1982: 157–59); practices, laws, and regulations discouraging the registration of new unions or of federations of smaller unions, as in Singapore and Malaysia; the recent trend toward privatization, which effectively destroys previously powerful unions in the public sector; public intimations by political leaders that unions are Communist led, therefore threaten national security, and thus must be resisted in their demands—all are examples of options that fall short of the outright use of force. More extreme measures, a history of our supraregion suggests, also have been used and will be resorted to again on occasion. The violent breaking up of strikes; arrests and imprisonment of labor leaders, including women; and the decertification of labor unions, all are justified by various laws, regulations, and ad hoc fiats (Boulanger 1991; Pineda-Ofreneo 1987; Enloe 1983; Charoenloet 1991). Thus a range of state and capitalist stratagems are aimed explicitly against the formation of independent labor unions and seek to neutralize the collective gains of labor, both formal and informal. It has been argued that in the first tier of Asian "newly industrializing countries"—Hong Kong, Singapore, South Korea, and Taiwan—there has been a transition from earlier (1950s, 1960s) repressive state controls of laborers to recent corporatist stratagems (Deyo 1987)—but this tendency, if general, is far less in evidence in other, peripheral regions within the supraregion.

With some exceptions, such as in the United States and Japan, these actions by the states of the regions of the "Asia-Pacific" make sense because the paramount political and military leaders and bureaucratic functionaries directing these states are of all groups those who most benefit from the accommodations reached with offshore capitalists to situate their operations locally. For example, the ruling bureaucratic and military elites of Malaysia, Indonesia, and the Philippines have aggrandized their economic positions by engaging in joint ventures with transnational corporations, and have received lucrative directorships, exclusive licensing privileges, and graft in return for the concessions of various kinds they have made to transnational investors—measures that discourage labor unions, offer tax vacations, provide free modern infrastructure, and so on (see Mehmet 1986; Robison 1986: 131–210; Bello, Kinley, and Elinson 1982: 183–95).

PETTY-COMMODITY PRODUCTION: RESISTANCE TO EXPLOITATION?

I claimed above that certain features of the new regions did not facilitate but rather impeded the spatial displacements carried out by the capitalist order in the "Asia-Pacific" since the mid-1970s. What are these blockages? These obstacles to the successful realization of profits by offshore investments are connected to the fact that the regions are not completely capitalist in a variety of senses, although they are "dominated" by the capitalist mode of production. In particular, the existence of well-developed petty-commodity productive relations may provide an alternative to participation by young women and other disadvantaged groups as labor in the new capitalist enterprises, at least for some groups in some countries of our supraregion.

The new workers are drawn from substantial populations of past or continuing land-owning peasantries. The willingness of persons from these populations, women and men, to engage in production in the new export-oriented factories depends in large part on the preexisting economic, political, and social conditions prevailing in the countrysides and urban areas of the "rim" regions to which transnational capitalists have been drawn. Neither the seductive blandishments of commodities nor the exercise of local patriarchal power are per se sufficient to ensure that rural populations in these regions will be "attracted" to factory labor; other options may exist. One fundamental feature that determines the "willingness" of these populations is the history of the "primitive accumulation" process (Marx 1967)—of the changes in political economy that lead to rural proletarianization, marginalization, and displacement of peasants; in the course of this process, actions by colonial and postcolonial states against peasant cultivators have been crucial and decisive (see Arrighi 1973; Nonini in press). Here, of course, there has been much variation within and across the regions and over time within our supraregion. I would go so far as to argue that the presence of an advanced process of primitive accumulation is a necessary if not sufficient condition to "attract" rural laborers in sufficient numbers into the new factories.

A sober examination of agrarian conditions in the countries of Southeast Asia and East Asia in the "rim" does not lead one to sanguine conclusions about the alternatives to such "attraction." Most of the countries in capitalist Southeast Asia (i.e., ASEAN) show a long-standing and massive displacement of peasants out of agriculture due to Green Revolution innovations and the sociopolitical changes accompanying them, to stagnating rural pro-

ductivity (often the result of past state policies), or to a colonial legacy of neglect of and discrimination against the masses of rural farmers; and in countries such as Malaysia, the Philippines, and Indonesia, there can be found
large populations of marginalized and displaced peasants made "willing" to
enter the gates of the new factories (Nonini in press; Limqueco, McFarlane,
and Odhnoff 1989; Mather 1983; also see Pincus 1990).

But there are two sets of conditions under which rural farmers may prove
more reluctant to take upon themselves the factory labor offered them by
transnational capitalists. The first would be where the process of primitive
accumulation has not sufficiently advanced and large populations of land-
owning peasants still engage in petty-commodity production in *articulation*
with large-scale capitalist enterprise, but not either directly employed by it as
rural proletarians nor otherwise under its control.[10] Such may be the case in
certain regions of contemporary Thailand. More promising for an alternative are the new mixed socialist/market economies of non-capitalist Southeast Asia, especially that of Vietnam, where rural decollectivization and the
emergence of the "product contract system," devolving both productive responsibilities and incomes down to individual households, will increase
peasants' commitment to maintain their cultivation, rather than leave their
farms for city work, even as Vietnam has recently established special zones to
encourage foreign industrial investment (Beresford 1990).

A second set of conditions prevails for Taiwan, where there was significant rural land reform in the 1950s, and for Hong Kong and the New Territories, where British laissez-faire rule has not sought to disrupt but rather to
rationalize rural land tenure (Chun 1991), leaving the rural population
largely to develop on its own. In both countries, the peasantry combines
agrarian petty-commodity production with family-based commercial ventures and small-scale industrial production (Hu 1983; Deyo 1987). Although both countries are known for their successful export-oriented industrialization, one could predict that in times of global recession, their still
viable agrarian economy may provide enclaves of return to absorb re-
trenched ex-peasant workers and may confer a measure of protection
against extreme wage reductions and intensified exploitation by the new factories of the transnationalists. This could allow workers to say to employers,
in effect, "Lower than this we will not go, for we would rather go back to the
rural natal household." Such at least has been the experience of earlier historical examples (see Loh 1988).

The forms of life associated with petty-commodity production thus represent a reservoir out of which oblique resistance to the exploitation unleashed
by transnational capital can grow. The implications of this for the successful
transplantation of offshore capital to the regions of "Asia-Pacific," and more
generally for the theory of capitalist crisis discussed above, need substantial
exploration, and soon.

THE STATE, ETHNICISM, AND DOMINANT GROUPS IN THE NEW INDUSTRIAL ORDER

How the tendencies toward spatial displacements just discussed interact with pressures toward ethnic discrimination in the new capitalist regions is an interesting question. The mediating agency here is of course the states of these regions and the groups who control these states. In general, the political and administrative elites who assumed power with the end of colonialism brought with them specific ethnic allegiances (Thomas 1984; see also Geertz 1973). They have enacted state policies and practices that formally and informally label, segregate, discursively divide off, and structurally advantage or disadvantage specific ethnic populations within their territories. These forms of state ethnicism constitute and refashion ethnic differences more than any other factor.[11] Thus there have been, for example in Malaysia, the New Economic Policy of the state that discriminates against non-*bumiputera*, that is, ethnic Chinese and Indians; in Taiwan, Guomindang loyalties to "mainlanders" and the exclusion until recently of native Taiwanese from political leadership and from certain business sectors (Gates 1987: 50–67); in Singapore, the implicit practices of exclusion directed against non-Chinese (Li 1989); and in Indonesia, state bureaucratic favoritism toward Javanese and against non-Javanese—extended at one extreme to the point of ethnocide against recently conquered "West Irian" and East Timorese indigenous peoples (see e.g., Chomsky 1987).

One consequence of these forms of state ethnicism is that certain ethnic groups are systematically excluded from collaboration with the new offshore capitalist enterprises and from participation in the side benefits (e.g., contracts for services) these generate. What began as a stigmatized civil status then becomes a matter of economic disadvantage as well. In consequence, capitalists, technicians, intellectuals, and other members of these groups either attempt to change their ethnic identities to join dominant ethnic groups, out-migrate (and thereby engage in their own petty spatial fixes), or are relegated to the petty-commodity-producing sectors of these regions. In any event, over time these pressures of exclusion predictably lead to characteristic deformations in capitalist development, particularly in the "newly industrializing countries" of our supraregion. These need urgently to be investigated.

CONCLUSION

I would like to conclude by merely asserting without demonstration the sense that the "Asia-Pacific"/"Pacific Rim" neologisms have been taken as seriously as they have been—in the symposium for which this chapter was originally written and elsewhere—because they stand as tropes of a certain kind. They are tropes of the obverse side to the multifarious constructed national identities and perceived national traditions that have heretofore divided off the regions within our supraregion from one another. These national identities and traditions have been, as has been repeatedly pointed out, invented and constituted *ab novo*, puffed up as it were by various "state-forming" elites aiming at power (see Robertson 1990). As Benedict Anderson (1983) so tellingly demonstrates, national communities are *always* imagined, limited, and sovereign—and specific elites are always implicated in these imaginings. But one problem with such factitious identities and traditions is that many people also come to take them very seriously—in a certain sense, through history, the imaginings take on a life of their own.

But what do those in power within the "Asia-Pacific" imaginary do when the contemporary connections of benign commerce and friendly investment aimed at "economic development"—rather than colonialism and war, as was so long the case previously—ostensibly define the economic relationships between regions, but these connections are in fact contradicted by fierce and at times desperate competition between increasingly mature capitalist regions and states—the United States, Japan, Korea, Taiwan? They respond by finding a way of drawing everyone into a new ecumenium. They invent the "Asia-Pacific" and demand that we take it very, very, seriously.

NOTES

1. Were, for instance, Chinese communities in Hong Kong, Taiwan, and Southeast Asia parts of a "residual China," as claimed by the sinological anthropologist Maurice Freedman in the early 1960s (orig. 1969; 1979: 413–17), or did these communities constitute a "residual China" only in the sense that although second best, they were still available for study at a time when Western social scientists had no access to the "real" unresidual China that had gone "Red" under Mao Zedong?

2. For instance, graduate programs have emerged in something called "Pacific Rim Studies," scholarly centers (e.g., the East-West Center in Hawaii) have appeared, and conferences such as the one for which this chapter was written have been held.

3. Thus much of contemporary anthropology since the 1960s has consisted of attempts to confront the many theoretical issues about the relationship between these small spaces and "systems" of region and nation—and how such articulation has changed over time. In this connection, see Skinner 1964, 1977; Smith 1976; and Lomnitz-Adler 1991.

4. "This structured coherence ... embraces the forms and technologies of production (patterns of resource use, inter-industry linkages, forms of organization, size of firm), the technologies, quantities, and qualities of consumption (the standard and style of living of both labour and the bourgeoisie), patterns of labour demand and sup-

ply (hierarchies of labour skills and social reproduction processes to ensure the supply of same) and of physical and social infrastructures. ... The territory within which this structured coherence prevails is loosely defined as that space within which capital can circulate without the limits of profit within socially necessary turnover time being exceeded by the cost and time of movement" (Harvey 1985: 146).

5. The evolutionary theorists who see the putting-out system as belonging to an earlier and "more primitive" stage of capitalism are of course completely refuted by the frequency of its contemporary use under the new regime of accumulation.

6. Tracing the sources and modes of diffusion of this notion through our imaginary would be a worthwhile research task. The costs to workers of the prevalence of this notion are great. For instance, of the 6,200 industrial accidents reported in the state of Penang in Malaysia in 1991, "about 60 percent ... caused injuries to the fingers of female workers" (*Star* 1992: 20).

7. "The time of production together with the time of circulation of exchange make up the concept of 'the turnover time of capital.' This, too, is an extremely important magnitude. The faster the capital launched into circulation can be recuperated, the greater the profit will be. ... There is an omnipresent incentive for individual capitalists to accelerate their turnover time *vis-à-vis* the social average, and in so doing to promote a trend towards faster average turnover times" (Harvey 1989: 229).

8. By invoking Gramsci's concept of "hegemony," I do *not* mean to imply that resistance to hegemony or resistance to class exploitation are absent. However, it appears consistent with Gramsci's use of this concept to distinguish the former from the latter very clearly. Resistance to hegemony takes place in a variety of cultural sites (see Willis 1981 for an example of such resistance by working-class "lads" in British schools), whereas resistance to exploitation in the labor process is in general much more narrowly focused and more often than not manifested in "everyday forms of resistance" (cf. Scott 1985). This distinction is as valid for the "Asia-Pacific" imaginary as elsewhere. The issues involved are complex (see Nonini n.d.).

9. Other sites of exercised hegemony throughout the supraregion can only be noted in passing, but deserve separate treatment: state inculcation of industrial values of obedience, diligence, etc. through the primary and secondary schools; the claims of citizenship and nationality imposed by the state and envisioned to override class differences; and the appeal of consumption-oriented individualism, which would appear to make these differences irrelevant. These elements of hegemony are, I would argue, contra Gramsci (1971), not only ideologies, but also include discourses and their associated practices (Nonini n.d.).

10. For example, in the 1920s and 1930s, independent Malay peasant rubber smallholders in colonial Malaya were able to compete successfully with large-scale European rubber plantations on the international market—until the British rulers intervened with policies favoring the European plantation sector (Nonini in press).

11. By using the term "ethnicism" I wish to distinguish the discourses, ideologies, and practices that order everyday life in terms of ethnic group membership from racism or racialism, which is a sociopolitical and ideological transformation of physical differences between human beings into categories of humanity marked by ranked and incommensurate essences. Racism/racialism is in this sense a post-Enlightenment phenomenon largely unique to the preexisting core states of the "Asia-Pacific," though its effects have been widely disseminated abroad by colonialism.

REFERENCES

Ackerman, Susan. 1984. The impact of industrialization on the social role of rural Ma-
lay women: A case study of female factory workers in Malacca. In *Women: A Ma-
laysian Focus*, edited by Nik Safiah Karim. Kuala Lumpur: Oxford University Press.
Anderson, Benedict. 1983. *Imagined Communities: Reflections on the Origin and
Spread of Nationalism*. London: Verso.
Arnold, Fred, and Suwanlee Piampiti. 1984. Female migration in Thailand. In *Women
in the Cities of Asia: Migration and Urban Adaptation*, edited by James T. Fawcett,
Siew-Ean Khoo, and Peter C. Smith, pp. 143–64. Boulder, CO: Westview.
Arrighi, Giovanni. 1973. Labor supplies in historical perspective: A study of the prole-
tarianization of the African peasantry in Rhodesia. In *Essays on the Political Econ-
omy of Africa*, edited by J. Saul and J. Woods, pp. 180–234. New York: Monthly
Review Press.
———. 1990. Marxist century—American century: The making and remaking of the
world labor movement. In *Transforming the Revolution: Social Movements and the
World-System*, edited by Samir Amin et al., pp. 54–95. New York: Monthly Review
Press.
Arrigo, Linda Gail. 1984. "Taiwan electronics workers." In Janet Salaff (ed.), *Lives:
Chinese Working Women*. Bloomington: Indiana University Press.
Bello, Walden, David Kinley, and Elaine Elinson. 1982. *Development Debacle: The
World Bank in the Philippines*. San Francisco: Institute for Food and Development
Policy/Philippines Solidarity Network.
Beresford, Melanie. 1990. Vietnam: Socialist agriculture in transition. *Journal of Con-
temporary Asia* 20(4): 466–86.
Bluestone, Barry, and Bennett Harrison. 1982. *The Deindustrialization of America:
Plant Closings, Community Abandonment and the Dismantling of Basic Indus-
tries*. New York: Basic Books.
Boulanger, Clare. 1991. "Working the system": Constructive relations within the West
Malaysian workforce. Unpublished Ph.D. dissertation, University of Minnesota.
Charoenloet, Voravidh. 1988. Factory management, skill formation and attitudes of
women workers in Thailand: A comparison between an American and a Japanese
factory. In *Daughters in Industry: Work, Skills and Consciousness of Women
Workers in Asia*, edited by Noeleen Heyzer, pp. 209–36. Kuala Lumpur: Asian and
Pacific Development Centre.
———. 1991. Thailand in the process of becoming a NIC: Myth or reality? *Journal of
Contemporary Asia* 21(1): 31–41.
Chomsky, Noam. 1987. East Timor. In *The Chomsky Reader*, edited by James Peck,
pp. 303–12. New York: Pantheon.
Chun, Allen. 1991. "*La terra trema*." *Dialectical Anthropology* 16(3–4).
Cohen, Robin. 1987. *The New Helots: Migrants in the International Division of La-
bor*. Aldershot, UK: Avebury.
Davis, Mike. 1989. *City of Quartz*. London: Verso.
Deyo, Frederic C. 1987. State and labor: Modes of political exclusion in East Asian De-
velopment. In *The Political Economy of the New Asian Industrialism*, edited by F.
C. Deyo, pp. 182–202. Ithaca: Cornell University Press.

———. 1989. *Beneath the Miracle: Labor Subordination in the New Asian Industrialism*. Berkeley: University of California Press.

Elson, D., and R. Pearson. 1981. Nimble fingers make cheap workers: An analysis of women's employment in Third World export manufacturing. *Feminist Review* 7:87–107.

Enloe, Cynthia. 1983. Women textile workers in the militarization of Southeast Asia. In *Women, Men, and the International Division of Labor*, edited by June Nash and Maria Patricia Fernandez-Kelly, pp. 407–25. Albany: State University of New York Press.

Eviota, Elizabeth, and Peter C. Smith. 1984. The migration of women in the Philippines. In *Women in the Cities of Asia: Migration and Urban Adaptation*, edited by James T. Fawcett, Siew-Ean Khoo, and Peter C. Smith, pp. 165–90. Boulder, CO: Westview.

Fernandez-Kelly, Maria Patricia. 1983a. Mexican border industrialization, female labor force participation, and migration. In *Women, Men, and the International Division of Labor*, edited by June Nash and Maria Patricia Fernandez-Kelly, pp. 205–23. Albany: State University of New York Press.

———. 1983b. *For We Are Sold, I and My People*. Albany: State University of New York Press.

Freedman, Maurice. 1979. Why China? In *The Study of Chinese Society: Essays by Maurice Freedman*, edited and introduced by G. William Skinner, pp. 407–22. Stanford, CA: Stanford University Press.

Galarza, Ernesto. 1971. *Barrio Boy*. Notre Dame, IL: University of Notre Dame Press.

Gates, Hill. 1987. *Chinese Working-Class Lives: Getting by in Taiwan*. Ithaca, NY: Cornell University Press.

Geertz, Clifford. 1973. The new integrative revolution. In *The Interpretation of Culture: Selected Essays*. New York: Basic Books.

Gordon, David M., Richard Edwards, and Michael Reich. 1982. *Segmented Work, Divided Workers: The Historical Transformation of Labor in the United States*. Cambridge, UK: Cambridge University Press.

Gramsci, Antonio. 1971. *Selections from the Prison Notebooks*, edited by Geoffrey Nowell Smith and Quintin Hoare. New York: International Publishers.

Green, Susan S. 1983. Silicon Valley's women workers: A theoretical analysis of sex-segregation in the electronics industry labor market. In *Women, Men, and the International Division of Labor*, edited by June Nash and Maria Patricia Fernandez-Kelly, pp. 273–331. Albany: State University of New York Press.

Grossman, Rachel. 1978–79. Woman's place in the integrated circuit. *Southeast Asia Chronicle* 6/*Pacific Research* 9(5–6).

Haggard, Stephan, and Tun-jen Cheng. 1987. State and foreign capital in the East Asian NICs. In *The Political Economy of the New Asian Industrialism*, edited by F. C. Deyo, pp. 84–135. Ithaca, NY: Cornell University Press.

Hamilton, Clive. 1983. East Asia's four little tigers. *Journal of Contemporary Asia* 13.

Harvey, David. 1985. The geopolitics of capitalism. In *Social Relations and Spatial Structures*, edited by Derek Gregory and John Urry, pp. 128–63. New York: St. Martin's.

———. 1989. *The Condition of Postmodernity*, Oxford: Basil Blackwell.

Horowitz, David. 1971. Politics and knowledge: An unorthodox history of modern Chinese studies. *Bulletin of Concerned Asian Scholars* 3(3–4): 139–68. (See esp. Appendix: Development of foreign affairs research centers: A selected chronology, pp. 167–68.)

Hu, Tai-li. 1983. The emergence of small-scale industry in a Taiwanese rural community. In *Women, Men, and the International Division of Labor*, edited by June Nash and Maria Patricia Fernandez-Kelly, pp. 387–406. Albany: State University of New York Press.

Huang, Nora Chiang. 1984. The migration of rural women to Taipei. In *Women in the Cities of Asia: Migration and Urban Adaptation*, edited by James T. Fawcett, Siew-Ean Khoo, and Peter C. Smith, pp. 247–68. Boulder, CO: Westview.

Jamilah, Ariffin. 1984. Migration of women workers in Peninsular Malaysia: Impact and implications. In *Women in the Cities of Asia: Migration and Urban Adaptation*, edited by James T. Fawcett, Siew-Ean Khoo, and Peter C. Smith, pp. 213–26. Boulder, CO: Westview.

Kingston, Maxine Hong. 1980. *China Men*. London: Pan Books.

Lefebvre, Henri. 1988. Toward a leftist cultural politics. In *Marxism and the Interpretation of Culture*, edited by Cary Nelson and Lawrence Grossberg, pp. 78–80. Urbana: University of Illinois Press.

Li, Tania. 1989. *Malays in Singapore: Culture, Economy and Ideology* (East Asian Social Science Monographs). Singapore: Oxford University Press.

Lim, Linda Y.C. 1983. Multinational export factories and women workers in the Third World: A review of theory and evidence. *Third World Studies Dependency Papers*, Series 51.

Limqueco, Peter, Bruce McFarlane, and Jan Odhnoff. 1989. *Labour and Industry in ASEAN*. Manila: Journal of Comtemporary Asia Publishers.

Lin, Vivian. 1984. Productivity first: Japanese management methods in Singapore. *Bulletin of Concerned Asian Scholars* 16(4): 12–25.

Loh, Francis Kok Wah. 1988. *Beyond the Tin Mines: Coolies, Squatters and New Villagers in the Kinta Valley, Malaysia, c. 1880–1980*. Singapore: Oxford University Press.

Lomnitz-Adler, Claudio. 1991. Concepts for the study of regional culture. *American Ethnologist* 18(2): 195–214.

Marx, Karl. 1967. *Capital: Vol. 1, A Critical Analysis of Capitalist Production*. New York: International Publishers.

Mather, Celia E. 1983. Industrialization in the Tangerang Regency of West Java: Women workers and the Islamic patriarchy. *Bulletin of Concerned Asian Scholars* 15(2): 2–17.

McGee, Terry. 1987. Mass markets—little markets: A call for research on the proletarianization process, women workers, and the creation of demand. In *Geography of Gender in the Third World*, edited by Janet H. Momsen and Janet G. Townsend, pp. 355–58. Albany: State University of New York Press.

Mehmet, Ozay. 1986. *Development in Malaysia: Poverty, Wealth and Trusteeship*. London: Croom Helm.

Nash, June. 1983a. Introduction. In *Women, Men, and the International Division of Labor*, edited by June Nash and Maria Patricia Fernandez-Kelly, pp. vii–xv. Albany: State University of New York Press.

————. 1983b. The impact of the changing international divison of labor on different sectors of the labor force. In *Women, Men, and the International Division of Labor*, edited by June Nash and Maria Patricia Fernandez-Kelly, pp. 3–38. Albany: State University of New York Press.

Nolan, Peter. 1990. Assessing economic growth in the Asian NICs. *Journal of Contemporary Asia* 20(1): 41–63.

Nonini, Donald M. 1983. The Chinese community of a West Malaysian market town: A study in political economy. Unpublished Ph.D. dissertation, Stanford University.

————. In Press. *British Colonial Rule and Malay Peasant Resistance, 1900–1957*. New Haven, CT: Yale Southeast Asia Monographs.

————. n.d. Beyond hegemony, beyond resistance: The dialectics of "disputatiousness" and "rice-eating money." Unpublished manuscript, University of North Carolina.

O'Connor, James. 1984. *Accumulation Crisis*. Oxford: Basil Blackwell.

Ong, Aihwa. 1983. Global industries and Malay peasants in Peninsular Malaysia. In *Women, Men, and the International Division of Labor*, edited by June Nash and Maria Patricia Fernandez-Kelly, pp. 426–39. Albany: State University of New York Press.

————. 1987. *Spirits of Resistance and Capitalist Discipline: Factory Women in Malaysia*. Albany: State University of New York Press.

Piampiti, Suwanlee. 1984. Female migrants in Bangkok metropolis. In *Women in the Cities of Asia: Migration and Urban Adaptation*, edited by James T. Fawcett, Siew-Ean Khoo, and Peter C. Smith, pp. 227–46. Boulder, CO: Westview.

Pincus, Jonathan. 1990. Approaches to the political economy of agrarian change in Java. *Journal of Contemporary Asia* 20(1): 3–40.

Pineda-Ofreneo, Rosalinda. 1987. Women in the electronics industry in the Philippines. In *Technology and Gender: Women's Work in Asia*, edited by Cecilia Ng, pp. 92–106. Serdang, Malaysia: Women's Studies Unit, Universiti Pertanian Malaysia and Malaysian Social Science Association.

Pineda-Ofreneo, Rosalinda, and Rosario del Rosario. 1988. Filipino women workers in strike actions. In *Daughters in Industry: Work, Skills and Consciousness of Women Workers in Asia*, edited by Noeleen Heyzer, pp. 308–26. Kuala Lumpur: Asian and Pacific Development Centre.

Rajah, Rasiah. 1981. Reorganization of production in the semi-conductor industry and its impact on Penang's position in East Asia. In *Images of Malaysia*, edited by Muhammad Ikmal Said and Johan Saravanamuttu, pp. 203–23. Kuala Lumpur: Persatuan Sains Sosial Malaysia.

Roberts, Moss. 1971. The structure and direction of contemporary Chinese Studies. *Bulletin of Concerned Asian Scholars* 3(3–4): 113–38.

Robertson, Roland. 1990. After nostalgia? Wilful nostalgia and the phases of globalization. In *Theories of Modernity and Postmodernity*, edited by Bryan S. Turner, pp. 45–61. London: Sage.

Robison, Richard. 1986. *Indonesia: The Rise of Capital* (Southeast Asia Publication Series, 13, Asian Studies Association of Australia). North Sydney: Unwin Hyman.

Rodan, Garry. 1989. *The Political Economy of Singapore's Industrialization: National State and International Capital*. London: Macmillan.

Rosa, Linda. 1990. The Singapore state and trade union incorporation. *Journal of Contemporary Asia* 20(4): 487–508.

Scott, James C. 1985. *Weapons of the Weak: Everyday Forms of Peasant Resistance.* New Haven, CT: Yale University Press.

Singhanetra-Renard, Anchalee. 1987. Non-farm employment and female labour mobility in northern Thailand. In *Geography of Gender in The Third World*, edited by Janet H. Momsen and Janet G. Townsend, pp. 258–74. Albany: State University of New York Press.

Skinner, G. William. 1964. Marketing and social structure in rural China. *Journal of Asian Studies* 24: 3–43.

———. 1977. Cities and the hierarchy of local systems. In *The City in Late Imperial China*, edited by G. William Skinner, pp. 275–351. Stanford, CA: Stanford University Press.

Smith, Carol A. 1976. Regional economic systems: Linking geographical models and socioeconomic problems. In *Regional Analysis: Vol. 1, Economic Systems*, edited by Carol A. Smith, pp. 3–63. New York: Academic Press.

Snow, Robert. 1979. Multinational corporations in Asia: The labor-intensive factory. *Bulletin of Concerned Asian Scholars* 11(4): 26–39.

———. 1983. The new international division of labor and the U.S. workforce: The case of the electronics industry. In *Women, Men, and the International Division of Labor*, edited by June Nash and Maria Patricia Fernandez-Kelly, pp. 39–69. Albany: State University of New York Press.

Southeast Asia Chronicle/Pacific Research. 1978–79. Changing role of S.E. Asian women. Special joint issue of *Southeast Asia Chronicle 6/Pacific Research* 9(5–6): 1–27.

Star. 1992. Socso: Industrial mishaps on the rise in Penang. *Star* (Penang), May 13, 1992, p. 20.

Stivens, Maila. 1986. Becoming workers: The social context of female labour migration in Rembau, Negri Semibilan. In *Women's Studies in Malaysia*, edited by Wendy Smith and Ariffin Jamilah. Singapore: Institute of Southeast Asian Studies.

Strauch, Judith. 1984. Women in rural-urban circulation networks: Implications for social structural change. In *Women in the Cities of Asia: Migration and Urban Adaptation*, edited by James T. Fawcett, Siew-Ean Khoo, and Peter C. Smith, pp. 60–80. Boulder, CO: Westview.

Takaki, Ronald. 1983. *Pau Hana: Plantation Life and Labor in Hawaii, 1835–1920.* Honolulu: University of Hawaii Press.

Thomas, Clive. 1984. *The Rise of the Authoritarian State in Peripheral Societies.* New York: Monthly Review Press.

Wad, Peter. 1989. Socio-cultural aspects of working-class formation: A study of industrial and labour relations in Malaysian manufacturing enterprises. In *Southeast Asia Between Autocracy and Democracy*, edited by Mikael Gravers et al., pp. 150–74. Aarhus, Denmark: Aarhus University Press.

Weston, Kath. 1990. Production as means, production as metaphor: Women's struggle to enter the trades. In *Uncertain Terms: Negotiating Gender in American Culture*, edited by Faye Ginsburg and Anna Tsing, pp. 137–51. Boston: Beacon.

Willis, Paul. 1981. *Learning to Labor: How Working Class Kids Get Working Class Jobs.* New York: Columbia University Press.

NEFERTI XINA M. TADIAR

10

Sexual Economies in
the Asia-Pacific Community

WITH THE celebrated emergence of the Asia-Pacific community, the Philippines is confronted with the tensions of its historical identity and the political and economic crisis that is its persistent reality. As a region, the Asia-Pacific designates a political and economic constituency represented primarily by the United States, Japan, Canada, Australia, and New Zealand, a group known as the OECD (Organization for Economic Cooperation and Development) Five, and secondarily by newly industrialized countries such as South Korea, Taiwan, and Singapore. Such a representation and the excitement for regional prosperity that it generates, however, elide the contradictory Third World status of the rest of the Asia-Pacific—developing countries like the Southeast Asian nations that threaten to disrupt the congenial unity that the dream of "community" conjures. Once a dominantly geographical area composed of dispersed political territories, the Asia-Pacific is increasingly sold on the idea of constituting a purely economic network among its member nations. Indeed, the dream of "community" is steadily being realized as a transnational corporation with the power to regulate and determine national as well as individual lives. For the fantasy of the Asia-Pacific community is one that takes form and force within a particular global purview, namely, the First World fantasy of the Free World, or international community, that shapes international relations through the political and economic practices of individual nations. It is, in other words, the shared ground upon which the actions and identities of its participants are predicated—it is a field of orientation, an imaginary determining the categories and operations with which individuals as well as nation-states act out their histories. Among these categories is sexuality—in this fantasy, the economies and political relations of nations are libidinally configured, that is, they are grasped and effected in terms of sexuality. This global and regional fantasy[1] is not, however, only metaphorical, but real insofar as it grasps a system of political and economic practices already at work among these nations.

183

Individuals as well as governments act not only as if a unified global community did exist, but as if nations were individual citizens who compose this
community and who, like individuals, behave in particular (sexual) ways
and act with particular desires.[2] That international community in effect
works in the way it is imagined, but only because it is realized as this totality
through the displacement of its constitutive contradictions onto Third
World bodies; that is, capitalism is impelled by desire (visibly demonstrated
by the endless processes of accumulation and consumption)—desire, in
other words, for surplus wealth/pleasure, produced by and producing a fantasy of political-libidinal economies that regulate individual and national
lives. The Asia-Pacific community is predicated on this fantasy of a global
(Free World market) economy. Indeed, as a regional reproduction of an ideal
international community, it reproduces the same sexual economies and relations at work in global capitalism, intensifying them to the greater profit of
its main promoters and to the greater loss of the populations whose labor
must pay for it. It is the logic of these libidinal processes that I would like to
trace in this rendering of the fantasy of the Asia-Pacific community.

PACIFIC DESIRES

Invoking the Asia-Pacific as a leader and symbol of an emergent international order, therefore, obscures the intensification of globalized capitalism
to which this community is dedicated. It is, in effect, to invoke international
cooperation without the competition and violence necessary to this global
organization. I argue that the Asia-Pacific, as a dream and an actuality, functions as a locus of containment of the threat the region poses to the dominant
powers who benefit from its promotion. With the Vietnam War and other
anti-imperialist revolutionary struggles being waged in Southeast Asia (as
well as in Africa, the Middle East, and Latin America) from the late 1960s to
the mid-1970s, the Asia-Pacific region emerged as a threat to the global
power of the United States, that is, to its political authority as well as to economic superiority. The end of the cold war and the burgeoning economy of
Japan and the newly industrialized countries only increased this economic
and political threat and the necessity of its containment. Hence, the intensified efforts to push for the realization of the Asia-Pacific community, a
dream dedicated to the greater dream of global capitalism.

Thus Prime Minister Nakasone could wholeheartedly claim: "In the Pacific we are witnessing the birth of a new kind of capitalism. Here the vigour
and competitiveness of Western—particularly American—capitalism has
been enriched by the Asian cultural heritage." Furthermore, "Asian free enterprise has shown itself capable of fostering a competitive dynamism of its
own. The distinguishing mark of the Pacific Basin countries has been their

commitment to free enterprise economics."[3] More than fifty years ago, Japan was advocating the founding of a very different Asian empire, a desire that all but ended in World War II. But forty years earlier, the United States had already set its sights on the very same region, which was to whet its appetite for global power: "The Pacific is the ocean of the commerce of the future. Most future wars will be conflicts for commerce. The power that rules the Pacific, therefore, is the power that rules the world. And, with the Philippines, that power is and will forever be the American Republic."[4] This desire to be a Pacific power has brought about these two wars: the "war of pacification," as Americans used to refer to the Philippine–U.S. war at the turn of the century, and the "Pacific war," as they called the war between themselves and Japan at mid-century. One might well argue, however, that this war over the Pacific continues to be waged today, but in a very different way. Global conflict is no longer envisioned in the fantasy of East-West relations (i.e., relations of the Orient and the Occident, or for that matter, of the two power blocs, the United States and the USSR); nor is it envisioned in the fantasy of the First and Third Worlds, or of North and South. These global unities have ceased to function in the same way in a decidedly post–cold war, post–Gulf War era. Japan and the United States are no longer up in arms over the Pacific or even over "the last land left in all the oceans," the Philippines; instead, they are now in cooperation. This new mode of relation realized through incorporation is libidinal/economic in character and thus can be truthfully described as a marriage of interests.

THE PACIFIC MARRIAGE

It has been claimed that the idea of a Pacific community is "a baby whose putative parents are Japanese and American and whose midwife is Australian."[5] This marriage between Japan and the United States, however, masks as well as reveals the particular global desires and tensions still at play in the Free World. War has been consummated in a sexual relationship that stabilizes the tenuous unity of the international community. In this arrangement, sexual union is war through economic incorporation. Indeed, what this marriage evinces is an unequal and potentially antagonistic relation at the heart of the economic union, whether this union refers to the Asia-Pacific or to the larger international community. What it further reveals is the desire for incorporation into these global unions. Hence the Japanese initiative in proposing the formation of the Pacific community during the late 1960s, confirming what Nakasone could later admit as "Japan's need to become an '*international* nation'; that is to say, a nation that must bear a heavy share of international responsibilities in keeping with its international position."[6] The desire for incorporation might thus be seen as a desire for citizenship in the international community, a citizenship that entails more than an allegiance to the ideals of internationality, that entails also buying into the preconditions of the Free World. But the Japanese have only lately begun to see themselves as attaining this citizenship that persons in other nations, such as the United States, have long since held—with the idea that there are nation-citizens with more rights and responsibilities than others, that is, with more power than others. If there is such a thing as an international state, clearly the United States is seen to hold some kind of presidential power. Hence the uneasiness of the marriage. For in desiring inclusion, the Japanese show themselves to be lacking in political power in spite of their economic wealth (a condition secured with Japan's disarmament as a consequence of her losing to the United States in World War II). The Asia-Pacific community is, in this light, a way for Japan to marry into power and the United States to domesticate her desires for power. For in the transformation of this international community into a multinational corporation, the preoccupation with the balance of power becomes the participation in the bargain for power; that is, power becomes a matter of negotiating economic shares and political management or control.

I say "her," because in this scenario, Japan is the wife and the United States her husband. The antagonism that the fantasies of East-West, First World–Third World, and North-South relations have historically addressed (as frameworks of global contradictions) has been transmuted into libidinal cooperation, that is, into the fantasy of masculine-feminine relations. Deterritorialized, these global polarities are now predominantly enacted according to a prevailing mode of heterosexual relations. But the allies and partners that territories and possessions of a past age have been transformed into are not categories that pertain to particular nations at all times. As it is well known in the Philippines with reference to the United States, "There are no permanent friendships, only permanent interests." More than this wavering interest, the positions in partnerships, that is, of masculine and feminine, are continually in flux and dependent on what parties are in relation. In other words, masculine and feminine are defined against each other and function according to the specific historical relation at work. Hence, in relation to the United States, Japan may occupy a feminine position, but in relation to the Philippines, a masculine position. Since nations maintain simultaneous and crossing international relations, masculine and feminine should be seen not as essential features of even specific relations, but rather as diacritical marks of certain political practices and economic modes of operation within and between nations that are libidinal in character, such as investment of capital and extraction of interest.

The logic of this sociolibidinal economy at work among nations can be demonstrated in the "special relations" of the Philippines and the United States. The fantasy of this particular relationship is paradigmatic not only because of the intimate history shared by these two nations and the sexual form it has taken, but also because of the tremendous difference between them in national wealth and global power. In effect, they encapsulate two extreme positions within the Asia-Pacific community and thereby make more glaring the antagonisms it must contain. Furthermore, the role of the Philippines in relation to the United States and Japan evidences the costs entailed by the offspring of the latter's marriage of interests, that is, by the realization of the Asia-Pacific community.

THE PHILIPPINE-AMERICAN ROMANCE

The Philippines is second only to Bangladesh as the country with the worst growth rate in Asia.[7] She owes this position to a large extent to her enormous debt to and dependence on the United States, together with the World Bank and the International Monetary Fund, a relation that is "secured" through various policies and treaties, not the least significant of which is the U.S. military bases agreement. This "involvement" of the United States in the Philippines is as a territory to be invested in (whether in capital or in arms) in the name of national and regional *security*. Although "security" has long been touted as being an issue of military defense of political sovereignty, the end of the cold war and the move to steer clear of "politics" in the promotion of the Asia-Pacific community have brought out the full implications of its economic and financial significance. As an economic arrangement, "security" also has its romantic overtones, inasmuch as it means the cementing of a relationship or the insuring of its stability. But the question to be asked of the international arrangements being made in the Asia-Pacific is: Who is getting off on this? Who is getting screwed and by whom?

In the case of Japan, clearly some leverage, that is, some bargaining power, is gained in her marriage of interests with the United States. In the case of the Philippines, that "security" is at least questionable. For the "special relationship" of the Philippines and the United States is no marriage, and the Philippines is no wife; she is, rather, the mistress of the United States. Feminized in this relationship of debt and dependence, the Philippines produces the surplus pleasure (wealth) that the United States extracts from her bodily (manual) labor. It is indeed her inexhaustible labor and her abundant natural resources that draw the United States to her, that is used to "attract" the latter's interest and investments. Philippine security therefore comes to mean the political stability necessary to attract foreign investors, the source of capital. An advertisement the Philippine government took out in the *New York Times* (July 28, 1974) demonstrates the sexual marketing of the country's domestic attractions:

We've put our house in order. ... There are attractive investment packages for you if you want to explore, develop and process mineral resources. ... Easy entry for expatriate staff. ... Doesn't that sound like an offer you can't refuse? We like multinationals. Manila's natural charms as a regional business center have been enhanced by a special incentive package ... your expatriate-managers will enjoy Asia's lowest living costs among the most outgoing people in the Pacific. ... Accountants come for $67, executive secretaries for $148. Move your Asian headquarters to Manila and make your cost accountants happy. ... The country is lovely. And loaded. Beneath the tropical landscapes of our 7,000 islands lies a wealth of natural resources. ... [8]

The prostitution of the Philippines that is attendant upon such rhetoric is made possible by and perpetuates a logic in which certain divisions of labor and patterns of sexual relations converge and collaborate in the driving of the national economy. Those who are at the wheel of the nation are its representatives, and the behavior they exhibit bespeaks the character of the nation. Thus does the Philippine-U.S. relationship appear as a romance-fantasy that has each government courting and manipulating the other for his or her security and happiness:

> Philippine presidents, out of tradition but more of necessity, have always had a love-hate relationship with the Great White Father in Washington. Cory Aquino is no exception. Right now, she is displaying the classic behavior of a spurned lover, one who not too long ago was playing beautiful music with no less than George Bush himself.
>
> What explains this cyclical and all too predictable behavior of virtually everybody who has ever lived in Malacañang? First, there is the realpolitik aspect. Nobody gets to be president of this country without, more or less, the imprimatur of whoever happens to call the shots in the White House. Second, Washington tends to keep a tight leash on Philippine presidents, especially on the matter of keeping American bases in this part of the world. Third, America's love is never constant, never enduring; Filipino presidents come and go, but American interest in this country is eternal. Or so it seems.[9]

The article from which this extract was taken goes on, relating the "tragic pattern of presidential love-hate for America" in which the various presidents experienced "the sweet love of American support, followed by an acrimonious parting of ways," sharing "the common fate of being at the mercy, if not in the physical custody of America." This custody that makes Filipinos a kept people, however, is actively pursued by those who in their desire to share in the rights and privileges of the international community buy into this economic arrangement (free enterprise, free love)—this open relationship that economically means the letting down of protectionist barriers and "liberalization" of imports, that is, easy entry and exit.

This "special relationship" is the manifestation and consequence of an imperialistic dream that at the turn of the century was steeped in sacred tones. As Senator Beveridge exclaimed:

We will not repudiate our duty in the archipelago. We will not abandon our opportunity in the Orient. We will not renounce our part in the mission of our race, trustee under God, of the civilization of the world ... of all our race He has marked the American people as his chosen nation to finally lead in the regeneration of the world. This is the divine mission of America, and it holds for us all the profit, all the glory, all the happiness possible to man. We are trustees of the world's progress, guardians of its righteous peace. The judgement of the Master is upon us: "Ye have been faithful over a few things; I will make you rule over many things."[10]

The religious rhetoric of U.S. colonization has become today the libidinal action of U.S. capitalism. The goal of economic and political conversion was also zealously expressed by Senator Beveridge:

American soil is producing more than Americans can consume. ... The trade of the world must and shall be ours. American law, American order, American civilization and the American flag will plant themselves on shores hitherto bloody and benighted but by the agencies of God henceforth to be made beautiful and bright.[11]

This process of evangelization has today become explicitly the process of seduction. But although the form has changed, the dream yet seeks the same coveted object, the Philippines—a body resistant to its desire and to its ideals of democracy and freedom, that is, free enterprise. The Philippines needs to be converted and seduced because she is a contradiction to these ideals to the extent that she is residually feudal or precapitalist and threatening to become communist or anticapitalist. As a colony she therefore had to be "emancipated" and granted independence, converted to that U.S. order that has become today a global order in order to contain the potentially eruptive antagonism that could develop from the contradiction she poses (by serving as a locus for her displacement), a contradiction that is nevertheless necessary for the motoring of capitalism. What one might glean from this history of decolonization is the same logic at work in the granting of autonomy to the Asia-Pacific region. Now constituted as a self-governing unit, it could thereby be more efficiently engaged in the global economy.

The coveting of former colonies, however, did not cease with "liberation." These recalcitrant bodies, now members of an independent region, must continually be lured into feeding the desires of power. As Luz del Mundo observed:

The Western powers are now reaping the effects of their ignoring "nationalist" aspirations of Arab countries and their greedy grabbing of spheres of influence on Arab oil resources in the past several decades, thus triggering retaliatory moves from OPEC. Now they turn their attention to the Asia-Pacific region. ASEAN is now at a stage where it has more countries from Europe, the Middle East and Latin America interested in entering into partnership with ASEAN. Japan sees this and wants to preempt the ASEAN as its own preserve; a prize and plum to be won permanently by persuading its other OECD partners, particularly the US and Australia, that through the creation of a Pacific community, Japan will be certain to remain an ally of the West.[12]

Part and parcel of this "prize and plum to be won" that is the ASEAN is the Philippines. Thus, the Philippines plays a curious role in the marriage of Japan and "the West"—"won" back from Japan in World War II by the United States, she must now be shared as the price of alliance and as insurance of Japanese fidelity. But this price is paid neither by the United States or Japan, that is, neither by "the Great White Father" or his recent spouse—but by the Philippines, mistress-infant to one, stepdaughter-servant to the other, the body that keeps the two in relative harmony by acting as a membrane for the coursing of their desires and as a locus for the playing out of their antagonism. Such is a typical international triangle: an incestuous ménage a trois as well as a perverted oedipal affair.

A MODEL ASIAN-PACIFIC FAMILY

As Aida Fulleros Santos and Lynn F. Lee show in their analysis of the Philippine Aid Plan (PAP), a current project of the United States and Japan, the marriage of the two powers is convenient but uneasy. There are obvious tensions in this "triangular relationship between institutions in the United States, Japan and the Philippines": Japan has not agreed entirely that aid to the Philippines be conditioned by the U.S. perception of their common regional interests, and that Japan be "guided" by the United States while giving the bulk of ODA [Official Development Assistance] funds. ... Japan sees its strategic interests as similar to the United States but does not have exactly the same view on the best ways of furthering these mutually shared interests. For the United States, the PAP concretises a political strategy for the U.S. and Japan to work together to further their mutual interests in the Asia-Pacific region and globally. ... PAP shows the U.S. strategy—U.S. political direction and Japanese funding."[13]

In spite of the tensions, however, the U.S.-Japan cooperative effort is bound to make the Philippines pay, for aside from giving the two more leverage with the Philippine government in defining and determining "regional security," it also increases the Philippine foreign debt. "In the long term, foreign investment that may flow on from PAP will contribute to the net outflow of money from the Philippines."[14] Indeed, what the PAP scheme shows is that such marriage of powers only augments their individual exploitation of the country of their desires.

In her relationship to the United States, the Philippines is an exploitable body, an industry hooked up to the U.S. desiring machine through a system

of flows of labor and capital in the guise of free exchange (export oriented, capital and import dependent), but functioning in the mode of dialysis, which gives one the strength and life depleted from the other. As such, the
Philippines is the hooker of the United States who caters to the latter's demands (ostensibly demands of global production and consumption); in other words, a hospitality industry, a hostess to U.S. desires, a prostitute. As the greatest of her foreign investors, that is, the most powerful of her multinational clients, the United States establishes free trade zones on the body/land of the Philippines over which he exercises a considerable degree of monopoly (the way he derives his pleasures) by obtaining free entry and exit rights (investment of capital and repatriation of profits). This mode of relations between the Philippines and the United States operates according to a fantasy of relations between masculine and feminine ideals that has become dominant in economically advanced nations—a sexual masquerade in which the Philippines serves as a feminine ideal for the United States, servicing his power the way the Philippine prostitutes service U.S. military men, symbols of U.S. national (masculine) strength. The fantasy is shared, of course, and the United States in turn becomes a masculine ideal for the Philippines, determining the kind of desires expressed by this "bar waitress" who might speak for the Philippines as well: "Sure I would like to marry an American! I want to help my family. If I marry a Filipino, it will be the same; but if I marry an American, maybe it will be better."[15] The fulfillment of the prostitute's desire to marry into a better life (i.e., foreign, American), however, is not forthcoming, as it has been pre-empted by other partners of the United States.

New investment flows in the Philippines are dominated by Japanese as well as Taiwanese capital. "For both Japan and Taiwan, the motives for investment are primarily the need to recycle trade surpluses and the exploitation of advantages offered by the Philippines, e.g., a cheap labour force, natural resources, trade preferences vis-à-vis the developed countries, as well as a location for polluting industries."[16] In other words, the interest Japan and Taiwan take in the Philippines is not very different in form from the interest the United States takes in her, for the attractions the Philippines holds are all the same for these capital-bearing nations. In this scenario, speaking of interest and involvement is the same as speaking of investment, and to speak of any of these things is to use the language of politics and economics as well as the language of love and sexual exploitation. Thus with the increase of Japanese loans and grants to the Philippines, Japan joins in the feminization of the Philippines: "As Japan chalks up more trade surpluses, Japanese penetration of the country's economy will, no doubt, increase."[17] Adopting the Free World fantasy of the advanced nations of the West in order not only to enter the international community but also "to step out of the shadow of the U.S."[18] and exercise equal if not greater power in a new global order, Japan is yet determined by the threat of an emasculation similar to that which she participates in effecting on developing nations such as the Philippines. Thus the protectionist measures she adopts in the form of high tariffs on processed or semiprocessed products are in effect a successful defense against getting screwed, that is, penetrated.[19] Who is penetrating whom—in translated terms, which countries export capital, technology, and finished products to which countries—hence becomes a gauge by which to measure economic strength. It is no surprise then that even those in developing nations who want to get in on the action that the Asia-Pacific community promises point out the necessity of correcting the uneven trade among member nations—demonstrated, for example, by the fact that "tropical products from the Pacific Developing Countries (PDCs) suffered from low import penetration into the American, Japanese, Canadian and Australian markets"[20]—a problem whose proposed solution lies merely in an equalization of flows through political reform ("national goodwill") rather than in a transformation of the mode of relations among these nations. Furthermore, development is always seen in terms of inside and outside, feminine and masculine, domestic and international. Hence the possibility of critiquing the economic growth registered by the Philippines in recent years in the following way: "One finds that most of the permanent or 'structural' features of the growth have originated from the outside. These have come in the form of loans, official assistance, and the expansion in world markets ... the impetus has come mainly from without."[21]

Thus subjected to extensive and intensive penetration of her economy by powers such as the United States, Japan, and the rest of the OECD Five, as well as the newly industrialized countries, the Philippines finds herself hyperfeminized in her relations. It is not an accident that the U.S. expression "to fuck someone over" means to exploit or abuse someone. The way in which this dominant fantasy of sexual relations has developed as an essential condition of advanced capitalism might be traced through the history of imperialism up to the present. Indeed, one could show that the hyperfeminization of certain countries signifies their condensation of the contradictory symptoms of patriarchy, colonialism, and imperialism. Thus the hyperfeminization of the Philippines is a historically new phenomenon, which is not to say that this process of objectification did not exist earlier, for it might be argued that the production of the prostitute as a feminine ideal is a cultural corollary to commodity fetishism in the age of capitalism, and feminization is the process of management through investment (such was the new mode of control of the colonies in the age of imperialism). But what is new is the way in which prostitution has become a dominant mode of production of neocolonial nations in late capitalism—that is, neocolonial nations are now like prostitutes to be invested in for the extraction of surplus pleasure (wealth)[22]—and the extent to which this feminizing process has intensified on a global scale since the mid-1970s. Indeed, it is the intensification of global capitalism that has led to the visible manifestation of its internal contradictions in the catastrophe of developing nations—the sexual fantasy is henceforth literally realized on the bodies of women. That is to say, this hyperfeminization is not merely metaphorical, but translates into the concrete exploitation and abuse of actual women.

SEXUAL LABOR AND COMMERCE

In the case of the Philippines this phenomenon is most clearly seen in the feminization of exploited labor. "The export-oriented, debt-propelled strategy has given rise to the global commodification of Third World women in the form of female labor export, exploitation of their cheap labor power and their utilization through sexual trade, whether it be in the legitimate 'tourism' or hospitality and mail-order bride business or in prostitution which has phenomenally spread."[23] Indeed, what the case of the Philippines and other Southeast Asian nations demonstrates is the veritable feminization of the Third World of Asia (rather than simply the Third World, which was once synonymous with Asia). In these countries the sexuality of commerce thus necessarily means the commerce of feminine sexuality, that is, the selling and trading of women forced into prostitution through poverty or physical abuse, not only within these countries but internationally as well.

In the Philippines, there are 300,000 to 500,000 prostitutes,[24] working not only in the areas surrounding the U.S. bases servicing U.S. military men on leave, but also in Japanese-owned hotels catering to Japanese businessmen on vacation. The "boom of the sex industry" is only the necessary consequence of the "development" of a larger hospitality industry, that is, one that hosts the capital and arms of touring men[25] and multinationals. In fact, the establishment of the Ministry of Tourism in 1973 was a key achievement of the Marcos state in its revitalized efforts to transform the nation into a lucrative business beginning with the declaration of martial law:

> Before 1973 the Philippines was not much of a tourist spot. The combination of street crime and well-organized demonstrations aginst American imperialism and the Vietnam war created a less-than-friendly environment for a fun seeker. When President Ferdinand Marcos declared martial law on September 21, 1972, a lot of that changed. Criminals were rounded up and the political opposition jailed. In 1973 the Ministry of Tourism was established with former Marcos press agent Jose Aspiras in charge, and the number of visitors rapidly increased from less than 150,000 in 1971 to more than a million in 1980.[26]

With the military imposition of stability in an otherwise crisis-ridden country, the number of hotels and tourists, multinationals and investors increased rapidly. Martial law was not, however, merely the whim of a dictator in pursuit of power (although that was undoubtedly at work as well), but part of the engineering of a new economic order necessary to meet the intensified demands of global capitalism. Marcos's indebtedness to the World Bank and the IMF, for which the Filipino people are still paying dearly, is only the logical consequence of the latter's instrumental role in this cooperative prostitution of the country through "authoritarian modernization":[27]

> The Bank set in motion in the Philippines a development program with two key objectives: "pacification" and "liberalization." The pacification component consisted of rural and urban development programs aimed at defusing rural and urban unrest. Liberalization referred to the drastic restructuring of Philippine industry and external trade strategy to open up the country more completely to the flow of U.S. capital and commodities. To implement this strategy of "technocratic modernization," the Bank encouraged the formation of an authoritarian government and carefully cultivated a technocratic elite.[28]

Mostly educated in the United States, this elite was heavily influenced by the Keynesian revolution in economics during the 1950s and the principles of technocracy "fine-tuned" during the 1960s. Thus the technocrats who replaced the industrial elite in the 1970s could be said to share "a strong sense of fraternity with their World Bank and IMF counterparts."[29] As one columnist wrote in 1981, "Now we're completely under the thumbs of the IMF because our principal planners are IMF boys."[30]

This situation hardly changed when Aquino came into power in 1986—the fraternal identification with these governing bodies of international finance transcended national changes. Hence Aquino's finance minister, Jaime Ongpin, could sincerely claim, "I don't blame the IMF for what they did. If I were in their shoes, I would have been tougher."[31] Such are the outstanding young men of the nation whose consolidation with the government and fraternal bonding with international economists, financiers, and other managers of nations was the single-handed, multi-armed achievement of martial law. Part of the legacy of martial law is the desire for authoritarian (masculine) rule evidenced in the repeatedly expressed desire on the part of many Filipinos for a "strong leader" (in complaints, for example, that Aquino is not "man enough" for the position), a desire stoked not only by the absence of Marcos and fueled by the tradition of patronage politics, but now especially attractive in light of the ostensible success of authoritarian regimes in newly industrialized countries.

With Marcos and his boys and cronies manning the nation, modernization and militarism went hand in hand in restructuring the economy, now characterized by import liberalization, privatization, foreign capital dependency, and export orientation. Free trade zones and tourist belts were essential components of the government's "incentive packages" to attract capital to the Philippines and thus similar in constitution. Both relied on a predominantly female and wholly feminized labor force. Both employed a "get laid or get laid off" policy. In the case of the tourist industry, labor and raw material were the same: women. It is not an accident that "Sin-city," Manila, the "sex-capital of the world,"[32] was touted and fashioned by Imelda Marcos as "the City of Man." The "beautification" projects meant to raise Manila to the level of a modern metropolis to compete for international attention and capital only evidences the veritable prostitution of the Philippines. This means not only the selling of women but the feminization and parceling out of the land: in Ermita, the red-light district in Manila, different zones of bars and clubs are owned and primarily patronized by different nationalities, so that one could identify, for example, an Australian strip, a German one, and so forth—a free trade zone that makes Manila into a multinational brothel.[33] Thus one could in all truth declare, "The government is not only selling women to foreigners, but also the sovereignty of the nation itself."[34]

IMPERIAL SONS, NATIONAL PIMPS

The rise of a "strong-man" regime was a World Bank-endorsed response to the growing and intensifying crises felt in the nation as a result of the political and economic system installed by United States colonization being pushed to its limits by the acceleration of global capital. Other developing countries underwent similar postwar crises and responded with similar "strong-man" regimes.[35] The nationalist tenor of these Third World dictatorships only made manifest that in the age of imperialism, nationhood is figured and operates in masculine terms. The early experience of the Philippines with nascent nationalism in the late nineteenth century evidences this form of masculinization, a masculinization that found its symptomatic expression in the militarism of interimperial rivalry. Given these conditions and the infantilization of the colonies that predominated in an earlier age, early anti-imperialistic nationalism could only be articulated as a son's demand for independence and sovereignty:

> The nation is gendered and domesticated within the circle of sacrifice and the idealization of loss that binds the child-patriot to this motherland. By doing so, the patriot not only expresses his love but also reverses the relationship of dependency between mother and child. He posits his future authority over her, imagining himself and others like him as potential patrons, "bequeathing" to the *patria* the legacy of freedom. In this way, the motherland inherits from her sons an "immense fortune"—a surplus of symbolic wealth with which to nurture future sons. Offspring and lover, the patriot is now also father to the na-

tion. It is thus wholly without irony that Filipinos have regarded Rizal as the "father" of Philippine nationalism and that one of his biographers has referred to him as the "first Filipino."[36]

The infantilization of the Philippines continues to be felt. Senator Estrada expressed it when he spoke against the presence of the U.S. bases: "Our current relations with the U.S. is not untarnished. It's not the relation of two friends, but the relation between the master and a ward who is forcibly being suppressed to remain a child."[37] The representation of this relation is the result of the general mode of exchange between the Philippines and the United States; it is a discourse built up also from an exchange of representations that is most evident in the media. The *New York Times,* for example, recently wrote:

> Even among Filipinos who want the United States military to stay, it is commonly said that this is a nation that has never been allowed to progress beyond adolescence, beyond an immature need to hide behind someone or something else for protection. ... many Filipinos admit that too often they seek out godfathers rather than take responsibility for their own actions.
>
> Led by several fierce, hard-headed nationalists, who say with a touch of pride that they are willing to buck popular opinion, the Philippine Senate seems poised to try to end the country's dependence on what is being portrayed as the biggest godfather of them all, the American military. ... [38]

The patronizing recognition of that "touch of pride" is then explained (and thus legitimated) by a Filipino political analyst whose understanding of the significance of rejecting the bases affirms his identification with this infantilized image: "It will be therapeutic, a national primal scream that may mature us."[39] In all such attempts to articulate the problems of the Philippine national identity, the motherland seems, however, to have disappeared; the maternal has vanished, leaving only traces of a feminine body transposed over the national territory.

Thus are the national resources configured for exploitation—as raw material for processing or export. With the government's model of development necessarily bolstering "domestic industrialization" and other economic activities considered "productive," that is "infrastructure and other capital investments that have long-term impact on the economy," women-dominated activities have to suffer. "There is no budget support for women's subsistence and income substitution/generation economic activities, the budget makes their work, and contribution to the local and to the national economy, effectively invisible."[40] In effect, their productive capacity is erased and their increasingly bodily labor must henceforth function as raw material for the national industries. Small-scale industries and firms, subsistence agricultural production, education, the "underground economy," all of whose labor force is predominantly comprised of women, these are activities that must be sacrificed in the name of development. The destruction of domestic income-generating activities results in the effective dispossession of the female and feminized labor force, thus making it more accessible for exploitation and circulation as commodified products. At the same time that the feminized labor force is deterritorialized—forced to seek employment abroad, pushed out of the country by the sheer absence of means of living, pulled into advanced countries by the spaces of demand for cheap and tractable labor—it is also further grounded in the female body.

With the erasure even of the reproductive function of the nation, all its resources are extricated from any organic life or vital community of their own, processed and packaged, and made ready for circulation and unimpeded exploitation. Thus is labor produced for the export-oriented policy of authoritarian modernization. In the export processing zone, there is not much distance between human labor and raw material. Furthermore, the replacement of manual strength by machines eliminates unskilled males from the newly tailored definition of human labor, since within an already patriarchally divided society, unskilled females are the preferred operators of those unfulfilled functions of the machines requiring physical dexterity, patience, tractability, and long periods of immobility, all learned in the domestic sphere. As one manager explained, "We hire girls because they have less energy, are more disciplined, and are easier to control."[41] Supervisors and managers, on the other hand, are male, thus reinforcing the configuration of industrial, technologically advanced countries where the necessary intangible services and skills, education and information technology for such positions are produced, as masculine. This gender division of symbolic capital and bodily labor into, respectively, masculine and feminine, thus results in a diaspora of unemployed, unskilled men.[42] It also enables the "sons of the nation," that is, the technocratic and political elite at the hub of the nation, to cooperate fraternally with international capital in the stimulation and regulation of trade flows, thereby at once becoming supervisors and pimps of the nation.

In the actual export of women forced into the "entertainment industry," there is no more difference between raw material and labor, for the prostitute applies her labor power to her own body in the production of herself as a commodity. A testament to the ever-increasing efficiency of multinational capital, prostitutes are at once the raw material, labor, and machines of new national industries in advanced countries such as Japan: "Filipino women in Japan are grist to Japan's 10-trillion-yen-a-year sex mills. The boom in the sex industry in Japan is an indication of the economic prosperity enjoyed by that country."[43] One might add that it is this economic prosperity without military prowess that has made Japan the leader among national sex industries. Sex takes on a crucial role in the domestic staging of political fantasies and economic realities of nations.

Global conditions have taken another shift. With the increase of hostilities in the Philippines, not only in the sense of antagonism to Japanese sex tours and to the presence of the U.S. bases, but also in the sense of military and insurgent fighting, the climate has become largely unfavorable or at least precarious for foreign investments of any kind. Hence the necessity of drawing labor and raw material into the developed countries that now employ the strategy of import liberalization. Nowhere is this strategy more clearly visible than in the case of Japan; Japan, however, cautiously confines her definition of imports to "non-traditional semiprocessed products" meaning, labor material—in other words, women. The increase of hostilities within the Philippines is also symptomatic of the World Bank–determined economic strategies for development reaching their effective limits. The depletion of natural resources and destruction of the productive capacity of outmoded economic forms, especially those that have been female dominated, have forced the transformation of an already feminized labor force into the semiprocessed products that await final processing for the realization of surplus value. In this sense, women are the last abundant resource of the nation—they are like the surplus products they themselves sell for subsistence, now sold themselves by their own feminized nation. Free floating, they are "excess liquidity" that is "mopped up" in "stream-lining operations" at the injunction of "international capital,"[44] their mobility now regulated by their sex (more accurately, their sexual function, which is their penetrability[45]) and their passport. Sexuality and nationality thus become deterritorialized indicators of vulnerability to exploitation, as well as instruments of such exploitation.

EXPORT ORIENTAL LABOR

The fate of Filipino women exported to other countries as domestics and prostitutes demonstrates the logic that subjects their own feminized nation to the same treatment. The cruel scenario that becomes typified from the accumulation of recounted individual experiences presents itself as the same operations that have cohered through the process of history into a system of exploitation of the Third World. Yayori Matsui, a Japanese journalist, reports that in 1988 there were 7,000-8,000 Filipinas who were working as domestic helpers in Singapore and 30,000 working in Hong Kong.[46] She also reports that nearly 100,000 Asian migrant women working as "entertainers in the booming sex industry" enter Japan each year, 90 percent of whom come from the Philippines, Thailand, and Taiwan, and 80 percent of that total coming from the Philippines.[47]

Usually they are picked up by recruiters in their own countries and sent to Japan with a promise or contract stating that they will work as waitresses, models or ordinary hostesses (not engaging in prostitution). However, in reality, they are sold out by the recruiters to promoters in Japan. ... The women are then sold again, by the Japanese promoters, to clubs or other sex business owners, at double the price. Sometimes they are simply rented at a monthly charge of US$1,600 to US$6,400. In order to cover such expenses, the owners force the women into prostitution, taking advantage of their vulnerability, the prime cause of which is their illegal visa status. Without the protection visa status affords, there is no limit to the abuse and exploitation that these women may have to face.

The sexual relations that marked the political and economic links of the Philippines with the United States have become literally realized in the case of Japan—military prowess and domination has in Japan become masculine prowess and domination, international politics acted out by male sexual violation, military arms translated into raping penises. As one reporter described:

> I visited the tiny theater where Maria was working. On the stage of the smoke-filled room, just big enough for 40 people, she stood naked. Then an announcement was heard: "We have something special tonight, a direct import from the Philippines! Come and get it, quick!" An office worker type climbed up to the stage, and dropped his pants. I saw Maria raped again and again, in full view of the audience.[48]

But the international economy of forced prostitution is not merely a symptom of Japan's repressed political fantasies—it is in fact a constitutive part of the current mode of relations between Japan and the Third World populations[49] from which she derives her economic prosperity. The series of transactions between recruiters, promoters, and sex business owners are analogous to the series of transactions between national and multinational bodies regulating trade flows of capital, goods, and labor. With intangible services, information, and technology dominated by multinational production, nations such as the Philippines and other Southeast Asian countries are reduced to providing physical labor, which makes the national government no more than a recruiting agency for the sale of its feminized labor to markets in more advanced economies. Indeed, it is the government that does the "mopping up of excess liquidity" for smooth transfers and expedient profits. To the extent that it functions as a multinational corporation, the Asia-Pacific community acts as the promoting agency that secures the uninterrupted flows between the recruiters and the business owners by functioning as a regional membrane managing individual national interests. Finally, multinational companies and industries function like the sex business owners—the employers of feminized labor from various developing countries.

The women are kept in physical and financial bondage—locked in cells, their passports and airline tickets confiscated, desperate to earn money for

their families as well as for themselves (if only to buy a ticket home); they are
in no position to resist the brutally enforced prostitution for which they were
imported. In fact, those who do resist are physically and sexually abused—
raped, beaten, and starved, often to the point of critical or fatal injury. The
irony of this situation is that their bodies abroad are worth more than their
skills and education at home. Produced as physical commodities, they cease
to be treated as humans. They are indeed what they are advertised (on t-
shirts around the U.S. bases) to be: "little brown fucking machines powered
by rice." More than a hundred years ago, Gustave Flaubert observed that
"The oriental woman is no more than a machine: she makes no distinction
between one man and another man."[50] The equivalence of the oriental
woman and a sexual machine was already functioning then in congruence
with the relations of imperial nations and their colonies. It only took a global
shift in those relations in the age of neocolonialism to equate the two terms
with the entire economy of the colony, now an "independent" developing nation. But it is precisely because of the historical development of these colonies from political appendages to economic dependents that developing nations, particularly their labor, now serve their developed "masters" (the word
used to designate the club owners).

Like the women who are rented out to clients, developing nations operate
through the subcontracting of their properties, whether buildings, facilities,
land, or labor, to client companies. In the words of Finance Minister Ongpin:
"We are paying special attention to ... international subcontracting, where
we provide facilities for large multinationals to come in and do the more labor-intensive aspects of their operations in this country."[51] What this provi-
sion of facilities entails, however, is a specialization that destroys the nation's
productive capacities and reduces it to a field of operations, a place "to come
in and do ... "—very much as these women are reduced to a sexual function.
Short-term investments and limited time horizons are merely economic
equivalents of the "short-times" clients enjoy with their prostitutes, a practice that belies the promise of permanent friendships and financial security.
This is a lesson the United States continually teaches because he has epito-
mized the practice in the actions of his servicemen. As one bar waitress asserted: "While they are here, they love you very much. Then they return to
the States and you are forgotten. They take no more notice of you. They
might support you for one year, but they tire of that and see someone new in
the States."[52] The difference between this relation, however, and that of
transnational corporations and their feminized labor is in the latter there is
neither pretense nor hope of love. The relations have been streamlined into
efficient versions of what they always were: strictly economic transactions.
Corporations are not personified in the same way nations are, hence their
operations manifest more blatantly the mode of relations they are founded
upon. Again this is demonstrated by Japan's sex industry.

Although transnational corporations seem to transcend the ideologies and boundaries of nations, their existence and prosperity nevertheless do depend upon them. The possibility, for example, of extracting and enslaving labor rests on the nation-state and its institutions. Passports and visas become both a means of protection and a means of exploitation. National differences also become a means of disempowerment. Immigrant women in Japan are imprisoned in the confines of their national languages and cultures. At the same time, however, national unities also function as a means of empowerment. Thai women in Japan are apparently more victimized than Filipino women because the Thai community is smaller than the Filipino community and therefore its members have less access to organized efforts to address their problems.[53] Nevertheless, nationalities are used as instruments of exploitation. The fact that Filipino girls are imported in Japan to replace the Japanese prostitutes who used to service U.S. soldiers in Okinawa demonstrates that certain national ideologies of discrimination are at work.

It is curious that although the Japanese have historically been referred to as "orientals" by Westerners, it is other Asians, specifically people from developing nations within Asia, who are referred to by the Japanese as "orientals." Statements in the Japanese press like "Asian women are favorite goods with 'Oriental Charm' and an exoticism for Western and Japanese men" and "Japan's sex industry has need of Asian women, especially Filipinas"[54] shows the extent to which Japan has come to distinguish herself from Asia. The feeling of racial superiority is not new to Japan, nor is the culture of patriarchy. What is new is the merging of these discourses of race, sex, and capital in multinational industries and in the production of a new species of inferior beings:

> There is a general feeling among the Japanese that they are superior to other races, but especially to the peoples of the Southeast Asian region. A Japanese priest confessed in a meeting with Filipino priests that Japanese Catholics looked down on Filipinos in Japan, who as a rule are Catholics, as "the kind of people who would do anything for money."
>
> "Most Japanese are allergic to Filipinos who scare them as bearers of some infectious disease," said the Japanese priest.[55]

Indeed, what in the prevailing fantasy defines prostitutes and orientals in their inferiority is financial parasitism, moral depravity, sexual proclivity and communicable disease. And since the political weakness and economic dependence of nations marks them as inferior, it is not difficult to see how the equivalence between developing nations, orientals, and prostitutes can be made. Japan herself has not been immune to this hierarchic configuration of nations. Thus at another time, "In order to convince the West that it was really in earnest and civilized enough to be treated as an equal, Japan had to fight and win a war."[56] One might hence explain the heavily-documented

Japanese bestial treatment of imported prostitutes in part by the historical
emasculation of Japan, for equality in the international community requires
proof of a certain kind of masculinity and the debasement of a certain kind
of femininity or, better, feminization. However, one must also bear in mind
that for Japanese women the imported prostitutes are not merely feminine
but altogether a different species. As Matsui describes:

> Men buying prostitutes is never socially condemned, nor is women's acceptance
> of it condemned—women often say: "If my husband goes to a 'professional'
> woman, it's not a problem, but if he is attracted to an ordinary woman, I get
> hurt and jealous." Such a double standard of women is still deep-rooted among
> the Japanese and they consider the prostitute as a special kind of woman, and
> fail to treat them as human beings and to accord them their human rights.[57]

The double standard is a result not only of Japan's patriarchal structure, feudal history, and tradition of prostitution, but also of the new configuration
of these systems of relations within an advanced capitalist economy. The ele-
vation of women's status in Japan in areas not traditionally open to them ne-
cessitates the displacement of the contradictions of capital, which they have
historically borne, on other peoples. At the same time, women in Japan can
find their place in society by either joining the white-collar work force, the
masculine sphere, or remaining in the home as housewives and mothers, the
feminine sphere; in other words, in this economy there are two paths that are
open for those who have the means of staying human whether one is male or
female: to act productive or to be reproductive, to act masculine or to be
feminine. Anything outside of this dichotomy becomes relegated to the less
than human, reduced to the "professional" animal or thing.

FAMILIAL AND PEDOPHILIC EXPLOITATION

So far I have been speaking of the feminization of developing labor. But as
the relations of the Philippines with the United States and Japan (as paradigms of power) show, in this context feminization also necessarily means
dehumanization, and emasculation necessarily means debasement. Within a
Japanese-style management system in which the company takes on a feudal
familial structure, those who are not seen as productive sons or reproductive
daughters are food for machines. Feminized objects can have no human role
in this system. Increasingly multinational corporations are adopting this
family mode—hence the call for "families of nations." Soon the international
community will be dominated by "first families" of the world. The Asia-Pacific community is one such bid to becoming a first (world) family-corporation, one that will rival the other family-corporation building up in Europe.
But within this family are collectives of labor that embody all the historical

contradictions of international capital and therefore cannot "mature" and compete with or equal the nations that have established themselves as their parents. At the same time they are rendered incapable of producing or reproducing their own means of subsistence, like children or things. This is the condition of the Philippines within the Asia-Pacific family—subject to a sociolibidinal economy that deploys deterritorialized relations of power through sex and money.

Ward, child, mistress, commodity—the Philippines is a historical condensation of these different relations tending toward equivalence, an equivalence that does not rest easy but which must continually be secured through systematic violence. But the tendency toward equivalence is evident in the mass production of a new commodity, the child prostitute. The phenomenal scale of forced prostitution of children in Southeast Asian nations is yet another testament to the subordination, infantilization, and feminization at work in the production of labor material necessary to maintain the level of prosperity attained by advanced economies such as Japan and the NICs. Lured by promises of prosperity and familial security and forced by the dire circumstances of their lives if not by their own desperate parents, children are turning into the raw material of an intensified prostitution industry. In Japan the average age of imported prostitutes is decreasing rapidly due to several related factors: the increasing fierceness of competition in the sex industry, the increasing organized resistance of women, and the increasing risk of AIDS.[58] Hence the great demand for young, tractable, virgin boys and girls.

What this phenomenal explosion of forced child prostitution demonstrates is the constant need for capital to produce new commodities and the desire to consume them. The debt-servicing policy of developing nations is using up all traditional and nontraditional (such as feminized labor) resources and is now exploiting new nontraditional products: children. Hence in 1990 the United Nations Children's Emergency Fund (UNICEF) could truthfully report that "the heaviest burden of the debt crisis is falling on the growing minds and bodies of children in the developing world."[59] UNICEF's concern, however, only reveals itself as a concern for capital. As a deputy executive of UNICEF put it: "Human capital is a far more important factor in economic growth than physical capital. Investment in a human capital in the form of nutrition, basic education, and health cannot be postponed. ... The underemphasized tragedy of the disinvestment in human capital in the 1980s is that the results will be carried forward in stunted bodies and deficient educations well into the 21st century."[60] In other words, children are another resource for multinational capital to invest in. But as child prostitution attests, children need not be long-term investments—they are marketable now. If the price of production of a prostitute is minimal, the cost to produce a child prostitute is even less. Such is the cold logic of the Free World.

Within the Free World, therefore, pedophilic exploitation is only an intensified mode of the relations already prevailing between multinational corporations and their developing labor. With these international pedophilic tendencies in mind it is difficult to see how any familial harmony can be achieved within the Asia-Pacific community. For the regional security it promises means the abuse and exploitation of weaker, dependent, feminized, and infantilized collectives—the poor Southeast Asian relations of the OECD Five and the NICs. The call for privatization in the current movement toward global incorporation is therefore a call for the privatization of the antagonisms and crises of nations. It is, in effect, a privatization of the violence endemic to global capital. With the effacement of nations in the creation and incorporation of new global families emerges a deterritorialized Third World—a new race of infantilized, feminized, commodified peoples distributed over the world, motoring globalized production. It is no longer, therefore, a matter of nations acting like people, but of people embodying their nations. The libidinal character of national economies makes it easier for the crises of nations to become at once deterritorialized and grounded in the bodies of people. Those who occupy the masculine ranks of global management are free to move and accumulate profit like capital, but those who remain in the feminized terrain of labor must passively bear the burden of their nations.

Such is the prospect of the laboring populations of developing nations such as the Philippines. It is indeed a dim prospect. And yet the existence of other such collectives leaves space for hope, for other desires to emerge within this already overdetermined region. Hence the efforts to redefine the community, to seek alliances with the collectives that share the burden of capital's contradictions. Instead of the desire for "security," which prostitutes nations like the Philippines, condemning them to an increasingly oppressive existence, alternative voices are calling for solidarity among Third World collectives—solidarity based not on a shared region or a common investment in the Free World, but on common interests and a cooperative political strength yet to be founded. As one such voice expressed:

> There is an international network in Asia and the Pacific of advocacy for a wide range of social, economic, and political issues heretofore unimagined, much less articulated: denuclearization, demilitarization or disarmament, rights of indigenous or ethnic peoples to their ancestral domain, human rights as guaranteed by international covenants to individuals and groups, development with consultation and consent, environmental protection (which daily grows into a universal concern of critial proportions), and increasingly, women's and children's rights and welfare.
>
> It is incumbent upon the governments of ASEAN and the Pacific community of island states to seriously consider the possibility of a continuing dialogue with these advocates, whose rallying cry has been "regional solidarity" based on

common causes and shared problems, instead of the more unstable and potentially more volatile ideal of "regional security" which has traditionally drawn strength from the realpolitik of confrontation, containment and the balance of power.[61]

This is the challenge that the concept of the Asia-Pacific poses—not as an economic network of dominant classes, but as an emergent political constituency composed of peoples desiring an alternative community. Instead of a nonaligned movement that only secures the citizenship of these countries in the Free World, laboring populations within the Asia-Pacific (and not their representative governments) must engage in a movement of alliances not for aggression but for the assertion of shared desires for self-determination and for the strength to forge an alternative international community that does not buy into another fantasy of the Free World. In other words, we must struggle against the practices that reproduce the political-libidinal relations of our present lives and engage in alternative modes of production to realize a more just form of community. But we can only begin working for this if in our actions we are already dreaming other worlds in other ways.

NOTES

1. The concept of fantasy that I employ here derives from Slavoj Zizek, for whom a fantasy construction "serves as a support for our 'reality' itself: an 'illusion' which is structuring our effective, real social relations and which is masking thereby some insupportable, real, impossible kernel" ("The Real of Ideology," *PsychCritique* 2, no. 3 [1987], p. 265). In the global fantasy, that impossible kernel would be the Third World, that is, the nonindustrialized, residually feudal, pre- or anticapitalist sectors of the world.

2. The possibility of grasping the actions of nations as citizens or international subjects is founded precisely on the historical colonization and decolonization of the world. The entire debate on imperialism since the turn of the century might be seen to turn on the issue of world citizenship, that is, whether the colonial peoples were fit for self-government and thus inclusion in the world community of nations. As present global divisions show, however, inclusion did not in any case mean equality with imperial nations. The divisions of the world into First, Second, Third also signify a hierarchy among nations in the eyes of the Free World. There is no room for me here to elaborate on the historical process of oedipalization of nations, that is, in the creation of nations as modern subjects. But the strong identification peoples have with their nation and the state actions and popular movements that are predicated upon this identification should point to a shared process of identity formation for individuals and nations as subjects in the modern world. Hence there is more than metaphorical truth in the observation not only that nations act like men and women, but that men and women act like nations. Inasmuch as sexuality is a central axis of subject identities, nations are configured sexually. Sexuality is endemic, however, not only to the individual

modern subject, but to the modes of production that have produced him (the modern subject is configured as masculine) as such, other individuals who do not quite qualify as modern subjects (women, colonials, ethnic and sexual minorities, the masses), as well as all modern nations, and countries that do not qualify as international subjects. These modes of production of modern identities to which sexuality is endemic include patriarchy, colonialism, orientalism, imperialism, and global capitalism.

3. "The New Asia-Pacific Era: A Perspective from an International Nation Building for the 21st Century," *Britannica Book of the Year 1986* (Chicago: Encyclopedia Britannica, 1986), p. 14.

4. Senator Alfred J. Beveridge, "Our Philippine Policy," in *The Philippines Reader,* ed. Daniel B. Schirmer and Stephen Rosskamm Shalom (Boston: South End Press, 1987), p. 24.

5. Purificacion Valera-Quisumbing, "Towards an Asia- 'Pacific Community': Varying Perceptions," in *The Pacific Lake,* ed. Jose P. Leviste, Jr. (Manila: Philippine Council for Foreign Relations, 1986), p. 81. Abrino Aydinan also asserts this U.S.-Japanese parentage of the Pacific idea: "The idea of organizing the nations lying along the basin or rim of the Pacific is a Japanese and American notion which has been embraced by the Association of Southeast Asian Nations (ASEAN), with the United States and Japan only too willing to yield the cares of paternity" ("Doubts Plague Pacific Basin Organization" in Leviste, ed., *The Pacific Lake,* p. 119). It is interesting to note that this expression of lineage or history is one used in the discourse of law (Valera-Quisumbing is a law professor) as well as in the discourse of business (Aydinan is a writer for a business-economics review).

6. "The New Asia-Pacific Era," *Britannica Book of the Year 1986,* p. 14.

7. Edgardo B. Maranan, "Peace, Development and Solidarity Through Initiatives from Below," in *Diliman Review* 37, no. 4 (1989), p. 21.

8. Philippine Government, "*New York Times* Advertisement," in Schirmer and Shalom, eds., *The Philippines Reader,* pp. 227–229.

9. Nelson Navarro, "Accidental Saints of Filipino Nationalism," *Malaya* (13 May 1990). The fantasy is one maintained by Americans as well. George Bush's ludicrous toast to Marcos after the latter effected his reelection in 1981 ("We love you, sir") attests to this. U.S. government support of the popular ousting of Marcos five years later also attests to the inconstancy of that love.

10. Schirmer and Shalom, eds., *The Philippines Reader,* pp. 23–26.

11. Quoted in Epifanio San Juan, Jr., *Crisis in the Philippines* (South Hadley, MA: Bergin and Garvey, 1986), p. 18.

12. "Disadvantages of a Pacific Community," in Laviste, ed., *The Pacific Lake,* p. 116.

13. *The Debt Crisis: A Treadmill of Poverty for Filipino Women* (Manila: Kalayaan, 1989), p. 16.

14. Ibid.

15. Lolita, quoted in Joseph Collins, *The Philippines: Fire on the Rim* (San Francisco: Institute for Food and Development Policy, 1989), p. 271. This was her response to the question whether she wanted to marry an American, which was posed to her during a discussion of her illegitimate child whose father is American. Two significant things come out of this contextualization: first, the option of marriage is a question

posed to Lolita by an American, that is, the form of her desire is predetermined by a dominant logic; second, the wish expresses the need for legitimation and financial support, both of which mean the same thing and are the result of a preexistent relation. In other words, the desire to marry is the consequence of already being fucked.

16. Emmanuel S. de Dios, "The Philippine Economy: A Conspectus of Recent Developments," *Diliman Review* 37, no. 2 (1989), p. 5.

17. Raffy Rey Hipolito, "Japanese Economic Power, Philippine Setting," *Diliman Review* 37, no. 2 (1989), p. 23.

18. This possibility is one that Aydinan ("Doubts Plague Pacific Basin," p. 121) sees as necessary if Japan is to serve as a model for other Asian countries.

19. This successful defense has, however, roused Japan's international partners to action, into forcing her open: "The yearly trade surpluses of Japan with the U.S. and European Economic Community members have angered the latter. Japan has been subjected to strong-arm tactics by her Western allies to open her economy" (Hipolito, "Japanese Economic Power," p. 22). The leverage that the United States and the EEC have, of course, is the "international community," a global superego over which they exercise dominant control through ownership of greater symbolic shares. As a U.S. political economist asserted: "If there is one country that is criticized for not playing by these emerging global rules, it is Japan. But the logic of the global web is so powerful that the Japanese will either be forced to comply over time or else face a stiff penalty from the marketplace, the talent pool, and competitors and governments" (Robert B. Reich, "Who is Them?" *Harvard Business Review* (March-April 1991), p. 81.

20. Jose P. Leviste, Jr., Introduction, p. 19.

21. de Dios, "The Philippine Economy," p. 5.

22. As Walker, the character in Pontecorvo's film *Burn* who argues for and effects the transformation of the fictional colony Quemada into a neocolony (that is, the transformation of a slave-labor economy into a wage-labor economy), asks its colonizers, "Gentlemen, which would you rather have? A wife whom you must clothe and feed even when she is no longer of any use to you? Or a whore who you need only pay for so long as she pleases you?"

23. Liza Maza, "Equity in the Philippines: Development Strategies and the Impact on Philippine Women," *Gabriela Women's Update* 7, no. 3 (July-September 1990), p. 15.

24. Santos and Lee, *The Debt Crisis,* p. 36.

25. In the 1970s, about 200,000 Japanese visited the Philippines annually, 90 percent of whom were male (*Japan Christian Activity News* [29 August 1980]).

26. A. Lin Neumann, "Tourism Promotion and Prostitution" in Schirmer and Shalom, eds., *The Philippines Reader,* p. 182.

27. Walden Bello, David Kinley, and Elaine Elinson, *Development Debacle: The World Bank in the Philippines* (San Francisco: Institute for Food and Development Policy, 1982), pp. 13–39. The authors argue that the World Bank emerged as a central influence in Philippine affairs as a consequence of an economic and political crisis. "In the late 1960's and early 1970's, Philippine society underwent a fundamental crisis. In its economic dimension, the crisis was precipitated by the intersection of three developments: the failure of the strategy of import substitution as a path to sustained industrialization, the increasing inability of agriculture to meet the country's basic food

needs, and the growing pressure from foreign capital to 'open up' the economy more completely." Added to this was a growing class and national consciousness, the breakdown of patronage politics, and the intensified competition within the oligarchy for political power. With the declaration of martial law and the blessing of U.S. businesses whose interests the World Bank represented, Marcos reconsolidated his position and centralized power, commandeering the state for the desires of capital.

28. Ibid., p. 198.

29. Ibid., p. 28.

30. Quoted in Ibid., p. 14.

31. Quoted in Paul A. Gigot, "Manila's Economic Revolutionary," in Schirmer and Shalom, eds., *The Philippines Reader*, p. 375.

32. "Under Marcos, promotion of tourism resulted in Manila's competing with Bangkok for the title of 'International Sex City'; Manila's reputation has become well-known, particularly to the Japanese." (Yayori Matsui, *Women's Asia* [London: Zed Books, 1987], p. 70.)

33. This division of the land into prostitution colonies also occurs with beach resorts, a practice that might be traced as a libidinal-economic practice to the mistresses' salons in late-nineteenth-century Europe. In the Philippines, these brothels and other owned land and businesses are generally acquired by expatriate men marrying a Filipino wife or adopting a Filipino child, under whose name the property is registered.

34. Karina David, quoted in Neumann, "Tourism Promotion and Prostitution," p. 185.

35. "In the Philippines, Chile, and Uruguay—all countries renowned for long-standing democratic traditions—there emerged from the wreckage the same formula pioneered by the Brazilian junta in the late 60s: a military or presidential-military dictatorship 'sanitizing' the social situation with massive repression, justifying its existence with the ideology of controlled modernization with the indispensable participation of foreign capital, and resting on a social coalition of technocrats, officers, local bureaucrat-capitalists, and foreign investors" (Bello, Kinley, and Elinson, *Development Debacle*, pp. 35–36).

36. Vicente L. Rafael, "Nationalism, Imagery, and the Filipino Intelligentsia in the Nineteenth Century," *Critical Inquiry* (Spring 1990), p. 602.

37. Schirmer and Shalom, eds., *The Philippines Reader*, p. 453.

38. Philip Shenon, "How Subic Bay Became a Rallying Cry for Philippine Nationalism," *New York Times* (15 September 1991), p. 2.

39. *New York Times*, 15 September 1991, p. 2e.

40. Santos and Lee, *The Debt Crisis*, p. 23.

41. Sr. Mary Soledad Perpiñan, "Philippine Women and Transnational Corporations," in Schirmer and Shalom, eds., *The Philippines Reader*, p. 239.

42. Many of these men find employment and the opportunity to regain lost masculinity in the army or vigilante groups, both running rampant over the countryside. Extreme militarization is evidenced by the creation of the Citizens Armed Forces Geographical Units in 1987 by the executive order of President Aquino and other vigilante groups (Arnel de Guzman and Tito Craige, "Counterinsurgency War in the Philippines and the Role of the United States," *Bulletin of Concerned Asian Scholars* 23, no. 2 [1991], p. 41). The armed forces of the Philippines plans to have 80,000 "combat-

ready forces" in the CAFGUs when the master plan is fulfilled. The human rights abuses (including torture, mutilation, and canibalism) of the 600 vigilante groups that exist at the present are well documented. Given that the insurgency movement is also growing steadily, absorbing the dispossessed, the unemployed, and the abused—all refugees of the state of political and economic war being waged to motor international capital—the military is a secure occupation. The regional community proposed by the Asia-Pacific can only exist in its present form through the maintenance of this war. That "the United States provides 83 percent of the procurement, operations, and maintenance budget (excluding salaries) of the Philippine military" (p. 46) attests to its interests in this community.

43. M. Dueñas, "Filipina as Japayuki-San," *Philippines Free Press* (April 4, 1987), p. 40.

44. " 'Mopping up excess liquidity' was the term Central Bank (CB) Governor Jobo Fernandez, currently the CB head and former Marcos government official, used to justify an increase in domestic rates, which made credit hard to come by. Small companies and factories with little capital had to close down and hundreds of workers were laid off. By IMF standards, but with extreme hardship for the people, the 'mopping up' resulted in improved financial capacity so the Philippine government could better service its foreign debt obligations" (Santos and Lee, *The Debt Crisis,* p. 9). The analogy is accurate inasmuch as the export of women is directly tied to the debt-servicing policy of the government—not only as an outcome but also as a necessary function of this policy. Not only does the policy result in inadequate funding for local income-generating activities, which forces the women to seek employment abroad, but also the earnings abroad that they remit are used for debt payments (p. 40).

45. This qualification is important when we consider the phenomenon of forced child prostitution, which manifests that feminization cuts across biological and age differences and depends more on the tractability and economic dependence of the feminized subject.

46. Matsui, *Women's Asia,* p. 52.

47. "Asian Migrant Women Working at Sex Industry in Japan Victimized by International Trafficking," *In God's Image* (June 1990), p. 6.

48. Mainichi Shimbun, quoted in *Philippines Free Press* (4 April 1987), p. 15.

49. The economic and ideological contradictions of the harmonious Asia-Pacific community become most visible in the fate of the Third World, an appellation that increasingly refers to peoples marked by poverty, infantilization, and feminization; in other words, in the fate of the poorest of the global poor, notably indigent, nonwhite women and children. The feminization and infantilization is unambiguous and intensified in the case of Third World Asian nations because of the combination of two independently feminized units, that is, Third World and Asia.

50. Quoted in Edward Said, *Orientalism* (New York: Vintage Books, 1979), p. 187. Flaubert was one of the more notable writers who contributed to the simultaneous idealization and debasement of prostitution in nineteenth-century France. I discuss elsewhere the relation between this representation and the role of France in the age of imperialism. Suffice it to say that prostitution as a mode of discourse of international relations was already evident in France at the time because of the latter's particular "sentimental relations" with the colonies until then—relations defined more by capital investments than by physical and military presence.

51. Quoted in Bello, Kinley, and Elinson, *Development Debacle,* p. 153.

52. Marlyn, quoted in Brenda Stoltzfus, "The Sale of Sexual Labor in the Philippines: Marlyn's Story," *Bulletin of Concerned Asian Scholars* 22, no. 4 (1990), p. 19.

53. Matsui, "Asian Migrant Women," p. 8. Compare this with another assessment: "Filipinos, mostly women, accounted for about 70 percent of all offenses committed by Asians in Japan in 1985, followed by Thais, 20 percent, and Koreans, 9 percent, a dubious distinction consistently maintained by Filipinos since 1982—a phenomenon which a top official of the Japanese immigration office perceived as an indication of the depressed Philippine economic condition." (Tono Haruhi, quoted in *Philippines Free Press* [4 April 1987], p. 15).

54. Matsui, "Asian Migrant Women," p. 12; and Tono Haruhi in *AMPO,* quoted in Schirmer and Shalom, eds., *The Philippines Reader,* p. 15.

55. Dueñas, "Filipina as Japayuki- San," p. 42.

56. V. G. Kiernan, *The Lords of Human Kind* (New York: Columbia University Press, 1986), p. 182. In other words, Japan had to show it was man enough to be treated like an imperial nation.

57. "Asian Migrant Women," p. 9.

58. Compare this with the perception of Filipinos as bearing diseases. It is not merely coincidental that AIDS has been represented as having spread in the Philippines mainly through the U.S. bases. The "tainted" relation between the Philippines and the United States only legitimates and aggravates the system of exploitation that Japan engages in. This is achieved, however, through not only representation but actual practice. For Japan's mode of relation with the Philippines is built upon or made possible through the system of exploitation that the United States had already established in its "special relations" with the Philippines.

59. Quoted in "Debt Crisis Burden Heaviest on Children," *Daily Globe* (30 December 1989).

60. Ibid.

61. Maranan, "Peace, Development, and Solidarity," p. 4.

EDWARD FOWLER

Minorities in a "Homogeneous" State: The Case of Japan

HOW CLOSE do stereotypes of a society match the invariably more complex realities? In what ways should we be concerned about the gap between them? What is at stake in downplaying that gap—or bringing it into bold relief? These questions are the subject of the following discussion, which considers a well-known stereotype: Japanese ethnocultural homogeneity.

John Dower's study of race hatreds between Japan and the United States, which were nurtured by a variety of propagandistic reproductions of the Other during World War II, has shown us the sweeping purposes to which racial stereotypes can be put, how they can persist over time (in some cases transformed but never dispelled), and how they "remain latent, capable of being revived by both sides in times of crisis and tension."[1]

We are clearly witnessing such a revival today. Ever since Japan emerged as a major economic power, and particularly since the early 1980s, the issue of race or ethnicity has been invoked almost reflexively both in the United States and in Japan, as if it provided all the answers to what makes the two countries different and why mutual antagonism is only natural. The recent flurry of Japan-bashing (*Nihon-tataki*) and America-bashing (*kenbei*) episodes demonstrates, moreover, both sides' keen awareness of the way in which facile appeals to racial/ethnic stereotypes can conceal a variety of potentially damning domestic ills, ranging from mediocre economic performance to misguided political leadership.

Important and useful though it is to examine the contrasting image that one society produces of its Other, it would not do to overlook certain similarities in either side's depiction of one and the same society. It is curious to note, for example, that *both* sides subscribe uncritically to the argument (to take, as shall be done here, the case of Japan) that the Japanese are a homogeneous race and therefore a harmonious people and that Americans are not; and that the argument is generally presented in a way designed to close discussion about national "essences," rather than to open it up.

211

But just what is meant here by "homogeneity"? I will try to get at that question by examining its obverse, as it is conceived in a society that frequently claims, at both official and private levels, to have no first-hand knowledge of ethnocultural or social diversity. An obvious place to begin is with foreign residents in Japan.

Throughout the postwar years and until as recently as a mere decade ago, "foreigner" to a Japanese was nearly synonymous with the colloquial expression *gaijin* ("outsider"), and *gaijin*, for all intents and purposes, meant American. This was hardly because Americans were the only foreigners in Japan. Rather, it was because the Americans were the one group of foreigners that the Japanese felt they had to contend with—the one group that demanded their undivided attention—for a variety of historical, political, and military reasons well known to anyone the least bit familiar with Japan's experience of war and occupation in the mid-twentieth century.

Significantly, *gaijin* was not used in reference to just any American. It meant, with few exceptions, white Americans, as well as Europeans in Japan who were mistaken for them. An African American, for example, was not a *gaijin*: he or she was a *kokujin*, or black. Descendants of Japanese living in the United States (and elsewhere outside Japan) were called *Nikkeijin*, or people of Japanese lineage—the emphasis being on the blood relation to their country of origin rather than on their non-Japanese nationality. In short, it was inconceivable in the Japanese worldview for two or more races or ethnic groups to occupy the same sociopolitical space.

This is perhaps understandable in a country where race and nationality have been taken throughout the modern period to be indivisible—the warp and woof of the same ideological cloth—and where the concept of ethnopolitical unity has served as the cornerstone of nationhood ever since the Meiji state began promulgating it in the interest of blunting provincial loyalties and buttressing the centralized rule of the state. Emerging from a long period of relative isolation and a system of government that for all its power more resembled a confederation than a nation-state, the Meiji oligarchy seized on the antiquity of the single, "unbroken" imperial line[2] (which ironically had grown nearly defunct after centuries of neglect) as the basis first for creating an "imagined community"[3] whose relative ethnic homogeneity transcended the cultural, linguistic, and economic diversity of the various feudal domains, and second, for mobilizing that community against the unprecedented danger of Western encroachment.

The identity of race/nation as conceived in the Meiji oligarchs' political imagination of course never fully matched the social reality (Japan has had its foreign and ethnic minorities since the beginning of recorded history); but it grew even more problematic with the advent of what is popularly called "internationalization" in the late 1970s. First, Japan became more cognizant of a variety of often conflicting definitions of social organization (i.e., those not necessarily predicated on the identity of race/nation). Second, citizens at the grass roots level began to recognize with the increase in foreign traffic (especially from other parts of Asia) to their country that "internationalization" meant the global circulation of *humans* as well as of goods and capital, and that there was considerably more to foreigners than *gaijin*. One read and heard with greater and greater frequency in the 1980s the appellation *gaikokujin* standing in for "foreigner." Like *gaijin*, the term denotes a noncitizen; unlike the latter, however, it does not connote a specific racial or ethnic background.

This was only natural: non-*gaijin* foreigners were visiting Japan in record numbers by the mid- to late-1980s; and the vast majority were clearly not tourists. They had come looking for work, and finding it, they remained, primarily in the major urban centers and often for extended periods, overstaying their visas and supporting themselves (and usually relatives in their homelands) as illegal aliens.[4] They were in Japan illegally because relatively few foreigners qualify for working visas, which are made available only to those with special "expertise" not in the possession of the domestic population.[5] It is these people—the Asian and African *gaikokujin* rather than the American and European *gaijin*—and their tenuous yet pivotal position in Japanese society that I wish to focus on here.

JAPAN'S GROWING ILLEGAL IMMIGRANT POPULATION

It should be noted that there is nothing new about the presence of illegal foreign workers in Japan. Thousands of *gaijin* (mostly Americans, of course) have worked in recent decades primarily as English teachers on nothing more than a tourist or student visa with the tacit approval of (or at least benign neglect by) authorities who like the employers gave first priority to the native English speakers' scarcity value (without giving a thought, it often seemed, to quality control). The determination of scarcity value itself derived from notions of what Japanese businessmen and bureaucrats deemed to be the requisite skills for emulating and competing with a technologically advanced culture. These notions were of course instilled in the Meiji period (1868–1912), when the state-sponsored program of rapid modernization, which included the hiring of European and Americans (*yatoi*) by the bureaucracy, was instituted.[6]

The phenomenon of illegal *gaikokujin* workers is an outgrowth of a decade-long trend that has made fellow Asians the largest single group of visitors overall to Japan.[7] Documentation is still sketchy, but one thing is certain even at this early stage: illegal workers have migrated to Japan in great numbers to fill the jobs that go begging in many of Japan's labor-intensive industries. Perhaps 200,000 to 300,000 *gaikokujin*, mostly Asians, work in thousands of shops and small factories, usually without even the minimum of benefits, in every major industrial area around Tokyo—from Kawaguchi to Kawasaki—and in many other of the country's metropolises as well.[8] They may be in less visible positions than the *gaijin* from the West (who typically work in schools or corporations or even on television), but they are far more numerous and hardly less needed. Indeed, the demand for labor in small industry greatly exceeds that for the field of English teaching, which is for *gaijin* the most plentiful source of jobs in Japan.

The demand will not slow down in the foreseeable future. In the midst of what is commonly characterized as a high-tech, postindustrial age, the need for manual labor and low-tech production persists unabated. In a recent survey, the Industrial Bank of Japan estimated that despite the massive entry of women into the labor force, the country could be short by as many as two million workers by the year 2000.[9] In the last few years male *gaikokujin* (the focus of this discussion), working primarily in manufacturing and construction, have come to outnumber female *gaikokujin*, who work primarily in the "water trade" (*mizu shôbai*) of bars, hostess clubs, strip joints, and cabarets.[10] That foreigners working in small and medium-sized corporations have become a major presence is revealed by a survey (compiled March-April 1990) of over two thousand firms in the greater Tokyo metropolitan area: one firm in seven employs foreigners, and 70 percent of those firms are hiring illegal workers.[11]

The numbers, in other words, are large enough to have effected a structural impact on these firms and by extension on the entire lower tier of Japan's so-called two-tiered economy, in which subcontractors compete for the business of the major firms by using cheap labor and thus help the latter control their costs in the national and international markets.[12] Foreign laborers are a boon in particular to firms lacking the capital to automate, since their services can be had for substantially less than what it costs to hire a Japanese for the same position. (Even when hourly wages for a Japanese are no higher, the benefits package and bonuses provide a much higher income overall.)

Two events in particular, both occurring in the mid-1980s, helped change the face of labor in Japan: the drop in oil prices and the rise in value of the yen. Lower oil prices caused the demand for foreign labor in the Middle East to dry up, and Japan became the labor market of choice for many of these workers, especially from such South Asian countries as Pakistan and Bangladesh. Meanwhile, Japanese industry, reeling from the strong yen and rising domestic wages and looking for ways to remain competitive in the international market, saw in foreign labor a way out of its difficulties.

The picture sketched here is based as much on personal observation and journalistic accounts as it is on sociological or other scholarly studies. The phenomenon under discussion is too recent, the data too scant and undigested, not to require a more "hands-on" form of research, however lacking in statistical corroboration. Anyone living in metropolitan Tokyo in the late 1980s (as I did, from 1988–1990) could not help but notice the rapid influx of Asian and African workers into Japan—and (perhaps more important) the media's reaction to what was identified more and more frequently as a "problem."[13] It was a problem, of course (although the media rarely hinted at why), because the presence of these recently immigrated foreigners inevitably brought attention to the foreigners and ethnic minorities *already* living in Japan. This latest influx of foreigners, in other words, supplied the catalyst for reexamining Japan's celebrated myth of ethnocultural homogeneity.

My own acquaintance with foreign workers originated with explorations of several neighborhoods in Tokyo's "Low City" (Shitamachi). I took particular interest first in a run-down district northeast of Ueno known as San'ya, home to most of Tokyo's large day laborer population, and second in a small section of Sumida Ward, where the nation's principal leather-tanning district is located (roughly two out of every three pigskins in Japan are processed here) and where central Tokyo's largest population (2500) of *burakumin*, the descendants of outcastes, is concentrated.[14]

Explorations of these and other sections of the city have made me realize just how much our (and by "our" I mean we scholars, journalists, and other visitors of privilege) view of Tokyo and of Japan in general is colored by the people we typically associate with: educators, intellectuals, and other defenders of majority culture, as well as the urban samurai of corporate businessmen and bureaucrats. Associations with such like-minded groups have led, not surprisingly, to mere corroborations of the Japanese state's presentation of itself as a seamless ethnopolitical entity.[15]

My own associations in recent years have provided a different perspective, however. We often hear that "the Japanese are different from you and me,"[16] and this may be true as far as it goes; but what too frequently gets lost in the discussion is the fact that the Japanese are also quite different from each other. This, at any rate, is the lesson that my perambulations have taught me. The myth of Japanese homogeneity—still perpetrated by cultural arbiters keen on preserving a nostalgic vision of racial "purity" and bent on mobilizing diverse groups for the benefit of the state—is easily shown for the distortion that it is as soon as one takes to the streets, and if one is in Tokyo, moves beyond the corporate, financial, bureaucratic, and political centers of, say, Marunouchi, Ōtemachi, Kasumigaseki, and Nagata-chô.

THE MEANING OF SOCIAL DIVERSITY IN JAPAN

For Japan scholars who have made a considerable career investment in presenting the subject of their study as a political or ethnic or cultural monolith, it is tempting to ignore the actual diversity. The problem of describing contemporary Japanese society, however, in ways that make good sense empirically as well as enable us to recognize the interconnectedness between Japan and the world community requires that we begin reading the country in a radically different manner from the way we have read it in the past. As for the nature of this radicality, we might take a hint from Edgar Allen Poe's well-known story, "The Purloined Letter," in which the amateur detective C. Auguste Dupin is able to track down an incriminating letter that has been invisible to everyone else, including the prefect of the Parisian police, even though it has been lying virtually under everyone's nose all the while. I am not so interested here in the Lacanian claim for this story that the signifier can function independently of the signified (i.e., a letter can generate effects even when its contents are unknown)[17] as I am concerned with how the sign itself (the statist message of "homogeneity," in the context of this discussion) becomes a subterfuge for a separate agenda altogether.[18]

The following example provides an illustration. In the fall of 1986, Nakasone Yasuhiro, who was then prime minister of Japan, lectured to members of his own ruling Liberal Democratic party on why Japan had been so successful as an economic power. Among the factors he stressed was education—not simply the curriculum per se, but also the receptivity to that curriculum, that is to say, the ability of students to learn it. He argued that education was an easier task in Japan because the country had a homogeneous population, unlike that of the United States, which was facing difficulties because of its large numbers of blacks and Hispanics.[19]

The foreign press soon picked up Nakasone's comments, prompting an immediate reaction from various minority groups in the United States, who condemned Nakasone for ignoring the political and economic determinants of educational discrepancies in favor of a bogus biological determinism. Jesse Jackson visited Japan to protest personally what he termed an "insult" to African Americans.[20] Yet what no one seemed to notice during the entire exchange was how poorly Nakasone's characterization of Japan actually fit Japanese society—and here of course I am talking about the sign as subterfuge. It is precisely this description, too often taken as a neutral "given," that we must scrutinize in order to decode the message of homogeneity. The invocation by politicians, educators, and other cultural arbiters of Japanese society's essential difference *from* other societies (in short, the discourse of *Nihonjin-ron*, of which Nakasone's remarks are merely one recent example)[21] has been the state's most consistently reliable and powerful means of concealing—and ultimately suppressing—differences *within* society.

By difference I am referring first of all to ethnic diversity. There are perhaps two and a half million people living in Japan who are not ethnically Japanese: the aboriginal Ainu (now mostly mixed blood), for example; the migrant workers discussed above, mostly illegal aliens from South and Southeast Asia; legal resident aliens such as the Koreans and Chinese; and

Okinawans, who are Japanese nationals with a history of state-sanctioned suppression.[22] This is admittedly a small percentage of a population of some 125 million, but still large enough to call into question the popular image of a racially "pure" nation-state.

The suppression of difference appears in less obvious ways with various other groups, disenfranchised not by ethnicity but by occupation, who live at the margins of Japanese society. For them to become visible to us, however, we must effect a change in our hermeneutic register, much as Dupin did in "The Purloined Letter." We cannot think simply in terms of ethnicity as the basis for social heterogeneity, as we commonly do in the United States. We must also think in terms of class and even of caste.

An example of the former is the lumpen proletariat, comprising largely day laborers, numbering in the hundreds of thousands and concentrated in the larger urban areas. Although quite recognizable as a group, these people (nearly all men) remain curiously out of the view of society at large, because they are generally kept to themselves in centrally located but physically isolated areas like San'ya in Tokyo or Kotobuki-chô in Yokohama or Kamagasaki in Osaka.[23] Day laborers rarely venture out to other parts of these cities except to work and generally change into their livery only after making the commute to the work site. Unnoticed or ignored by majority society, they are known only by their work—the countless construction and road-building projects that dot the landscape. Majority Japanese likewise rarely venture *into* the haunt of the day laborer. My own experience from talking with Tokyo residents—and these include academics and even newspaper reporters—is that surprisingly few even know exactly where a neighborhood like San'ya is. It turns out that this and other day laborer quarters are at once eminently accessible and yet nearly invisible.

An example of caste is provided by the two to three million descendants of outcastes known as *burakumin*.[24] The rigidly hierarchical system of social organization that characterized the Tokugawa Period (1600–1868) was officially outlawed more than a century ago. In 1869, the year after the Meiji Restoration, the samurai were disenfranchised and put on an equal legal footing with the other three classes of peasants, artisans, and merchants. (They retained exalted status as *shizoku,* which, however, had no legal privileges.) Two years later, in 1871, the outcastes were given full rights of citizenship in the new nation-state.[25] But to take this legal assimilation at face value is to ignore the grim reality of a minority living even today in apartheid-like conditions and still largely restricted to certain hereditary occupations—including slaughtering, leather tanning, sewage treatment, and garbage collecting—that no other group in Japan will undertake.

No other *Japanese* group, that is, as is immediately apparent from a walk through Higashi Sumida in Tokyo's Sumida Ward, home to more than two hundred tiny factories and sweatshops that make up the city's principal leather-tanning center.[26] An informal count taken at perhaps two or three dozen of these factories, which typically open right out onto the streets, revealed about half the workers to be foreigners.[27] The majority are from South Asia, but many hail from Southeast Asia and Africa as well. I encountered workers from Bangladesh, Sri Lanka, Pakistan, Iran, and Nigeria, but many other countries are also no doubt represented.[28] Indeed, they are there in such great numbers now that the industry would face collapse without them.[29]

Male foreign laborers are by and large still in their twenties, attracted by wages that are astronomical compared to what might be offered at home. One Sri Lankan, a three-year resident of Japan and a two-year veteran of pigskin tanning, told me that he could earn in two weeks at his Tokyo shop what it would have taken him a whole year to earn in Colombo. His dream was to build a house near his parents' home on the money he had earned in Japan.[30] In his late twenties, he had already had considerable experience in the international labor market, having worked in Switzerland and Hong Kong before coming to Japan. His two brothers (one fresh out of school; the other, with a wife and children in Sri Lanka, who had quit his subsistence-level job with the postal service to earn more money for his family) also worked in the same neighborhood. Like many of his counterparts from other Third World countries, he is a relatively well-educated member of his home country's middle class.[31] Workers changed jobs frequently, using brokers (often foreigners themselves) as middlemen. They were commonly housed on the factory premises for convenience and to avoid detection and possible deportation by immigration agents during a commute.[32] They typically worked nine or ten hours a day, six days a week, earned two to three hundred thousand yen a month, and sent half to two-thirds of their earnings home to their families.

IMMIGRANTS: JAPAN'S NEW OUTCASTES?

With the rise in affluence since the Tokyo Olympics in 1964, but especially since the late 1970s, when the country recovered from its second "oil shock," Japanese have become less willing to soil their hands in occupations associated with the three Ks: *kiken, kitanai,* and *kitsui.* Let us call them the three Ds: dangerous, dirty, and physically draining—to which we could add a fourth D: demeaning. In recent years the younger generation of *burakumin* have become less involved in the kinds of work that are so deeply stigmatized by tradition. The Sri Lankan mentioned above expressed his awareness of the majority society's distaste for the sort of job in which he was employed. He also confirmed what was obvious even to the casual observer:

that there are very few Japanese under the age of forty working in any of the factories.

The Sri Lankan's remarks hint at a major transformation taking place in Japanese society. What we are seeing here, I think, is the creation of a new pariah class: that of the Asian and African *gaikokujin*. This new social configuration, defined by nationality, is no doubt less onerous in the minds of Japanese looking for ways to rid society of its domestic caste system, because the immigrant population is readily identifiable (and thus "naturalized" objects of discrimination) as alien in a way that *burakumin*, of course, never were.

The work of foreign laborers is by no means limited to the traditional occupations of the *burakumin*. Yet the fact remains that they are generally employed in the kind of demeaning occupations that however valuable to the economy, invite the contempt of majority Japanese. Prejudice is the result of another factor as well. That it did not occur to most Japanese to discriminate against the *gaijin* who preceded the wave of *gaikokujin* laborers is due not merely to the relative prestige of the jobs they hold but also to the position enjoyed by the countries they came from in the geopolitical hierarchy as interpreted by the Japanese. *Gaijin* came from countries on which Japan has based its political and cultural aspirations. In short, Japan has looked down on the rest of the world precisely to the degree to which it has looked up to the West; regions in which Japan has extended its political, military, or economic influence during the course of this century, moreover, are precisely those which supply the bulk of foreign labor to Japan.[33]

And here is the rub, of course. Japanese officialdom, still caught up in the social and political myths of its own making about homogeneity (which foreground the more obvious racial differences such as those between "Oriental" and "Caucasian" in an attempt to obscure, in a far more subtle and systematic way, the ethnic, political, and even linguistic similarities that exist between Japanese and other Asians), is trying to figure out ways to slow down or even prevent the flow of *gaikokujin* into Japan—even as Japanese (and other) multinationals and a "borderless" economy have helped create an environment in places like South and Southeast Asia that has in effect hampered internal development and forced workers to earn hard currency abroad.[34] Officials in Tokyo worry about the example of "guest workers" (southern Europeans, mostly Turks, Yugoslavs, and Italians) in countries like the former West Germany, and this is the lesson they have drawn: people who migrate for economic reasons often stay on for social ones, at times to the irritation of the home population.[35]

The oft-cited "failure" of the German example turns out on closer inspection to be in part a convenient misconstrual: Germany's economy, facing a severe labor shortage from the 1950s on, was aided immensely by the massive influx of foreign workers, many of whom decided to stay permanently.

If there was a "failure," it was due to the misguided faith in a rotation system designed to treat foreign laborers like replaceable machine parts and to hinder long-term residency.[36] Or, as one Swiss writer succinctly observed of his own country, where at least one quarter of the labor force is non-Swiss: "What we wanted was a labor pool. What we got were human beings."[37] Human beings who interact with their social environments; who remain longer than planned; who get married (sometimes to nationals of the host country) and have children; who come to expect the benefits accruing to other members of that society.

Fearing the logical consequence of opening Japan's doors to foreign workers—their assimilation into Japanese society—the bureaucracy has dragged its feet on policy decisions, calling for more and more studies while tightening immigration laws.[38] It has overlooked one thing, however, in its effort to legislate control of immigration: policy has consistently lagged behind reality. Asian and African *gaikokujin* are *already* in Japan in great numbers, and they are there because Japanese industry needs them desperately. The issue, as Hachiya Takashi so aptly puts it, is not how to prevent the influx of immigrants—an impossible task given the high demand for unskilled and semi-skilled labor in Japan and the limited capacity to stop the flow[39]—but how best to accommodate the many foreigners, who are very willing and capable workers, to the needs of small and medium-sized industry in Japan. Moreover, as Tessa Morris-Suzuki argues, the accommodation should naturally result in fair compensation and respect for human rights.[40] Instead of looking to other countries plagued by their own xenophobia and pointing to failed examples of integration, the Japanese ought to be examining the successes, like that of the Dutch assimilation of Indonesians in the immediate postwar period, which are the direct result of aggressive national planning.[41] Indeed, Hachiya provocatively suggests that the policies instituted henceforth will determine the kind of country Japan will become in the twenty-first century.[42]

The bureaucrats have other reasons to worry, of course. The presence of illegal foreign laborers has ironically drawn attention to another population of *legal* yet extremely marginalized aliens who are neither *gaijin* nor *gaikokujin* and who have been in Japan since the early twentieth century. I am referring to Japan's Korean minority, (*zai-Nichi Kankokujin, zai-Nichi Chôsenjin*), the legacy of Japan's military and economic adventurism on the Asian continent earlier in this century, and more specifically, of its colonization of Korea from 1910 to 1945.[43] About 680,000 North and South Koreans reside in Japan, and roughly 300,000 more have become naturalized Japanese. Most of them are the descendants of Koreans who were removed, often by force, to Japan before and during the Pacific War and have never set foot in their "native" land. The majority live in the Kansai region (western Japan), and the largest community is in Osaka. Although born and raised in

Japan, they enjoy few of the economic and social benefits available to majority Japanese and are victims of discrimination in education, employment, and marriage.[44]

The situation of Koreans (and of the Chinese, another minority whose history of residency also dates to the prewar years) in Japan differs considerably, of course, from that of the *gaikokujin* workers from South and Southeast Asia. The former are legal and usually long-term residents, whereas the latter are usually temporary and nearly all illegal. But this distinction should not obscure the general trend of Asians from various parts of the continent being called on to do more and more of the work in Japan that the Japanese are unwilling to do. Koreans have for decades been doing in the Kansai area, centering on Osaka, what South and Southeast Asian *gaikokujin* in particular have been called on to do more recently in the Kantô area, centering on Tokyo: namely, work in the small factories and sweatshops that subcontract work from the industry giants and that in effect subsidize the latter's competitiveness on the international market by recruiting the cheapest labor available.

It hardly needs mentioning how deeply this particular configuration of labor has affected and will continue to affect the Japanese view of what might be termed the "Asian community," if only in the ironic mode. By equating the person with the occupation, the Japanese have assigned the people from an entire continent to membership in an inferior race, as if they were naturally suited to the demeaning tasks for which they have been recruited. Michael Weiner's description of Korean laborers in Japan before World War II has relevance for the present situation of Third World workers in Japan. "While Koreans were for the most part excluded from the skilled labor market, they were regarded as, *by nature,* ideally suited for dirty, taxing and often dangerous work in industries which were normally avoided by Japanese workers. ... But, above all, it was their status as colonial workers which determined ... relations between Koreans and the Japanese majority society."[45] Korea is of course no longer a Japanese colony. But migrant workers from Korea and other parts of Asia that were formerly under Japanese domination almost inevitably confront a legacy of prejudice that long preceded their journeys to Japan.

JAPANESE ''HOMOGENEITY'': RHETORIC AND REALITY

It is not my intention here to become preoccupied with the peculiarity or particularity of the Japanese case. Indeed, readers will no doubt detect certain parallels to the experience of other developed countries that make use of migrant labor.[46] I simply wish to call attention to the fact that the Japanese state's well-publicized project of socialization has not been the complete success story that it is often made out to be both in Japan and abroad. What success it has had, moreover, has frequently been made at the cost of denying numerous groups, through various acts of nonaccommodation, the benefits of assimilation and forcing other groups to assimilate with no regard whatsoever to their ethnic integrity.

To dwell at all on the Japanese myth of homogeneity is of course to beg a larger question: does it really matter that Japanese society is a more varied, a more diverse, a more heterogeneous society—in terms of race and class and caste—than is generally acknowledged? Does it matter that Japan, too, has its ethnic minorities, for example, if not on the scale of a United States or a China or the former Soviet Union, then at least on a scale comparable to many European or some of the smaller Asian nations? Needless to say, I think that the answer is Yes, it does matter, it matters crucially. The reason has to do with the country's place in the global community.

Ever since the Meiji Restoration in 1868, the ruling regime has sought to mobilize the Japanese citizenry in an effort to meet the challenge of modernization and Western imperialism. It succeeded in large measure by exploiting another myth—that of an unbroken imperial line[47]—that could claim the loyalty of all Japanese of the blood and unite them against the outside threat. Differences between groups within Japan—however real and exacerbated they might be—were downplayed in the interest of focusing the country's attention on what was insistently (and sometimes hysterically) presented as the *overriding* difference: that of being Japanese or non-Japanese. Interests between these two last groups were seen as either mutually exclusive or only coincidentally convergent.

This cult of nation served its purpose well in the Meiji period when the state was trying to extricate itself from the threat of foreign domination and the bind of extraterritoriality. But this totalizing narrative of an embattled Japanese race engaged in the quest for political legitimacy in the eyes of the West tended to suppress any energies that ran counter to statist goals. When those goals took an imperialist turn, particularly after the annexation of Korea in 1910, and Japan had to look for a more universal value than ethnic or racial purity on which to base its colonial rule, it faced the inevitable contradiction of appealing to its Asianness abroad in its confrontation with Western imperialism, even as it engaged in a repressive containment of Asian minorities at home.

After the war, faced with territorial dissolution and economic collapse, an occupied Japan rallied to pull itself up from the ashes of its burned-out cities and forge ahead with the task of rebuilding. Nearly a half century after war's end, however, the prewar ethos appears to have survived virtually intact. Government leaders continue to nurture a siege mentality vis-à-vis a vaguely defined but seemingly ever-present external threat and to channel people's resources and energies into activities that however "privately" motivated, have neatly dovetailed with the "public" good: investing personal income, for example, on a scale little known elsewhere in the world into savings (thus helping fuel corporate Japan's capital development, but necessitated in large part by Japan's unrelentingly exorbitant housing market); working overtime (in an environment that often makes extra labor compulsory) to meet organizational and production goals; nursing children through the "examination hell" in the competition (if successful) for them to become members of the educated elite and in preparation (if unsuccessful) to follow docilely the elite that has succeeded; buying an ever-increasing number of frenetically marketed consumer goods (often at prices that subsidize their cheaper sale abroad). This quasi-official, semipermanent mobilization that underwrites Japan's policy of "export or perish" has continued long after any threat to the nation's survival disappeared. The ramifications of this policy for the world economy are too well known to require comment here.

But there is another aspect of this "us"-versus-"them" policy that is less obvious yet perhaps even more significant. Japan's self-perception of living in a hostile international environment—that it is a nation forever embattled—helps promote ideological conformity at home and a united front in dealing with the outside world. The active (indeed, obsessive) nurturing of this self-perception by the state demonstrates the stakes involved in the claim to homogeneity. The myth of Japanese uniqueness, then, goes hand in hand with the ideological construct of a beleaguered nation that must forever circle its wagons in an attempt to minimize the impact from abroad—even as it asserts its own expansive presence around the globe. In short, the belief in ethnopolitical homogeneity directly serves the rhetoric of continuous national crisis: intranational issues, however pressing, are strictly subordinated to the international agenda. The lack of an outside threat therefore poses a great danger for the ideologues of homogeneity. Indeed, in the absence of such a threat, the state is in effect compelled to invent one. Thus, Japan continues to operate, even in peacetime, in a constant state of yellow alert.

It goes without saying that any parallels that might be drawn between what I am calling here Japan's rhetoric of national crisis and the cold war rhetoric of the United States are entirely intentional, for the strategy of creating external enemies and of mobilizing domestic resources to confront these so-called threats for the profit of a small segment of society is hardly unique to Japan. Recent revelations about the constructed nature of the cold war have made us more cognizant of how deeply a totalizing worldview affects the domestic political culture. Mary Kaldor notes, for example, how "The idea of an East-West conflict, the invocation of the 'other,'"[48] was a means by which governments could manage domestic conflicts *within* East and West:

I use the term "imaginary war" to describe this process. "Deterrence" did not represent preparation for some future war; rather, it was a way of acting out the East-West conflict day after day throughout the postwar period. Through military exercises, the deployment of troops and weapons, the scenarios of military planners, the games of espionage and counterespionage, and the research, development and production of military technology we behaved as though we were in a war situation, as though World War II had never really ended. This imaginary war had profound consequences for the way society was organized in both East and West. There were two distinct systems in East and West. ... But [they] were not in conflict. On the contrary, they complemented each other. They shared a need for an imaginary war.[49]

Kaldor does not mention Japan in her description; but it is surely no coincidence that Japan has loomed and will no doubt continue to loom particularly large on the horizon as U.S. policymakers scramble to construct a new enemy in the wake of the cold war. If Japan has not skipped a beat while the United States frantically shifts gears, it is because the antagonist for Japan has remained intact: the entire outside world, which has for all intents and purposes meant the West.

A new "antagonist" for Japan, however, may be slipping in through the back door. The flood of migrant workers has forced Japan to recognize that its global policies can no longer be passed off as "business as usual," because they have direct domestic repercussions that strike at the very heart of the nation's identity. A Dutch official's lament about the Netherlands in the 1970s is if anything even more relevant to the situation in present-day Japan: "We're up against a new problem: that of economic refugees. The Third World is coming to us, not for political reasons but simply because the economic prospects are so poor if they remain."[50] What Japan is learning, of course, is the social dimension to these "economic" refugees. Japan's policies of global expansion, quite suddenly in historical terms and quite without explanation by the leadership to the general public, have, in short, come home to roost.

In 1885, Fukuzawa Yukichi, the celebrated educator and leader of the Japanese "enlightenment," wrote an oft-cited editorial in *Jiji shimpô* advocating that Japan extricate itself from the legacy of its geographic proximity to the Asian mainland:

Not only have we escaped the old habits of Japan, but we have devised a new strategy concerning Asian countries; its fundamental idea is "escape from Asia." ... Today China and Korea are no help at all to our country. On the contrary, because our three countries are adjacent we are sometimes regarded as the same in the eyes of civilized Western peoples. ... It is really a great misfortune for our country. It follows that in making our present plans we have not time to await the development of neighboring countries and join them in reviving Asia.

Rather, we should escape from them and join the company of Western civilized nations. Although China and Korea are our neighbors, this fact should make no difference in our relations with them. We should deal with them as Westerners do. If we keep bad company, we cannot avoid a bad name. In my heart I favor breaking off with the bad company of East Asia.[51]

Today, a century after Fukuzawa proposed that Japan leap out of Asia and embrace the cultural hegemony of the west, Asian *gaikokujin* threaten to leap into Japan, and in doing so, reveal the character of Japanese culture in a way that *gaijin* employees, official and unofficial, have never been in a position to do.

CONCLUSION

In early October 1990, riots broke out in the streets of Kamagasaki, the Osaka counterpart of San'ya and the largest day laborer ghetto in Japan, and continued for a week. The events were reported widely in the U.S. press. Typical of these reports is a *New York Times* article that I believe sets quite succinctly the tone for how the situation was viewed in this country: "On the surface, most Japanese view their country as a classless society prizing harmony and consensus among its many contending forces. Every once in a while, however, an incident occurs that exposes stresses, conflicts and antisocial behavior underneath the placid exterior."[52] The article reports that the riot was the largest to have taken place in Osaka in thirty years. It fails to suggest, however, that it was only the latest of several dozen disturbances that have shaken the country's day laborer ghettos during those decades.[53] If reporters in the United States passed over earlier incidents silently, it is only because Japan itself was not "news" in the way that it has become of late.

What I wish to suggest in conclusion, then, is that terms like "harmony," "consensus," and "placid exterior," which are so often employed in accounts of Japan, do not do an honest job of describing the society *even under ordinary circumstances*. The Japanese, it turns out, are like any nation: an amalgam of diverse groups with sometimes radically conflicting interests. In trying to achieve a better understanding of those groups and those interests, we must be wary of explanations by Japanese sources and even by many Japan watchers, who in deferring to the ideology of consensus have generally abetted the image of the monolithic Japanese state. The need for reading minorities—both Japanese and non-Japanese—in ways that avoid the pitfalls of the Parisian prefect's investigation in "The Purloined Letter" is perhaps more urgent than ever before. Whether or not our success is as spectacular as that of

Dupin remains to be seen, but the time has surely come for us to change our hermeneutic register.

NOTES

1. John W. Dower, *War Without Mercy: Race and Power in the Pacific War* (New York: Pantheon Books, 1986), p. 13.

2. See, for example, Changsoo Lee and George DeVos, *Koreans in Japan: Ethnic Conflict and Accommodation* (Berkeley: University of California Press, 1981), pp. 3–13, for a brief review of recent archaeological evidence *against* an "unbroken" imperial line "unsullied" by non-Japanese blood and for a description of the Shintô role in constructing "a sense of uniqueness for Japanese ethnicity" (p. 13).

3. The term, of course, is Benedict Anderson's. See his *Imagined Communities: Reflections on the Origin and Spread of Nationalism* (London: Verso, 1983), esp. pp. 89–93, for a discussion of Japanese nationalism.

4. Hachiya Takashi, in *Soredemo gaikokujin rôdôsha wa yatte kuru* (Tokyo: Nikkan Kôgyô Shimbunsha, 1991), p. 6, notes that the influx of foreign laborers in Japan became particularly noticeable around 1987.

5. As of 1989 approximately 60,000 foreigners (or roughly 0.1 percent of the total labor force) were working in Japan legally, mostly in entertainment but also in sports and certain professions. See Shigeru Shimoyama, "The Shadow Work Force," *Intersect*, Vol. 5 (July 1989), p. 12.

6. See H. J. Jones, *Live Machines: Hired Foreigners and Meiji Japan* (Vancouver: University of British Columbia Press, 1980), for a history of this small (roughly 3,000) but influential group of foreign workers.

7. Asians had become a majority of the total by 1988. See Shimoyama, "The Shadow Work Force," p. 11.

8. The life of a *gaikokujin* day laborer, for example, is described in Ray Ventura, "The Color of Life in Japan: A Filipino Day Laborer's Diary," *AMPO Japan-Asia Quarterly Review,* Vol. 20, No. 4 & Vol. 21, No. 1 (1989), pp. 50–53. See also the special issue on foreign workers, "Japan's Human Imports," *AMPO Japan-Asian Quarterly Review,* Vol. 19, No. 4 (1988), pp. 2–37; and Shimoyama, "The Shadow Work Force," pp. 11–18.

9. Shimoyama, "The Shadow Work Force," p. 17. This demand has occurred at a time when Japanese labor is in shorter and shorter supply. The decline in the pool of young domestic workers is to reach its lowest ebb in 1995; the overall supply, in 2000. See Hachiya, *Soredemo gaikokujin rôdôsha wa yatte kuru,* p. 3. See also Kantô Bengoshikai Rengôkai, *Gaikokujin rôdôsha no shûrô to jinken* (Tokyo: Akashi Shoten 1990), p. 176 ("Shiryô 3").

10. For a discussion of female workers in Japan, see Yayori Matsui, "Asian Migrant Women Working at Sex Industry in Japan Victimized by International Trafficking," *In God's Image* (June 1990), pp. 6–13.

11. Hachiya, *Soredemo gaikokujin rôdôsha wa yatte kuru,* pp. 37–38.

12. Dorinne K. Kondo, *Crafting Selves: Power, Gender, and Discourses of Identity in a Japanese Workplace* (Chicago: University of Chicago Press, 1990), p. 51, notes

that this economic distinction translates into significantly "disparate images of life-style, stability, and cultural worth."

13. See, for example, a five-part series on foreign laborers, entitled "Atarashii rinjin: gaikokujin rôdôsha mondai o kangaeru," *Yomiuri shimbun,* May 19–July 25, 1990.

14. Kawamoto Shôichi and Fujisawa Yasusuke, *Tôkyô no bisabetsu buraku: jittai, rekishi, genjô* (Tokyo: San'ichi Shobô, 1984), p. 23. Known prior to the Meiji Restoration as *eta,* this group was excluded along with *hinin* in the Edo Period from the hierarchical caste system of samurai/peasant/artisan/merchant. *Eta,* whose leather (used in footwear and armor) was highly valued by the samurai, were the objects of severe discrimination due to socioreligious taboos on the killing of animals. *Hinin* included a variety of outcastes, from executioners to prostitutes, whose social position was actually lower than *eta* but who could be reinstated into their previous social stations. Both groups are ethnically identical to majority Japanese, but tend even today to live in separate communities known as *buraku.* See Kawamoto and Fujisawa, *Tôkyô nohisabetsu buruku,* passim, for information on Tokyo *buraku.*

For a succinct discussion of *buraku* and other minorities in Japan, see David Coates, ed., "Shattering the Myth of the Homogeneous Society: Minority Issues and Movements in Japan," *JPRN Monograph Series,* No. 4 (Berkeley, CA: Japan Pacific Resource Network, 1990), which includes a useful bibliography.

15. Ezra Vogel, *Japan As Number One: Lessons for America* (Cambridge, MA: Harvard University Press, 1979), for example, although acknowledging minority groups and ethnic discords in Japan, tones them down considerably in the interest of presenting his model for a smooth-running postindustrial society. See pp. 198, 239.

16. I allude to an article by James Fallows by the same title, *Atlantic Monthly,* Vol. 258 (September 1986), pp. 35–41. See also two other articles by the same author, "Playing by Different Rules," and "Containing Japan," *Atlantic Monthly,* Vol. 260 (September 1987), pp. 22–32; and Vol. 263 (May 1989), pp. 40–54, respectively, for some perceptive social analyses that, however, are too preoccupied with differences *between* Japan and the United States to take much note of the diversity *within* Japanese society.

17. See for example, Jacques Lacan, "Seminar on 'The Purloined Letter'" (trans. Jeffrey Mehlman), in John P. Muller and William J. Richardson, eds., *The Purloined Poe: Lacan, Derrida & Psychoanalytic Reading* (Baltimore: Johns Hopkins University Press, 1988), pp. 28–54, esp. pp. 45–46; and Muller and Richardson, "Lacan's Seminar on 'The Purloined Letter': Overview," in Miller and Richardson, eds., *The Purloined Poe,* pp. 55–76, esp. pp. 57–58.

18. In using the word "sign," I am thinking in particular of the notion of exemplarity embedded in it, as articulated by Irene Harvey: "Transforming something into an example of something else can be seen as on the one hand, making it into a *sign* for something else and, on the other, making it into a *case* or a particular instance of something more general for which it stands and which, as an example or illustration, it concretizes." See "Structures of Exemplarity in Poe, Freud, Lacan, and Derrida," in Muller and Richardson, *The Purloined Poe,* p. 253.

19. Nakasone Yasuhiro, "Zensairoku: Nakasone Shushô 'chiteki suijun' kôen," *Chûô kôron* (November 1986), p. 152.

20. Tomoji Ishi, "Nakasone's Racial Remarks and International Dynamism in Race Relations," *JPRN Monograph Series*, No. 1 (Berkeley, CA: Japan Pacific Resouce Network, March 1987), p. 8.

21. For a review of the literature, see Peter N. Dale, *The Myth of Japanese Uniqueness* (New York: St. Martin's Press, 1986).

22. For recent accounts of Okinawa's position within the Japanese state, see Norma Field, *In the Realm of a Dying Emperor* (New York, Pantheon Books, 1991), pp. 33–104; and Steve Rabson, trans., *Okinawa: Two Postwar Novellas by Ôshiro Tatsuhiro and Higashi Muneo* (Berkeley, CA: Institute of East Asian Studies, 1989), pp. 1–31.

23. For a description of life in these ghettos, see for example, Brett de Bary, "Sanya: Japan's Internal Colony," in E. Patricia Tsurumi, ed., *The Other Japan* (Armonk, NY: M. E. Sharpe, 1988), pp. 112–118; Edward Fowler, "San'ya: Reflections on Life at the Margins of Japanese Society," *Transactions of the Asiatic Society of Japan*, Series 4, Vol. 6 (1991), forthcoming; and Miyashita Tadako, *San'ya nisshi* (Tokyo: Ningen no Kagaku Sha, 1977).

24. The official estimate of just over one million takes into account only the census figures for clearly identified *buraku* ghettos and fails to include several prefectures (most notably Tokyo) at all, nor does it include the very large number of *burakumin* who have "passed," at least temporarily, into majority society. See Roger Yoshino and Sueo Murakoshi, *The Invisible Visible Minority: Japan's Burakumin* (Osaka: Buraku Kaiho Kenkyusho, 1977), pp. 63–65.

25. For background information on this group, the standard work is George DeVos and Hiroshi Wagatsuma, *Japan's Invisible Race: Caste in Culture and Personality* (Berkeley: University of California Press, 1967). See also Yoshino and Murakoshi, *The Invisible Visible Minority;* John D. Donoghue, *Pariah Persistence in Changing Japan: A Case Study* (Washington, DC: University Press of America, 1977); and Ian Neary, *Political Protest and Social Control in Pre-war Japan: The Origins of* Buraku *Liberation* (Manchester, UK: Manchester University Press, 1989). Frank K. Upham, *Law and Social Change in Postwar Japan* (Cambridge, MA: Harvard University Press, 1987); and Susan J. Pharr, *Losing Face: Status Politics in Japan* (Berkeley: University of California Press, 1990), also include sections on *burakumin* (Ch. 3, "Instrumental Violence and the Struggle for Buraku Liberation"; and Ch. 5, "Burakumin Protest: The Incident at Yôka High School," respectively).

26. Kawamoto and Fujisawa, *Tôkyô no hisabestu buraku*, p. 24.

27. Hachiya's estimate of two hundred foreign laborers working in this area would seem to be a conservative one. Figures are unstable at best, because of periodic government raids and deportations. See *Soredemo gaikokujin rôdôsha wa yatte kuru*, p. 25.

28. Other likely nationalities, based on foreign residents in Japan with trainee (*kenshû*) visas, would include: China, Ghana, India, Indonesia, Malaysia, the Philippines, and Thailand. (See Hachiya, *Soredemo gaikokujin rôdôsha wa yatte kuru*, p. 112 and passim.)

29. Hachiya quotes an industry leader as saying that the presence of foreign laborers is a matter of life and death for the leather industry, and that he regrets the Tokyo prefectural government's unwillingness to advocate legalization of unskilled foreign labor in Japan. See *Soredemo gaikokujin rôdôsha wa yatte kuru*, p. 26. The extent of the foreign laborers' impact on the industry is realized upon a reading of Kawamoto

and Fujisawa (*Tôkyô no hisabetsu buraku,* pp. 29–30), who predicted only a few years earlier the industry's decline in the face of liberalized import laws and a vigorous foreign market.

30. This dream is not only realizable but also fairly typical. See Hachiya, *Soredemo gaikokujin rôdôsha wa yatte kuru,* p. 58.

31. I met one worker in the same area who holds a doctorate. Hachiya also observes that foreign workers tend to come from middle-class backgrounds, for only those with some means can afford the 400,000- to 500,000-yen cost (airplane ticket, broker's fee, and settling-in expenses) involved in traveling to Japan. See *Soredemo gaikokujin rôdôsha wa yatte kuru,* pp. 29, 39–40. Hachiya quotes a survey of thirty metal-galvanizing firms employing illegal aliens that reveals 90 percent to have at least a high school education. Tessa Morris-Suzuki also notes the generally high level of education among immigrant workers to Japan. See "Imin rôdôsha—shinwa to genjitsu: Oranda to Eikoku no rei kara," *Sekai,* No. 542 (June 1990), pp. 332, 337.

32. Communal apartment living, in which as many as half a dozen men share a small room, is a more typical arrangement in other areas of Tokyo, including the so-called ethnic triangle (Ikebukuro/Ôkubo/Kabuki-chô) on the city's west side and several older industrial neighborhoods on the east side.

33. This is the observation of a number of commentators. See for example, Tessa Morri-Suzuki, "Imin rôdôsha—shinwa to genjitsu," p. 333.

34. John Berger puts it this way: "Migrant workers come from underdeveloped economies. The term 'underdeveloped' has caused diplomatic embarrassment. The word 'developing' has been substituted. 'Developing' as distinct from 'developed.' The only serious contribution to this semantic discussion has been made by the Cubans, who have pointed out that there should be a transitive verb: to underdevelop. An economy is underdeveloped because of what is being done around it, within it and to it. There are agencies which underdevelop." John Berger and Jean Mohr, *A Seventh Man: A Book of Images and Words About the Experience of Migrant Workers in Europe* (Harmondsworth, UK: Penguin Books, 1975), p. 21.

35. Japanese readers were introduced to the lives of *Gastarbeiter* through a West German journalist's explosive exposé: Günther Wallraff, *Saiteihen: Torukojin ni henshin shite mita sokoku Nishi Doitsu,* trans. Masako Schöneck (Tokyo: Iwanami Shoten, 1987). The title in German is *Ganz unten.*

36. Several Japanese groups have looked to some sort of rotation system as a solution to the country's labor shortage: to wit, a proposal by the Tokyo Chamber of Commerce and Industry for the country to "establish a system of receiving a maximum of 600,000 foreign laborers—about one percent of Japan's total labor force—on condition that they return home within two years." Quoted in Kyoichi Miyagawa, "Question of Opening Japan's Doors to Foreign Workers," *Japan Times Weekly International Edition,* March 5–11, 1990, p. 6.

37. The writer is Max Frisch. Quoted in Wolfgang Herbert, "Monko o hiraki, kanzen na kenri hoshô o," in *Buraku kaihô,* No. 307 (March 1990), p. 102. See also Wolfgang Herbert, "Nihon de hataraku Ajiajin-tachi wa ima," in *Gakuin nyûsu,* No. 278 (September 1, 1990), pp. 3–4, which offers a shrewd analysis of the foreign laborer phenomenon in Japan. Both articles provide a counterargument to received notions in Japan of the guest worker phenomenon in West Germany.

38. The Revised Immigration Law (promulgated June 1990) held *businesses* responsible for illegal workers in their employ, causing, ironically, an exodus of foreign laborers to Narita Airport prior to enactment (Hachiya, *Soredemo gaikokujin rôdôsha wa yatte kuru*, pp. 77–99).

There is one exception to this general tightening: the *Nikkeijin* now working in Japan, mostly from South America (Peru, Argentina, and especially Brazil, who alone number upwards of 100,000). There are no legal restrictions on their activities in Japan, making them the object of enthusiastic recruiting by Japanese corporations.

39. Seven hundred immigration agents police the entire country for an illegal worker population that now numbers in the hundreds of thousands (Hachiya, *Soredemo gaikokujin rôdôsha wa yatte kuru*, p. 108).

40. Tessa Morris-Suzuki, "Imin rôdôsha—shinwa to genjitsu," p. 339.

41. See Morris-Suzuki, "Imin rôdôsha—shinwa to genjitsu," pp. 337–38. Jonathan Power comments further on the Dutch example: "Job training and recruitment was planned, and over a 15-year period, this large racial minority was virtually completely integrated into Holland. The massive allocation of finance and housing to help the process is indeed a lesson for today, when the Dutch government is spending only a seventh per foreign worker on similar programmes, and at a guess is experiencing seven times the problems." Cited in Power, *Migrant Workers in Western Europe and the United States* (Oxford: Pergamon Press, 1979), p. 92.

42. *Soredemo gaikokujin rôdôsha wa yatte kuru*, Preface, p. 5.

43. See Lee and DeVos, *Koreans in Japan*, and Michael Weiner, *The Origins of the Korean Community in Japan: 1910–1923* (Manchester, UK: University of Manchester Press, 1989), for a detailed description of Koreans in Japan. I have gleaned current statistical data from Sun-hae Bae et al., *Japan's Subtle Apartheid: The Korean Minority Now* (Tokyo: Research/Action Institute for Koreans in Japan, 1990), which has more recent figures.

44. For a trenchant account of life in Japan as a Korean national, see Kyô Nobuko, *Goku futsû no zai-Nichi Kankokujin* (Tokyo: Asahi Bunko, 1989). Until the mid-1980s, a Korean or any foreign national had to adopt a Japanese name and register it with the authorities in order to qualify for Japanese citizenship.

45. *The Origins of the Korean Community in Japan*, p. 201. Emphasis in original.

46. Both proximity and the colonial legacy have been major factors in the flow of immigrants into countries like Great Britain (Commonwealth nations), France (Algeria), the Netherlands (Indonesia, Surinam), and the United States (Mexico) since the mid-twentieth century. Japan resembles the United States more than the northern European countries because of its high percentage of illegal immigrants. See Power, *Migrant Workers in Western Europe and the United States*, pp. 70–122, which compares the experiences of the United States and half a dozen European countries.

47. In his introduction to Kitabatake Chikafusa's *Jinnô Shôtôki*, H. Paul Varley notes some of the stray threads in the "unbroken" imperial line. See *A Chronicle of Gods and Sovereigns: Jinnô Shôtôki of Kitabatake Chikafusa* (New York: Columbia University Press, 1980), pp. 15–20.

48. "Cold War Europe: Taking the Democratic Way," *Nation* Vol. 252, No. 15 (April 22, 1991), p. 517.

49. Ibid., pp. 517–18.

50. Quoted in Power, *Migrant Workers in Western Europe and the United States*, p. 93.

51. Quoted in Kenneth B. Pyle, *The New Generation in Meiji Japan: Problems of Cultural Identity, 1885–1895* (Stanford University Press, 1969), p. 149.

The same year that Fukuzawa wrote his editorial ironically marks the beginning of the first wave of emigration from Japan to the Americas. Even as the Japanese state was trying to "escape" the Asian continent, Japanese citizens were escaping their homeland by the thousands in search of a better economic life and working in a variety of menial tasks as temporary laborers. That their search was often fraught with difficulties, many of them racially motivated (for a history of Japanese emigrants abroad, see for example, Yuji Ichioka, *The Issei: The World of the First Generation Japanese Immigrants, 1885–1924* [New York: Free Press, 1990], which focuses on the U.S. experience), has not been lost on Japanese bureaucrats who wish today to insure the "purity" of their country's new immigrant population. They have offered, for example, favorable treatment to *Nikkeijin* from South America, particularly Brazil, and to the employers that hire them. What businesses have found in the Japanese-Brazilians they have recruited, however, are Japanese-*Brazilians* who not only speak a different language but have been acculturated into a national ethos in which ethnocentricism can have no place. Instead of witnessing a return of the "blood," Japanese are finding in *Nikkeijin* immigrants a new challenge to their national identity and a reminder of their own century-long history as human capital on the world labor market.

52. Steven R. Weisman, "Japan's Urban Underside Erupts, Tarnishing Image of Social Peace," *New York Times,* October 10, 1990, p. A-1.

53. See Tôkyôto Jôhoku Fukushi Sentâ, ed., *Jigyô gaiyô* (Tokyo: Tôkyô-to Jôhoku Fukushi Sentâ, 1990, esp. pp. 63–69), a government publication that cites twenty major disturbances in or pertaining to the San'ya area alone.

WORKS CITED

BOOKS AND ARTICLES

Anderson, Benedict. *Imagined Communities: Reflections on the Origin and Spread of Nationalism.* London: Verso, 1983.

Bae, Sun-hae, et al. *Japan's Subtle Apartheid: The Korean Minority Now.* Tokyo: Research/Action Institute for Koreans in Japan, 1990.

Berger, John, and Jean Mohr. *A Seventh Man: A Book of Images and Words About the Experience of Migrant Workers in Europe.* With the assistance of Sven Blomberg. Harmondsworth, UK: Penguin Books, 1975.

Coates, David, ed. "Shattering the Myth of the Homogeneous Society: Minority Issues and Movements in Japan." *JPRN Monograph Series,* No. 4. Berkeley, CA: Japan Pacific Resource Network, 1990.

Dale, Peter N. *The Myth of Japanese Uniqueness.* New York: St. Martin's Press, 1986.

de Bary, Brett. "Sanya: Japan's Internal Colony." In E. Patricia Tsurumi, ed. *The Other Japan.* Armonk, NY: M. E. Sharpe, 1988, pp. 112–18.

DeVos, George, and Hiroshi Wagatsuma. *Japan's Invisible Race: Caste in Culture and Personality.* Berkeley, CA: University of California Press, 1967.

Donoghue, John D. *Pariah Persistence in Changing Japan: A Case Study.* With the collaboration of Anna Acitelli-Donoghue. Washington, DC: University Press of America, 1977.

Dower, John W. *War Without Mercy: Race and Power in the Pacific War.* New York: Pantheon Books, 1986.

Fallows, James. "Containing Japan." *Atlantic Monthly,* Vol. 263 (May 1989), pp. 40–54.

———. "Playing by Different Rules." *Atlantic Monthly,* Vol. 260 (September 1987), pp. 22–32.

———. "The Japanese Are Different from You and Me." *Atlantic Monthly,* Vol. 258 (September 1986), pp. 35–41.

Field, Norma. *In the Realm of a Dying Emperor.* New York: Pantheon Books, 1991.

Fowler, Edward. "San'ya: Reflections on Life at the Margins of Japanese Society." *Transactions of the Asiatic Society of Japan,* Series 4, Vol. 106 (forthcoming).

Hachiya, Takashi. *Soredemo gaikokujin rôdôsha wa yatte kuru.* Tokyo: Nikkan Kôgyô Shimbunsha, 1991.

Herbert, Wolfgang. "Nihon de hataraku Ajiajin-tachi wa ima." *Gakuin nyûsu,* No. 278 (September 1, 1990), pp. 3–4.

———. "Monko o hiraki, kanzen na kenri hoshô o." In *Buraku kaihô,* No. 307 (March 1990), pp. 99–105.

Ichioka, Yuji. *The Issei: The World of the First Generation Japanese Immigrants, 1885–1924.* New York: Free Press, 1990.

Ishi, Tomoji. "Nakasone's Racial Remarks and International Dynamism in Race Relations." *JPRN Monograph Series,* No. 1. Berkeley, CA: Japan Pacific Resource Network, 1987.

Jones, H. J. *Live Machines: Hired Foreigners and Meiji Japan.* Vancouver: University of British Columbia Press, 1980.

Kaldor, Mary. "Cold War Europe: Taking the Democratic Way." *Nation,* Vol. 252, No. 15 (April 22, 1991), pp. 514–19.

Kantô Bengoshikai Rengôkai, ed. *Gaikokujin rôdôsha no shûrô to jinken.* Tokyo: Akashi Shoten, 1990.

Kawamoto Shôichi and Fujisawa Yasusuke. *Tôkyô no hisabetsu buraku: jittai, rekishi, genjô.* Tokyo: San'ichi Shobô, 1984.

Kondo, Dorinne K. *Crafting Selves: Power, Gender, and Discourses of Identity in a Japanese Workplace.* Chicago: University of Chicago Press, 1990.

Kyô Nobuko. *Goku futsû no zai-Nichi Kankokujin.* Tokyo: Asahi Bunko, 1990.

Lee, Changsoo, and George DeVos. *Koreans in Japan: Ethnic Conflict and Accommodation.* Berkeley: University of California Press, 1981.

Matsui, Yayori. "Asian Migrant Women Working at Sex Industry in Japan Victimized by International Trafficking." *In God's Image* (June 1990), pp. 6–13.

Miyagawa, Kyoichi. "Question of Opening Japan's Doors to Foreign Workers." *Japan Times Weekly International Edition* (March 5–11, 1990), p. 6.

Miyashita, Tadako. *San'ya nisshi.* Tokyo: Ningen no Kagaku Sha, 1977.

Morris-Suzuki, Tessa. "Imin rôdôsha—shinwa to genjitsu: Oranda to Eikoku no rei kara." *Sekai,* No. 542 (June 1990), pp. 331–39.

Muller, John P., and William J. Richardson, eds. *The Purloined Poe: Lacan, Derrida and Psychoanalytic Reading*. Baltimore, MD: Johns Hopkins University Press, 1988.

Nakasone, Yasuhiro. "Zensairoku: Nakasone Shushô 'chiteki suijun' kôen." In *Chûô kôron,* (November 1986), pp. 146–62.

Neary, Ian. *Political Protest and Social Control in Pre-war Japan: The Origins of Buraku Liberation*. Manchester, UK: Manchester University Press, 1989.

Pharr, Susan J. *Losing Face: Status Politics in Japan*. Berkeley: University of California Press, 1990.

Power, Jonathan. *Migrant Workers in Western Europe and the United States*. In collaboration with Marguerite Garling and Anna Hardman. Oxford, UK: Pergamon Press, 1979.

Pyle, Kenneth B. *The New Generation in Meiji Japan: Problems of Cultural Identity, 1885–1895*. Stanford, CA: Stanford University Press, 1969.

Rabson, Steve, trans. *Okinawa: Two Postwar Novellas by Oshiro Tatsuhiro and Higashi Muneo*. Berkeley, CA: Institute of East Asian Studies, 1989.

Shimoyama, Shigeru. "The Shadow Work Force." *Intersect,* Vol. 5 (July 1989), pp. 11–18.

Tôkyô-to Jôhoku Fukushi Sentâ, ed. *Jigyô gaiyô*. Tokyo: Tôkyô-to Jôhoku Fukushi Sentâ, 1990.

Upham, Frank K. *Law and Social Change in Postwar Japan*. Cambridge, MA: Harvard University Press, 1987.

Varley, H. Paul, trans. *A Chronicle of Gods and Sovereigns: Jinnô Shôtôki of Kitabatake Chikafusa*. New York: Columbia University Press, 1980.

Ventura, Ray. "The Color of Life in Japan: A Filipino Day Laborer's Diary." *AMPO Japan-Asia Quarterly Review,* Vol. 20, No. 4 & Vol. 21, No. 1 (1989), pp. 50–53.

Vogel, Ezra F. *Japan As Number One: Lessons for America*. Cambridge, MA: Harvard University Press, 1979.

Wallraff, Günter. *Saiteihen: Torukojin ni henshin shite mita sokoku Nishi Doitsu*. Trans. Masako Schöneck. Tokyo: Iwanami Shoten, 1987.[*Ganz unten.*]

Weiner, Michael. *The Origins of the Korean Community in Japan: 1910–1923*. Manchester, UK: University of Manchester Press, 1989.

Weisman, Steven R. "Japan's Urban Underside Erupts, Tarnishing Image of Social Peace." *New York Times,* October 10, 1990, pp. A-1, A-8.

Yoshino, Roger, and Sueo Murakoshi. *The Invisible Visible Minority: Japan's Burakumin*. Osaka: Buraku Kaiho Kenkyusho, 1977.

SPECIAL REPORTS

AMPO Japan-Asia Quarterly Review. "Japan's Human Imports," Vol. 19, No. 4 (1988), pp. 2–37.

Yomiuri Shimbun. "Atarashii rinjin: gaikokujin rôdôsha mondai o kangaeru." A series of thirty articles in five parts. May 19–July 25, 1990.

12

Pacific Island Responses to U.S. and French Hegemony

MORE THAN any other place on the globe, Oceania has been portrayed and popularized as an earthly paradise. Captain Cook's logs, Gauguin's canvases, Mead's anthropological tracts, Michener's tomes, and Hollywood films all contributed to the South Seas stereotype of "happy campers" living harmoniously in a sensuous nirvana. Yet, the highly militarized Oceania of the 1990s is one of the most nuclearized and colonized geopolitical regions in the world. In this chapter, I propose to lift the "coconut curtain" that has romanticized and distorted the Pacific for most people by challenging the Western popular images of these island people.

The anthropologist Bengt Danielsson—a Norwegian member of the 1947 Kon-Tiki expedition—has been residing in Tahiti for more than four decades and has been active (along with his wife, Marie-Therese) in the Pacific antinuclear and independence movement. According to Danielsson, the naming of the Pacific islands occurred this way:

> The term Polynesia was coined by Charles de Brosses in 1756 and applied to all the Pacific islands. The present restricted use was proposed by Dumont d'Urville during a famous lecture at the Geographical Society in Paris in 1831. At the same time he also proposed the terms Melanesia and Micronesia for the regions which still bear those names. The terms are not particularly good, considering that all three regions have "many islands" (polynesia) and "small islands" (micronesia); in Melanesia, it is not the islands, but the people who are black. (personal communication, 1991)

As for colorful names, the ambassador to the United Nations from Papua New Guinea, Renagi Lohia, has popularized the term "aquatic continent" to represent all of the Pacific islands (Lohia, 1989).

The more than 10,000 islands of the Pacific are home to roughly 6 million indigenous peoples in twenty-three microstates. Scattered over one-third of the earth's surface—but comprising a mere 0.5 million square kilometers of

235

land—the Pacific islands were first encountered by European explorers 400 years ago (Walker and Sutherland, 1988, p. 6). Although the United States and France were late entrants into the Pacific region—preceded by the Spanish, the Dutch, and the British—their presence (along with Japanese investment) dominates the "Ocean of Peace" in the late twentieth century.

It will be my aim in this chapter to search beyond the tempting—but static—Western representations by analyzing the real politik interests of the United States and France in the Pacific region. An examination of how military and intelligence operations by these two Western nations have tampered with the postwar decolonization process will be featured. Additionally, I will explore the historic responses by the indigenous islanders to these metropolitan incursions in this vast (and underpublicized) oceanic expanse.

PAX AMERICANA IN THE PACIFIC

Early U.S. expansion into the Pacific was limited to Hawaii and the islands of Micronesia north of the equator: annexed in 1900, American Samoa (which became independent in 1962) was the sole island entity seized by the United States in the South Pacific. Congress annexed Hawaii in 1898, following the 1894 military coup by U.S. soldiers from the USS *Boston* overthrowing Queen Liliuokalani.

As booty in the Spanish-American War, the United States acquired Puerto Rico, the Philippines, and Guam in the Mariana Islands, an island outpost that has well served U.S. strategic interests for nearly a century. Nearby Tinian Island acted as the stationary aircraft carrier for the *Enola Gay* en route to Hiroshima.

The 2,100 islands of Micronesia were awarded to Japan at the Paris Peace Conference of 1919 as a class C mandate under the League of Nations (Heine, 1974, p. 14). Instrumental in its island outpost campaign, the Japanese mandated islands proved to be strategically useful for Japan's World War II military planners: the attack on Pearl Harbor was launched from aircraft carriers based in Micronesia.

In the Cairo Declaration, December 1, 1943, Churchill and Roosevelt announced that after the war, Japan would be relieved of the Pacific islands (north of the equator) granted in 1920. Of the 50,000 Micronesians living at the time, about 10 percent were killed in the bitter crossfire between foreign belligerents on island soil (Stanley, 1989a, p. 33).

At war's end, the United States engaged in an internal debate about the future administration of its newly won Micronesian isles. The War Department under Stimson advocated outright annexation of these useful isles, stretching past Hawaii and nearly to the Philippines; the State Department under Hull won out, getting them declared an unprecedented "strategic" trust territory under the newly spawned United Nations (McHenry, 1975, p. 56). Of the eleven newly created trust territories at the war's end, only Micronesia was designated a "strategic" trust and thus placed under the supervision of the Security Council.

The Pentagon had fixed its attention on the furtherance of its nuclear monopoly. A year before the United States formally signed the 1947 UN Trust Agreement, the 167 Marshall Island people of Bikini were forcibly evacuated from their ancestral atoll by the U.S. navy in preparation for the first series of postwar nuclear tests, "Operation Crossroads." The Bikinians today remain an exiled community awaiting return to their revered Eden.

From 1948 to 1958, at least sixty-six atomic and hydrogen bombs were exploded at Bikini and Eniwetok, another atoll similarly relieved of its original inhabitants in 1947. A monstrous series of hydrogen bombs designed by Edward Teller was exploded at Bikini and Eniwetok in spring 1954. The first H-bomb of the Castle series, code-named "Bravo," had a yield of fifteen megatons (over 1,000 Hiroshimas); this largest and dirtiest of U.S. hydrogen bombs blanketed countless inhabited atolls in the Marshalls with radioactive fallout. Aside from the Marshallese evacuees who were exposed on Rongelap and Utirik, U.S. service personnel on an adjacent atoll were likewise irradiated from the Bravo behemoth (Alcalay, 1987a, p. 237). Twenty-three Japanese fishermen were also caught in the lethal radioactive fallout.

The United States was eager to collect scientific data on how humans are affected by hydrogen bomb fallout and was quick to establish long-term health studies of the irradiated Marshallese: the Atomic Bomb Casualty Commission (now called the Radiation Effects Research Foundation) provided *only* data on the direct effects of radiation exposure. In his 1958 follow-up report, the chief scientist from Brookhaven National Laboratory (under contract with the Atomic Energy Commission [AEC], now the Department of Energy) said:

> Greater knowledge of [radiation] effects on human beings is badly needed. Considerable research is being carried out on animals, but there are obvious limitations in extrapolating such data to the human species. The habitation of these people on the island will afford most valuable ecological radiation data on human beings. (Conard, Zarsky, and Belloe, 1958, p. 22)

More recently, another document on Bravo from previously classified minutes of an AEC meeting revealed in the most bare-knuckled manner the actual rationale for conducting the follow-up Marshallese radiation studies. In January 1956, two years after Bravo, Merril Eisenbud, the AEC director of Health and Safety, addressed the radiation problems in the Marshalls:

> Now that island [Utirik] is safe to live on but is by far the most contaminated place in the world, and it will be very interesting to go back and get good environmental data. Now data of this type has never been available. While it is true

that these people do not live, I would say, the way Westerners do, civilized people, it is nevertheless also true that these people are more like us than the mice.
(Eisenbud, 1956, p. 232)

With several island communities remaining sociologically disrupted as "nuclear nomads" (Bikini, Eniwetok, and Rongelap), a key question today concerns the full extent of radiological contamination. A congressionally mandated Nuclear Claims Tribunal is currently attempting to sort out the
radiation legacy in the Marshall Islands (Nuclear Claims Tribunal, 1992, p.
3).

The Marshall Islands continue to serve U.S. strategic interests. Kwajalein
Atoll, 4,200 miles west of California's Vandenberg Air Force Base, is well
sited for a U.S.$2 billion secret Pentagon laboratory. Used for development,
missile testing, and perfecting ICBM warhead accuracy, the facility is key to
"Star Wars" and the new emphasis on "smart" weaponry (Johnson, 1984, p.
23).

Now that the United States has been forced to vacate Clark Air Base and
Subic Naval Base in the Philippines, the importance of Guam's strategic location just off the Asian mainland will increase dramatically. The largest island
in Micronesia, Guam was originally claimed by the explorer Magellan in
1521 after Spanish troops waged a war of extermination against the indigenous Chamorro people. With the help of introduced diseases like smallpox
and syphilis, the Chamorros were reduced from an original population of
80,000 in 1668 to fewer than 5,000 in 1741. By 1783 their numbers had
been further decimated to a mere 1,500 (Stanley, 1986, p. 180).

The Pentagon stations 21,000 U.S. military personnel, spends U.S.$750
million a year, and controls one-third of Guam's 216 square miles. The current population of 130,000—composed of mixed blood Chamorros, Japanese, Filipinos, Chinese, and Koreans—has been Westernized and disrupted
by this overbearing presence.

The indigenous Chamorros have been protesting to the United Nations
and the U.S. Congress for years about environmental contamination from
the military bases and along with the other people of Guam have intensified
their campaign to retake land seized by the United States for military purposes. With growing Chamorro nationalism pitted against a huge influx of
military hardware and personnel expected over the next few years (principally from the Philippines), and as the Pentagon pushes to militarize the adjacent islands of Saipan, Tinian, and Rota in the Northern Marianas, increased social and political unrest is practically guaranteed in this distant
colony of the United States.

When the New Zealand Labour government under David Lange declared
its ports and airfields off-limits to nuclear-laden ships and aircraft in 1984,
the United States perceived its interests threatened in its "American Lake."

Three years later, a military coup in Fiji—the first in the region—crushed another Labour government's threat to likewise adopt an antinuclear policy. The antinuclear thrust originated within the more progressive and newly independent Pacific microstates of Vanuatu (formerly New Hebrides), Papua New Guinea, and the Solomon Islands, known within the region as the Melanesian Spearhead Group.

While in New Zealand in 1987, I spoke with Graham Kelly, a New Zealand member of Parliament, about outside interference in the Pacific region. Because of the insights Kelly offered, I shall quote at some length from my interview with him:

> I worked for 25 years in the trade union movement, and it doesn't take you very long when you see events taking place to politicize you very quickly about the very subtle—and sometimes not so subtle—activities of people and organizations from outside your own country that want to determine your future and the way you should operate. There was a scandal that broke in Australia in 1975 where the CIA was known to be involved in the trade union movement there. The labor attache working out of the U.S. Embassy in Canberra was CIA-trained, as they are in New Zealand and elsewhere.
>
> These labor attaches work to influence the course of elections and to influence the policy of unions at the national level on their political and economic international issues. We found in New Zealand in 1977 a spin-off of that. In my own case with my own union we were challenging the then-Tory government over some national legislation on shop trading hours, and in the course of that we shut New Zealand down for two days; it was unprecedented. It was a golden opportunity for those who would like to see some dissent within the union to capitalize on that, and they did. We later learned that the dissenters were being orchestrated with the help of the U.S. labor attache from the embassy, and we resented the heavy-handed nature of U.S. involvement in our internal affairs.
>
> Various U.S. agencies have poured money into third world countries, whether it is Turkey or South American nations, or Asia and the Pacific. The American Federation of Labor–Congress of Industrial Organizations in fact financed an office in Fiji for the trade union movement—the Asian-American Free Labor Institute (AAFLI). It was an offer that was too good to be missed by the Fijians who haven't got much money, and in fact, they're doing this in other Pacific island countries as well. AAFLI, as it is called, is one of three foreign affairs arms of the AFL-CIO; there is AAFLI in the Asian-Pacific region. These have been known to have CIA involvement from its formation during the Cold War.
>
> Also, we now know about the National Endowment for Democracy, which has been used around the world to intervene in the electoral affairs of many nations. Now we know that all of these things are going on, so, for example, when the Fiji coup occurred [in May 1987], it didn't happen in isolation. (Kelly, 1987)

Further evidence of U.S. clandestine activities in the Pacific may be gleaned from the following passages contained in documents released under the Freedom of Information Act. For example, funding submissions from the AFL-CIO's Free Trade Union Institute, AAFLI's parent, to the National Endowment for Democracy, state:

> The trade unions located in the island nations of the South Pacific are fragile institutions. ... Their ability to draw distinctions between the Soviet bloc and the democratic nations of the world is sometimes clouded, especially when emotional issues such as colonialism, nuclear testing and economic protection zones are introduced. (Wypijewski, 1987, p. 684)

Another document recounts the proceedings of a 1985 Pacific conference of the International Confederation of Free Trade Unions:

> The Australian and New Zealand representatives attempted to gain approval for a political resolution endorsing a Pacific "nuclear freeze" [sic] zone and supporting New Zealand in its dispute with the U.S. However, only one South Pacific delegate spoke up in favor of their approach, and the conference rejected it. This was in no small measure due to close collaboration and friendship nurtured between AAFLI and the South Pacific trade union leaders. (Wypijewski, 1987, p. 684)

U.S. concerns about Soviet and Libyan influence gained currency during the Reagan administration. One of the clearest statements came in the Hawaii Declaration issued in December 1987 at a major conference organized by the Moonie-funded International Security Council in New York City. In the Hawaii Declaration, the thirty-six scholars who signed the final document had these ominous and chilling things to say:

> The results of this comparative description and analysis provided a compelling picture of a Soviet strategic design to dominate the entire basin. That drive for preeminence employs a variety of means including intimidation, manipulation, regime transformation, subversion, the support of anti-American nationalism, and the promotion of chaos. The evidence of the Soviet commitment to hegemony includes its own policy statements, naval deployments, covert activities, basing patterns, support of insurgencies and activities of its clients. (Hawaii Declaration, 1988, p. 218)

In 1984 the State Department commissioned the University of Hawaii anthropologist Robert Kiste and the New Zealand political scientist R. A. Herr (1984) to research Soviet penetration in the South Pacific. Their study, "The Potential for Soviet Penetration of the South Pacific Islands: An Assessment," concluded that Soviet influence in the Pacific was rather limited, and the authors pointed to the nearly universal perception by Pacific peoples that the United States and France posed a much greater threat to stability in the region. In their conclusion, Kiste and Herr noted:

> By the usual objective criteria, the South Pacific ranks as one of the most vulnerable regions in the world and yet it has perhaps the least Soviet influence of any

area of the globe. Further, as evidenced by Namaliu's [i.e., the former Prime Minister of Papua New Guinea] assessment of threat, the prospect of a physical or political danger from the Soviet Union was not regarded as high. (pp. 66–67)

This sentiment was shared by none other than Admiral William Crowe, the former chairman of the Joint Chiefs of Staff. In the July 26, 1986, issue of *U.S. News and World Report,* Crowe stated:

The Soviets are in real trouble in the Pacific. They haven't been able to make much headway ideologically or politically. They have acquired some shabby allies [e.g., Vanuatu and Kiribati, with whom the Soviets entered into fishing agreements] ... whose economies are either stagnant or declining. The whole Far East—not just Japan—is becoming the most active, most prosperous market in the world, and the Soviets can't even penetrate it. (p. 23)

As the cold war quickly fades into memory, the U.S. military continues to show itself out of touch. According to the vice chairman of the Joint Chiefs of Staff, Admiral David Jeremiah, the United States has "absolutely no intention of ending its military presence in Asia and the Pacific." Addressing the Australian Royal United Services Institute in Canberra in September 1991, Jeremiah explained that despite troop reductions in Japan and Korea, the United States expects to "remain fully engaged in Asia through a program of frequent exercises, short term deployments and visits by units based in the U.S." (*Wellington Pacific Report,* 1991, p. 2). For an excellent analysis of the U.S. defense posture in the Asia-Pacific region, see *American Lake: Nuclear Peril in the Pacific* by Hayes (1986).

LA BOMBE AND LA FORCE DE FRAPPE

France's encroachment into the Pacific isles commenced in 1843 when Tahiti-Polynesia (known as "French Polynesia") was wrestled from the British and declared a French protectorate. This wide area, comprising the Society islands (including Tahiti), the Australs, the Tuamotus, the Gambiers, and the Marquesas, consisted of over five million square kilometers of French territory in the South Pacific (Stanley, 1989b, p. 15).

Additionally, with the idea of creating a penal colony similar to that in New South Wales in Australia, Emperor Napolean III ordered the annexation of New Caledonia in 1853. When nickel was discovered there in 1864—the world's third largest nickel deposit—France saw economic advantage along with another far-flung strategic outpost.

The success of the Algerian independence struggle in 1962 meant that France had to move its nuclear weapons program from the Sahara Desert in that former colony. Beginning in 1966, France shifted its atmospheric nuclear experiments to its convenient Polynesian colony, and until 1974 ex-

ploded more than forty neutron and hydrogen bombs above the balmy la-
goons at Moruroa and Fangataufa atolls near Tahiti. Following much
regional protest—including litigation by New Zealand and Australia (which
were hit with radioactive fallout from the French N-tests) before the International Court of Justice in the Hague—France drove its nuclear testing underground. Since 1966, France has exploded over 150 nuclear weapons in this
Pacific colony more than 8,000 miles from Paris as part of its *force de
frappe,* the French policy of nuclear deterrence.

In 1963, when all local political parties in Tahiti protested the invasion of
Polynesia by thousands of French troops and technicians sent to create a nuclear test center, President Charles de Gaulle simply outlawed political
parties. Since then the territorial assembly of Tahiti-Polynesia has adopted
numerous resolutions asking the French government to halt the testing,
without response (Stanley, 1989b, p. 33).

Indigenous protest in Tahiti was led by Pouvanaa a Oopa, an outspoken
World War I hero. In 1949 Oopa became the first Polynesian to occupy a seat
in the French Chamber of Deputies. In 1957 he was elected vice-president of
the Government Council. A dedicated proponent of independence, Oopa
was arrested in 1958 on trumped up charges of arson and was sentenced to
an eight-year prison term. Eventually freed in 1968, Oopa won the "French"
Polynesia seat in the French Senate, a post he held until his death in 1977.
Tahitians refer to Oopa as *metua* ("father") and his statue stands in front of
Papeete's Territorial Assembly (Stanley, 1989b, p. 33). Other Tahitian independence leaders have since filled the vacuum, including Oscar Temaru, the
mayor of Tahiti's second largest city, Faaa, and Charlie Ching, who has been
repeatedly jailed and beaten for leading antinuclear and independence pro-
tests.

As part of its international antinuclear campaign, Greenpeace planned a
1985 protest of France's nuclear weapons program in the Pacific (the United
States ended its Marshall Islands nuclear tests in 1958, but tested H-bombs
at Johnston Atoll [near Hawaii] until 1962). To draw attention to past as
well as present nuclear testing in the Pacific, the Greenpeace flagship *Rainbow Warrior* helped to evacuate the Rongelap islanders in the Marshalls to
another island in May 1985. As a member of the *Rainbow Warrior* evacuation team, I conducted interviews with the Rongelap people. A representative view about the Rongelap evacuation was expressed to me by Liam
Anjain:

> The United States came and poisoned our islands and the people living here, and
> have thereby contaminated our once-untouched environment. We have had
> many problems over the years with our health and the health of our children.
>   You have to understand that this is the island of my greatgrandparents,
> grandparents, and parents. Our decision to move was based on our concern for
> our children and the persistent fears we have about diseases that will affect the

children in the future. We feel that the radiation from the Bravo bomb is still too dangerous for us to continue living here without fears and anxieties. (Liam Anjain, 1985, p. 27)

After the Rongelap evacuation in the Marshalls, the *Rainbow Warrior* headed south to New Zealand en route to completing the Greenpeace campaign of protest at the French nuclear test sites near Tahiti. While docked in Auckland, French military intelligence commandoes sabotaged the ship, killing one crew member in the bombing. French fears of drawing international attention to its clandestine N-testing in the Pacific were revealed when it became known that France's intelligence agency—the General Directorate for Foreign Security (DGSE)—carried out this terrorist act against Greenpeace (Robie, 1986, p. 105). Ironically, the world's attention was drawn to the French N-tests in the Pacific by its bungled act of violence against the environmental organization. In 1987 the UN Secretary General Javier Perez de Cuellar brokered a settlement between New Zealand and France, whereby the latter paid US$3 million in damages for the sunken ship and the death of a crew member.

New Caledonia, France's other Pacific colony, is a simmering cauldron waiting to explode. Located about 800 miles east of Australia, New Caledonia's tensions revolve around demography and land disputes. The indigenous Kanaks, like the Melanesian Fijians, have become a minority in their own land. They make up about 42 percent of the total population of 150,000, but reside on only 15 percent of the habitable land, in reservations not unlike South Africa's bantustans.

French settlers, known as Caldoches, have been migrating to the colony for more than a century. Included in this group are hundreds of right-wing militarists who fled Indochina in 1954, Algeria in 1962, and most recently Vanuatu (a former French-British colony) in 1980 and now view New Caledonia as their last stand. Today there are some 55,000 Caldoches. Centered around the "Paris of the Pacific" capital of Noumea, the heavily armed Caldoches control the lion's share of the economy.

The remainder of the population consists of 30,000 Pacific islanders and Asians who were lured to the Melanesian nation by lucrative employment opportunities in the now-depressed nickel industry. Included in the ethnic brew are some 10,000 French soldiers stationed in the island outpost to "maintain order."

Following a series of violent skirmishes between the Kanaks and the Caldoches, the majority of Kanak factions merged into the Kanak Socialist National Liberation Front (FLNKS) in 1984. In December of that year, the FLNKS swore in a provisional government as the first step in creating the independent state of Kanaky and installed independence leader (and Catholic priest) Jean-Marie Tjibaou as president. The organization demanded an immediate referendum on independence in which only Kanaks could vote, real-izing that they would be outflanked by a coalition of the more numerous Caldoches, Polynesians, and Asians, who are economically linked by the nickel industry. Clashes between anti-independence Caldoche factions and the FLNKS erupted in late 1984, and by January of the following year vio-lence brought the death toll of twenty, including two of Tjibaou's brothers (Robie, 1989, pp. 92–104).

Violence continued in France's Pacific outpost of New Caledonia with scores of new fatalities, and in May 1988—following repeated setbacks for the independence struggle—hooded Kanak militants seized a heavily armed French gendarme post on the island of Ouvea in New Caledonia. Armed with machetes, axes, and a handful of sporting guns, the Kanak militants killed four gendarmes who resisted, injured five others, and captured twenty-seven as hostages.

The Kanak militants hid their hostages underground in a cave on Ouvea Island. Flying in additional gendarmes from Tahiti, France launched an at-tack on the cave, and in the ensuing violence killed nineteen Kanaks. After the dust settled from the "Ouvea massacre," French President Mitterrand of-fered a ten-year plan of development for New Caledonia, known as the Matignon Accord. Under the accord, a referendum on independence would be offered at the end of the ten-year period in 1998. A controversial provi-sion called for the stepped-up acculturation of the Kanaks into the Caldoche (French) culture, a proposal detested by many indigenous Melanesians.

For many within the FLNKS coalition there was a feeling that Jean-Marie Tjibaou had compromised too much with the French government, especially by postponing a referendum on independence for ten long years. In 1989, one year after the Ouvea massacre, hard-line FLNKS radicals assassinated Jean-Marie Tjibaou—known affectionately as the "Gandhi of the Pacific"—and his deputy Yeiwene Yeiwene at point-blank range (Robie, 1989, pp. 275–80).

Today, New Caledonia simmers in ethnic and economic turmoil, and the volatile Melanesian nation is known throughout the region as the Pacific's tinderbox. Likewise, the mineral-rich island of Bougainville is embroiled in a violent struggle to secede from Papua New Guinea. And the island of East Timor (astride the lucrative oil-rich Timor Gap) is the continuing site of on-going genocidal policies conducted by the Indonesian army. It has been re-ported that about one-third of East Timor's population of 700,000 has been killed since 1975. Portugal, which retains internationally recognized sover-eignty over the island, is currently involved in an attempted negotiated settle-ment with the Jakarta government.

Interestingly, the former director of French intelligence provided a candid picture of French attempts to destabilize the region. In a revealing 1988 in-terview with the conservative *New Zealand International Review*, Count

Alexandre de Marenches, who departed from the DGSE in 1981 (well before the *Rainbow Warrior* bombing), boasted that "During my eleven years (1970–1981) we carried out about fifty successful operations in the region. Now to me an intelligence operation is only successful if you never hear about it" (*Wellington Pacific Report,* 1988, p. 5).

THE ISLANDERS' RESPONSE

Having suffered the most in the nuclear age—from Hiroshima and Nagasaki to Bikini, Eniwetok, and Christmas Island (where the British conducted nuclear tests in the 1950s), Pacific islanders are intimately aware of the destruction wrought by the atom. When the push for independence gained momentum in the 1970s (with Fiji becoming independent in 1970, Papua New Guinea in 1975, the Solomon Islands in 1978, and Vanuatu in 1980), the movements contained an admixture of national pride and opposition to French nuclear testing. This political thrust led ultimately to a dynamic grass roots drive for a nuclear-free Pacific.

This movement took organizational form in 1970 with the founding of the ATOM (Against Tests on Moruroa) committee in Fiji. The group was made up of activists from the University of the South Pacific in the Fijian capital of Suva, the Pacific Conference of Churches, and the Pacific trade union movement.

The ATOM committee organized the first nuclear-free Pacific conference in Fiji in 1975. The meeting drafted a People's Charter calling for the creation of a nuclear-free zone in the Pacific on the model of the 1959 Antarctic Treaty and the 1967 Treaty of Tlatelolco for a Latin American nuclear-free zone. A second conference on the Micronesian island of Pohnpei in 1978 officially endorsed the People's Charter. In addition to demanding a ban on all nuclear tests and other nuclear-related activities, the charter asked that the dumping of nuclear waste into the Pacific be prohibited. At the time, Japan and the United States were actively seeking such dumping rights.

A third nuclear-free Pacific conference in 1980 drew fifty-five delegates from twenty Pacific Rim countries.

The 1983 regional conference expanded its scope to include ongoing Pacific independence struggles. Fittingly, delegates met in newly independent Vanuatu, considered the region's most progressive nation (and denounced by the U.S. State Department as the "Cuba of the Pacific"). There the more than 100 delegates renamed their campaign the Nuclear-Free and Independent Pacific (NFIP) movement, to stress their concern over the liberation struggles under way in New Caledonia, French Polynesia, East Timor, and West Papua.

Regional representatives came together again in 1987 in Manila to hammer out a concrete twenty-four-point program. This program focused on economic justice and independence as integral features of the campaign for a nuclear-free Pacific.

The 1987 Manila conference examined three Pacific "hot spots"—Belau in Micronesia, postcoup Fiji, and New Caledonia—and condemned the United States and France for blocking the indigenous struggles for nuclear sovereignty and independence.

The most recent NFIP meeting was held in New Zealand in 1991, where the concerns centered around indigenous peoples from the Pacific, including the plight of the Maoris, the Australian Aboriginals, and Native Hawaiians. Native Americans—who refer to North America as "Turtle Island"—have merged their quest for sovereignty within the NFIP movement.

Following the UN Law of the Sea Treaty, the Pacific microstates in 1979 declared 200-mile exclusive economic zones (EEZs) around their archipelagoes in order to protect their valuable marine and mineral resources. Seabed minerals—especially manganese and cobalt—are abundant near many Pacific archipelagoes, and it is expected that at the turn of the century the potato-like nodules that contain them will be mined from the ocean's depths, with unknown environmental consequences. These EEZs greatly enlarge the territorial size of the tiny Pacific states, and help to explain why France and the United States are loath to relinquish their Pacific holdings.

The South Pacific Commission based in New Caledonia, the region's first governmental organization, was founded in 1947 by six metropolitan powers (Australia, France, the Netherlands, New Zealand, Great Britain, and the United States) to promote regional economic (i.e., fisheries and agriculture) and social development of the Pacific island nations.

The South Pacific Forum, founded in 1971, grew out of dissatisfaction with the South Pacific Commission, which was perceived as being dominated by Great Britain and France. The forum is currently composed of fifteen member nations and meets annually to discuss pressing issues in the region. Agencies of the forum meet more frequently.

In 1973 the forum created the South Pacific Bureau for Economic Cooperation (SPEC, now called the Forum Secretariat and based in Suva, Fiji), which focuses on economic problems of the region.

The forum established a regional shipping line in 1976 (the Pacific Forum Line), a fisheries bureau (the Forum Fisheries Agency based in the Solomon Islands), and the South Pacific Trade Commission in 1979. The forum negotiated the South Pacific Regional Trade and Economic Agreement (SPARTECA) in 1980 to provide preferential nonreciprocal access to Australian and New Zealand markets. Also, the Forum Secretariat participates in the South Pacific Regional Environment Programme (SPREP), a cooperative effort of the forum, the South Pacific Commission and the United Nations started in 1986.

The South Pacific Forum has consistently called for an end to French nuclear testing. Crafted by the forum nations—and inspired by the grass roots NFIP movement—the South Pacific Nuclear Free Zone Treaty was finally endorsed by the Pacific nations on August 6, 1985 (exactly forty years after Hiroshima), in Rarotonga, the capital of the Cook Islands. The accord, known as the Treaty of Rarotonga, has been signed by Beijing and Moscow; France, Great Britain and the United States remain the noteworthy recalcitrants, and are thus perceived as pariahs in the Pacific.

What is especially troubling about the U.S. refusal to sign the treaty is that the treaty would not restrict U.S. military activities insofar as it only applies to the South Pacific and therefore does not encroach upon U.S. missile testing at Kwajalein, militarization of Guam, and so on, which are occurring north of the equator and are not covered by the treaty. It has become apparent that the U.S. refusal to sign the Treaty of Rarotonga in part stems from its stand of nuclear solidarity with France.

Quite unexpectedly, France announced on April 9, 1992, that it was suspending its program of nuclear weapons testing at Moruroa until the end of the year and suggested that it would extend the moratorium in 1993 if other nuclear powers followed suit (Riding, 1992, p. A-5).

CONCLUSION

In the late twentieth century, some interesting political developments are taking place in the Pacific. The five smallest members of the South Pacific Forum—the Cooks, Niue, Kiribati (formerly the Gilbert Islands), Nauru, and Tuvalu (formerly the Ellice Islands)—recently held their first summit at Rarotonga in January 1992 to form a new organization to increase their visibility in the region as they try to address concerns common to them (*Washington Pacific Report,* 1992, p. 1). Calling themselves the Small Islands States (SIS) the group initially will involve itself in negotiating fishing rights in EEZs, looking at the global warming issue, and surveying the potential of renting air space to aircraft overflying their countries. Also mentioned was the possibility of initiating a SIS development bank. The five nations have a combined population of only 100,000 people living on less than 1,300 square kilometers of land. However, their territories encompass more than seven million square kilometers of ocean, about two-thirds the size of the continental United States.

Another interesting development is the newly created Alliance of Small Island States (AOSIS, including the Seychelles in the Indian Ocean and others), formed by Vanuatu's UN representative. Based in New York, AOSIS is an ad hoc group of diplomats from island states all over the world who wish to maximize their impact at the UN-sponsored environmental summit to be held in Brazil in June 1992.

In the wake of the cold war, and with major trading blocks forming (Japan and the so-called Asian tigers; the European Community; the North American block of Canada, the United States, and Mexico), the island nations of the Pacific will increasingly expand their role as markets and sources of raw materials in a still-unraveling post–cold war world. Moreover, the potential for tourism has been accelerating in the Pacific microstates, as infrastructure development (including ultramodern airports and hotels) and hefty Japanese investment continue. But even tourism will bring severe social, economic, and psychological disruptions to the Pacific region, as described in Cynthia Biddlecomb's excellent 1981 monograph *Pacific Tourism: Contrasts in Values and Expectations.*

Because this chapter focused on the Pacific incursions by the French and U.S. governments, very little was mentioned about the influence of Western capital in the region. For an astute analysis of the role of transnational corporations in the Pacific Islands, the reader is directed to James Winkler's 1982 *Losing Control: Towards an Understanding of Transnational Corporations in the Pacific Island Context.*

It is to be hoped that with the diminishing militarization of the Asia-Pacific region—as recently evidenced by France's cessation of nuclear testing and the drawing down of U.S. forces in Korea and the Philippines—the island peoples of Oceania will finally begin to achieve a measure of true sovereignty in the postcolonial Pacific. If the next century fulfills the prediction that it will be known as the "Pacific Century," the indigenous island people of the region should fare better than they have under the brutal ravages visited upon them by the militaristic and marauding metropolitan powers of centuries past.

REFERENCES

Alcalay, Glenn. (1987a). "Nuclear Hegemony: America in Micronesia," *Third World Affairs 1987*, pp. 236–50.
_____. (1987b). "South Pacific Regionalism: Connecting the Dots on the Map." *Nation,* August 1–8, 1987, pp. 84-86.
_____. (1988). "The Ethnography of Destabilization: Pacific Islanders in the Nuclear Age," *Dialectical Anthropology,* Vol. 13, pp. 243–51.
Anjain, Liam. (1985). Interview conducted by Glenn Alcalay aboard the *Rainbow Warrior* in the Marshall Islands.
Biddlecomb, Cynthia. (1981). *Pacific Tourism: Contrasts in Values and Expectations.* Suva, Fiji: Pacific Conference of Churches.

Conard, R. A., Lyuba Zarsky, and Walden Belloe. (1958, June). "March 1957 Medical Survey of Rongelap and Utirik People Three Years After Exposure to Radioactive Fallout." Brookhaven National Laboratory, BNL 501 (T-119).

Crowe, William. (1986, July 26). "Interview with Admiral William Crowe," *U.S. News and World Report*, p. 23.

Eisenbud, Merril. (1956, January 13–14). "Minutes of Advisory Committee on Biology and Medicine." U.S. Atomic Energy Commission.

Hawaii Declaration. (1988). *Global Affairs*, Spring 1988, pp. 217–20.

Hayes, Peter. (1986). *American Lake: Nuclear Peril in the Pacific*. New York: Penguin Books.

Heine, Carl. (1974). *Micronesia at the Crossroads: A Reappraisal of the Micronesian Political Dilemma*. Honolulu: University of Hawaii Press.

Johnson, Giff. (1984). *Collision Course at Kwajalein: Marshall Islanders in the Shadow of the Bomb*. Honolulu: Pacific Concerns Resource Center.

Kelly, Graham. (1987, October). Interview conducted by Glenn Alcalay in Auckland, New Zealand.

Kiste, Robert, and R. A. Herr. (1984). "The Potential for Soviet Penetration of the South Pacific Islands: An Assessment." Report commissioned by the U.S. State Department.

Lohia, Renagi. (1989, September 6–9). "Search for Genuine Security in the Aquatic Continent." Keynote address at the Global Security Studies conference, Seattle.

McHenry, Donald. (1975). *Micronesia: Trust Betrayed*. Washington, DC: Carnegie Endowment for International Peace.

Nuclear Claims Tribunal. (1992, January). *Executive Summary*. Majuro, Marshall Islands.

Riding, Alan. (1992). "France Suspends Its Testing of Nuclear Weapons," *New York Times*, April 9, 1992, p. A-5.

Robie, David. (1986). *Eyes of Fire: The Last Voyage of the Rainbow Warrior*. Auckland: Linden.

_____. (1989). *Blood On Their Banner: Nationalist Struggles in the South Pacific*. London: Zed Books.

Stanley, David. (1986). *South Pacific Handbook*. Chico, CA: Moon Publications.

_____. (1989a). *Micronesia Handbook: Guide to the Caroline, Gilbert, Mariana, and Marshall Islands*. Chico, CA: Moon Publications.

_____. (1989b). *Tahiti-Polynesia Handbook*. Chico, CA: Moon Publications.

Walker, Ranginui, and William Sutherland. (1988). *The Pacific: Peace, Security and the Nuclear Issue*. London: United Nations University and Zed Books.

Washington Pacific Report. (1984–1992). Published biweekly in Washington, DC.

Wellington Pacific Report. (1987–1992). Published monthly in Wellington, New Zealand.

Winkler, James. (1982). *Losing Control: Towards an Understanding of Transnational Corporations in the Pacific Islands Context*. Suva, Fiji: Pacific Conference of Churches.

Wypijewski, JoAnn. (1987). "What's It All About AFFLI?" (Letter to the Editor), *Nation*, December 5, 1987, p. 684.

13

Latin America in
Asia-Pacific Perspective

ALTHOUGH Latin America enjoys a long Pacific coastline, because of its relative economic and political insignificance in the late twentieth century, it can be overlooked easily in discussions of the Asia-Pacific region. In point of fact, from Mexico to Peru, and across the South American continent to Brazil, there has been a long and continuous historical connection between this large region of first Iberian, and later Latin, America and Asia. Asians established small communities in Mexico already at the beginning of the seventeenth century, and most recently in 1990, a Peruvian of Japanese descent, Alberto Fujimori, was elected president of his adopted homeland.

Here I sketch out a history of the relationships between Latin America and societies across the Pacific, especially China. The discussion focuses on the most prominent aspect of these relationships: Chinese immigration into Latin America beginning in the mid-nineteenth century, first as coolie, then from the late nineteenth century, as free labor. Labor migrations, I argue, were initially tied in with developments in Latin America as part of a larger world economy, specifically, the need for labor in plantation economies once the abolition of slavery cut off sources of labor in the Atlantic region. The migrations themselves contributed to the formation of a "Pacific" and encouraged further flows of population. By way of conclusion, I will say a few words on Asian immigrants' contributions to Latin America in spite of a social and cultural environment that was frequently hostile to their presence there.

SPANISH AMERICA AND THE
INITIAL FORMATION OF THE PACIFIC

In 1513, Spanish explorer Vasco Núñez de Balboa's "discovery" of the Mar del Sur (the Southern Sea), the first European name for the Pacific Ocean, set

251

in motion Spain's "discovery" and exploration of the Pacific coast of South America. By mid-century, Spanish conquistadores had conquered the Inca empire, renaming it the colony of New Castille, or Peru.

In 1518, Hernán Cortés arrived on the Atlantic coast of Mexico near present day Veracruz, sailing not directly from Spain but from the already established Spanish foothold in Santiago de Cuba. Three years later, the Aztec empire collapsed from the combined weight of internal disintegration and external pressures; from its ashes arose the Spanish colony of New Spain, or Mexico. Together, the silver-producing colonies of Peru and Mexico constituted the core of the extensive and long-lasting Spanish empire in the New World.

In 1540, the Spanish Crown sent its first viceroy to New Spain, which extended from today's U.S. Southwest to today's Central America. During the preceding two decades, Cortés and other early conquistadores sent expeditions north from Acapulco and other points along the Pacific coast to Baja California and California, culminating with Vázquez de Coronado's exploration (1540-1542) of the Colorado River and the Gulf of California (then known as the Sea of Cortés) and Juan Rodríguez de Cabrillo's long voyage to present day San Francisco in 1542.

By the end of the sixteenth century, the Spanish finally figured out how to accomplish what Columbus had failed to achieve—finding a way to the Orient by sailing westward. Spain established the Manila galleon trade, which lasted some three centuries, linking China and Japan via the Philippines (which Spain had also acquired as a colony) to Europe in an exchange of Mexican silver for Oriental luxury goods. Acapulco on Mexico's Pacific coast was developed specifically for this purpose.

Not long after the Manila trade was established, the first Asian colony in the Americas appeared. In 1635, a group of Spanish barbers in Mexico City complained about excessive competition from Chinese barbers in that colonial capital city. They petitioned the viceroy to remove these bothersome Asian barbers to special quarters at the outskirts of town, so that they, the Spaniards, would not have to compete with the *chinos de Manila* for business.[1] Although this early settlement of Asians never grew into a large colony during the colonial period, it left legacies now firmly entrenched in Mexican folklore, notably the embroidered blouse known popularly as the *china poblana*, worn by Mexican women in central Mexico.[2]

Thus, it can be said that long before any North Europeans laid eyes on the Pacific coast region of what is now the United States, the "Spanish-Pacific" was already a well established geographical and political entity. Moreover, this Spanish-Pacific was the result not only of Spanish settlement along the Pacific coast from California to Chile, a settlement sparse at both ends but dense and intense in the middle (Mexico and Peru)—it early established a continuous link with Asia through trade and some migration across the Pacific.

ASIAN LABOR IN LATIN AMERICA

After Mexico and Peru's independence from Spain in early nineteenth century, the reality of a Spanish-Pacific, though briefly interrupted by the cessation of the Manila galleon trade in the late eighteenth century, was renewed by first Peru and Cuba, and later Mexico. In the creation of a "Latin American-Pacific" in the nineteenth and twentieth centuries, material trade continued to play a role, but this time it was secondary to international labor migration and other forms of population movements from Asia across the Pacific. Chinese labor was initially most prominent in these population movements, staring around the turn of the twentieth century and later joined by Japanese labor. Peru, among the countries of Spanish America, took the lead in attracting Japanese labor, but the largest number of Japanese immigrants in Latin America would end up not in Spanish America but in Brazil on the Atlantic coast.

CHINESE COOLIE LABOR IN CUBA AND PERU

In the middle of the nineteenth century, Peru, which had become independent of Spain, and Cuba, which remained a Spanish colony in the Caribbean, both actively promoted the importation of Chinese coolies or contract laborers to work on sugar plantations. Known in Spanish as *la trata amarilla* (the yellow trade), it bore remarkable resemblance to the African slave trade, which both countries, especially Cuba, had practiced extensively. From 1847 to 1874, as many as 250,000 Chinese coolies under eight-year contracts were sent to Peru and Cuba, with 80 percent or more destined for the plantations. In Peru, several thousand coolies also helped build the Andean railroad and worked in the offshore guano mines south of Lima. In the 1870s escaped coolies and free Chinese were among the pioneers who penetrated the Peruvian Amazon, building settlements; introducing trade activities; cultivating rice, beans, sugar and other crops; manufacturing on a small scale; and brokering communication between the native Amazonian peoples and later European arrivals. Finally, although demand for cheap plantation labor remained high, international outcry against this brutal human traffic abruptly terminated the coolie trade in 1875, with the last contracts expiring by the 1880s.[3]

The British were the first to experiment with the exporting of Chinese, then East Indian, laborers under contract to their overseas colonies. As early as 1806, a precisely the time when the British ended the slave trade, two hundred Chinese were sent to Trinidad. Although this experiment was a failure, British entrepreneurs continued to press for the export of Asian labor, turning from China to India by the 1830s. By 1838, some 25,000 East Indians had been exported to the new British East African colony of Mauritius and successfully adapted to the plantation system there. In 1845, the first cargo of East Indians was shipped to British Guiana, Trinidad, and Jamaica in the West Indies. They were under contract to the plantations for five years, a period known euphemistically as "industrial residency," after which they could presumably ask for passage home or remain in the colonies as free men and women. During the same time, the French also acquired East Indians under indenture to their colonies in East Africa and the Caribbean.[4]

Between 1763, the year the British captured Havana, occupied the city for ten months, and opened this Spanish colony to international trade and the emerging North American market, and 1838, when the Cuban industry mechanized significantly, Cuban society was transformed from "the relatively mixed economy based on cattle-ranching, tobacco-growing, and the small-scale production of sugar" to the "dominance of plantation agriculture based on the large-scale production of sugar and coffee."[5] Cuba surpassed its British West Indian neighbors to become the preeminent sugar producer in the world. Along with new markets; improved technology; capital availability; a responsive political climate; a modern, entrepreneurial spirit among the planters; and other factors, African slave labor was crucial to the success of the plantation economy. The slave population had grown from 38,879 (22.8 percent of the total population) in 1774, to 436,495 (43.3 percent of total population) by 1841. Despite British efforts already under way to end the international slave trade, Cuba continued to import large numbers of Africans during the early nineteenth century, as many as 25,841 in 1817.[6]

The transformation of Cuban society was not just an economic phenomenon, it was social as well, for the population became not only increasingly slave and colored, but the planter class—often *hacendado* (landowner), *esclavista* (slave owner) and *negrero* (slave trader) all in one—reigned supreme, with its interests driving most policymaking, and its authority, particularly on the estates, largely unquestioned.

In Peru, the coastal sugar economy declined after independence due to the ravages of war and labor shortage brought on by the end of African slavery. The slave trade to Peru ended in 1810, and slavery itself was formally abolished in 1854. But the guano trade of the 1840s generated new capital, some of which was transferred to agriculture and revitalized it. Referring to the rise of this new *burguesía agraria,* Peruvian historian Jorge Basadre stated:

> El poderío económico de la nueva plutocracia costeña tuvo su base en parte en contratos de individuos aislados con el Estado enriquecido por el guano, en especulaciones bursátiles o en dividendos en bonos, así como también en propiedades urbanas y, a la vez, en el auge que supieron dar a sus haciendas trabajadas principalmente por los chinos.[7] (The economic power of the new coastal plantocracy had its base in part in isolated individual contracts with the state, enriched by guano, stock market speculations, and dividend earnings, as well as in urban properties, and at the same time, in the economic surge that they knowingly gave their plantations as worked principally by the Chinese [my translation].)

Together with the guano merchants, coastal planters went in search of cheap labor overseas, unable to find it among the small coastal peasantry or the faraway *serranos.* When slavery was officially abolished in Peru in 1854, there were only 17,000 slaves left. Even if willing to remain as salaried workers, they were hardly enough to meet the growing labor demand. Between 1839 and 1851, the Peruvian government paid 450,000 pesos in premiums to encourage importation of foreign labor to replace slaves.[8] Two-thirds of this money was directly invested in labor for the sugar plantations.

In Cuba, planter interests were represented by the powerful Real Junta de Fomento y de Colonización, presided over by the eminent landowner and international businessman Julián Zulueta. An agency of the junta was the Comisión de Población Blanca, charged at first with promoting the immigration of free European workers to Cuba, as these farsighted planters were already preparing for the imminent end of Africa as their source of labor and the need to adjust to free white labor. But free men and women in Europe were not attracted to a plantation society with slave labor. So, in 1844, when the British coolie trade was in full swing, the junta sent an agent to China to study the possibility of importing Chinese coolies. The Spanish government was also familiar with Chinese agricultural labor in the Philippines. An agreement was concluded in 1846 between Zulueta in London and the British in Amoy, a treaty port in Fujian province, South China. On June 3, 1847, the Spanish ship *Oquendo* docked in Havana with 206 Chinese on board, after 131 days at sea. Six died at sea and another seven shortly after arrival. Nine days later, a British ship, the *Duke of Argyle,* arrived with 365 Chinese on board, after 123 days at sea.[9] Thirty-five persons had died at sea. Both human cargoes were consigned to the Junta de Fomento, which proceeded to distribute the coolies in lots of ten to the island's most prominent planters and a railroad company.

Shortly after the Cubans initiated the Chinese coolie trade, Peruvian planters emulated their Cuban counterparts. An immigration law of November 1849 granted exclusive license (called *asiento* as in the African slave trade) for four years to two planters, Domingo Elías and Juan Rodríguez, to introduce Chinese into the departments of Lima and La Libertad after they had imported an initial experimental group of 75 Chinese *colonos* in October 1849. During the Elías-Rodríguez license period and continuing until 1854, 4,754 Chinese were imported.[10]

Initial response to the Chinese as workers in both Cuba and Peru was not enthusiastic. The Peruvian government suspended the trade in 1856, although a few hundred more trickled in between 1857 and 1860. Cuba also suspended the trade after the first contract with Zulueta and spent the next few years promoting other forms of immigrant labor, including Yucatecos (Mayan Indians) from Mexico and Gallegos, Catalans, and Canary Islanders from Europe. But these failed to meet the ever-growing labor demand. The Chinese trade was officially resumed in 1853 to Cuba and in 1861 to Peru. By then, in response to harsh international criticism of an already infamous human experiment, the British prohibited their subjects from participating in the particularly notorious passage to Cuba and Peru, forcing the trade to the Portuguese colony of Macao off the China coast, where Portuguese colonial authorities for the right price fully cooperated with the European coolie traders until 1874, when even Portugal succumbed to international pressures to end it. By then, over 200,000 Chinese had been sent from Macao, although of course, the ultimate origins of the Chinese remained in South China, in Guangdong and Fujian provinces. Table 13.1 summarizes the figures for the duration of the trade to Cuba and Peru, correlated with slave importation for Cuba and sugar production for both Peru and Cuba.

In the case of Peru, about half of the total number of coolies arrived during the first twenty years of the trade, 1849–1869. The other half arrived during the last five years, 1870–1874. This was also a time when sugar production mounted rapidly, from 13,475 metric tons in 1870, to 31,940 metric tons in 1874—more than doubling. It skyrocketed to 56,102 metric tons in 1875. Although the trade had ended by then, most of the Chinese were still under contract. During this time, the Chinese constituted almost the exclusive labor force on the plantations, as Peru had no slaves and few other forms of labor. It is undeniable, therefore, that coolie labor was a significant factor in the growing success of sugar production.

A similar correlation can be observed in the case of Cuba. As the African slave trade wound down and ended with the last shipments in 1865 of just 145 and in 1866 of 1,443 slaves, the size of the coolie imports rose markedly, reaching as many as 12,391 and 14,263 in 1866 and 1867. From 1865 to the end of the coolie trade in 1874, 64,500 coolies arrived, constituting over 50 percent of the total number imported. During this period, sugar production climbed steadily, reaching a high of 768,672 metric tons in 1874. Coolies constituted the source of labor replenishment, delaying the crisis that

TABLE 13.1 Coolie Imports and Sugar Production in Peru and Cuba, 1847–1878

	Peru		Cuba		
Year	Coolies	Sugar (metric tons)	Slaves	Coolies	Sugar (metric tons)
1847				571	
1848	4,754				
1853			12,500	4,307	391,246
1854			11,400	1,711	397,713
1855	2,355		6,408	2,985	462,968
1856	4,220		7,304	4,968	416,141
1857	405		10,436	8,547	436,030
1858	300		19,992	13,385	426,274
1859	321		30,473	7,204	469,263
1860	1,092	618	24,895	6,193	429,769
1861	2,116	885	23,964	6,973	533,800
1862	1,691	1,257	11,254	344	454,758
1863	1,620	1,615	7,507	952	445,693
1864	6,562	2,864	6,807	2,153	525,372
1865	5,943	1,463	145	6,400	547,364
1866	6,725	5,111	1,443	12,391	535,641
1867	3,360	3,431		14,263	585,814
1868	4,307	9,352		7,368	720,250
1869	2,861	12,479		5,660	718,745
1870	7,544	13,175		1,227	702,974
1871	11,812	13,141		1,448	609,660
1872	13,026	14,022		8,160	772,068
1873	6,571	21,696		5,093	742,843
1874	3,827	31,940		2,490	768,672
1875		56,102			750,062
1876					626,082
1877					516,268
1878					553,364

SOURCES: Peru, coolies—Humberto Rodríguez Pastor, *Hijos del Celeste Imperio en el Perú (1850–1900): Migración, Agricultura, Mentalidad y Explotación* (Lima: Instituto de Apoyo Agrario, 1988), Table 4 and Anexo I, pp. 27, 296; Peru, sugar—Rodríguez Pastor, *Hijos del Celeste Imperio*, p. 296; Cuba, slaves—Rebecca Scott, *Slave Emancipation in Cuba: The Transition to Free Labor, 1860–1899* (Princeton, NJ: Princeton University Press, 1985), p. 10; Cuba, coolies—Scott, *Slave Emancipation*, p. 29; Cuba, sugar—Scott, *Slave Emancipation*, pp. 36, 240.

would have set in with the end of the slave trade and making it possible for the plantation economy to continue to prosper. It is also noteworthy that after 1875, when both the slave and the coolie trade had ended, sugar production displayed a pattern of general decline, a crisis brought on certainly in large part by the shortage of labor.

When the coolie trade was cut off to Cuba and Peru in 1874, many of those already in these two countries still had to work off their terms of servitude. Moreover, in both places mechanisms were put in place to extend the term of service by forcing or enticing the Chinese to continue working under some kind of contract primarily on the plantations, where demand for labor continued to be high.

In Cuba, forced recontracting began early, with the *Reglamento* of 1860, which obligated those coolies who had completed their first eight years to re-contract (for an unspecified period of time) or leave Cuba at their own ex-pense. Only those whose contracts expired before 1861 were exempt. To critics such as Cuban historian Juan Pérez de la Riva, recontracting simply further confirmed his conclusion that the coolie system was slavery, in that compulsory and successive recontracting perpetuated servitude to the point that the legal distinction between indenture and slavery became blurred in practice.

There is no doubt that the Cubans issued the recontracting regulation in order to keep as much as possible of this captive foreign labor force on the plantations, knowing full well that very few of the coolies could have saved enough from their meager wages to pay for their passage home. Equally un-deniable a factor was racism, for the question of race definitely figured in this decision to keep the Chinese unfree. Cuban slavers and abolitionists alike had trouble dealing with a free nonwhite population and were concerned about the further mongrelization of Cuban society with the admission of an-other undesirable colored race—more on this point later. Recontracting suc-ceeded well as a device to keep Chinese labor in agriculture. The 1872 Cuban census noted 58,400 Chinese, of whom 14,046 were "free," that is, had com-pleted their original contracts. Nevertheless, of this number, 10,044 re-mained in agriculture.[11] Records uncovered by historians in the People's Re-public of China, reveal that from 1880 to 1885, a period when many of the coolies sent to Cuba and Peru during the height (also the last thrust) of the coolie trade in the first half of the 1870s would have completed their original contracts, only 1,887 Chinese managed to make their way back home to China. This was an insignificant number, given that over 100,000 left China in the 1870s for Cuba and Peru.[12]

In Peru, recontracting began in the early 1870s, a time of many expired and expiring contracts. No law per se forced the coolies to recontract, al-though compulsory recontracting was proposed by a Peruvian lawmaker in 1870. The planters resorted to debt or other forms of coercion. One frequent practice was the *sobretiempo,* or *yapa,* an extension attached to the original term on grounds that the coolie had not worked all the days due the *patrono* (some planters argued that work was due them on Sundays, in spite of the contracts consistently exempting Sunday work) or owed money to the *patrono,* which then had to be paid off by more work. The debt could have been incurred as a result of loans, advances, or even costs involved in recap-turing coolies who ran away.[13] More likely, however, the wages offered and the short term of the recontract—ranging from as short as six months to no more than one or two years at the most, with the option of recontracting several times under these terms—enticed many coolies to recontract voluntarily in their desire to accumulate more savings and ultimately break free from the plantations. What made savings more feasible under the recontracting system was the planter's offer to pay the wages in advance, up to year's worth, as incentive. In the late 1870s and 1880s, as the trade came to a close but demand for labor remained high, planters offered other concessions to lure the Chinese to remain longer on the estates. As early as 1870, in Santa province, in the labor force of twenty haciendas that relied almost exclusively on Chinese labor, 930 laborers or 77.1 percent, were under contract; 117 (9.7 percent) were recontracted, and 160 (13.2 percent) were *libres* (free), living and working in nearby pueblos.[14]

In both Peru and Cuba, recontracting took a significant new turn, beginning as early as 1870 in Cuba and appearing around 1880 in Peru. Although the original recontracts were between the individual coolie whose contract had just expired and the planter or estate administrator, usually the same persons who made the original contracts, a new contracting system involved a free Chinese—operating as an *enganchador* (labor contractor or broker)—who engaged and organized fellow free Chinese (*chinos libres*) into *cuadrillas*, or gangs. This entire group of *cuadrilleros* was then hired out to a plantation for a specified period of time or a specific piece of work, such as the evaporating room (*casa de calderas*) in the *ingenios* (sugar factory on the estate) of Cuba.[15]

In Peru, the Chilean invasion in 1880 during the War of the Pacific created chaos along the coast and led to the destruction of numerous estates. The displaced Chinese, both those still serving out contracts and those already freed, became readily available clients of the Chinese *enganchadores*. The Chinese *enganchador* negotiated all terms of work for a squad and handled all aspects of employment for the workers, including obtaining advances from the planters to pay them; handing out tools; and arranging for lodging and food and was responsible for discipline, control, and supervision. The *enganchador,* who also assumed the risks of all losses and damages, was likely once a coolie, now an independent merchant trading in goods and people. Michael González, who studied the Aspíllaga planter family and their estate Cayaltí, found that the Aspíllagas also offered their Chinese contractors the right to operate small stores on site to cater to the needs of the Chinese workers, who were each paid sixty centavos per day without rations.[16]

In Cuba, by the census of 1872, 14,064 coolies had completed their original contract and become naturalized or registered as a foreign resident. Under contract were 34,408 coolies; 7,036 were runaways still missing, 864 were captured runaways, and 684 were sentenced criminals. Awaiting recontracting in the *depositos* (pens where slaves were held, awaiting sale) were only 864.[17] Thus, the planters welcomed the Chinese *cuadrillas* in 1870 as an innovative device to keep the Chinese working on the estates after their contract expired. But the planters also realized that the presence of these *chinos libres* posed a severe problem of control over slaves and especially coolies still under contract. An editorial in the *Boletín de Colonización,* an official organ of the colonial government that represented sugar interests, concerned about the high rate of *marronismo,* or runaways, charged that the *cuadrillas* were the principal cause of flight. The writer asserted that the runaways could easily hide among the *cuadrilleros,* and that their presence "demoralized the workers."[18] Thus, the colonial authorities banned the use of *cuadrillas,* seeing the need for control as more important than economic flexibility. But the system was revived in 1879 at the end of the Ten Years' War, when the coolie trade as well as slave imports had been terminated for several years and labor was in short supply.[19]

For the Chinese, given the 1860 regulation forcing them to recontract or leave the island, joining one of these *cuadrillas* was one way to stay in Cuba without resorting to the much-hated individual contract with a planter. And as in Peru, the Chinese contractor accumulated capital for business through this process.[20]

As the decade of the 1880s drew to a close, both Peru and Cuba saw the end of dependence on slave and coolie labor on the plantations. Very simply, after 1885, an aging Chinese population whose ranks were not being replenished by younger immigrants, was increasingly replaced by Peruvian *peones libres;* Chinese disappeared almost entirely from the plantations by the end of the century. By then, Peruvian *hacendados* had learned how to entice and keep native Peruvian workers with the use of advance wages and debts, much the same way they had enticed and coerced free Chinese to work for them. In Cuba, the old plantation system gave way to the *colonos,* or independent small farmers, who cultivated and supplied the newly modernized mills with the raw canes. Many of these *colones* were new immigrants, mostly Canary Islanders and Gallegos.

During the chaos of the War of the Pacific, when the invading Chilean army sacked a number of Peruvian coastal haciendas and liberated coolies (whether under original contract or recontracted), other *hacendados* eagerly hired the Chinese, usually by agreement with a Chinese contractor, "incorporating them as peones," or wage workers, to supplement what the coolies that remained under contract on the estates. "It would not be exaggerated to say that for a period of time, very short to be sure, the great sugar estates depended on these Chinese contractors and those Chinese engaged by them, that is, the same people who years before had worked as forced laborers and been treated like slaves." These outside-contracted Chinese workers (*chinos enganchados*) became an "embryo" of Peru's "rural proletariat," and an "initial form of peonage" or wage labor.[21]

The *enganche* system in Peru gave way entirely to a free, or wage labor system, involving many Chinese until these died or moved out of agriculture into commerce and other urban occupations. They were succeeded in the fields of Peruvian *serranos* contracted by labor brokers emulating the example of the Chinese.

An official inspection of the coastal provinces of 1887 located 8,503 Chinese, of whom the vast majority, 6,245, were excoolies now free, who worked in agriculture, and whose condition "was similar to that of the *peon libre nacional.*" They received the same wages and rations as other workers, although wages varied from hacienda to hacienda. Another 1,182 Chinese on the coast were individually recontracted, and only 838 were tied to a labor contractor. There were also 40 *yanaconas,* or sharecroppers, 193 *arrendatarios,* or renters, 5 shopkeepers and innkeepers. The commission of inspection even located one excoolie who had become an *hacendado* himself, and who hired eighty or ninety free Chinese to work for him.[22] The work force of one important plantation as early as 1883 had become predominantly Peruvian and Chinese wage laborers—373 of the total of 550, or 68 percent.[23] The transition to an authentic free labor system was clearly in progress. If coolies—that is, Chinese workers during their eight-year term—were more slave than free in the way they were treated, excoolies earning a wage did become the country's early free workers, paving the way for other *peones.*

Although the major imprint of the Chinese in Peru was unquestionably on the coastal export economy (guano and sugar) and later in retail commercial development, they also ventured into the largely Indian *sierra* as well as joined the pioneer efforts into the Peruvian Amazon.[24] It is for their contribution to Amazon settlement and resource development that the Chinese have been least known, most neglected, and as one new study suggests, deliberately suppressed in official Peruvian historiography due to a prevailing nineteenth-century Peruvian attitude that only European pioneers were capable of bringing "civilization" to the jungle.[25]

As early as 1873, Chinese colonies were established in the Amazon. By the end of the century, Chinese had built colonies in major towns such as Iquitos, Huánuco, Chanchamayo, and Pucallpa, as well as scattered all over the Amazon region. Some of these first pioneers and settlers very likely were fugitives from coastal masters, joined later by coolies who had completed their contract and free immigrants.

These early colonies were small—around one hundred persons each—but prosperous, and in the sparsely populated underdeveloped Amazon region, assumed a significance above their size. The Chinese acquired urban lots as well as rural land; they manufactured basic consumer items as well as growing food to provision the towns. In the towns and regional markets, as itinerant peddlers (muleteers) and shopkeepers, they not only sold their own crops (principally rice, but also beans, peanuts, sugar cane) and manufactured goods (clothing and shoes), but also took on an intermediary role in the exchange of natural, artisanal, and agricultural products between the highland and the jungle. When cash was not available, they bartered.

In these activities, the Chinese covered a lot of territory, occasionally suffered Indian attacks, and also became much sought after as expeditionary guides and interpreters. Not only did the Chinese adapt with alacrity and facility to the Amazon environment, but as early pioneers and trailblazers, they acted the role of cultural broker between the "uncivilized" Indian natives and the Peruvian and European settlers.

Rubber and gold in Loreto province, with its capital in Iquitos on the Amazon River, attracted Chinese from all over Peru, directly from China, and from California. They spread over the vast jungle to tap wild rubber trees; they washed for gold in the tributary rivers; and they established themselves in business in Iquitos. By 1899, the Chinese community of Iquitos, numbering 346, was the largest of many foreign groups in that most cosmopolitan of Peruvian cities, isolated to be sure from the national capital of Lima, but well connected to Europe, the United States, and especially Brazil.

CHINESE IMMIGRANTS IN MEXICO

After the coolie trade, some Chinese continued to go to Peru and Cuba, now as free immigrants, but a much larger number voluntarily migrated to Mexico, particularly to the northern frontier zone bordering the United States. Not coincidentally, this new migration occurred just when the United States enacted the first Chinese Exclusion Act in 1882, by which the Chinese became the first group specifically designated by race to the barred from entering the country.

Chinese immigrants, mostly young males, began arriving on the west coast of Mexico in 1876, coinciding with the military coup of Porfirio Díaz, who ruled Mexico with an iron hand for thirty-five years and promoted its rapid economic development by foreign investors. This immigration accelerated following the passage of the Chinese Exclusion Act in the United States. Entering through the Pacific coast ports of Mazatlan and Guaymas, the Chinese spread throughout Mexico but primarily the northern border states, no doubt attracted by their proximity to the United States. An initial tendency to cross illicitly into the United States abated, however, as the Chinese perceived and moved swiftly into a widening economic space in the rapidly developing frontier region, where the bulk of U.S. investment in Mexico was concentrated. Unlike the Chinese north of the border, those in northern Mexico did not take up laboring jobs, which were filled by Mexicans, but rather entered commerce as small independent entrepreneurs or occasionally in partnership with U.S. mine and railroad owners in the company towns. Chinese shopkeepers followed the trail of Yankee capital.

Nowhere was this pattern clearer than in the northwestern state of Sonora, which bordered the then territory of Arizona. Astutely avoiding competition with established European and Mexican merchants in old towns such as Guaymas and Hermosillo (the state capital), the Chinese ventured into some remote villages of the interior, but mostly into new working-class settlements that sprang up along railroad and mining sites, and later, modern agricultural colonies. These were the new towns that grew in the wake of foreign, mainly U.S., investment in northern Mexico during the last quarter of the nineteenth century. The Chinese were often the first *comerciantes* to reach these new localities, thus the first shopkeepers to cater to the needs of the workers.

Within two generations, they succeeded in monopolizing the small commercial sector of the state's economy. Far from being a hindrance, the Mexican Revolution of 1910–1917 actually furthered their commercial growth in several ways. First, with most Mexicans engaged in the civil conflicts, the revolution retarded the emergence of Mexican small businesses to compete with the Chinese. Second, even during these turbulent times, towns, including mining and railroad centers that continued to operate, needed to be supplied with goods and services. Third, the various revolutionary armies needed to be provisioned. As aliens, the Chinese remained officially "neutral" and willing to do business with all revolutionary factions. Although some of the sales were on "forced loan" bases, whereby Chinese merchants were given a credit slip for future payment by revolutionary generals who commandeered goods and supplies, the Chinese figured these inconveniences to be part of the cost of doing business in the midst of chaos. Fourth, further solidifying the Chinese position in Sonoran commerce was the weakening of traditional commercial links between Mexico and Europe during World War I, which coincided in time with the Mexican Revolution. Some of the departed German, French, and Spanish commercial houses were replaced by Chinese firms, which turned to U.S. suppliers, thereby forging new Mexican-U.S. commercial ties. This in turn strengthened the existing symbiotic relationship between Chinese merchants and U.S. interests in Sonora, and explains the actions frequently taken by U.S. consuls to protect Chinese persons and businesses when they came under violent attack by Mexicans.

Most of the Chinese immigrants were young males, who arrived in Mexico nearly penniless, armed with only a willingness to work long and hard. However, a small number of Chinese capitalists also went early to Mexico to set up merchant houses in Guaymas and Hermosillo, with branches in important new towns such as Magdalena along the Sonoran railroad and Cananea of the Greene Consolidated Copper Company. In some cases, they added factories next to the stores to manufacture cheap shoes and clothing.

These large merchants hired almost exclusively fellow Chinese in the stores and factories. They also, significantly, extended goods on credit to enterprising but poor compatriots to peddle in small, remote mining towns and to set up new stores throughout the state. By the twentieth century, the Chinese controlled the trade in groceries, dry goods, and general merchandise. Some Chinese truck-farmed on land they leased, then carted the fruits and vegetables to local markets, which were often dominated by Chinese-owned stalls. Other Chinese worked as artisans and small-scale manufacturers, producing shoes, clothing, brooms, *masa* for tortillas, pasta, and sweets. In these multiple ways, the Chinese succeeded in creating a production, purchasing, supply, and distribution network among themselves, a closed system with characteristics of vertical integration that in effect became the state's first commercial infrastructure. This remarkable system endured until early 1931, when most of the Chinese were expelled from Sonora and their businesses nationalized.[26]

By the end of the Porfiriato, in 1910, the Chinese population in Sonora had reached 4,486, in a total population of 265,383, making them the largest foreign colony in the state, surpassing the 3,164 U.S. nationals by over a thousand and well above the 259 Spaniards and 183 Germans. In 1910, according to Mexico's official census, there were 13,203 Chinese throughout Mexico, in every state except Tlaxcala. Table 13.2 summarizes demographic data for Chinese immigration to Mexico, by state, from 1900 to 1930.[27]

The Chinese colony in Sonora—as in all of Mexico—was almost exclusively male. Even as late as 1930, the census noted only 412 women among the 3,471 Chinese recorded for Sonora. Not even all these four hundred or so women were necessarily Chinese, for Sonoran law had begun to strip Mexican women married to Chinese men of their citizenship and nationality, consigning them to their husband's ethnic group.

The highest number of Chinese in Sonora was recorded in 1919, when the Chinese colony itself supplied the count of 6,078. The sharp drop to the 3,571 noted for 1930 can be explained in a number of ways, aside from unreliable statistics. It reflected declining new immigration into the state at a time when Sonora had begun expulsion proceedings against established residents, many of whom were nationalized Mexican citizens. During the 1920s, as anti-Chinese campaigns mounted in intensity and frequency, many Chinese fled the state—back to China, illegally across the border to the United States, south to Sinaloa, and it appeared, especially across the gulf to Baja California, which recorded 5,889 Chinese in 1927 compared to 3,785 for Sonora.

When the Chinese first began arriving in Sonora in the last quarter of the nineteenth century, they congregated in Guaymas, the port of entry, and in the capital of Hermosillo. Then they moved to newer towns, notably the railroad hub of Magdalena north of Hermosillo, and to the state's leading min-

TABLE 13.2   Chinese Population in Mexico, 1900–1930

State	1900	1910	1921	1927	1930
Aguascalientes	102	21	14	31	47(18)
BC Norte	188	532	2806(14)	5889	2982
BC Sur		319	175(3)		139(3)
Campeche	5	70	61(1)	108	113(38)
Coahuila	197(5)	759(14)	523(16)	707	765(153)
Colima	5	80(2)	32(1)	43	38(14)
Chiapas	16	478(1)	645(30)	1261	1095(238)
Chihuahua	328(2)	1325(9)	533(16)	1037	1127(229)
Méx.D.F.		1482(5)	607(18)	1062	886(141)
Durango	147(1)	242(2)	46	197	229(33)
Guanajuanto	11	102	21(3)	37	37(12)
Guerrero	3	27	3	7	10(3)
Hidalgo		38	50(1)	98	70(18)
Jalisco	20	70(1)	53(1)	192	151(48)
México	15	58(1)	25	78	24
Michoacán	4	26	5	8	12(1)
Morelos	5	18	3	9	3
Nayarit			152	164	170(27)
N. León	90	221	89(2)	216	165(4)
Oaxaca	81	262	158(6)	254	158(50)
Puebla	11	31	17(1)	22	44(12)
Queretaro	1	5	1	1	2
Quin.Roo		3	3	2	10(4)
San Luis P.	32	109	105(2)	288	271(18)
Sinaloa	233(1)	667(4)	1040(4)	2019	2123(438)
Sonora	850(9)	4486(37)	3639(66)	3758	3571(412)
Tabasco	2	36(1)	48(4)	67	64(23)
Tamaulipas	38	213(2)	2005(21)	2916	2117(242)
Tepic	29	173			
Tlaxcala					
Veracruz	116	434(1)	847(10)	1908	1238(162)
Yucatán	153	875	773(5)	1726	972(153)
Zacatecas	19	41	19	113	142(25)
Total	2,719	13,203	14,498	24,218	17,865
	(18)	(80)	(185)	(1,772)	(2,522)

NOTE: Women in parentheses.
SOURCES: Mexican Censuses for 1900, 1910, 1921, 1930. For 1927, see "Extranjeros residentes Estados Unidos de México. Resúmen del censo practicado por la Sría. de Gobernación en 1927, y extranjeros, distribución por estados, 14 marzo 1928," Archivo Histórico del Gobierno e Estado de Sonora (AHGES), vol. 50, 1930.

ing town of Cananea on the northeast corner of the state close to the U.S. border. By 1904, Chinese could be found in all nine districts of the state, although unevenly distributed. Still prominent in Guaymas, Hermosillo, and Magdalena, by far the largest number had gone to Arizpe district, which included Cananea as well as a number of smaller mining camps and border towns. Of Arizpe's 1,106 Chinese, 800 resided in Cananea. By contrast, the districts of Altar, Sahuaripa, and Ures, which had no significant mining or railroad activities, had only a few Chinese residents each. The informative 1919 census, the data for which was provided by the Chinese Fraternal Union to the federal Department of Labor, noted 6,078 Chinese distributed across all nine districts and in fifty-eight of the state's sixty-two municipalities. Only four very small towns in Sahuaripa and Ures districts had no Chinese at all.

The 1919 community was composed overwhelmingly of young to middle-aged men, that is, men of working age. Eighty-four percent were between twenty-one and forty-five, the percentage increasing to an astonishing 91 percent if the upper limit is raised to fifty. Only 331 individuals, or 5.4 percent, were under twenty, and only 170, or 2.8 percent, were older than fifty-one. In years of residency in Mexico as of 1919, 41 percent had been in Mexico for ten to fifteen years, and another 37 percent for five to ten years. Thus the vast majority, almost 80 percent, had at least five years experience in Mexico. The data also suggest that a significant number, 1,459 or 24 percent, had entered Mexico during the active revolutionary years of 1912–1915.

The first year for which there is good commercial data on the Chinese was 1913, published by the International Chinese Business Directory.[28] For Sonora, 279 Chinese businesses were noted, most of them in general merchandise or groceries, located in twenty-six towns. There were also forty restaurants, sixteen laundries, four hotels, two dry goods businesses, two clothing factories, one shoe factory, and two pharmacies (probably Chinese herbal goods).

In 1919, of the 6,078 Chinese residents in Sonora, 70 percent (4,258) were listed as *comerciantes* by occupation, which probably included store owners, partners, and clerks (see Table 13.3). Common or day laborers, *jornaleros,* were a distant second, with 12.8 percent. There were very few cooks or launderers. Artisans and craftworkers of various kinds—tailors, shoemakers, jewelers, carpenters, bakers, tanners—constituted another two percent.

By 1925, although the Chinese population had declined sharply as noted above, the Chinese maintained a solid hold on local small businesses throughout the state.[29] Only a handful of traditional communities in Ures, Altar, and Sahuaripa districts had no Chinese presence. What is important is that these towns had *probably no stores whatever.* In other remote communities, such as Atil, Tubutama, and San Pedro de Cueva, with only one or a few commercial outlets, *all* were Chinese owned and operated. Even more significant, the commerce of certain mining towns, such as Nacozari de García near Cananea, was also exclusively in Chinese hands. The same was true for rapidly developing commercial agricultural towns in the southern part of

TABLE 13.3   Chinese Occupation in Sonora, 1919

District	(1)	(2)	(3)	(4)	(5)	(6)	(7)	(8)	(9)	(10)
Moctezuma	514	25	75	5	6	8	2	4	5	75
Guaymas	1156	50		5	15	8	2	1	9	65
Sahuaripa	46	2		1	1				1	6
Altar	146	15	1	4	2	1	1		3	15
Alamos	492	2	15	5	6	5	2		2	100
Ures	51	3		1	1			1	1	8
Arizpe	758	20	120	15	18	15	8	6	10	287
Magdalena	516	53		15	12	8	4		7	147
Hermosillo	579	24		7	8	24	4	3	1	75
Total	4258	207	196	58	69	69	23	15	39	778

(1) Merchants (fixed or traveling); (2) Truck farmer; (3) Mine worker; (4) Cook; (5) Launderer; (6)Shoemaker (or repairer); (7) Tailor; (8) Confectioner, butcher, tanner; (9) Baker; (10) Day Laborer. In addition, there were 8 "industrialists" (probably meaning someone who owned some kind of manufacturing business); 3 jewelry maker/repair, carpenter; 100 "minors"; and 255 "vagrants" (probably meaning someone without a fixed or stable occupation).
SOURCE: Departamento de Trabajo. Sección de Conciliación. "Informe que rinde el Jefe de la Sección sobre la situación República," 1919 (E. Flores, Commissioner). Archivo General de la Nación/Trabajo. México, D.F.

the state, such as Cócorit in the Yaqui Valley, with forty-two Chinese merchants, and Etchojoa and Huatabampo in the Mayo Valley.

The widespread distribution of Chinese businesses must also be noted in the context of their capitalization. In 1913, only 15 Chinese businesses were capitalized at $20,000 pesos or above, for a total of $721,830, compared to 238 non-Chinese businesses, with a total of $18 million.[30] The average Chinese in this group had capital of $48,789, compared to $75,630 among the others. Only three of the Chinese had over $50,000; by contrast, ninety-eight non-Chinese firms were capitalized at over $50,000. If this group can be characterized as Sonora's "grande bourgeoisie," then the Chinese were only an insignificant part of it. Chinese participation at this level of economic activity did not grow with time. From 1917 to 1920, Chinese entrepreneurs formed some eighty "mercantile societies," or companies.[31] The vast majority of the eighty were capitalized under $5,000 pesos. Mexican, European, and U.S. companies, by contrast, were typically capitalized at $25,000, $50,000, in the hundreds of thousands, and up to one or two billion for the big mining, railroad, land, and agricultural enterprises.

The detailed report prepared by the Mexican Labor Department on capital invested in the Sonoran economy in 1919 further confirms the low Chinese presence among the large enterprises and the fundamentally petit bourgeois nature of the Chinese business community. Total Chinese-owned capital did not lag far behind all other capital combined, $2,186,935 pesos compared to $2,813,540 (see Table 13.4). However, there were almost twice as many Chinese establishments as all others combined—North American,

TABLE 13.4   Commercial Establishments and Capital in Sonora, 1919

District	Chinese		Mexican and All Others	
	No.	Total Capital	No.	Total Capital
Moctezuma	81	$220,520.00	28	$522,270.00
Guaymas	248	854,110.00	54	936,805.00
Sahuaripa	6	27,000.00	29	40,550.00
Altar	30	61,404.00	42	73,810.00
Alamos	102	185,100.00	44	104,400.00
Ures	25	48,900.00	28	45,400.00
Arizpe	110	196,320.00	67	546,555.00
Magdalena	107	320,621.00	54	168,400.00
Hermosillo	118	272,960.00	88	375,350.00
Total	827	2,186,935.00	434	2,813,540.00

SOURCE: Departmento de Trabajo. Sección de Conciliación. "Informe que rinde el Jefe de la Sección sobre la situación de las colonias asiáticas en la Costa Occidental de la República," 1919. Archivo General de la Nación/Trabajo. México, D.F.

German, French, Arab, Japanese and other foreigners, and Mexican. The average Chinese business capital was $2,644, compared to $6,482 for others. Of the 827 Chinese businesses distributed over sixty communities, 740 were capitalized under $5,000.

Finally, in 1925, in the midst of a vigorous anti-Chinese campaign that called for their expulsion from Sonora, the state government once again took stock of the Chinese business profile, this time comparing it to Mexican industrial and commercial holdings.[32] By this time, it should be noted, a Mexican industrial and large commercial bourgeoisie had firmly established itself in Sonora, home to President Plutarco Elias Calles and former President Alvaro Obregon as well as many other revolutionary leaders who all laid claim to land and other properties in the state except for what the Chinese still held. Mexican-owned enterprises can be characterized as falling within the medium to large range: twenty-seven capitalized at $5,000 to $10,900 pesos; twenty-eight at $11,000 to $99,000, and five over $100,000. Among the Chinese, a considerable number—forty-one—fell in the $5,000 to $10,900 range, but only four between $11,000 and $99,000, and only one above $100,000. The vast majority of Chinese businesses were capitalized under $5,000, with most of them actually worth $1,200 to $2,500. There was only one Mexican-owned business in this modest category. Moreover, the 517 Chinese businesses were spread over sixty-five of the state's seventy municipalities; the 61 Mexican firms were to be found in only fourteen towns.

In short, this commercial/industrial survey conducted by the state government conclusively demonstrated the Chinese monopoly of the small commercial sector, to the practical exclusion of Mexicans. The situation was not particularly alarming to the large Mexican capitalists who in turn controlled the large commercial industrial sector of the economy, but it would provide fodder for the average Mexican who could, and did, aspire to the small commercial sector that was firmly in Chinese hands. The ubiquitous nature of these Chinese *comerciantes,* although providing a necessary service to all Sonorans, also became a thorn on the side of middle- and working-class Mexicans. Modest in fact, but prosperous in comparison to ordinary Sonorans still struggling to improve their lives well after the revolution in which many of them fought in the name of social justice, the Chinese also reminded Sonorans just how much foreigners had historically controlled their destiny, and how much farther they would have to go to reclaim Mexico for the Mexicans. Understandably, Mexican workers, landless peasants, and their families formed the backbone of the campaigns to remove the Chinese from their midst.

Where did the expelled Chinese go? It is hard to trace their steps. Some tried to enter the United States surreptitiously; some returned to China; and others resettled in more hospitable parts of Mexico, notably Baja California Norte, a territory and Mexico's last frontier.

Like Mexico's other frontier and border regions, such as Sonora in the north, the Yucatan and Tapachula in the south, Baja California also experienced an influx of Chinese. But well before Sonoran Chinese fled to Baja California in the late 1920s and early 1930s, Chinese workers had been brought there under rather unique circumstances at the beginning of the twentieth century to develop the virgin land of the fertile Mexicali Valley. U.S. landowners and entrepreneurial Chinese formed partnerships to clear this rich valley, an extension of California's Imperial Valley, for large-scale cotton cultivation. U.S. landowners leased land to California Chinese merchants and labor contractors who brought in the workers to do the backbreaking work. By 1920, Chinese lessees and their Chinese workers were raising 80 percent of Mexicali's cotton crop. Details of the relationships between U.S. landowners and Chinese lessees, and between Chinese labor contractors and workers have been recounted elsewhere.[33]

OTHER ASIA-PACIFIC LABOR IN LATIN AMERICA

My concern in this discussion is primarily with Chinese immigrants. I would like to note here, however, Chinese were not the only Asia-Pacific people to end up in Latin America. Equally important in numbers and activity have been Japanese immigrants. In contrast to Chinese labor, the emigration of Japanese labor into Latin America, as into the United States, was much more closely regulated and supervised by the Japanese government. The first Japanese laborers began to arrive in Latin America—in Mexico and Peru—just about the turn of the twentieth century and increasingly after 1908, in Brazil. By the second and third decades of this century, Peru and Brazil were the foremost recipients of Japanese labor in the Western hemisphere. By 1940, there were 234,574 immigrants of Japanese origin in Latin America, nearly 48 percent of all Japanese living abroad outside of Asia. By far the largest number were in Brazil (around 200,000), followed by Peru and Mexico. Also noteworthy is the fact that among Japanese immigrants to Latin America were large numbers of Okinawans and Ryukyu Islanders.[34]

The majority of Japanese immigrants to Latin America arrived initially also as contract laborers on coffee plantations in Brazil, sugar plantations in Peru, and rubber plantations in Bolivia. Although the Japanese, like the Chinese in Peru, Cuba, and Mexico, would gradually move into urban small businesses (and after World War II, the professions), in Brazil in particular they were to achieve prominence as independent landed proprietors ("middle-class farmers," as historian James Tigner describes them) pioneering settlement in frontier regions, which made them a crucial sector of the agrarian economy in Brazil.[35]

One other group must be mentioned here not because it played any significant part in the development of Latin America, but because of what its presence in Latin America reveals about the underside of an Asia-Pacific formation. These are the Easter Islanders, who were nearly exterminated by labor needs in Peru. In 1862–1863, for a period of a few months, private entrepreneurs "recruited" by force and guile Easter Islanders (among other Polynesians) to work in the guano fields in Peru. In the end, the islanders proved not to be suitable for the job. Many perished on the voyage or of disease and suicide after arrival. In a few months, the population of Easter Island came to the verge of extinction, about to follow in the wake of the Arawaks of the Caribbean and the Tasmanians of the Pacific. Luckily for the Easter Islanders, their labor proved "useless," and the trade created such disgust in Peru that it came to an end while some of them still lived.[36]

Asian laborers contributed in significant ways to Latin America's development. As coolies and workers, they provided much needed labor in mines, guano fields, and plantations. As free laborers and small entrepreneurs, they opened up new frontiers of settlement and contributed to the vitality of urban economies.

As the earliest modern agriculturalists in Baja California who cleared the land for commercial crops, as coolies who moved progressively from semislavery to wage labor in Peru, the Chinese in Latin American agricultural and labor history have not been adequately recognized and fully documented. Yet the prosperity of both Baja California Norte and the Peruvian coast could not have been realized without Chinese sweat. The exact relationship of varius categories of Chinese workers to production needs further research and more in-depth analysis.

As free immigrants to northwest Mexico and the Amazon, the Chinese proved adaptable to strange physical and cultural surroundings as well as harsh work regimens. They demonstrated an uncanny ability to detect and move swiftly into new economic spaces, often in "untamed" and underdeveloped frontier and border regions, where they usually found little or no competition from locals. They also tended to avoid conflict with entrenched, more powerful white or European interests. Rather, they were instrumental in both Mexico and Peru's frontiers in clearing land to grow food for local consumption and crops for export. And with their production and distribution system and their widespread retail network, they in effect helped create in both countries a modern commercial infrastructure.

LATIN AMERICA AND THE ASIA-PACIFIC

The fragileness of the small Easter Island population nearly drove it to extinction in a short period of recruitment for labor in Peru. There was no such danger for Chinese and Japanese. The experiences of immigrant laborers from China and Japan, however, were also revealing of the economic exploitation, racist discrimination, and cultural suppression of Asia-Pacific peoples that attended the formation of the Asia-Pacific region.

Although the coolie labor of the nineteenth century must be distinguished from slavery, it is quite clear that Chinese laborers were imported to Cuba and Peru to substitute for African labor that was lost with the abolition of slavery, and at least initially, they were barely distinguishable from slaves in the conditions of labor as well as in the treatment to which they were subjected.

The eventual success of Chinese in converting themselves into small urban business proprietors and the influx of free Asian immigrants to Latin America in ensuring decades were accompanied everywhere by anti-Asian agitation and mob action, as well as more organized state campaigns and persecution. In emulation of the U.S. Exclusion Act, Latin American governments in the early twentieth century enacted laws to severely limit further Asian, especially Chinese, immigration.

In Mexico, again echoing what had occurred earlier in California, anti-Chinese persecution culminated in 1929–1931, the onset of the Depression, with mass expulsion from Sonora and to a lesser extent Baja California. The once ubiquitous and relatively prosperous Chinese community of Sonora never recovered, although the Chinese have continued to be a viable commercial force in Baja California.

In Peru at the end of the twentieth century, Chinese Peruvians remain a visible minority, their presence illustrated by the numerous and popular *chifas,* or Chinese restaurants, in Lima and other Peruvian towns big and small. Shortly after the triumph of the Cuban Revolution of 1959, a large number of the Cuban Chinese left the island as part of the massive exodus of the Cuban middle class.

Although Japanese communities in Latin America survived more intact than Chinese communities, in some ways anti-Japanese persecution in Latin America reached even greater heights. In Peru, anti-Japanese sentiments led to the government's willingness to allow the U.S. government during World War II to round up and transport 1,429 Japanese Peruvians to the United States for internment in special concentration camps. In spite of this infamy, Japanese immigration resumed after World War II to Peru and especially Brazil. Significantly, from the beginning and throughout its history, Japanese migration to Latin America included more women and children. New immigration and natural reproduction allowed Japanese communities in both Peru and Brazil to continue to grow, until in both countries they came to constitute the largest immigrant community in the postwar period, numbering over 50,000 in Peru and 700,000 in Brazil by the 1970s.[37]

Against this historical background, Alberto Fujimori's election to Peru's presidency is truly extraordinary. On the other hand, the Japanese Peruvians are only cautiously proud of their fellow son of immigrants, fully aware that in the extremely difficult economic condition and volatile political situation of the country, Fijimori could well fail to govern effectively. Should that happen, another round of anti-Asian violence would not be beyond question.

In sum, the Latin American Pacific from the mid-nineteenth to the late twentieth century has been a mixed and often bitter experience for most Asian immigrants. Until Fujimori's election in 1990, Asian Latin Americans led a mostly quiet existence, trying hard not to call excessive attention to themselves.

For the past 150 years, from the California Gold Rush days on, the Pacific has been defined by another kind of Latin American migration. Led by Mexicans, but since the 1960s increasingly joined by Central and South Americans, a stream of legal but mostly undocumented Latin Americans have been streaming across the Mexican border into the United States. Largely in search of better economic opportunities, they also come to escape from civil war and political persecution at home.

At the time of Mexican independence from Spain in 1820, both the United States and Mexico had wide and sparsely settled frontiers rich in natural resources and open land. Both frontiers were also inhabited by hostile indigenous peoples determined to protect their distinctive way of life, land, and environment, and whose resistance to white encroachment made colonization difficult for EuroAmericans in both countries.

With a series of disastrous territorial losses by Mexico (amounting to three-fifths of its national territory) to the United States in the mid-nineteenth century—Texas independence in 1836, the Treaty of Guadalupe Hidalgo in 1848, the Treaty of La Mesilla (Gadsden Purchase) in 1853—the U.S. frontier expanded greatly at the expense of Mexico, and the U.S. government increasingly assumed responsibility for pacifying this broad zone. The long and violent process culminated with the pacification of the Apaches in the 1880s, opening up the final chapter of U.S. conquest of the west and Mexico's colonization of its by then much reduced north.

When the two frontiers finally met along the Rio Grande, they were also transformed into an international border.[38] But far from separating two countries, this border has functioned to integrate Mexico and the United States far more closely than they had ever been before. For twentieth-century Mexicans, this border and the land beyond is known as *El Norte*.[39] The *El Norte* phenomenon has created in Los Angeles the second largest Mexican city in the world, second only to Mexico City.

Driven from their homeland by landlessness and unemployment, twin results of dependent capitalist development, and by revolutions and civil wars, Mexicans have been going north since the days of the California Gold Rush. They continued crossing the border when mining gave way to agriculture, factories, manufacturing, assembly, and service industries in the late nineteenth and throughout the twentieth century. With jobs and economic opportunities constantly beckoning on the other side of the border, Mexicans have become the reserve labor force of the U.S.-Pacific. For Mexicans, this border has always been porous, a legal fiction never intended to keep them out permanently, but merely to control their movement to conform to vicissitudes of the U.S. economy and its changing labor demands.[40]

Although population movements back and forth across the border have involved mostly Mexican laborers, equally significant since the 1880s has been the massive flow of U.S. capital investment into Mexico and the resultant trade with Mexico. Initially concentrated in mining and railroads, since the 1940s it has diversified into commercial agriculture—culminating in the highly technified Green Revolution—and manufacturing. More recently, since 1965, U.S. capital has erected labor-intensive border plants known as *maquiladoras,* which utilize mostly young female labor to assemble products from parts imported duty free into Mexico; the finished products are then shipped back into the United States, also duty free. Touted as an ingenious mechanism to contain surplus Mexican labor within Mexico and hence stem the flow of Mexican workers across the border, the *maquiladoras* have actually served to integrate the Mexican economy even more closely with that of the United States and further consolidate Mexico's dependent status.

Any current and future conceptualization of the Asia-Pacific must contend with the *El Norte* phenomenon and integrate at least Mexico, if not the rest of the Pacific Rim of Latin America, into its configuration. With an equally massive post-1965 migration from Asia, Mexicans and Asians have transformed the demographic makeup of the U.S.-Pacific. According to the 1990 census, these two ethnic/racial minorities already exceed 35 percent of California's total population of nearly thirty million. Through continuous immigration and high reproductive rates, their growth will continue to outstrip that of other EuroAmericans, and their presence severely challenge the preservation of the dominant ethnic composition of U.S. society.

NOTES

1. H. H. Dubs, "The Chinese in Mexico City in 1635," *Far Eastern Quarterly* 1 (1942): 387–89.

2. The popular historian Stan Steiner asserted that a Chinese from Mexico City helped found Los Angeles in the 18th century. A seductive idea undoubtedly, but I believe he made a mistake, based on a misreading of colonial Spanish terminology, specifically a reference to a *chino* named Antonio Rodríguez who was a member of a motley crew of marginalized, mostly mixed-race individuals—8 Indians, 3 mulattos, 2 Blacks, 1 mestizo and 2 Spaniards—seeking their fortune on New Spain's far northern frontier and founding a settlement they named "Ciudad de Los Angeles" (City of Angels). In colonial Spanish terminology, the term *chino* by itself did not refer to a Chinese or an Asian, but rather, a dark-skinned person of mixed racial heritage. To refer to a Chinese or a person from Asia, the colonial records used the term *chinos de Manila.* Stan Steiner, *Fusang: The Chinese Who Built America* (New York: Harper & Row, 1979).

3. Watt Stewart, *Chinese Bondage in Peru: A History of the Chinese Coolie in Peru, 1849–1874* (Durham, NC: Duke University Press, 1951); Evelyn Hu-DeHart, "Coolies, Shopkeepers, Pioneers: The Chinese of Mexico and Peru (1849–1930)," *Amerasia* 15 (1989): 91–116. During this period, about 1.5 million Chinese went overseas, to Southeast Asia, North America, as well as South America and the Caribbean, and other parts of the world. See Arnold Joseph Meagher, "The Introduction of Chinese Laborers to Latin America and the 'Coolie Trade,' 1847–1874" (Ph.D. dissertation, UC Davis, 1975), p. 55. (This is an excellent piece of research that should have been published as an important contribution to an aspect of the international migration of labor in the 19th century.)

The approximately 225,000 Chinese who went to Cuba and Peru were almost exclusively males. So few women went under contract that they were statistically insignificant. A few women went as prostitutes (possibly sent from California by enterprising California Chinese) or free women. The Cuban census of 1872 noted 58,400 Chinese, of whom only 32 were females, 2 under contract, and 30 free. Of the 34,650 noted in the 1862 census, 25 were females. Of the 24,068 in the 1877 census, 58 were females (some possibly born in Cuba and Peru). These figures taken from C. M. Morales papers, vol. 3, no. 19, Biblioteca Nacional José Martí, Havana: Vidal Morales y Morales, "Inmigración de chinos en la Isla de Cuba. Datos que ha proporcionado el que suscrita a Mr. Sanger, Inspector General del Censo" (Collection of clippings, n.d.). The Peruvian census of 1872, which is incomplete, notes 12,849 Chinese in the four coastal provinces of Pacasmayo, Trujillo, Chiclayo, and Lambayeque where the Chinese population was concentrated; only 15 of them were females (Censo de 1872, Archivo General de Peru [AGP]).

4. After experimenting briefly with Chinese coolies in the early 19th century, the British exported massive numbers (1-2 million) of East Indian coolies to the West Indies and East Africa; for a comprehensive study of this coolie trade, see Hugh Tinker, *A New System of Slavery: The Export of Indian Labour Overseas, 1830–1920* (London: Oxford University Press, 1974).

5. Franklin Knight, *Slave Society in Cuba During the Nineteenth Century* (Madison: University of Wisconsin Press, 1970), p. 6.

6. Ibid., p. 22.

7. Cited in Humberto Rodríguez Pastor, *Hijos del Celeste Imperio en el Perú (1850–1900): Migración, Agricultura, Mentalidad y Explotación* (Lima: Instituto de Apoyo Agrario, 1988), p. 32.

8. Michael J. Gonzáles, *Plantation, Agriculture and Social Control in Northern Peru, 1875–1933* (Austin: University of Texas Press, 1985), p. 23.

9. Archivo Nacional de Cuba (ANC), Junta de Fomento, 147/7278. Also, Juan Jiménez Pastrana, *Los chinos en la historia de Cuba, 1847–1930* (Havana: Ed. Ciencias Sociales, 1983), pp. 13–17.

10. Watt Stewart, *Chinese Bondage in Peru*, pp. 13–17; he gives the number of Chinese imported in 1849–1854 as 2,516. The figure of 4,754 taken from Rodríguez Pastor, *Hijos del Celeste Imperio*, p. 27, Cuadro no. 4.

11. *Boletín de Colonización*, I: 18, 15 October 1873. The Boletín, published in 1873 and 1874, was the official organ of the powerful Junta (or Comisión) de Colonización, which had jurisdiction over the coolie trade and the coolies, whom it always and consistently termed *colonos* or *inmigrantes*. The president of the junta was the prominent planter and international businessman, Julián Zulueta, the same who introduced the first coolie cargo to Cuba in 1847. Zulueta exemplified what might be termed vertical integration in the sugar industry of Cuba.

12. Zhang Kai, "Guba Huagong yu ZhongGu jianjiao shimo" (Chinese Labor in Cuba and Establishment of Sino-Cuban Diplomatic Relations), *Huaqiao Huaren Lishi Yanjiu* (Overseas Chinese History Review) 4 (1988): 3–11.

13. Rodríguez Pastor, *Hijos del Celeste Imperio*, p. 39; Stewart, *Chinese Bondage in Peru*, pp. 117, 123.

14. "Actas de la comisión inspectora de asiáticos en la provincia de Santa," *El Peruano*, 29 April 1870; Rodríguez Pastor, *Hijos del Celeste Imperio*, p. 52. Many examples of recontracts in Cuba can be found in the ANC, Misc. de Exp., e.g. 4193/Cs, which contains several for 1868. The Archivo del Fuero Agrario account books for Peruvian plantations also contain much information on recontracted Chinese in the 1870s and 1880s.

15. Antonio Chuffat Latour, *Apunte histórico de los Chinos en Cuba* (Havana: Molina y Cia., 1927), p. 93. *Boletín de Colonización* I:9, 30 May 1873, contains an editorial on the *cuadrillas*, describing them as dedicated "colectivamente a las faenas de la finca."

16. Gonzáles, *Plantation, Agriculture and Social Control*, pp. 71, 93.

17. *Boletín de Colonización* I:18, 15 October 1873. By law, anyone residing in Cuba but not naturalized must be registered as an alien or foreign resident. As most

Chinese in Cuba embarked from Macao, they registered generally with the Portuguese consul in Havana. Besides, there was no representation of the Chinese government in Havana at the time of the census (1872).

18. *Boletín de Colonización* I:9, 30 May 1873 (Editoria); Denise Helly, *Ideólogie e ethnicité. Les Chinois Macao a Cuba, 1847–1886* (Montreal: Les Presses Universitaires de Montréal, 1979), pp. 231–37.

19. Rebecca Scott, *Slave Emancipation in Cuba: The Transition to Free Labor, 1860–1899* (Princeton, NJ: Princeton University Press, 1985), pp. 99–100, 110, 120.

20. Helly, *Ideólogie e ethnicité*, pp. 237–40.

21. Rodríguez Pastor, *Hijos del Celeste Imperio*, pp. 108, 121.

22. "Expediente sobre la averiguación practicada por la Comisión China asesorada por funcionarios del gobierno, respecto a la situación de sus connacionales que prestan sus servicios en las haciendas," Lima, 9 de mayo 1887–diciembre 1888. Biblioteca Nacional, Lima, Peru. This document, also based on testimonies taken from the Chinese (in this case, mostly excoolies, given the late date), is the Peruvian equivalent of the Chinese Commission to Cuba.

23. Rodríguez Pastor, *Hijos del Celeste Imperio*, pp. 145–46, 165.

24. A study of a small but important Chinese community in a sierra town is contained in Isabel Lausent, *Pequeña propiedad, poder y economía de mercado. Acos, Valle de Chancay* (Lima: Instituto de Estudios Peruanos, 1983).

25. Lausent is also the one who has published on the Chinese in the Peruvian Amazon: "Los inmigrantes chinos en la Amazonía Peruana," *Bulletin Institut François d'Etudes Andines* 15 (1986): 49–60.

26. Elsewhere I recount more fully the establishment of the Chinese community in Sonora and Mexican reaction: "Immigrants to a Developing Society: The Chinese in Northern Mexico, 1875–1932," *Journal of Arizona History* 21 (Autumn 1980): 49–86; "Racism and Anti-Chinese Persecution in Mexico," *Amerasia* 9 (1982): 1–28. See also Charles Cumberland, "The Sonoran Chinese and the Mexican Revolution," *Hispanic American Historical Review* 40 (1960): 191–211; Leo H. D. Jacques, "The Anti-Chinese Campaign in Sonora, Mexico, 1900–1931" (Ph.D. dissertation, University of Arizona, 1974).

27. The demographic discussion is based on the following sources: Mexican censuses for 1900, 1910, 1921, 1930; "Extranjeros residentes Estados Unidos de México. Resúmen del censo practicado por la Sría de Gobernación en 1927; y extranjeros, distribución por estados, 14 marzo 1928," Archivo Histórico del Gobierno e Estado de Sonora (AHGES), vol. 50, 1930; Consul A. Willard to State Department, Guaymas, 31 December 1887, U.S. National Archives, General Records of the Department of State, Record Group 59, M284, Roll 4, no. 851; Willard to State, 8 May 1890, RG59/M284/Roll 4, no. 983; Ramon Corral, *Memoria de la administración pública del estado de Sonora* (Guaymas, 1891), vol. I, pp. 586–602; "Comisión oficial encargado del estudio de la inmigración asiática en México, 18 noviembre 1903," reports submitted by district prefects in 1904, AHGES, vol. 1900; Sonora State Government, Census of Chinese residents, submitted by municipal presidents, 1919, AHGES, vol. 3345; "Estado de Sonora, Seccion de Estadística, Año de 1925, Censo Chino," AGHES, vol. 3741; Departamento de Trabajo. Sección de

Conciliación. "Informe que rinde el Jefe de la Sección sobre la situación de las colonias asiáticas en la Costa Occidental de la República," 1919, Archivo General de la Nación/Trabajo, México, D.F.

28. International Chinese Business Directory, 1913.

29. Estado de Sonora. Sección de Estadística. Año de 1925. "Censo Chino," AHGES, vol. 3741.

30. "Lista de los causantes sujetos a la contribución directa ordinaria que tienen capitales de $20,000 en adelante," AHGES, vol. 2968.

31. "Sociedades civiles y mercantiles en Sonora, 1912, 1917, 1918, 1919, 1920," taken from the *Registro Público de la Propiedad* (property registration) of each district, AHGES, vol. 3432.

32. "Noticia estadística comparativa de los giros comerciales e industriales con especificaciones de su capital invertido, de Nacionales y Chinos establecidos en el Estado de Sonora," 2 junio 1925, AHGES, vol. 3758.

33. For a fuller discussion of the Chinese in Baja California Norte, see my article: "The Chinese of Baja California Norte, 1910–1934," *Baja California and the North Mexican Frontier,* Proceedings of the Pacific Coast Council on Latin American Studies, vol. 12 (San Diego, CA: San Diego State University Press, 1985–1986). This pattern of Chinese leasing land from U.S. landowners and contracting Chinese labor gangs to work the land is similar to what happened in California as described in Sucheng Chan, *This Bittersweet Soil: The Chinese in California Agriculture, 1860–1910* (Berkeley, CA: University of California Press, 1986).

34. James L. Tigner, "Japanese Immigration into Latin America: A Survey," *Journal of Interamerican Studies and World Affairs* 23 no. 4 (November 1981): 457–82. Despite their number and importance, little has been published in Spanish or English on the Japanese in Brazil and Peru (though more may be published in Japanese). Among available works, in addition to Tigner, are the following: José Tiago Cintra, *La Migración Japonesa en Brasil (*1908-1959) (México: El Colegio de México, Centro de Estudios Orientales, 1974); C. Harvey Gardiner, *The Japanese and Peru, 1873–1973* (Albuquerque: University of New Mexico Press, 1975); Amelia Morimoto, *Los Inmigrantes Japoneses en el Perú* (Lima: Taller de Estudios Andinos, Universidad Nacional Agraria, 1979); C. Harvey Gardiner, *Pawns in a Triangle of Hate: The Peruvian Japanese and the United States* (Seattle: University of Washington Press, 1981).

35. Tigner, "Japanese Immigration," p. 476.

36. Grant McCall, "European Impact on Easter Island: Response, Recruitment and the Polynesian Experience in Peru," *Journal of Pacific History* 11, pt. 1 (1976): 90–105. See also H. E. Maude, *Slavers in Paradise. The Peruvian Slave Trade in Polynesia, 1862-1864* (Stanford, CA: Stanford University Press, 1981).

37. Evelyn Hu-DeHart, "Asians in Latin America," *Encyclopedia of Latin American History* (forthcoming).

38. For an elaboration of this thesis on the two frontiers becoming an international border, see Friedrich Katz, *The Secret War in Mexico: Europe, the United States and the Mexican Revolution* (Chicago: University of Chicago Press, 1981), Chapter 1.

39. Since the 1960s, Mexicans have been joined by increasing numbers of Central Americans going to *El Norte*. A good depiction of this migration is the film *El Norte*.

40. For a fuller discussion of Mexican labor immigration into the United States and the idea of the border as legal fiction, see James D. Cockcroft, *Outlaws in the Promised Land. Mexican Immigrant Workers and America's Future* (New York: Grove Press, 1986).

PART FOUR

Cultural Formations
in the Asia-Pacific

14

Blue Hawaii: *Bamboo Ridge* as "Critical Regionalism"

PLACE AND DISPLACEMENT

When I look around the island space of Oahu where I have lived and worked at the University of Hawaii since 1976, toward lush green Manoa Valley in Honolulu or the expanding commercial area of Ala Moana and the military complex that is Pearl Harbor, I can no longer think "east" and "west" as primary geographical orientations. I have learned to posit *mauka* (Hawaiian for "toward the mountain") and *makai* ("toward the sea") as bioregional directions, though the interactions of East and West, Pacific and Atlantic, local and international, in cultural and economic senses, are so commingled that ocean-front Waikiki looks like a fusion of the Ginza malls of Tokyo and the sun-lotioned streets of Miami Beach. As Wing Tek Lum, a Chinese-American poet of *Bamboo Ridge* affiliation who lives in his native Honolulu, has phrased this problem of geopolitical *dislocation* and historical *displacement* while trying to figure his own tiny place, as a child growing up in multiethnic Hawaii, upon the map of world history and postcolonial torment:

O
East is East
and
West is West.

but
I never did
understand
why
in Geography class
the East was west
and
the West was east

and that no
one ever
cared
about the difference.[1]

Using a micropolitics of careful perception and slow-moving syntax, Lum's poem defamiliarizes for readers of this "East/West Issue" of *Hawaii Review* that Kipling's late imperial project of Anglo-Saxon global redemption has in certain respects been discredited: where are "East" and "West" in a Pacific region wherein such Eurocentric orientations and EuroAmerican formations of "the Orient" and "the Far East" into commercial unity dissolve into social contradiction and fade into the horizon of the surrounding ocean?[2] In terms of world system, how can anyone map or totalize the unstable relationship of core (center) and margin (periphery) when Tokyo, New York City, Hong Kong, Los Angeles, and Vancouver all override Lum's Honolulu with claims to be the financial and metropolitan "center" of this Asian/Pacific region? In a postmodern context, with universalizing tactics of "Orientalism" undermined and postcolonial politics of ethnic and racial identity emerging as strategies of resistance, a stance of local implication and global import has managed to worry and "care about" theorizing/imagining this very fate of regional *difference* as the Pacific Rim serves as testing ground and crossover site for currencies and standardized products (not the least simulacrous of which are the atomic bombs still tested by France in the oceans of Micronesia) from Asia, the Atlantic, and the Pacific. Lum's questioning of who he is as a Chinese American in Honolulu requires a concrete sense of where he and his community are classed in the "Asian and Pacific Rim" as a blissful/ tormented space of cultural production/ difference/ resistance not only to the much dreaded/admired "Mainland" of Los Angeles and New York City but also in relation to those main-capital and high finance (yen) interactions of Tokyo, Hong Kong, Toronto, Sydney, and Kuwait.

This matter of geopolitical *dislocation* remains a plight of identity, audience, and commitment for writers in Hawaii as they try to imagine and figure forth, in literature as in ordinary language, their (un-represented or under-represented) place, literally, on or off the global map, as well as their exclusion/token inclusion within multicultural canons of national representation such as the *Heath Anthology of American Literature* (1990).[3] Some 2,397 miles west of San Francisco and Los Angeles, "place" (as well as particularities of language, history, and value) remains an enchanted ground and enigma of the imagination for such local authors. For Hawaii is a state whose special, noncontiguous location off the continental mainland cannot gainsay the fact that it abides within the U.S. historical project of Manifest Destiny as a site substantiating some outpost of imperial outreach in the Asian/Pacific region. Hawaii was annexed in 1898, five years after Queen Lilioukalani was deposed by white U.S. business/military interests, and this place remains the site, unavoidably, of the ongoing battle for modern supremacy that was initiated at Pearl Harbor by rival powers (Western/Asian) for Pacific regional hegemony.[4]

Though this threat of "haolification" through the white culture of English and its attendant dilemmas of self-division registers a theme of much of the literature of Hawaii, this enigma of Hawaii's relationship to "the Mainland" U.S.A. is diagnosed in a poem by Joe Balaz from the recent *Aloha 'Aina Concert* film, "Da Mainland to Me." Balaz uses a stubbornly pidgin English that embodies the very linguistic marginality (dialogue) of being identified as outside, minor, other, different, exotic, distant, unreal to a distant place of cultural domination (in this context, Northern California):

> *Eh, howzit brah,*
> *I heard you goin mainland, eh?*
>> No, I goin to the continent.
> *Wat? I taught you goin San Jose*
> *for visit your bradda?*
>> Dats right.
> *Den you goin mainland brah!*
>> No, I goin to da continent.
> *What you mean continent brah?!*
> *Dah mainland is dah mainland,*
> *dats where you goin, eh?!*
>> Eh, like I told you,
>> dats da continent—
>> Hawai'i
>> is da mainland to me.[5]

So reconfigured, which one is the *mainland* of power, work, community, and family, as providing a sense where one's language and culture fits in: Hawai'i or California, "the mainland" or "the island" of a (globalized, international, intertextual) workaday existence? Balaz's punning retort to his unquestioning friend is staunch, terse, and admirably *local* in a committed sense that speaks as grounded in the body and place of regional identity: "Hawai'i is the mainland to me" becomes a slogan of regional resistance. Written in a minority diction, though, Balaz's pidgin poem of place was not published in the *New Yorker* or *Zyzzyva* (with workshop poets Garrett Hongo and Cathy Song, for example, who are used by Norton and Heath to represent—in token and palatable form of ethnic formality—the literature of Hawaii). Instead he was published in one of the staunchly local journals that has helped to promote and circulate such a "local" aesthetic. After the "Talk Story" conference of 1978 and 1979, this literature emerged and flourished, belatedly, in keeping with decolonizing trends in the "American Pacific."[6]

At least since the mixed blessings of U.S. statehood accelerated the impact of technocratic culture and imposed a tourist-driven economy of high rises, urban sprawl, and cash nexus upon the islands in 1959, "Hawaii" has remained a place/sign up for grabs within the literary and filmic capitals: something Hollywood or Joan Didion could inject as backdrop for a detective series to work, use as an exotic landscape parading a Royal Hawaiian Hotel trope of pink-lady paradise and vacation bliss that airline companies refuse to let die, or disseminate around the globe as an ad-poem to sell punch and condominiums with. In short, Hawaii became a region that Westerners could reimagine as a place of surfer girl lyrics and guru initiation movies such as *North Shore* and *Joe and the Volcano* and so on. Against native opposition, Diamond Head, in fact, is slated to become the site of Hawaii's first state film studio, to fund and stimulate such commercial representations as Hawaii shifts from an agricultural to an all-out tourist mode.

So imagined within U.S. discourse, "Hawaii" gets dominantly projected as a region of fantasy and vacation and deployed as an ahistorical Eden of sexual excess that can situate longings for some precapitalist paradise of bodily fulfillment, tribal community, or release from the traumas of overwork in Tokyo or underemployment in Boston. Whatever its troubled history of colonization and plantation settlement, Hawaii flips into the stereotypical moviescape of "Blue Hawaii": a garden of the South Pacific as filmed in these islands, but scripted and made (conceptualized, narrated, and banked upon) for Elvis to play crooning tour guide "local," with lots of strings from the metropolis gleefully attached. Thus this Pacific region has been exoticized, reclaimed, and circulated from these troubled and racially conflicted islands, but made in Hollywood, Tokyo, and New York City. This reduction of history and cultural difference to lush backdrop or seascape of sublimity set apart from the migratory patterns and contradictions of social reality needs to be interrogated, challenged, if not undone by postmodern writers and subjects for whom "Hawaii" is more than a postcard from afar or a chunk of exoticism/orientalism full of lazy Kimos and sexy Suzy Wongs. Drive in along Pearl Harbor and the Nimitz Freeway from Honolulu International Airport, with its neon "Aloha," and your senses will soon confide an alternative message: Oahu and the Outer Islands are far from the simple pastoral "paradise" you had been promised from the snowy streets or toxic sunsets of afar. Neither is Maui just a suburb of California or site of Sierra Club rejuvenation sessions in what Lawrence once labeled "the void Pacific."[7]

THE LOCAL MEETS THE GLOBAL

The fears and desires that accompany this politics of regional identity formation as positing some act of local resistance to metropolitan centers of hegemonic culture have accelerated, by capitalist hook and cybernetic crook in these decades of postmodernism, into an even more decentered geopolitics of *dislocation* and *displacement*. "All that was local becomes increasingly glob-alized, all that is global becomes increasingly localized" as Edward Soja claims of urban transformations now taking place to restructure the Pacific Rim.[8] This push-and-pull aspect of postmodernity—argued in diverse cultural studies such as the formulation of the creolized recuperation of the anglophonic novel undertaken in "english" margins of the dismantled British commonwealth in *The Empire Writes Back,* Kenzaburo Oe's postwar commitment to the regional periphery of a residually imperial and centrist Japan, the literature of "the Pacific Way" as making up some region of post-colonial solidarity and resistance, as well as Kenneth Frampton's architectural advocacy of "a place-conscious poetic" of rearguard resistance to technocratic culture[9]—assumes that peripheral cultures are threatened, on several fronts, from pressures of global commodification and the push toward shopping mall unity. Even as these variously grounded "local" cultures try "to qualify the received consumerist civilization through a consciously cultivated 'culture of place,'" neighborhoods turn placeless and dissolve without trace of nostalgia, outside languages flow into and inhabit the inside, deregulated industry turns multiplex and liquid as flights of world capital flow into and out of any homegrown region with the speed of cyberpunk cowboys.[10]

If the "the local" encounters "the global" under pressures from these international reconfigurations of region, language, identity, and place, it needs to be recognized that this dynamic of fluid capital still *molests* the local with effects of cultural and economic uprooting that entail bewilderment; mimicry of the metropolitan or imperial center; creolized pastiche; tactical resistance; and an unequal distribution of information, profit, and pain. Drinking a glass of Meadow Gold milk or eating one of the Dole pineapples in Hawaii, for example, you consume the synthetic by-product of a Green Revolution with untoward local consequences. As Darrell Lum's anecdote of EDB trenchantly suggests, this version of "the local" may not be all that wholesome or natural and may, in fact, be toxic to your survival:

> Of course, there are the nature themes which, according to some visiting writers, appear too much and too often in local literature. But why shouldn't we [Hawaiian authors] write about nature when locals know that the EDB (ethylene dimethylbromide, more simply, ant poison) sprayed on the pineapples shows up in the drinking water years after they stop using the insecticide. This isn't standing-in-awe-of or ain't-it-beautiful nature writing that we're talking about.[11]

These Dole pineapples, too, have gone the way of global postmodernism, become a simulacrum of the dying agricultural market in Hawaii that is forcefully phasing out the entire island of Lanai as I speak into a totally planned and manipulated space of golf courses and tourist resorts, again to the chagrin (and impotence) of local workers who have labored for three or four generations in such fields and now are asked to service these new hotels. Remember, as Wing Tek Lum urges in "Local Sensibilites," this pineapple is another object that is invested with local labor and memory: "When I see a pineapple,/ I do not think of exotic fruit sliced in rings/ to be served with ham,/ more the summer jobs at the cannery/ driving a forklift or packing wedges on the line."[12]

The end result of such a drive to economic homogenization may be a reconfiguring of the native Hawaiian landscape of Oahu, that is to say, into an advanced tourist mode of shopping mall redemption. This will generate a space in "the American Pacific" fit for the well off of the First World such as Japan, the United States, and the EC to vacation in, stylize, pacify, simulate, parody, desacralize, and consume. Any version of the *local* or *regional,* as I am urging, will have to be spread upon the cognitive map of *global postmodernity* that Fredric Jameson, David Harvey, Stuart Hall, Edward Soja, and other "post-Fordist" geographers and critical theorists have conceptualized as that "world space of multinational capital" in which the material/tropological production of Asian/Pacific culture, in Los Angeles or Vancouver as in Honolulu, now takes place. Describing the by-now-lost U.S.\$15 billion that circulated in the seventy countries from Panama to Luxembourg, Hong Kong, and the Cayman Islands where the Bank of Credit and Commerce International (BCCI) was, as it were, located, a U.S. investigator puts the matter of this postmodern dislocation succinctly: "It [BCCI capital] was located everywhere but regulated nowhere," which recalls the medieval sense (still invoked by Emerson and William James) of an omnipotent Godhead whose "center [of power] was everywhere and whose circumference was located nowhere."[13]

Since places and languages no longer match or fit prior configurations of imperial domination, the spatial and temporal coordinates of such a condition of global/local interaction have to be imagined and brought to public consciousness, and culture as such "demands a priority of attention" as one site where such cognitive mapping, adjustment, and counterhegemonic resistance can take place.[14] Given these transformations of regional infrastructure, questions of where to locate emerging modes of postcolonial cultural production and strategies of "local literatures" within this globalizing economy of telematic instantaneity and environmental molestation can no longer be phrased as questions of "Who Am I?" or "Where Is My Origin?" but something like, "Where Are We?" or "Where Are We Going?" as a community with a disintegrating ethos of the tactile, natural, vernacular, and near. This dilemma of postmodern locality has been phrased contextually, as a rather Gramscian bumper sticker from the 1960s—"Think globally, act locally." Because local culture as such occurs within a boundary-bashing world system that goes on dismantling places and nation-states into transnational fusions, and more specifically, confuses and misrepresents whole regions of cultural and political-economic difference (such as that area that Japan and the United States have managed as "the Asia and Pacific Rim"), contemporary questions of "the local" or "regional" will have to be articulated in conjunction with thinking through these configurations of "the global" if any community of regional resistance is to have staying power.

Rejecting illusions of cultural purity or racial priority, those who promote cultural production in "the Pacific Way" aim to invent a syncretic culture of resistance grounded in place, language, and the will to collective decolonization. Albert Wendt argues from this Pan-Pacific perspective, using English as a language capable of regional linkage and historical solidarity between the Oceanic cultures of 1,200 indigenous languages, English, French, Hindi, and Spanish as well as various forms of pidgin: "Our quest should not be for a revival of our past cultures, but for the creation of new cultures, which are free of the taint of colonialism and based firmly on our own past." Since 1976, Wendt has called upon this collective process and named his work one of inventing the emerging postcolonial culture of "a new Oceania."[15]

As a cultural region, this formation of the Pacific (either in its hegemonic or counterhegemonic mode) remains a complex, contradictory, and multicentered space of production. As the Fijian critic Subramani has argued of these staggeringly complex cultures of the Pacific, "Each of the regions is oriented towards the power that colonized it: Papua New Guinea, after independence, is still linked to Australia; the French territories are connected to France; the American territories gravitate towards the United States; Easter Island is totally dependent on Chile"; whereas the Polynesian and Melanesian regions such as Fiji and Tonga that were grouped together during the British colonial era still look to London.[16] As one "American Pacific" case in point, I would elaborate "Hawaii" as exactly such a region of cultural imagining and site of critical resistance that must be situated, in the territories of the so-called Asian/Pacific Rim, within a global context of hegemonic domination that we can denominate, after the dismantling of the Berlin Wall, the ratification of START, and the technoeuphoric war in the Persian Gulf, "the New World Order." Drawing upon my involvement as a writer and critic of the local-literature scene for fifteen years, I will focus upon the "authentically local" culture of Hawaii as positing one such discourse of "critical regionalism." My goal is to articulate the regionally and ethnically inflected literature that has materialized in Hawaii since 1975 as a protopolitical ground, however illusory or fragile, for cultural resistance, projected community, and the recovery of a labor-troubled history and multivoiced critique of imperial domination.

In positing Hawaii as the space of counterhegemonic discourse and a "critical regionalism" capable of resisting, by means of community imagination, threats of external domination and internal sublimation, I will foreground certain qualities, attitudes, and aspirations that would make up this culture of the "authentically local." I will go on to focus upon two institutions in contemporary Hawaii that have been crucial to the formation of a distinctly Hawaiian literature hallmarked by these voices and tones of regional resistance: (a) *Bamboo Ridge,* the largely Asian-American journal formed in 1978 (in conjunction with the Talk Story conference in Honolulu) that has been the main outlet for the publishing and support of literary regionalism in the islands; (b) I will also touch upon the work of the Hawaii Literary Arts Council (HLAC), a statewide and town-grown coalition based in Honolulu that was formed in 1974 and has challenged, stimulated, and at times opposed this local regionalism with outside influxes of national and international pluralism.

"AUTHENTICALLY LOCAL"

One of the buzzwords in American education and literature today is "multi-cultural." But Bamboo Ridge has been multi-cultural from the beginning [1978]. We didn't follow any Mainland trends. In this case, they chased after us.[17]

One of the distinguishing marks of "local" cultural production that has emerged in Hawaii since the Talk Story conference of 1978 and 1979 started shaking up the by-products and forms of local literature and history, especially as this literary scene has centered around *Bamboo Ridge, Ramrod, Seaweeds and Constructions,* as well as other cultural journals of local commitment, has been the claim that "local literature" can *somehow* be recognized, by language, style, and cultural attitude, as "authentically local." All well and good—as strategic assertion of *difference.* But what exactly is this complex of qualities that can be validated as "authentically local"?

In a polemic for cultural authenticity called "Local Literature and Lunch" (1986), Darrell Lum brought some clarity to this unstable situation of defining the "authentically local" when he contended that "a number of Hawaii writers choose to describe themselves as local writers of 'local literature' (as opposed to 'Asian American' literature, largely a mainland term, or 'Hawaiian' literature, which the locals know means native Hawaiian literature."[18] By theory as well as expressive practice in pidgin-based works of striking originality such as *Sun* and *Oranges Are Lucky,* the novelist and playwright Lum (along with poets of diverse cultural and political commitment such as Eric Chock, Joseph Balaz, Dana Naone Hall, Richard Hamasaki, Juliet Kono Lee and others) has gone on to align himself with this distinct and mainland-resistant category we would now differentiate and commend as "authentically local." Of course any invocation of liberal pluralism can be an easy, fake cure to soothing the tensions and contradictions that drive and animate the "authentically local." It can be a way, finally, of absorbing and containing the drive to Hawaiian sovereignty, land rights, native religion, and cultural recovery now taking place by those who identify themselves not as hyphenated Americans but as indigenous "Hawaiians."[19] But Lum's troubled three-category separation of "the local" from both "Asian-American" and "Hawaiian" literatures suggests some of the difficulties and dangers any exclusionary definition of "the local" would confront when articulating the racial, linguistic, and historical dynamics of the overdetermined multicultural literature scene now emerging in contemporary Hawaii.

Furthermore, if we could identify such a complex of styles and attitudes, rooted in a sensibility for place or an enduring taste for pidgin English, for example, what would "local" mean anymore in an era of international finance and global molestation when a colorful and funky surf shop calling itself "Local Motion" can be bought out lock, stock, and stylistic barrel by a corporate conglomerate from Japan? In other words, what kind of purchase would "the authentically local" imply toward articulating and *resisting* the larger hegemonic forces of a shopping mall world? (Ironically, Lum had used this very same Local Motion shop in 1986 to stand for one aspect of the local-culture movement in "Local Literature and Lunch.")[20]

In "Waiting for the Big Fish: Research in the Asian American Literature of Hawaii," an early foray into historicizing local literature in *The Best of Bamboo Ridge Anthology* (1986), Stephen H. Sumida had first begun to challenge the tired colonial commonplace that Hawaii had produced no distinctive literature of its own with a crucial counterargument contending that an "authentically local, Hawaii literature began unmistakably to sound its voice in the postwar years."[21] As one of the organizational participants in the Talk Story scene, circa 1978–1981, Sumida at least knew the impetus driving this local culture of Hawaii as it emerged and sought to counter the fake paradise and erotic primitivism images circulating in the mass media and mainland literature of "Blue Hawaii" as seen, say, from a whiskey-hazed 747 window or the hegemonic view from a Hollywood Porsche. Sumida, Lum, Chock, and others wanted to seize the narrative apparatus, as it were, to recall, represent, and begin to circulate images and "talk story" of a Hawaii they could recognize as cultural home. Journals, presses, and coalitions soon emerged in the 1980s to fill in the literary gap when such outlets, prior to this time, did not broadly exist. Theory and cultural criticism lagged along rather than led the way in trying to articulate what needed to be done.

As a student of English and American Studies at the University of Hawaii in the 1970s, Sumida had been stung and wounded by a remark made by James Michener while putting *A Hawaii Reader* anthology to market during the first year of statehood (1959), the same year that Michener's *Hawaii* propagated his pseudo-history novel of "Hawaii." Michener had stupidly—and repressively—urged that those Hawaiian citizens "Oriental in ancestry" "having arrived in the islands as laboring peasants ... did not produce a literature of their own."[22] The blithe orientalism of such a remark helped to create a false canon and contributed to a dominant set of misrepresentations and cliches of Hawaii as propagated by mainland writers such as Twain, London, Taggard, and May Sarton, and Europeans like Stevenson and Maugham "shanghaied in Honolulu," as it were, or poets such as Rupert Brooke who amazingly wrote of "Waikiki" in 1913 that "Somewhere an ukelele thrills and cries/ And stabs with pain the night's brown savagery" [sic].[23]

In *And the View from the Shore: Literary Traditions of Hawai'i* (1991), arguing a more fully grounded *countermemory* to Michener, Magnum, and crew who work in the tourist industry of pastoral-paradise schmaltz so as to recall how "night's brown savagery" still threatens the Royal Hawaiian Hotel with racial and cultural otherness, Sumida has gone on to flesh out some of the genres, themes, tones, language tactics, authors, and works that have counted as and would make up a multicultural literature of what I am calling the "authentically local."[24] Drawing sweepingly upon extraliterary genres such as newspaper writing, songs, hula chants, histories, and the work of stand-up comics as well as critically reading important narrative examples of the "local-literature" tradition such as Milton Murayama's *All I Asking For Is My Body* (1975), John Dominis Holt's *Waimea Summer* (1976), and O. A. Bushnell's *The Return of Lono* (1956), Sumida has begun to articulate the specific textual/ideological and multicultural ingredients of what it means for the literature of Hawaii to become and remain "authentically local." For Sumida, "local" is not a racial nor even a geographical criterion so much as a sustained commitment to articulating a shared *ground* (Hawaii as place) and sense of *history* (one that recalls plantation history as well as forces of colonial appropriation) as well as embodiment in an authentic *language* (local style). As Sumida confessed to fellow local writer and critic, Tino Ramirez, while recalling his pastoral roots in his family's Aiea watercress farm, local means a commitment to *cultivate* the agricultural/cultural ground of Hawaii in both material and cultural senses: "You have to take care of the land because it supports you. If you don't, the island turns into a dump for imported resources and there's no life. Culture is the same: The word implies planting, tending and nurturing."[25]

And the View from the Shore is in the author's own words, "intended as a catalyst" to the cultivating, preserving, and transmitting of this local culture of the "Asian Pacific," and it is certainly—if unevenly—that. As the first scholarly narrative to attempt to describe, in sweeping summary for local and mainland consumption, the "literary traditions of Hawaii" as a distinct set of genres (primarily the so-called complex idyll and heroic), language styles (vernacular values rooted in pidgin English, though not exclusively so), and cultural attitudes (largely an ethos of family, community, and commitment to local ecology as well as *aloha aina,* for example), Sumida's pioneering book is bound to evoke and provoke hard-hitting critiques, counternarratives, and critical perspectives that would challenge many aspects of his ground-breaking summation. Whatever reservations emerge, many writers and scholars immersed in the local-literary scene, myself included, have much to be grateful for in this generous-hearted, brave, and category-defining study.

Admitting my overall respect for this important study, I nevertheless find much to contend with in Sumida's analysis, not the least of which is its sublation of the indigenously Hawaiian perspective into that of a dominantly Asian-American one, its liberal-American pastoralism of child, laboring swain, and place, as well as its very recognizably EuroAmerican urge to categorize if not to compell literature from the "pastoral" to the "heroic" as dominant modes of local-cultural production. Virgil and Milton may have moved from youthful pastoral to the more heroic epic modes of representation in the *Aeniad* and *Paradise Lost,* establishing the canonical pattern of the Western imagination, but why should Hawaii's writers follow this very Eurocentric pattern so rooted in imperial ambition and the will to historical domination? Oddly enough, Sumida seems to second the Asian-American and mainlandish claim of Frank Chin that in Sumida's words, Hawaii's writers should go "beyond the established limits to take pidgin [English] from the pastoral [as in Lum's short stories] into the heroic" [as in Bushnell's novels] (103). Resisting such a teleological use of generic categories, however, why should Hawaii's writers aspire to achieve works of "the heroic," that most Eurocentric, male-based, and even imperialist of forms as these literary prototypes come down "from da mainland" through Homer, Milton, and Whitman to these Polynesian shores?

In ironic respects, Sumida's study started out as a "view from the shore" of Hawaii to the mainland and thereby posited a perspective of marginalization, difference, and critique. But *And the View from the Shore* has ended up, by disciplinary reversal and the type-assimilating perspective and all-engulfing pluralism of American Studies, a "view from the shore" of the mainland to Hawaii as making up a rather recognizable literary territory after all. This scholarly pastoralism needs to be distanced and critiqued, however, because ("simple" or "complex," "hard" or "soft") such pastoralism remains, I would claim, the dominant ideology of liberal Americanists such as Sumida's mentor at Amherst, Leo Marx, who hovers over the central terms and literary mythology of this study.[26]

Emerging in the back-to-nature movement of the 1960s, American pastoralism would recycle a set of utopic conventions that allow "nature" to coexist as retreat from hegemonic forces of technology and industry, a green space of transcendence wherein (European) art and (American) nature could come into harmony and cultivation as an "earthly garden" that constitutes a recuperated Eden (at Walden Pond, for example). Such was and still is the dominant myth—or "myth at first sight"—of an American Studies beholden to the nineteenth-century romanticism of Thoreau and Muir. It is surprising and cumbersome to see Sumida read the literature of Hawaii through these very deeply *EuroAmerican* categories of pastoral/heroic and even posit the oddly aboriginal notion that pastoral seemingly sprang forth from Hawaiian volcanoes and indigenous chants, that is, that there was a primordial "Polynesian pastoral." "These concepts [of pastoral and heroic] were ready-made well before the arrival of James Cook's expedition in 1778" (4), Sumida claims, so that non-Western native mythologies and Eurocentric *haole* forms co-conspired to produce the (pastoral) illusion and (heroic) adventure first conjuring "Hawaii as paradise." A more critical genealogy of Pacific/American pastoral is called for, one situated within colonial dynamics of translation and exchange.

Not until Sumida gets to critiquing Mark Twain's abandoned novel of Victorian Hawaii, by way of the Western primitivist and "noble savage" fantasies of Melville, Cooper, and James Jackson Jarves, does he brilliantly begin to acknowledge and more fully confront the troubled colonialist dynamics of such uneven cultural exchanges. Sumida argues that though Twain promoted a soft-pastoral and tourist-like image of Hawaii as "the loveliest fleet of islands that lies anchored in any ocean," he had thought more darkly and historically in this contradictory novel of the antipastoral impact of disease, greed, legalized theft, racism, and industrial capitalism upon the "island kingdom sitting in the path of America's Manifest Destiny" (39). As Twain intuited, this place of Diamond Head and Pearl Harbor still has much to teach any American Adam innocent how deeply and how early the United States was already grounded in the history of colonial appropriation and the policing of the South Pacific.

I would concede, nonetheless, that Sumida's last chapter, "Hawaii's Local Literary Tradition," provides a splendid summary and survey of the themes and tactics that first emerged in the context of Talk Story and Bamboo Ridge. Trying to acknowledge as well as come to terms with the very distinct and distinctive *Hawaiian* traditions running through and energizing the local, Sumida urges that "the Hawaiian culture was rich in chants, dance, poetry, history, legend, and countless other arts" (272), and goes on to draw this future-oriented moral from such authentically local cultural production: "It seems to me that in this [cultural production by Hawaiians] is a recognition—from a people's actual hard experience of living on islands—that the arts, too, are absolutely necessary for survival." The local, so stated, is not a residual regionality (as often seems the U.S. South) but an emergent one capable of claims upon the national center.

BLUE HAWAII AND ''BAMBOO RIDGE''

This issue of "Hawaii" as indigenous territory is one that Hawaiians, in a biological as well as a geopolitical sense, refuse to see as just another forgotten metaphor or semiotic dance by white men on English-speaking Bibles. Rather, they see the issue as a life-and-death imposition on their very language and ecology, their culture as a way of life. Confronting this historical displacement, it should come as no surprise that contemporary Hawaiian writers, both indigenous and "local," remain spiritually *blue:* blue as that tour guide pseudo-Hawaiian Elvis in *Blue Hawaii,* blue as a plantation worker before the war, blue as an oblivion-inducing tourist drink, blue despite being in a so-called biological paradise of flowing mai-tais and see-through clothes, blue as the Delta blues of Robert Johnson despite the lure of surf, the call of body-bliss, the way of the ocean and sky.

Given the heteroglossic diversity ranging from work-ethic Japanese to land-grabbing developers to the slower paced, generous, live-and-let-live Samoans, say, or the Koreans who seem (even displaced in the United States) to run on ginseng, Confucius, and moral methedrine, "Hawaii" needs to be taken into U.S. consideration as a region with a distinct history and multicultural diversity worthy of wider recognition. *Bamboo Ridge* has managed sucessfully, within a decade, to serve these diverse audiences, styles, and tastes since its Talk Story conference beginnings in creating a narrative/poetic outlet. Cultivating "local writing" in the islands, *Bamboo Ridge* has given ground and place to help materialize, in distinct language, the spirit of "local writing" since its inception after the Talk Story conference. The magazine and press has functioned like the fishing place near the waters off Koko Head on Oahu and the particular style of slide-bait fishing it is named after: at once as a place of nourishment and as a place of manna, diverse voices (poles) who go "searching for his/her god [poem] off Bamboo Ridge" as Tony Lee writes in his flashback story on the ways of old, "Nowadays Not Like Before."[27] "Bamboo Ridge": it remains a place and metaphor of spirit power and ecological poetics, *local* only in some William Carlos Williams sense of loving the ground and body of place in full particularity. A place of daily love and fish-filled survival, hardly at all like the Hanauma Bay (not so far from Bamboo Ridge, actually) that served as the silly backdrop for that local tour guide, Elvis Presley, to croon his moonstruck love songs to while courting a moonstruck tourist wahine in *Blue Hawaii.*

This journal of Hawaii writers called *Bamboo Ridge* depends upon an ethos and center, which remains a hardworking, voluntary, and plural-spirited group of locals based around Eric Chock, Mari Hara, Wing Tek Lum, and Darrell Lum whose goal remains much the same since its founding—to promote the literary arts in the island, both by nurturing an intricate array of local talents, old and young, and by juxtaposing their work with better known talents from the outside world like William Stafford or Garrett Hongo to challenge the writing that goes on here to make larger claims upon "America" as a cultural artifact.

It should now be recognized, too, given the plight of pidgin English to be expressed for imaginative uses as well as the reign of commodity forms within the literary marketplace where poetry, say, seems self-enclosed if not publicly irrelevant, that this nurturing of "literary pluralism"—in some full sense allowing for radically mingled subjects, plural cultures resisting any master narrative of racial or technocratic unity—is no small feat in so-called melting-pot and hodgepodge-quilt Hawaii. This need to enlist a "literary pluralism" remains necessary in Hawaii given the sway of mainstream (and mainland) marketings and genre categories over such minority languages and (merely) regional literatures. Such literature is for the most part ignored or reprocessed, given the territorializing reach of U.S. empire, as it were, that can encode the ordinary lyric subject with liberal arguments and terms, reifications of capital, its own brand of add-one-more-ethnic-and-stir pluralism turning the nation into a gigantic shopping mall of which Oahu's Ala Moana or Newport Beach's Fashion Island are U.S.-sublime instances.

Despite these forces of U.S. marketing and liberal crisis management, these outlets for Hawaiian writing have cultivated in the 1970s and 1980s a literary "heteroglossia" of mixed voices and tongues that might otherwise starve out or have gone unrecognized in this state so far as it is (in a way, *luckily*) from the bright-lights-and-big-city voices of New York and Hollywood. Thus, *Bamboo Ridge,* as the main literary outlet of such localism and Asian-American heteroglossia since 1978, has nurtured not a "fantasy island" literature of the islands, written by clever (I could even say unwittingly imperialist) outsiders. An historically acute literature of Hawaii, "*local*" in this cutting sense means in touch with the traditions, forms, terms, the body and ground of this much-imaged and much-contested place. "Local," in this contestational sense, means the polyvocal enactment of critical regionalism, a strategy of resistance from postmodern architecture to which my argument will return.

Without committed journals such as Joe Balaz's pidgin-oriented *Ramrod* or Richard Hamasaki's Pan-Pacific *Seaweeds and Constructions,* which has aligned local literary production with the decolonizing literature of "the Pacific Way," many local writers would have been silenced or simply died off without writing. Not everybody can make the superwoman-like leap from teaching English at Midpac and UH to the Dick Cavett show through the worldwide distribution exposure of Random House like Maxine Hong Kingston. Not everybody, that is, has Max's amazingly graceful if not spiderlike patience and endurance, her touch of narrative genius and canny sense of market self-positioning—a "woman warrior" indeed who could even subvert the petunia elegies of the *New Yorker* with her tripmaster monkey rapping out urban trauma like a Chinese-American Whitman on acid. The eccentric fate of Milton Murayama, self-published and belatedly recognized, however, seems much more likely for any willfully local writer, committed to the terms and values of one place and off voices. Such a writer is committed, that is, to the narrating and lyric documenting of a particularly troubled history of Japanese-American plantation workers in wartime Hawaii, many of whom confronted cold war exclusion on into the 1950s and statehood, as Steve Sumida has exposed and as I have written about in my own analysis of Milton's multilanguaged novel of Japanese plantation life as a working-class pastoral.[28]

As for *Bamboo Ridge*, well, Bamboo Ridge is Bamboo Ridge. Spunky, vital, ongoing, recurring, broad hearted, ecological, political, spiritual, micropolitical, cosmic, poor, yet *blue: blue* in some sense early Elvis of Sun Records could figure out as heart tone; blue as the poetry of lyric Memphis and his gigantic-hearted mother; blue as the azure depths off Hanauma; blue as the uncapturable gratitude toward place; blue and refreshing in the glut and glamour of literary magazines like blue shave-ice or ice-shave. *The Best of Bamboo Ridge* anthology that came out in 1986 and is widely used in courses in Hawaii and on the mainland (for example, at UC Santa Cruz, where Sarah Wilson is studying "Asian-American Literature" and reading about her father's gratitude to Italian-American blue in "Anita Sky") is just one installment of an ongoing project in critical resistance and regional self-invention.[29] "Hawaii," as counterlanguage, is threatened by the antipluralist forces of homogenization. As Juliet Kono Lee portrays through her mishmash son in "Yonsei," U.S. pop culture threatens to abolish memory, override ethnic tradition, and render place unrecognizable to those who once inhabited it. The mother chides this fourth-generation son oblivious to Japanese-American traditions on the Big Island as he heads out to surf, "shouldering a radio,/ smouldering the speaker/ into your ear,"

> You live so far
> from what connects you.
> You have no recollection
> of old plantation towns,
> of rains that plummeted
> like the sheaves of cane,
> the song of flumes,
> the stink of rotting feet,

the indignities of hard labor.
Your blood runs free
from the redness of soil.[30]

But just putting koa wood counters at McDonalds in Waikiki or Peggy
Hopper sailboats on the McDonalds in the Hawaii Kai Shopping Mall does
not constitute a "local style" of critical-regional resistance; nor does putting
Suzy Wong dresses and white bucks on Hotel Street characters result in a distinctly "Hawaiian" literature, even if that convention-coded writer is/was
"Hawaiian" and readers on the mainland, especially New York City, cannot
tell or care to know the historically necessary *difference* as an act of critical/
stylistic resistance. This strategy of a "critical regionalism" in postmodern
culture would resist, through local styles and tones, the threat of technocratic modernization and Western "reason" to folk cultures and indigenous
traditions or regional locales. As Kenneth Frampton outlines, such an aesthetic of "rear-guard" [sic] architecture is enunciated as a counterhegemonic
discourse to Western modernity. As such, U.S. regionalism need not be the
code term for a neoromantic retreat from history into boyhood sentiment or
those hazy charms of pastoral submission. Frampton argues for deploying
such tactics of "local culture" to resist the threat of global homogenization
and Western modernism, assuming that counterlanguages and counterforms
to the "logic" of high-tech capital can be consciously voiced and inflected as
regional style without succumbing to decoration or decadence.[31]

Two works I would commend as exactly acts of such "critical regionalism" are the pidgin-rooted short stories of Darrell Lum in *Sun* (1980) and
the politicized lyrics of place and voice in Eric Chock's *Last Days Here*
(1990). Both of these authors have served, by necessity and vision, as founding editors of *Bamboo Ridge*. As Eric Chock depicts the sway of local culture
as a ground of commitment and critique to international capital in a recent
poem called "Home Free," for example, the sense of threat is imminent (as
his book title, *Last Days Here*, suggests):

I am like my father
who never left Hawaii,
working the dry docks at Pearl,
sending the ships back
to some foreign port
or out at sea.
He would rather go home after work
to the quiet place beside the stream. [...]
But now I stand beside
what used to be our stream:
the smell of grease or garbage reeks.
The influx of certain birds
limits the number of mangoes I can eat.

Even the tv, where he used to say,
"Come quick Mommy, we can go to Paris,
for free!"
is no longer clear enough
without a cable hook-up
so fenced in are we
with condominiums walking up from town,
into our valley.

Chock then turns from this register of local molestation to utter a future-oriented plea of entrenchment, the will to be "home free":

Now that I've grown up, and gone away,
I want to develop my own sense of green.
I want to be able
to cup my hands in a clear stream.
All I want
is to be home free.[32]

As ethnic writers such as Frank Chin, Richard Hamasaki, or Lawson Inada have done in different terms, I would reiterate that Americans of ethnic origin need *not* ride this hyphen of self-conflicted identity to mainstream marketings, self-positionings of "voice" still centered in New York. The stylistic result could be the authenticity of voice that the career of Milton Murayama embodies or the locally inflected poetry of Eric Chock, who registers this stance so far from the workshop spotlights of Wesleyan, Iowa, and Yale. The end result could as well be oblivion or regional marginalization, which means another form of national silence.

THE LABORS OF HLAC

Founded in 1974 with the institutional goal "to serve the literary arts in Hawaii," the Hawaii Literary Arts Council (HLAC), with funding from the State Foundation on Culture and the Arts and usually with supplemental funding from the National Endowment for the Arts, in addition to arranging an incredibly diverse program of readings for Oahu and the outer islands, has maintained such formative programs as the Poets in the Schools (again, under Eric Chock's leadership) and the useful Hawaii Children's Literature Conference and puts out a pluralistic magazine *Literary Arts Hawaii* (now called *Kaimana*) under the care of editors such as Jill Widner and Pat Matsueda in the past and Tony Quagliano, Anthony Friedson, and Joseph Stanton in the present.

The writers brought to read in Hawaii every month are strong in diversity and range: Margaret Atwood, Gary Snyder, Cathy Song, Albert Wendt, Arthur Sze, Ron Silliman, Victor Cruz, Milton Murayama, John Ashbery—just to name a few that remain vivid in my memory. Granted, most ot these writers came from the mainland and this provoked some local controversy and resistance, as Steve Sumida has documented. Yet with such a cantankerous inside grounding in tradition (*Bamboo Ridge* et al.) and an outside influx of techniques and agonistic challenges (HLAC et al.), is it any wonder that a new literature has emerged so fully in the 1980s? Audiences for such HLAC-sponsored literary readings over the years have ranged in size from full houses of around 150 at Korean Studies Center and 1,200 at Church of the Crossroads (Gary Snyder), to those attended by three or four friends of the author and a flickering candle (Edith Shiffert of Kona, now of haiku-laden Japan). The glut of these myriad readings go on until the would-be local poet might flee back to the oceans of the North Shore to get his/her head together; or to the sanctuary of actual fishing off Bamboo Ridge; or to drink alone with the radio; or (like myself) to play Robo-cop basketball on Roy Sakuma Productions' court on Sunday instead of going to mass or staying home to become an NBA couch potato.

Beyond such sponsored events, HLAC encourages and honors resident writers in the state through awards such as the Hawaii Award for Literature (which was given at the State Capitol to Reuel Denney for 1988, for example) and the Elliot Cades awards (given to Juliet Kono Lee and Darrell H. Y. Lum in October 1991)—two substantial awards to recognize "promising" and "middle-level" local writers at points in their careers when such honors can do their writerly souls and pockets maximal good. I call attention to this HLAC history to suggest, in local terms, that there is a link between literacy and literature. The cultivation of reading and writing skills not only by *Bamboo Ridge* and HLAC but by ordinary citizens needs to be encouraged "at both ends of the spectrum," as Frank Stewart of the UH writing program has noted. Young people can encounter not only the basics of language but the most challenging and imaginative uses of their language. The end result for Hawaiian-grown children will be that inward creativity, synthetic thinking, and metaphoric leaps across boundaries can come about in whatever field the student chooses to apply his/her talents.

I would like to narrate this collective work on the spirit-body of local literature and minority languages with one anecdote. In September 1987, I participated in a reading to celebrate the appearance of *Bamboo Ridge* 33. Such potluck-like readings to celebrate the appearance of *Bamboo Ridge, Hawaii Review, Ramrod,* or *Chaminade Literary Review* are sponsored by HLAC, often giving small funds for writers to come from the outer islands. These community-building readings of local imagination and regional commitment, like those of Language Poets in Berkeley, say, have become vital, necessary events for local writers to hear living tones, themes, terms, moves, images, challenges from the Outside—"voices"!

After I had read a few of my own poems on love and death in South Korea, I sat down next to Jonathan Penner (then a visiting novelist at UH Manoa from the U of Arizona) to hear other readers. I was struck by the usual diversity of voices and forms at any *Bamboo Ridge* event—the generational portraits of Mavis Hara, Diane Kahanu, and Wing Tek Lum; the growing-up-local narrative of Rodney Morales; the wry family images of Barbara Guerin; the highly aestheticized nature poems of Reuben Tam—but I was impressed, in particular, by a short story by Gary Pak—"The Valley of the Dead Air"—about a stench on a plantation that not even the old kahunas can remove. Pak's story uses a range of pidgin voices to capture folk culture, as well as a more sophisticated narrative voice with political insights that recalled the materialist perspectives into social community of Latin American novelists.

As place was given voice, I was really taken by this energetic Korean-American writer. I thought to my all-too-pedagogical soul, "Wow, here are new writers who are building on the narrative traditions of people like Milton Murayama and Maxine Kingston, but taking it further, in a new direction, writing about the state and its history in a way that still needs to be done. Hollywood watch out—Hawaii is so much more than the backdrop for a cops-and-robbers show with glitzy cars, Polynesian dolls, beach-bingo Republicans with Tiger caps whose ideal of U.S. womanhood is, well, Nancy Reagan."

As I mused upon this "local" story, Jonathan Penner turned to me, amazed, and asked, "Are your writers *all* this good here?" I wanted to say "Yes, of course," because my *local pride* had stemmed from a kind of maternal-paternal delight in *generativity*, the sense that I myself (through teaching, through supporting such vital outlets such as *Bamboo Ridge* or Joe Balaz's even more pidgin-based *Ramrod*, through participating in events such as magazine readings cosponsored by HLAC) had helped to hand on literary traditions and tools that could serve to shape the future, in specific ways that I or any jaded literary "old-timer" could not foresee.

Though it may sound like something you add to pluralize U.S. milk, "HLAC" is something you can add to literacy/ literature in Hawaii as a mysterious catalyst with benign effects. For, whatever contentious people are involved, this remains the kind of work that HLAC does: it is a kind of work upon and within the human spirit. The bottom line is, so to speak, these benefits are as real and as lasting as hotels or high-tech bombs, as the work of writers as diverse as Gary Park, Richard Hamasaki, or Milton Murayama can attest.

CONCLUSION: THINKING LOCALLY

In conclusion, I would invoke that bumper sticker refrain of regional pride/ identity that registers in tough-minded senses not yet coopted into a marketing strategy of local penetration by the *Harvard Business Review* and that more embittered writers of decadence or adaptation cannot grasp—"Lucky you live Hawaii [that is, *lucky you don't live in East Lansing!*]." Why remain "*local*"? Well, to my critical ally in San Francisco, Frank Chin, local is one rallying cry to get beyond some apolitical and white-left-brain generated "blue Hawaii" invented and marketed in Hollywood and New York for global distribution. Local in this dynamic and nomadic political sense means *thinking globally but acting locally,* as Darrell Lum's comment on the EDB sublime "nature" recognizes as the ground of Hawaii's commitment to preserve the land.

"Hawaii" is not just a trope of the South Pacific. It is not just a primitive myth of eros or native essence, nor a backdrop for Tom Selleck or Jack Lord to sport around in with some mixed-race locals. Hawaii is not just real estate; not just the site of "gee-aint-it-beautiful" postcards and plumeria-laden love-lyrics.[33] "Hawaii" remains capable of adhering to and broadening the support for a "place-specific poetic," and thereby expressing in multivoiced styles of history the lived-in spirit of a place and region worth preserving and passing on through literature as through other spiritual-material means of struggle.

NOTES

1. Wing Tek Lum, "East/West Poem," *Hawaii Review* Number 10 (Spring/Fall 1980): 140. Lum's commitment to forging a Chinese-American identity particularized in a language of regional location occurs more fully in his first collection of poems, *Expounding the Doubtful Points* (Honolulu: Bamboo Ridge Press, 1987). For related concerns, see *Pake: Writings by Chinese in Hawaii,* ed. Eric Chock and Darrell H. Y. Lum (Honolulu: Bamboo Ridge Press, 1989).

2. On the EuroAmerican production of "the Pacific" as a commercial and geographical region, "Basin," and "Rim," as well as the way this largely occidental invention obfuscated the Asian and Pacific content and motions of this same region, see Arif Dirlik, "The Asia-Pacific Idea: Reality and Representation in the Invention of a Regional Structure," *Journal of World History* 3 (Spring 1992): 55–79. Japan's hegemonic impact upon this region since the 1970s, culturally and economically, cannot be gainsaid.

3. *Heath's* canonization of Hawaiian writers occurs in the Asian-American guise of a Los Angeles/UC Irvine poet, Garrett Hongo, as well as through the work of Cathy Song, a poet from rural Oahu who has after a decade returned from Wellesley and Denver to teach in the state. Ethnically inflected in theme and imagery, both of these much-anthologized writers have much to admire in their work. Although both have appeared in *Bamboo Ridge,* however, their poetry is not tied to any "local-literature" discourse as such but to forms, rhetorical protocols, tones, and terms of logocentric imagery that can be better identified with "workshop" poetry. Responding to a sympo-

sium question on "For Whom Does the Poet Write?" Song reveals the nature of this (hegemonic) commitment: "Let's face it—you write for that cold girl in graduate school, the one in the Advanced Writing Workshop, you know the one who could rattle off Yeats and Hopkins at the drop of a hat, who smoldered poems with allegorical themes on Desire, Love, Jealousy, and Hate, who dismissed every poem you ever brought to class. ... You write with the hope that she'll read your gorgeous poems in *APR* and the *New Yorker*," *Manoa: A Pacific Journal of International Writing* 3 (1991): 108.

4. For a counterhistory of the state from a distinctly Hawaiian point of view and ecology, see Haunani Kay-Trask, "Hawaii: Colonization and Decolonization," in *Class and Culture in the South Pacific,* ed. Anthony Hooper, Steve Britton, Ron Crocombe, Judith Hunstman, and Cluny Macpherson (Suva, Fiji: University of the South Pacific and University of Auckland, 1987), pp. 154–175.

5. Joseph P. Balaz, "Da Mainland To Me," *Chaminade Literary Review* 2 (1989): 109.

6. For one of the first collective manifestations of the "local-culture" movement in Hawaii, see *Talk Story: An Anthology of Hawaii's Local Writers,* ed. Eric Chock, Darrell Lum, Gail Miyasaki, Dave Robb, Frank Stewart, and Kathy Uchida (Honolulu: Petronium Press/Talk Story Inc., 1978). The opposition between Maxine Hong Kingston and Frank Chin, her most forceful antagonist, accusing her (unlike Milton Murayama or Chin himself) of mainstream marketings that entail ideological mystifications of Asian-American dilemmas, was first staged at the Talk Story conference in Honolulu: see Edward Iwata's analysis of this ongoing confrontation of Kingston and Chin in "Word Warriors," *Los Angeles Times,* June 24, 1990, pp. E1–9.

7. In *West of the West: Imagining California,* ed. Leonard Michaels, David Reid, and Raquel Scherr (Berkeley, CA: North Point Press, 1989), D. H. Lawrence provides the Eurocentric orientation for such a *westward* march of culture across the continental frontier: "California is a queer place—in a way, it has turned its back on the world, and looks into the void Pacific." *West of the West* offers a feast of ideological imagining, starting with Theodore Roosevelt's closed-frontier lament for "the true west," "When I am in California, I am not in the west. I am west of the west" and ending with Christopher Isherwood's posthistorical glimpse of Edenic banishment into shopping mall sprawl, cinematic simulation, and freeway norm, "California is a tragic land—like Palestine, like every promised land." Needless to say, it never occurs to born-again Californians that there might be a U.S. geography west of their own Edenic dreaming, except to appropriate as a suburb or a mimic footnote, like Maui out glimmering in "the void Pacific." As Shiva Naipaul puts this hegemonic assumption, "What California is doing today, the rest of the United States will be doing tomorrow" (277). The local is posited exactly against such regional arrogance and vanguard domination of the periphery.

8. Edward Soja, "It All Comes Together in Los Angeles," *Postmodern Geographies: The Reassertion of Space in Critical Social Theory* (London and New York: Verso, 1989), p. 217. In a claim I will pluralize and dispute, Soja argues that this postmodernized Los Angeles has become "the financial hub of the Western USA and (with Tokyo) the 'capital of capital' in the Pacific Rim" (192) and later that "securing the Pacific rim has been the manifest destiny of Los Angeles" (225) from the U.S. financial and military perspective. (On such attitudes, see footnote 7 above.)

9. That " 'standard' British English" gets infiltrated with creolized pidgin "english" and "concerns with place and displacement" fill the postcolonial novel is outlined in Bill Ashcroft, Gareth Griffiths, and Helen Tiffin, *The Empire Writes Back: Theory and Practice in Post-Colonial Literatures* (London and New York: Routledge, 1989), pp. 8–77; Oe's poetic of Japanese regionality is articulated in Kenzaburo Oe, "The Centre and the Periphery," in *Writers in East-West Encounter: New Cultural Bearings*, ed. Guy Amirthanayagam (London: Macmillan, 1982), pp. 46–50, and Masao Miyoshi, → *Off Center: Power and Culture Relations Between Japan and the United States* (Cambridge, MA: Harvard University Press, 1991), pp. 238–241; the "Pacific Way" is articulated in Ron Crocombe, *The Pacific Way: An Emerging Identity* (Suva, Fiji: Lotu Pasifika Productions, 1976), and Subramani, *South Pacific Literature: From Myth to Fabulation* (Suva, Fiji: University of the South Pacific, 1985); and Frampton's position within postmodernity is outlined in "Towards a Critical Regionalism: Six Points for an Architecture of Resistance," in *The Anti-Aesthetic*, ed. Hal Foster (Port Townsend, WA: Bay Press, 1983), pp. 16–30.

10. See Kenneth Frampton, "Place-Form and Cultural Identity," in *Design After Modernism: Beyond the Object*, ed. John Thackara (London: Thames and Hudson, 1988), pp. 51–66. On restructurations of the "local" via tactics of flexible accumulation that have accelerated since the global recession of 1973, see David Harvey, *The Condition of Postmodernity* (Cambridge, UK: Basil Blackwell, 1989).

11. On this place-and-language ethos of "local writing" in Hawaii, see Darrell H. Y. Lum, "Hawaii's Literature and Lunch," *East Wind* (Spring/Summer 1986): 32–33.

12. Lum, *Exponding the Doubtful Points*, p. 67.

13. On the global preconditions of such postmodernity, see Fredric Jameson, *Postmodernism, or, The Cultural Logic of Late Capitalism* (Durham, NC: Duke University Press, 1990). On BCCI, I quote from Robert Jackson, "BCCI's Shadowy Web Aided Noriega in 'Shell Game,' " *Honolulu Advertiser*, August 12, 1991, p. D2.

14. Arif Dirlik, "Culturalism as Hegemonic Ideology and Liberating Practice," *Cultural Critique* 6 (1987): 13–19.

15. See Albert Wendt, "Towards a New Oceania," in *Writers in East-West Encounter*, pp. 202–215; and Albert Wendt, "Novelists and Historians and the Art of Remembering," in *Class and Culture in the South Pacific*, pp. 78–91.

16. Subramani, *South Pacific Literature*, p. x.

17. Darrell Lum, quoted in Ronn Ronck, "Write On," *Honolulu Advertiser*, October 24, 1991, p. B2, on the occasion of Lum's winning the 1991 Elliot Cades Award for Hawaiian Literature with Juliet Kono Lee.

18. Darrell Lum, "Local Literature and Lunch," in *The Best of Bamboo Ridge*, ed. Eric Chock and Darrell H. Y. Lum (Honolulu: Bamboo Ridge Press, 1986), p. 3.

19. See Richard Hamasaki's master's thesis in the Ethnic Studies Department of the University of Hawaii, *Singing in Their Genealogical Trees* (1990), for a distinctly "Hawaiian" take on this literature as emerging from a Pan-Pacific territory of ecological, linguistic, and political sovereignty as well as the important anthologies of Hawaiian literature and history edited by Rodney Morales (*Ho'i Ho'i Hou* [1984]) and Dana Naone Hall (*Malama* [1982]), both published by Bamboo Ridge Press in Honolulu.

20. As Lum proudly claimed in "Local Literature and Lunch," p. 3, "There's an island surf shop called Local Motion where you can buy T-shirts that say 'Locals Only.'

Anyone can shop there, even tourists. And locals and tourists alike buy 'Locals Only' shirts because they're brightly colored, full of geometric New Wave designs, and they say 'Hawaii' right there in front."

21. Stephen H. Sumida, "Waiting for the Big Fish: Recent Research in the Asian American Literature of Hawaii," in *The Best of Bamboo Ridge,* p. 312.

22. Michener's infamous comment from 1959 is quoted in Stephen H. Sumida, "Waiting for the Big Fish," p. 304.

23. See Rupert Brooke, "Waikiki," in *A Hawaiian Reader,* ed. A. Grove Day and Carl Stroven (Honolulu: Mutual, 1984), p. 217.

24. See Stephen H. Sumida, *And the View from the Shore: Literary Traditions of Hawaii* (Seattle: University of Washington Press, 1991). Subsequent references to this study will occur parenthically.

25. Tino Ramirez, *Honolulu Star-Bulletin,* April 13, 1991.

26. I argue a broadly counterpastoral way of looking at the U.S. landscape—and technoscape—in *American Sublime: The Genealogy of a Poetic Genre* (Madison: Wisconsin University Press, 1991), especially Chapter 9, "Towards the Nuclear Sublime." Simple or complex, *pastoral* can become a literary way of ignoring and containing the historical fact of how fully nuclearized, ecologically threatened, and commodified Hawaii and "the American Pacific" already are: we expect this from *New Yorker* poets writing landscape poems set in Hawaii, or racially obtuse movies like *North Shore,* but not from "authentically local" poets and critics of *Bamboo Ridge.* A study of "pastoral" that more trenchantly sets this literary mode (appropriated and transformed by Americans from Great Britain) within the class dynamics of labor, social community, and injustices of global capitalism remains Raymond Williams, *The Country and the City* (New York: Oxford University Press, 1973); but also see Lawrence Buell, "American Pastoral Ideology Reappraised," *American Literary History* 1 (1989): 1–29, for a more critical perspective on "pastoralism" as an American-liberal ideology. Neither of these works figure in Sumida's analysis of American/Hawaiian pastoral, however.

27. Tony Lee, "Nowadays Not Like Before," in *The Best of Bamboo Ridge,* pp. 167–174.

28. For a history of plantation communities and the ethnic determinations that marked the complex class warfare that dominated Hawaiian daily life from 1840 to 1960, see Ronald Takaki, *Pau Hana: Plantation Life and Labor in Hawaii* (Honolulu: University of Hawaii Press, 1983). On Murayama's plantation novel, in addition to the Sumida scholarship cited above, also see the heteroglossic analyis of dominant and minority "voices" in Rob Wilson, "The Language of Confinement and Liberation in Milton Murayama's *All I Asking For Is My Body*" in Eric Chock and Jody Manabe, eds., *Writers of Hawaii: A Focus on Our Literary Heritage* (Honolulu: Bamboo Ridge Press, 1981), pp. 62–65; and Rob Wilson, "Review: *All I Asking For Is My Body,*" *Bamboo Ridge* Number 5 (1979–1980): 2–5.

29. Rob Wilson, "Anita Sky," in *The Best of Bamboo Ridge,* p. 111.

30. Juliet S. Kono [Lee], "Yonsei," in *Hilo Rains* (Honolulu: Bamboo Ridge Press, 1988), pp. 102–103.

31. See Kenneth Frampton, "Towards a Critical Regionalism: Six Points for an Architecture of Resistance," in *The Anti-Aesthetic,* pp. 20–29.

32. Eric Chock, "Home Free," in *Last Days Here* (Honolulu: Bamboo Ridge Press, 1990), pp. 74–75.

33. Concerning this trope of Pacific domination—projected in EuroAmerican artists such as Paul Gauguin, Robert Louis Stevenson, Mark Twain, Wallace Stevens, and Marlon Brando—that "makes explicit the equation tropics/ ecstasy/ amorousness/ native," see Abigail Solomon-Godeau's analysis of Gauguin's French-colonial primitivism in "Going Native," *Art in America* 77 (July 1989): 119–128. As a "Pacific paradise" extending the nineteenth-century myths of U.S. Manifest Destiny, "Hawaii" still functions as this displaced incarnation of a U.S. Edenic eros. So runs the ad-myth for "the friendly skies" of United Airlines.

ARIF DIRLIK

15

The Asia-Pacific in Asian-American Perspective

*I*N THIS chapter, I discuss some issues arising from the conceptualization of an Asia-Pacific regional formation from an Asian-American perspective—by which I mean not just the perspective of Asian Americans, but a perspective on the Asia-Pacific region that recognizes an Asian-American presence within its field of vision. The issues are derivative of questions that writers on the Asian-American experience (themselves mostly Asian Americans) have raised in the course of elucidating and defining that experience. It is a fundamental assumption of Asian-American historiography that the locus of Asian-American history is imbedded in the history of the United States. I am quite aware that carrying these questions over into a discussion of the Asia-Pacific region idea takes them into a realm unintended by their authors and in some cases contrary to their intentions.

It is my contention, however, that problems of Asian-American history are also problems in the history of an Asia-Pacific regional formation. Although studies of the Asian-American experience do not usually relate their subject matter to an Asia-Pacific *problematic* (with the notable exception of migration studies), an Asia-Pacific context is unavoidably implicit in much of the writing on Asian Americans, and the relationship of Asian-Americans to their trans-Pacific origins is a matter of urgent, sometimes acrimonious, controversy. I suggest here that in an almost trivial sense the presence of Asian Americans (and the very term itself) invokes an Asia-Pacific regional formation—as both its condition and its effect. Rendering the regional dimension explicit is intended not to deny Asian Americans an integral part in the national history of the United States, but rather to re-view the national history within the context of a broader regional perspective and to question the ways in which it has been conceived and written. Conversely, the fact that Asian Americans have suffered racist subordination and cultural denial for their regional affiliation is revealing of a deep-seated contradiction that historically has characterized attitudes toward the Asia-Pacific region on the

part of the hegemonic culture in the United States and problematizes the part
the United States has played (or might play) in the regional formation. Finally, the efforts of Asian Americans to cope with their situation have produced cultural forms that may have much to tell us about Asia-Pacific as social and cultural construct—that point at once to a regional formation with
its own social and cultural features, and local formations that resist their in-
gestion into a homogeneous national or regional identity.

My discussion is of necessity illustrative rather than comprehensive. Although I do my best to be circumspect with generalizations, the very term
"Asian Americans" implies important blind spots that need to be spelled out
from the beginning, especially in a discussion that conjoins the Asian-American experience to an Asia-Pacific regional formation. First, the "American"
side of the term, which identifies a continental notation with a national entity. Although this usage has the sense of an almost unalterable convention, it
is necessary to note, especially in a discussion considering human motions as
a fundamental constituent of a regional formation, that the flow of Asian
peoples to the United States has been only part of the flow to the Americas,
which include not only Canada but Latin American societies; the latter are
barely included in discussions of Asia-Pacific in our day, even though the relationship between Spanish America and East and Southeast Asia played an
important part initially in the formation of a Pacific region. In the middle decades of the nineteenth century, the Chinese (the primary group of Asians at
the time) populations of Cuba and Peru exceeded in numbers that in the
United States.[1]

The "Asian" component is even more problematic, as it encompasses people of diverse national, cultural, linguistic, and racial origins who would
seem to share only two things in common: origins somewhere in Asia and a
common experience of oppression and discrimination peculiar to Asians at
the hands of a hegemonic culture that imposed a racist and culturalist homogeneity as "Asiatics" or "orientals" on otherwise vastly different peoples.[2]
The term "Asian Americans" is a product of the radical movements of the
late 1960s, when different groups of U.S. citizens of Asian descent sought to
counter such oppression and discrimination by establishing coalitions of
those who shared in the experience of this particular form of oppression—
the goal being less to assert their identity as "Asians," although that was inescapable, than to underline that in spite of its particular form, the oppression of U.S. citizens of Asian descent had much in common with the oppression of other "Third World" peoples, within and outside of the United States
(within the United States, these included Native Americans, Afro-Ameri-
cans, Latino Americans, and others).[3] The term, in other words, was not so
much a descriptive term as a product of a coalition-building political discourse; but as such, it was to enter the intellectual and academic discipline of
"Asian-American studies," which was itself a product of the radical move-

ment for social and cultural emancipation. Asian Americans themselves have been quite aware of the question of diversity ("Is there such an ethnic group?" queried a Filipino-American activist in the subtitle to a book on the subject)[4] as well as of the fact that different groups of Asians have been at odds with one another at different times. Viewing Asian Americans in Asia-Pacific perspective underlines this diversity, although the reverse is also true: common experiences in the course of a regional formation have brought together peoples originally quite remote from one another. Most important, the term requires sensitivity in light of the continued racist confounding of one Asian group for another. Finally, the term "Asian Americans" does not explicitly recognize the growing presence in the United States of peoples of Pacific origin, which has led one author recently to speak of "Asian Pacific Americans." It is not surprising that the author, Stephen Sumida, is of Hawaiian origin.[5] Once again, this is a reminder that is especially important in discussions of Asia-Pacific, which are on the whole oblivious to the Pacific islands around which, ironically, Asia-Pacific as a regional formation first took recognizable shape.

ASIAN AMERICANS AND ASIA-PACIFIC AS REGIONAL FORMATION

Writers on the Asia-Pacific region as a rule point to the intensity of capital and commodity flows, or political and military relationships to argue the reality of a regional construct. What is missing from most discussions of the subject is what may be the most fundamental—and enduring—element in an Asia-Pacific regional formation: the motions of people that have produced human networks that endow the region with a social reality and inscribed upon it the cultural features of trans-Pacific experiences. Asian Americans are prominently visible in these motions. Although the Asian-American experience bears upon it the stamp of its particular context in the history of the United States, it is important to note here that this experience shares certain common features with the experiences of Asian and Pacific peoples moving in alternative directions across the Pacific, for all these motions shared a common context in an Asian-Pacific regional formation, of which they were at once a product and an integrative ingredient.

I say "product," because a regional formation was the premise of Asian and Pacific peoples' migration to the United States. Asian and Pacific migrations coincide with the development of a capitalist world economy in the Pacific, which from the late eighteenth century on integrated the region economically (we might say *produced* the region as we know it today), gathering force by mid-nineteenth century with the development of the west coasts of the United States and Canada, of Australia and New Zealand, and of the plantation economies of Hawaii, Peru, and Cuba. This is not to say that there were no migrations in the region before capitalism. The Americas were initially populated by peoples from Asia (as were the Pacific islands). There were localized migrations and trade in the South Pacific. And of course, Chinese migrated to Southeast Asia in numbers from the fifteenth and sixteenth centuries onward, although that movement already coincided with the arrival of Europeans in the region. But the Pacific as we know it today did not exist until the late eighteenth century, and it was not until the nineteenth century that Asian migrations assumed a large scale and coherent direction: toward areas that with sustained economic development were emerging as economic cores.

Recent studies have adopted a world system approach as the most comprehensive framework for understanding Asian and Pacific migration to the United States. In the ground-breaking volume edited by Lucie Cheng and Edna Bonacich, *Labor Immigration Under Capitalism: Asian Workers in the United States Before World War II,* the editors described their theoretical framework "schematically" as follows:

> Capitalist development leads to imperialism, which in turn distorts the development of colonized territories. As a result, many people are displaced from their traditional economic pursuits, becoming available for emigration. Meanwhile, as the original capitalist society develops, its requirements for labor, especially cheap labor, increase. These two conditions, the displacement of colonized peoples and the requirement of more labor in the capitalist economy, arise out of the logic of capitalist development. And both result in pressure for people to migrate as workers to the more advanced capitalist countries. In other words, migration is a product not of discrete and unconnected factors in the sending and receiving societies but of historical connections between the countries. It is not fortuitous; it is systemic.[6]

A more recent study of migration patterns in the Pacific, *Pacific Bridges: The New Immigration from Asia and the Pacific Islands,*[7] although retaining a world system approach, introduces refinements into the analysis to account for complexities that have become evident in Asian migration since World War II (although the complexities were there before then), especially since 1965 when changes in the United States immigration laws led to a flood of Asian and Pacific immigrants to the United States. The dynamics of migration are still rooted in a world capitalist system and the motions of people from the peripheries to the core(s) of this system. In this more complex understanding of the world system, eschewing economistic reductionism, migration is no longer a direct function of the activities of capital, but is intermediated by the structures (not merely economic, but political, military, social, and cultural as well) of the capitalist world system. The approach also (implicitly) takes into account changes in structure that have accompanied the transnationalization of capital, which include the emergence to core status of formerly precapitalist states that have introduced considerable confusion into earlier notions of core and periphery. What Alejandro Portes describes in his contribution as the "relational dynamics within a global order" include in addition to labor flows induced by the motions of capital, international relations (among which political and military relationships are prominent), refugee movements spawned by wars and revolutions, and students, all of which may be accounted for by reference to the capitalist world system, but also have an autonomous dynamic of their own that is not reducible to capital-labor relations within the world system.[8]

Unlike "push-pull" analyses of migration (with factors "pushing" people out of the country of origin and factors "pulling" them to the country of arrival treated as if they were isolated from one another), the world system analysis of migration presupposes a regional formation. Factors of "push" and "pull" appear in this kind of analysis, therefore, as related outcomes of the regional formation. Even more important, perhaps, the regional formation provides the medium (through networks of interaction, organized formally or informally)[9] that makes migration possible. In this perspective, then, the very existence of an Asian-American population presupposes a regional formation rooted in the capitalist world system.

"Push-pull" analyses of migration stress local conditions in sending and receiving societies as if these conditions were independent of one another; world system analysis posits ties between these localities as parts of a broader regional formation. The contributors to *Labor Immigration Under Capitalism* do not deny differences between localities, but argue only that differences must be perceived within the context of a system dynamized by capital and the needs it creates for labor, which implies that large-scale migration is not fortuitous but is a product of those needs. Differences between localities in this approach are as likely to be creations of the regional formation as they are legacies to the regional formation of the precapitalist past.

The world system approach successfully explains a number of basic features of the motions of people across the Pacific, including the direction of these motions—which by the very premises of the analysis is from the less developed peripheries to the advanced core areas—and the timing of migration. The analysis shows that large-scale Asian migration to the United States coincides with the economic development of the North American West in the nineteenth century and the labor needs created by such development—mining and railroads on the continent and the plantation economy in Hawaii even before it became a part of the United States.[10] Incidentally, the situation was similar with Asian flows to other parts of the Pacific, such as Latin America and Australia.

This world system approach points to an important element in understanding the fate of Asian immigrants in the United States, which was bound up with conflicts between labor and capital. Labor opposition to Asian immigration was largely responsible for exclusionary policies toward Asian labor, beginning with the Chinese exclusion law of 1882 and culminating in the 1924 immigration law prohibiting the immigration to the United States of "aliens ineligible to citizenship." Although this opposition was most striking for the racist language in which it was expressed (of which more later), it is important nevertheless that the opposition was part of the struggle of labor against big business and the exploitation of Asian labor by the latter to hold down labor in general. In Hawaii, the competition took the form of competition among different Asian populations, with the plantation owners playing one against another to undercut labor resistance to exploitation; hence the importation successively of Chinese, Japanese, Koreans, and Filipinos to deal with labor problems.

Finally, a world system analysis also helps account for changes over the years in the *kind* of labor immigrating to the United States. In the early years of immigration to the United States, manual laborers predominated, although not all immigrants were manual laborers. By contrast, Asian immigrants to the United States over the past twenty-five years have included an increasingly significant number of professionals of one kind or another, reflecting changes both in Asian societies and in labor needs in the United States. The change, I might add, seems to correspond to changes in the capitalist world system as a whole and the increasing dependence of core countries on the importation of professional labor from peripheral societies.[11]

Two aspects to the Asia-Pacific regional formation do not appear in these studies with the importance they deserve, and I would like to stress them here. First, because they tend to employ world system analysis at a high level of abstraction, the authors show insufficient regard for differences between different regions of the globe. Neither study emphasizes what seems to me to be a peculiar feature of the Asia-Pacific regional formation: that although it was EuroAmerican capitalism that produced the region as an economic region, the people who filled out the region with their motions (and their labors) have been predominantly Asian and Pacific peoples.[12] The conflict between capital and labor (or core and peripheral societies for that matter) appears in this region therefore simultaneously as a racial and cultural conflict, which has determined the language in which social and political relationships are expressed. To complicate matters, given the racial and cultural diversity of the inhabitants of the region, such conflict has not been restricted to conflicts between labor and capital, or peripheral versus core societies, but has extended to conflict among the inhabitants of the region themselves, undermining, against the reality of economic integration, the possibility of a regional formation. I will return to this question below.

Second, in their preoccupation with the motive forces of migration, these authors do not emphasize with sufficient force that people's motions across the Pacific were not just a product of a regional formation, but were themselves an integrative ingredient of the region, because in the ties that migrant societies retained to their societies of origin, they contributed both to the formation of the region and to its consolidation at a fundamental, social level. In this perspective, the Asian-American presence is not merely an expression of an Asia-Pacific regional formation, but a fundamental constituent of such a formation because Asian Americans' relationships to their society of origin provide, to use a commonly encountered metaphor, "bridges" across the Pacific. Herein lies the Asia-Pacific element in Asian-American history.

This question is not unrelated to the first question above. There may be good reasons why Asian-American history has downplayed this Asia-Pacific aspect of Asian-American historiography. Regarded as "strangers" from the beginning because of their cultural and racial affinities, Asian Americans have suffered discrimination, oppression, and exclusion, which makes for a certain reluctance among Asian-American scholars to speak of this Asia-Pacific dimension of Asian-American history, emphasizing instead the "Americanness" of the Asian-American experience.[13] Further contributing to this reluctance, I suspect, is the diversity of Asian Americans that an emphasis on their Asia-Pacific affinities underlines, undermining the coalition-building political discourse to which I referred above. Sympathies for societies of origin that have been in conflict with one another on and off over the last century have also brought different groups of Asian Americans into violent conflict with one another, on occasion playing into the hands of the hegemonic culture of which they were all victims. The question nevertheless is important not only for understanding Asian-American history, but also for appreciating the role Asian Americans have played both in the constitution of an Asia-Pacific region and for what their diversity may reveal concerning the tenuousness of such a regional formation.

In the remainder of this section I will illustrate briefly Asian Americans' ties across the Pacific that justify a perspective that places their experiences within an Asia-Pacific context. I will return in later sections to the problems Asian Americans have faced because of these ties and what those problems may reveal about the relationship of the United States to Asia-Pacific, and the Asia-Pacific idea itself.

Most important among these ties are kinship and other social (such as regional) ties, which bound Asian immigrants to their society of origin and to some extent shaped their behavior in the United States. Portes has emphasized the role in migration of "network structures of migration," which he describes as structures that stabilize people's motions "by adapting to shifting economic conditions and by generating new opportunities apart from the original incentives."[14] Among these networks, kinship networks have played an especially significant part in the migration of Asian and Pacific peoples to the United States. It is easy to exaggerate the strength of such ties due to stereotyped notions about the "clannishness" of Asians, which long served as a reason for discrimination against Asian Americans (overlooking that "clannishness" might have been a product of discrimination). In their investigations among Chinese in Chinatown, San Francisco, Victor and Brett deBary Nee found that even among those who had come to the United States as "sojourners" (as was typical of early immigrants from Asia—and other places as well), memories of home faded with the passage of time and the realization that there would be no going back.[15] Nevertheless, where emigration abroad was not so much a matter of individual choice but of family survival strategy (as it was in most of these cases) by adding to the income of the family through the labor of members abroad, family ties retained considerable strength. It was even possible for families to exert pressure on wayward sons through formal or informal social networks when they failed to perform their duties, such as failing to send home the remittances that were expected of them.[16] These ties were reinforced by discriminatory laws against Asians in the United States. The prohibition of marriage between whites and "Mongolians" in many Western states forced Asian immigrants to look "home" to find mates. Such discrimination perpetuated the practice of arranged marriages and therefore the hold of the family on the individual.[17] Conversely, kinship ties provided a medium that facilitated further immigration. As June Mei has written of Chinese-Americans:

> It was well-known in Guangdong that a few Chinese emigrants did indeed "strike it rich" during their stay abroad. Some used their money to extend loans to others who needed funds to cross the Pacific. The most likely recipients of such loans would be people known either directly or indirectly to the creditor—in other words, people from his own district. Conversely, with a number of their kinsmen already in the United States and returning as lenders to China, job seekers from Siyi (one of the two major areas of emigration form Guangdong) had a better chance of obtaining loans through the credit-ticket system than did men from other parts of Guangdong. The importance of clan and regional ties in expediting emigration from certain areas should not be underestimated.[18]

Family ties have also played a major part in recent immigration from Asia, with family members of U.S. citizens and permanent residents constituting by far the predominant portion.[19]

An important economic by-product of kinship ties is the economic consequence of remittances. Although only a few would argue that remittances have contributed significantly to the economic development of the countries of origin, these remittances have been quite significant in volume and may have important consequences at the level of the local community, both in increasing the wealth of the community as a whole and in the redistribution of wealth in favor of emigrants' families.[20] They may also have long-term effects, I might add, both economically and culturally, as communities come to depend on outside sources for their income.

Finally, social ties between immigrant Asian communities and the countries of origin were not entirely haphazard, although the level of organization and its nature differed from one Asian group to another. In the case of Japanese Americans, social ties took the form almost of administrative control, as Japanese consuls became closely involved in the regulation of Japanese-American communities, in cooperation with local associations that were formed in the United States. The "Six Companies" in Chinatowns, a federation of locally oriented associations imported from China, were informal and yet they played a central part both in the organization of Chinatowns and the regulation of relationships between American Chinese and China.[21] Religious organizations of one kind or another have played comparable organizational roles in Korean and Indian communities.

Ironically, discrimination and oppression may have played an important part in perpetuating social ties of Asian Americans to countries of origin in another sense. Due to prohibitions against the immigration of women, Asian-American communities initially were bachelor societies. The prohibition against marriage with white women, as I noted above, forced them to look "home" for mates. But there was another product of such discrimination: it stunted the growth of a native Asian-American population, with the result that at any one time newly arrived immigrants have made up a substantial portion of the Asian-American population—except during the years of exclusion. After nearly a century and a half of Asian-American history, the newly arrived immigrants in most cases still make up half or more of the Asian-American populations today—with the exception of Japanese Americans, once the largest group among Asian Americans, but relatively ever smaller as there has been little immigration from Japan since 1965.[22] Given that newly arrived immigrants are more likely to have strong ties to their country of origin than native-born Asian Americans, it may not be surprising that social ties of the kind discussed above loom large as a characteristic of Asian Americans in the United States. They do contribute significantly, nevertheless, to the constitution of Asia-Pacific as a *social* entity.

In addition, ties across the Pacific are also visible in the movements and organizations of a political nature that over the years involved Asian Americans in the politics of their society of origin. The involvement of Chinese Americans in Chinese politics around the turn of the century, according to Eve Armentrout Ma, "altered their social structure and social order in a way that was probably more profound than anything that has taken place in the Chinatowns of the Americas up until the late 1970s."[23] The relationship of Chinese Americans to the People's Republic of China versus the Republic of China in Taiwan was to emerge as another divisive issue in the 1960s. Chinese Americans have also been involved in recent developments in Chinese socialism.

Similar ties are to be found among other Asian-American groups. Japanese Americans of the first generation (the *issei*) rallied to the support of Japanese government policies during the Sino-Japanese War (1894–1895), the Russo-Japanese War (1904–1905), World War I, and Japan's invasion of China from July 1937 to the beginning of the war between Japan and the United States. Conversely, radical and labor movements among Japanese Americans around the turn of the century had a significant impact on radical movements in Japan.[24] Political ties were most obsessively evident in the case of Korean Americans, for whom emigration to the United States appeared also as a political diaspora with Korea's annexation to Japan as a colony after 1910. As with Chinese Americans, the division of Korea (into north and south) after World War II was to complicate political ties to the society of origin among Korean Americans.[25] Issues arising from colonialism and national division have similarly affected Filipino and Southeast Asian Americans.

The issue of political ties is impossible to encapsulate in a brief space not just because of its complexities but more important because of its sensitivities for the groups involved and the whole question of Asian Americans as a group. More than one observer has suggested, validly in my opinion, that the exclusion of Asian Americans from politics in the United States helped perpetuate political ties across the Pacific; although such observations need to be qualified in light of the continuation of such ties even after World War II, when it became possible for Asian Americans to participate in U.S. politics.[26]

Most important, however, the question is sensitive both because of its implications for the status of Asian Americans in United States society and for its implications for the relationships of Asian Americans to one another. In the eyes of the dominant white population in the United States, which conveniently overlooked its denial of political rights to Asian Americans, the perception of political ties between Asian Americans and their society of origin rendered the former suspect as Americans, of which the most tragic consequence was the internment of Japanese Americans in concentration camps during World War II. These political ties also divided Asian Americans internally. The internment of Japanese Americans was welcomed by Chinese, Korean, and Filipino Americans, whose homelands had been colonized or invaded by Japan. Political ties on occasion even led to divisions within the same group. Chinese and Korean Americans have been divided over the years by conflicting loyalties to opposing political groupings in their society of origin. Ichioka has suggested that the support of first-generation Americans for Japan's policies in Asia even created a serious rift between the *issei* and their American-born children.[27] Such divisions imply that the various conflicts among and within Asian societies (as well as between the United States and Asian countries) have been replicated among Asian Americans and call into question the description of these peoples as a single ethnic minority. Divisions continue to this day as contests for power continues in the Asia-Pacific region.

As the Asia-Pacific region flourishes economically, another kind of tie between Asian Americans and their society of origin emerges to the foreground: economic ties. Such ties are not new; Asian Americans have been involved all along in the exchange of commodities between the United States and the various countries of immigrant origin. These ties have acquired a new significance, however, with the economic emergence of Asian societies and a simultaneous economic decline in the United States, which has intensified global competition for East Asian markets and capital. This has led to a new perception of Asian Americans as economic bridges between the United States and Asian countries, offering an edge for the United States within an overall regional economy.[28] The exact nature of these ties is yet unclear, and their significance probably belongs to a future yet to come. Suffice it to say here that this development may be more responsible than the factors described above for bringing to the foreground the Asia-Pacific ties of Asian Americans.

The final set of ties, and in my view the most fundamental, are cultural ties. They are fundamental not because they have played an integrative role in a regional formation comparable to the factors above—on the contrary, the issue of culture brings out fundamental ambiguities in the regional formation—but because culture, however perceived at different times by different protagonists, has provided the medium through which more concrete ties have been endowed with meaning. I will, therefore, return to the issue of culture after a few words on the national history of the United States as it appears in Asian-American perspective.

ASIAN AMERICANS, ASIA-PACIFIC, AND THE UNITED STATES: NATIONAL HISTORY IN REGIONAL PERSPECTIVE

Given the locus of Asian-American history within the national history of the United States, the trans-Pacific ties of Asian Americans would suggest that there has been all along an Asia-Pacific element in the construction of the United States as a national entity. Historically, however, a reverse image has been dominant. A culturally constructed definition of the United States has excluded any suggestion that the United States might be something other than a transplantation of a European civilization on the North American continent. To the extent that the trans-Pacific ties of Asian Americans have been recognized within the dominant culture, therefore, this recognition has served primarily to deny their "Americanness"—and their history. From the perspective of this dominant culture, the Pacific contrasts sharply with an Atlantic region. Ties across the Atlantic have derived their perceived cohesiveness ultimately from assumptions about a metahistorical cultural affinity between the United States and Europe. On the other side of the continent, even as the United States declared the Pacific to be an extension of its "Manifest Destiny," this same cultural self-image rendered the Pacific an alien territory, peopled by alien cultures that must be overcome in the realization of that destiny; the Pacific, in other words, must be conquered by remaking it in the U.S. image. The place assigned to Asian Americans in the history of the United States has been bound up with a profound ambivalence toward the Asia-Pacific articulated within the national history.

From the eighteenth century on, the United States was involved economically in the construction of an Asia-Pacific region, which set in motion the forces that would bring Asians to U.S. shores. Asian Americans in turn, in their trans-Pacific ties, introduced an Asia-Pacific element into the construction of the United States as a national entity. The history of the relationship of the United States to the Pacific, however, has been written entirely in terms of a U.S. expansion into the Pacific, an extension beyond the western shores of the continent of the same Manifest Destiny that had carried Americans across the continent, ultimately making the Pacific into a U.S. lake. The Asia-Pacific contribution to the construction of the United States has remained unacknowledged, suppressed beneath the cultural myth of a Manifest Destiny. The recovery of this Asian-American contribution to the history of the United States exposes a national history written as westward expansion as a hegemonic cultural construct; it also points to a profound ambivalence toward Asia-Pacific on the part of this hegemonic culture.

Asian-American scholarship has demonstrated that beginning with the Chinese in the middle of the nineteenth century, and well into the twentieth century, Asian labor made a significant contribution to the economic development of the North American West, from mining to railroad building to agriculture and fisheries.[29] One contemporary wrote, referring to the Chinese: "Without them the railroads could not have been built, nor the agricultural—and perhaps not even the mining—industries developed as they are."[30] The contribution was symbolized most dramatically in the contribution of Chinese labor to the building of the Central Pacific railroad, which when conjoined to the Union Pacific at Promontory Point, Utah, in 1869, symbolized the final unification of the continent. And as Chinese, and following them, Japanese laborers moved eastward from California and Washington with the railroads and expanding mining industries, they brought with them their trans-Pacific ties and their everyday cultures. Sam Wong's *English-Chinese Phrase Book,* printed in 1875, Frank Chin tells us, was distributed through Wells Fargo offices through nearly four hundred large and small Chinatowns scattered across the country west of the Mississippi.[31]

And yet even where such contribution was recognized, the Asian remained an exotic outsider. The same author who acknowledged the Chinese contribution to the building of the railroads observed that Chinese immigration had given San Francisco "the aspect of a settlement in the Flowery Kingdom."[32] Another contemporary observer, equally sympathetic, wrote in 1880:

> While gratifying my curiosity, and experiencing the pleasure of studying the habits and customs of a strange people during the recent Chinese civil and religious festival of the new year, it occurred to me that a short article giving the result of these observations might be of interest to readers, many of whom never have had, and possibly never will have, the opportunity to examine for themselves any of the peculiarities of this alien Asiatic race at present sojourning on the shores of the Pacific, apparently unaffected by contact with our Anglo-Saxon civilization. ... Within a circle whose radius is half a mile, in the heart of an intensely Western American city, itself the growth of little more than a quarter of a century, is found what we might call an Asiatic colony, and a colony bringing with it and retaining in its new home all the characteristics of its Chinese parentage. Traverse but a few feet, and the dividing line between a Mongolian and a Caucasian civilization, usually measured by an ocean, is crossed.[33]

Not without charm in their fascination with the exotic Chinese, these observations are testaments nevertheless to a generally agreed upon perception of the strangeness of the Chinese "sojourning" on the U.S. shore of the Pacific, separated by an "ocean" from "our Anglo-Saxon" civilization within the confines of the same city—a city that is itself only a quarter of a century old, but in the construction of which the Chinese population appears not as an integral part but rather as an exotic "Asiatic colony." It is not the status they assign to the Chinese in the growing civilization of the United States, but rather their sympathy for the exotic "Mongolian civilization" that distinguishes these writers from others who in the very same years called for and successfully achieved the exclusion of Chinese from immigration to the United States (1882). Those who wrote these lines objected to the rampant "anti-oriental" agitation in California, but the agitators themselves used the very same descriptions, in their case a cause for hostility to the Chinese, as the reason for their agitation.

As early as 1852, recent immigrants from Europe joined native-born Americans in demonstrating against the Chinese in San Francisco and calling for a "California for Americans."[34] The Chinese and subsequently other "Asiatics" were (in Ronald Takaki's term) "strangers," unassimilable to the "Anglo-Saxon civilization" that was to define United States culture. By 1924, all Asians, "ineligible for citizenship," were to be excluded from immigration to the United States. With that, their contribution to the construction of the United States was also "forgotten." In the recent fictional recreation of this history in Frank Chin's *Donald Duk*,[35] the Chinese-American boy

Donald wonders as he comes of age why there are no Chinese in the pictures from Promontory Point in 1869, although Chinese labor had been crucial to taking the Central Pacific to where it met the Union Pacific. As they were left out of the photographs, so were they taken out of history, not to be recalled into it until recently in Asian-American historiography.

In the exclusion of Asians from the United States, the struggle between labor and capital played a prominent part. White laborers, concerned with the use of "docile" Asian labor by capital to deepen the exploitation of labor, played a vanguard role in the calls for Asian exclusion. Although the concerns may have been legitimate, they were expressed in a racist language that led to the racist oppression of a minority and the suppression of the part that the latter had played (and continued to play) in the construction of the United States as a nation. Labor did not invent racism, of course, and in some ways to view the problem of Asian Americans merely as a problem of race is misleading. In the exclusion from the United States of East Indians, who technically speaking were of the same race as the "Anglo-Saxons," the legal decision specifically stated that it was color, not race, that was the issue.[36] From its founding, the United States was conceived as a "white" civilization, and nonwhites were to be excluded from it.[37]

In order to appreciate the U.S. Asia-Pacific "problem," however, neither race nor color are sufficient categories. What has distinguished the Asian-American experience from that of other minorities subjected to racist or color oppression is an additional element: the element of culture; or as stated in the quotation above, the confrontation between "Anglo-Saxon" and "Mongolian" civilizations, which rendered the situation into a metahistorical problem of a confrontation between Eastern and Western civilizations.

In a letter he wrote to the Secretary of State in 1920, arguing for the prohibition of landownership by Japanese Americans (in effect since 1913), then Governor of California William D. Stephens wrote:

> We stand today at this point of western contact with the Orient, just as the Greeks who settled in Asia Minor three thousand years ago stood at its eastern point. And while Mesopotamia and the country to the east thereof were the highways of the intercourse between the Orient of that era and the Occident of that era, and while historically, there was much of contact and conflict between the types representing the two standards of civilization, history does not show any material fusion of either blood or idea between the two peoples.[38]

To Governor Stephens history was irrelevant before a metahistorical confrontation between two civilizations, oriental and occidental. So was geography. Americans such as the governor, facing west on the shores of the Pacific, saw the East. Geography, no less than history, was culturally constructed. In this cultural construction U.S. history itself appeared not as a historical product, to the construction of which many diverse peoples had made significant contributions, but rather as a cultural construct that excluded from the history those who did not fit in with its culturalist premises. Essential to those premises was the Eurocentric premise of the United States as an Anglo-Saxon civilization, ever moving west. The Pacific, which seemed so inviting as a space in this westward march of European (or "occidental") civilization, became a threat when it appeared on western U.S. shores in the persons of an Asian population in a possible eastern expansion from the other side of the ocean.

A contributor to *Harper's Magazine* wrote in 1900 that it was California, with all its wealth, part of which at least came from its Pacific connections, that had made the United States possible:

> Our real West dates from California. It is not enough to remember that Minnesota, Oregon, Kansas, Nevada, Nebraska, Colorado, the two Dakotas, Montana, Washington, Idaho, Wyoming, Utah, have been admitted as States, and New Mexico, Arizona, Oklahoma, and Alaska organized as Territories, since California came into the Union. The pertinent question is how many of them we should have if there had been no California. ... The United States was mostly content to remain a narrow huddle of provinces when California, suddenly and almost empirically, unrolled our trivial halfway map to another ocean and gave us a national span, and pulled along population enough to vindicate the map. To this day there are many excellent people who never reflect what Uncle Sam's stature would have been if he had slept on with Canada as his head, Mexico for a foot-board, and his back against a British wall somewhere about the Platte.[39]

Arguing that "even American progress has to have reasons," the author went on to suggest that not only was California responsible for the physical unification of the continent by the railroads (without California, he stated, "there was not, nor has been, any other reason for mileages over three thousand"), but also for the shaping of the "American character" which was "woven of more threads than the stout one of birth."[40]

We may note here not only that the spaces between the eastern United States and California were filled thanks to California, as this author suggests, but also as Asian American writers have argued, that those spaces were filled out from the west as well as from the east, and Asian Americans played a significant part with their labors in filling out those spaces. Asian American historiography, in recalling Asian Americans into the history of the United States, has made a significant contribution to U.S. historiography by challenging its dominant paradigm of an expanding western frontier and showing that there was an eastern frontier as well, with a significant Asian presence on its outposts. This is not to deny the significance of a western frontier, but only to recall that that western frontier in addition to exterminating (physically or culturally) the Native Americans who stood in its way, also had to roll back an Asian-American presence that for a while promised to add a significant Asian aspect to the visage of the United States in the role it played in the U.S. West. As Victor and Brett deBary Nee have written:

> The arrival of ... Chinese pioneers to the shores of California signalled the beginning of the first large-scale migration of a free, non-white people to the North American continent and with it California became the final battleground for the borders of the European New World. The struggle that followed unleashed on members of the Chinese race the same fury and violence with which large regions of the continent had already been won from the American Indians. The struggle left on the North American continent an infinitesimal minority of a people whose settlements had once spanned the Far West from the Rocky Mountains and the Sierra Nevadas to the swamplands of California and the deserts of the Southwest ... through the defeat of Chinese migration by the passage of the Chinese Exclusion Act and the forceful expulsion of thousands of Chinese from the Far Western states, the entire North American continent had been secured as an extension of Western Europe and a preserve for the migration and regeneration of the European race.[41]

In the perception of the hegemonic "Anglo-Saxon" culture in the United States, Asian Americans were irretrievably Asians. Their trans-Pacific ties, of the kind discussed above, served not to further recognition of an Asian presence in the national formation of the United States, but to deny its members' "Americanness." The Asia-Pacific element they had introduced into the historical development of the United States was suppressed by a cultural construction of the United States as a western extremity of "occidental" civilization that faced the east in the west, as Asian Americans were suppressed in actuality by rolling back the inroads they had made into U.S. society thus conceived. The Asia-Pacific region, then, rather than a constituent of U.S. history, appeared as the next frontier to be conquered by this Occidental civilization.

CULTURAL HEGEMONY/CULTURAL RESISTANCE: REGION, NATION, AND LOCALITY IN ASIAN-AMERICAN DISCOURSE ON CULTURE

Denied their Americanness because of their Asian origins and ties, Asian Americans as they have claimed their place in the history of the United States have done so by also reasserting their identity as Asians. The constitution of an Asian American cultural identity, one that is at once Asian *and* American, has been problematic for two reasons. First, an Asian-American identity presupposes rejection of a U.S. history without Asians as well as of an Asian culture without history (implicit in the affirmation of the Asianness of American Asians), problematizing the notions both of Asianness and American-ness; the elements out of which such a new identity is to be constructed, in other words, must be reconstituted themselves in the very process of consti-tuting an Asian-American identity. Fixed notions of identity, therefore, give way to ethnic cultural identity as a historical process with unpredictable out-comes. This renders the process itself, into a contest both among Asian Americans themselves and between Asian Americans and the hegemonic cul-ture that provides the immediate context for the constitution of such an identity; especially over the question of whether such an identity in the pro-cess of its formation should seek assimilation into its cultural environment or assert itself as a culture of resistance that should seek in constituting itself also to reconstitute its cultural environment. The question of Asian Ameri-cans' relationship to the cultures of their society of origin has been inextrica-bly tied in with the question of their relationship to U.S. society.

These problems were sharply articulated early on in Asian-Americans' self-assertion in a remarkable essay, "Racist Love," written by two Chinese-American authors, Frank Chin and Jeffery Paul Chan. As the authors bluntly put it,

> White racism enforces white supremacy. White supremacy is a system of order and a way of perceiving reality. Its purpose is to keep whites on top and set them free. Colored minorities in white reality are stereotypes. Each racial stereotype comes in two models, the acceptable model and the unacceptable model. ... The unacceptable model is unacceptable because he cannot be controlled by whites. The acceptable model is acceptable because he is tractable. ... If the system works, the stereotypes assigned to the various races are accepted by the races themselves as reality, as fact, and racist love reigns. ... One measure of the suc-cess of white racism is the silence of that race and the amount of white energy necessary to maintain or increase that silence ... the people of Chinese and Japa-nese ancestry stand out as white racism's only success.[42]

Central to the white stereotyping of Asian men, according to Chin and Chan, was the feminization of Asians: "The white stereotype of the Asian is unique in that it is the only racial stereotype completely devoid of manhood. Our nobility is that of an efficient housewife."[43] The stereotype had been perpetuated by the objects themselves, who "euphemized" it "as being suc-cessful assimilation, adoption and acculturation."[44]

The authors rejected the "concept of dual personality" as a means of con-structing an Asian-American identity because rather than identify Asian Americans as Asian *and* American, the concept posited a "disintegrated per-sonality" that concealed the "self-contempt" that the internalization of the stereotype implied:

> The so-called "blending of East and West" divides the Chinese-American into two incompatible segments: (1) the *foreigner* whose status is dependent on his

ability to be accepted by the white natives; and (2) the *handicapped native* who is taught that identification with his foreignness is the only way to "justify" his difference in skin color.[45] (emphasis in the original)

Rather, the authors argued, negation of these abstract premises of the dual personality concept (East and West, Chinese and White American; abstract because they forced a self-definition in terms alien to immediate experience) and simultaneous affirmation of the historicity of Asian Americans' experience were crucial to the construction of an Asian-American cultural identity:

> The concept of the dual personality successfully deprives the Chinese-American of all authority over language and thus a means of codifying, communicating, and legitimizing experience. Because he is a foreigner, English is not his native tongue. Chinese from China, "real Chinese," make the Chinese-American aware of his lack of authority over Chinese, and the white American doesn't recognize the Chinese-Americans' brand of English as a language, even a minority language, but as faulty English, an "accent." The notion of an organic, whole identity, a personality not explicable in either the terms of China or white America (in the same way the black experience is not explicable in either the terms of Africa or white America), has been precluded by the concept of dual personality. And the development of Chinese-American English has been prevented, much less recognized. The denial of language is the denial of culture. ... Language is a medium of culture and the people's sensibility, including the style of manhood. Language coheres the people into a community by organizing and codifying the symbols of their own common experience.[46]

Neither Chinese nor white American, the Chinese-American sensibility was a product of the Chinese experience within United States history; and it was that historicity, imbedded in the very language of Chinese-American communities, that must be the point of departure for constructing a Chinese-American identity.

Such an identity, moreover, may be constructed only in resistance to white culture. Two decades later in another context, Frank Chin would refer to "death by assimilation."[47] A Chinese-American culture, he and Chan insisted at this time, would remain "emotionally-stunted" and "dependent" if it did not assert its autonomy of white culture in a relationship of antagonism:

> It is well-known that the cloying overwhelming love of a protective coddling mother produces an emotionally-stunted, dependent child. This is the Christian love, the bigoted love that has imprisoned the Chinese-American sensibility; whereas overt and prolonged expressions of hatred had the effect of liberating black, red, chicano and, to some degree, Japanese-American sensibilities.
>
> The hatred of whites freed them to return hate with hate and develop their own brigand languages, cultures, and sensibilities, all of which have at their roots an assumed arrogance in the face of white standards, and defiant mockery of white institutions, including white religion.[48]

In recent years, Frank Chin has engaged other major Chinese-American writers in acrimonious controversies, charging that in their urge to be assimilated to the hegemonic white culture, these writers have themselves assimilated, and perpetuated, white stereotypes of Chinese Americans. As he wrote recently,

> Kingston, Hwang and Tan are the first writers of any race, and certainly the first writers of Asian ancestry, to so boldly fake the best-known works from the most universally known body of Asian literature and lore in history. And to legitimize their faking, they have to fake all of Asian American history and literature, and argue that the immigrants who settled and established Chinese America lost touch with Chinese culture, and that a faulty memory combined with new experience produced new versions of these traditional stories. This version of history is their contribution to the stereotype.[49]

Chin's insistence on the need for "purity" in the Chinese-American relationship to a Chinese legacy, like his fear of "death by assimilation," yields the impression that he wishes to have nothing to do with U.S. culture, and seeks to isolate Asian-American culture from U.S. culture in general in order to construct an autonomous Asian-American culture from "purely" Asian ingredients. Although it is true, I think, that he insists uncompromisingly on the autonomy of Asian-American literature, it does not follow that this implies isolation from U.S. culture in general or a recovery of Asian purity.

What is at issue, I would like to suggest here, is an alternative vision of "Americanness" to that defined by the hegemonic white culture, one that resists assimilation into the received culture in order to create conditions for the reconstruction of U.S. culture in general. Chin has repeatedly pointed to the distance that divides Chinese Americans from Chinese in China; a distance that is at once the distance of history and language.[50] His own writing, arguably, is the most "American" of Asian-American writing in his incorporation of Western American lore into the Chinese-American experience; what he seeks to do, however, is to dissolve this lore into the Chinese lore that shaped the everyday culture of Chinese Americans.[51] Rather than repudiate "Americanness," his goal would seem to be to reject a hegemonic notion of Americanness that privileges white culture and to bring in an ethnic cultural formation as an equal partner in a redefinition of what it means to be American. He and Chan wrote in "Racist Love,"

> The concept of the dual personality deprives the Chinese-American of the means to develop his own terms of self-definition. It subjugates him by forcing him to define in terms he knows are not his. The tyranny of language has been used by white culture to suppress Chinese-American and Japanese-American culture and exclude the Asian-American sensibility from operating in the mainstream of American consciousness.[52]

Before an "Asian-American sensibility" can enter the "mainstream of American consciousness," the argument in "Racist Love" suggests, it must have its own space of cultural production; in other words, it must first develop fully as what we might call a "local" culture.

In a recent study of literary traditions in Hawaii, Stephen Sumida has explained that the term "local" may be understood in two senses. First is local in the sense of a parochial marginality, which is the sense in which it appears in hegemonic white conceptions of Asian-American literature. The other, the sense in which Sumida conceptualizes Hawaiian literature, is local in the sense of the articulation of a community's culture, which is central to the community itself:

> "Local" is today's shorthand by which people in Hawai'i—whether local or not, whether in pride or in derision-label a culture, a sensibility, an identity, and, often forgotten despite how strongly it is valued, a personal, family, and community history.[53]

Local in this sense, rather than a resignation to the existing structure of hegemony, is an assertion of the community's identity in resistance to hegemony; that in its self-assertion challenges the claims of white culture to centrality by localizing it as the culture of one ethnic group among others:

> Hawaii's locals know very well that they are members of American society, because Hawai'i is a state of the Union. By itself, the term "local" does not imply a desire for separatism from America; it is indeed quintessentially American to assert one's individualism within a representative group, to enjoy, for instance, eating noisily with one's family in a local chop suey house without feeling that one is partaking in something alien. The term is thus inherently pluralistic in concept—it abhors assimilation even though there is plenty of evidence of assimilation too in Hawai'i, where many still think that the "melting pot" preserves racial and cultural diversity, which it expressly does not. Assimilation is opposite to the concept of pluralism. With its inherent value on history and the processes by which a community comes to be, pluralism implies that the kaleidoscopic (not melted) local sensibility continually changes.[54]

And so must U.S. society, and what it means to be American, change continually, as new ethnic groups enter into it and rather than melt into one big white pot, assert their own identities in an ongoing redefinition of the United States. Carlos Bulosan may have been the first Asian American to make this point of the United States being an ongoing project rather than finished product when he wrote in *America Is in the Heart:*

> America is not a land of one race or one class of men. We are all Americans that have toiled and suffered and known oppression and defeat, from the first Indian that offered peace in Manhattan to the last Filipino pea pickers. America is not

bound by geographical latitudes. America is not merely a land or an institution. American is in the hearts of men that died for freedom; it is also in the eyes of men that are building a new world. America is a prophecy of a new society. ... [55]

CONCLUDING REMARKS

As an Asia-Pacific regional perspective, personified here by Asian Americans, offers novel perspectives on U.S. national history, the cultural struggles of Asian Americans within U.S. history also offer insights into the structure of Asia-Pacific as a potential region. The struggle of Asian Americans against homogenization into a hegemonic culture is paradigmatic of Asia-Pacific as a space for cultural production. There, too, it is possible to detect an ongoing struggle of local cultures against regional homogenization, whatever the source may be, of which Hawaii may be a prime example.

I started with the argument that the motions of people over the Pacific point to a constitution of an Asia-Pacific region as a social formation. In light of the discussion, I would like to qualify this observation. Although Asia-Pacific peoples have carried their cultural legacies across the Pacific, they also have been transformed by their host society without being absorbed into it beyond recognition. Rather, the histories of these peoples in their host society have produced a variety of local cultures. This has been the case with Chinese, who have moved across the length and breadth of the Asia-Pacific region in greater numbers than any other people, not just in the United States but in other societies as well.[56] The social constitution of the Pacific, in other words, ironically also points to a social dispersal when viewed from the perspective of these local cultural formations.

The Asia-Pacific idea has a significant social basis, which is evident in the motions of Asian and Pacific peoples as well as in their impact on the national histories of the societies that surround the Pacific or are located within it. As with the economic, political, and other relationships that endow the Asia-Pacific idea with some measure of material reality, however, socially, too, the region is as much a realm of contradiction and division as it is of mutuality of interest and unity. Cultural distance and dispersal articulate the contradictions that are built into the social dynamics of the regional formation. From this perspective, the Asia-Pacific idea appears simultaneously as an integrative discourse, one that suppresses its own contradictions in order to contain, hegemonically, the cultural formations that articulate community aspirations against the forces of cultural homogenization that emanate from the cores of the capitalist system that have shaped, and continue to shape, the region.

NOTES

1. Evelyn Hu-DeHart, "Chinese Coolie Labor in Cuba and Peru in the Nineteenth Century: Free Labor or Neo-Slavery?" (Unpublished paper presented at the annual meeting of the Association for Asian-American Studies, May 18–20, 1990, Santa Barbara, CA), p. 1. The number was 225,000. For comparable years (1847–1874), the number of Chinese immigrants to the United States was 171,171. See Fred Arnold, Urmil Minocha, and James T. Fawcett, "The Changing Face of Asian Immigration to the United States," in *Pacific Bridges: The New Immigration from Asia and the Pacific Islands,* ed. James T. Fawcett and Benjamin V. Carino (New York: Center for Migration Studies, 1990), p. 122.

2. Roger Daniels, *Asian America: Chinese and Japanese in the United States Since 1850* (Seattle: University of Washington Press, 1988), pp. 4–6.

3. See *Amerasia Journal,* Vol. 15, No. 1 (1989) (Commemorative Issue: Salute to the 60s and 70s), for these themes.

4. Ignacio Lemuel, *Asian-Americans and Pacific Islanders: Is there Such an Ethnic Group?* (San Jose, CA: Pilipino Development Associates, 1976).

5. Stephen H. Sumida, *And the View from the Shore: Literary Traditions of Hawai'i* (Seattle: University of Washington Press, 1991), Preface.

6. Lucie Cheng and Edna Bonacich, eds., *Labor Immigration Under Capitalism: Asian Workers in the United States Before World War II* (Berkeley: University of California Press, 1984), Introduction, p. 2.

7. Fawcett and Carino, eds., *Pacific Bridges,* fn. 1.

8. Alejandro Portes, "One Field, Many Views: Competing Theories of International Migration," in Fawcett and Carino, *Pacific Bridges,* pp. 53–70.

9. Fawcett and Carino, "International Migration and Pacific Basin Development," in Fawcett and Carino, eds., *Pacific Bridges,* pp. 8–12.

10. Edna Bonacich, "United States Capitalist Development: A Background to Asian Immigration," in Cheng and Bonacich, eds., *Labor Immigration,* pp. 79–129. For comparable arguments concerning other parts of the Pacific, see Charles A. Price, "The Asian and Pacific Island Peoples of Australia"; Andrew D. Trlin, "New Zealand's Admission of Asians and Pacific Islanders"; and Daniel Kubat, "Asian Immigrants to Canada," all in Fawcett and Carino, eds., *Pacific Bridges,* pp. 175–245.

11. William B. Johnston, "Global Work Force 2000: The New World Labor Market," *Harvard Business Review* (March-April 1991), pp. 115–127.

12. For an elaboration of this point, see Arif Dirlik, "The Asia-Pacific Idea: Reality and Representation in the Invention of a Regional Structure," *Journal of World History,* Vol. 3, No. 1 (Spring 1992).

13. For the application to Asian Americans of the concept of "strangers," originally from Georg Simmel, see Ronald Takaki, *Strangers from a Different Shore: A History of Asian Americans* (Boston: Little, Brown, 1989), pp. 11–12.

14. Portes, "One Field, Many Views," p. 57.

15. Victor G. Nee and Brett deBary Nee, *Longtime Californ': A Documentary Study of an American Chinatown* (New York: Pantheon Books, 1973), p. 19.

16. Ibid., pp. 17–19.

17. Ibid. For the case of another group, Japanese Americans, see Yuji Ichioka, *Issei: The World of the First Generation Japanese Immigrants, 1885–1924* (New York: Free Press, 1988), pp. 164–173.

18. June Mei, "Socioeconomic Origins of Emigration: Guangdong to California, 1850–1882," in Cheng and Bonacich, eds., *Labor Immigration,* pp. 219–247. Quotation on p. 237.

19. Peter S. Xenos, Robert W. Gardner, Herbert R. Barringer, and Michael J. Levin, "Asian Americans: Growth and Change in the 1970's," in Fawcett and Carino, eds., *Pacific Bridges,* pp. 249–284.

20. Carino, "Impacts of Emigration on Sending Countries," in Fawcett and Carino, eds., *Pacific Bridges,* pp. 407–426.

21. For discussions of associations for the different groups, see Ichioka, *Issei,* pp. 156–164; Nee and Nee, *Longtime Californ',* pp. 60–69; Takaki, *Strangers from a Different Shore,* pp. 270–314.

22. Xenos et al., "Asian Americans."

23. L. Eve Armentrout Ma, *Revolutionaries, Monarchists and Chinatowns: Chinese Politics in the Americas and the 1911 Revolution* (Honolulu: University of Hawaii Press, 1990), p. 1. See also Nee and Nee, *Longtime Californ',* pp. 72–74, 355–360.

24. Yuji Ichioka, "Japanese Immigrant Nationalism: The Issei and the Sino-Japanese War, 1937–1945," *California History,* Vol. 49, No. 3 (Fall 1990), pp. 260–274. See also Ichioka, *Issei,* Chapter 4, for the relationship between radical and labor movements in Japan and the United States.

25. Takaki, *Strangers from a Different Shore,* Chapter 7.

26. Ichioka, "Immigrant Nationalism," p. 274; Ma, *Revolutionaries, Monarchists and Chinatowns,* pp. 2–3.

27. Ichioka, "Immigrant Nationalism," pp. 273–274.

28. See for an example, Joel Kotkin, "The New Yankee Traders," *INC.* (March 1986), pp. 25–27. A recent conference on the Asian-American experience, sponsored by the Asia Society, included a panel on the role of Asian Americans in U.S.-Asian relations entitled, "Asian-Americans and U.S.-Asia Relations" (*The Asian-American Experience: Looking Ahead,* October 24–26, 1991, Los Angeles).

29. Ichioka, *Issei,* passim; Takaki, *Strangers from a Different Shore,* passim; Su Cheng-chan, *The Chinese in California Agriculture* (Berkeley: University of California Press, 1986).

30. William Henry Bishop, "San Francisco," *Harper's Magazine,* Vol. 66, No. 396 (May *1883*), pp. 813–832, reprinted in *The West: A Collection from Harper's Magazine* (New York: Gallery Books, 1990), pp. 75–92. Quotation on p. 92.

31. Frank Chin, "Come All Ye Asian American Writers of the Real and the Fake," in Jeffery Paul Chan, Frank Chin, Lawson Fusao Inada, and Shawn Won, eds., *The Big Aiiieeeee! An Anthology of Chinese American and Japanese American Writing* (New York: Penguin Books, 1991), pp. 1–92, 44. For the phrase book itself, see pp. 93–110. For the Japanese presence in the West, see, Tsurutani Hisashi, *America-Bound: The Japanese and the Opening of the American West,* tr. into English by Betsey Scheiner with the assistance of Yamamura Mariko (Tokyo: *Japan Times,* 1989).

32. Bishop, "San Francisco," p. 83.

328
ARIF DIRLIK

33. Catherine Baldwin, "The Chinese in San Francisco—the 6th Year of Qwong See [Guangxu]," *Harper's Magazine*, Vol. 62, No. 297 (December 1880), pp. 70–77, reprinted in *The West*, pp. 188–195. Quotation on p. 188.

34. Robert J. Schwendinger, *Ocean of Bitter Dreams: Maritime Relations Between China and the United States, 1850–1915* (Tucson: Westernlore Press, 1988), p. 92. For the role of labor in anti-Chinese agitation, see Alexander Saxton, *The Indispensable Enemy: Labor and the Anti-Chinese Movement in California* (Berkeley: University of California Press, 1975).

35. Frank Chin, *Donald Duk* (Minneapolis, MN: Coffee House Press, 1991).

36. *U.S. v. Bhagat Singh Thind* (1923). See Takaki, *Strangers from a Different Shore*, p. 299.

37. Ibid., pp. 15–16.

38. California Board of Control, *California and the Oriental* (Sacramento: State Printing Office, 1922), p. 10.

39. Charles F. Lummis, "The Right Hand of the Continent," *Harper's Magazine*, Vol. 100, No. 596 (January 1900), pp. 171–185, reprinted in *The West*, pp. 416–430. Quotation on p. 420.

40. Ibid., p. 421.

41. Nee and Nee, *Longtime Californ'*, p. 30. Roger Daniels expressed this point concisely: "To examine the Asian American experience involves, among other things, looking at American history the 'wrong way'; that is, from west to east rather than from east to west." *Asian America*, p. 3.

42. Frank Chin and Jeffrey Paul Chan, "Racist Love," in Richard Kostelanetz, ed., *Seeing Through Shuck* (New York: Ballantine Books, 1972), pp. 65–79. Quotation on pp. 65–66. I am grateful to Ken Berger of the Perkins Library, Duke University, for helping me locate this article.

43. Ibid., p. 68.

44. Ibid., p. 67.

45. Ibid., p. 72.

46. Ibid., pp. 76–77.

47. Edward Iwata, "Word Warriors," *Los Angeles Times*, June 24, 1990, Section E, pp. 1, 9. Statement on p. 9.

48. Chin and Chan, "Racist Love," p. 69.

49. Chin, "Come All Ye Asian American Writers of the Real and the Fake," p. 3. The references are to Maxine Hong Kingston, David Hwang, and Amy Tan. In approaching the problem here through Chin's writings I do not necessarily endorse Chin's views over that of these authors'. Indeed, Chin's approach is rather one dimensional and ignores the fact that cultural experience differs not only by ethnic group but also by gender, class, and generational differences. Denial of such differences has led Chin to contradict his own injunction to be mindful of the historicity of the Asian-American experience. Moreover, in stressing myth over history in his recent writing (and his insistence that he alone has direct and "pure" access to Chinese myths), he disguises his own historically conditioned reading of those myths (as a Chinese American rather than Chinese) and confounds what would seem to be the more fundamental question, which is the relationship of Chinese-American writing to the hegemonic culture; in other words, what readings of Chinese myths lends itself least to appropriation

by white culture and therefore to a cultural assimilation that undercuts Chinese-American cultural autonomy? It is because Chin has raised *this* question most insistently, from "Racist Love" to the present, that I have chosen here to emphasize his writings.

50. Chin and Chan, "Racist Love," p. 76; Nee and Nee, *Longtime Californ'*, p. 383.

51. Chin and Chan, "Racist Love," p. 77.

52. Sumida, *And the View from the Shore,* p. xvi.

54. Ibid., p. xvii.

55. Carlos Bulosan, *America Is in the Heart* (Seattle: University of Washington Press, 1990), p. 189.

56. For brief discussions of the cultural transformations of the Chinese in different parts of the Asia-Pacific region, see *Free China Review* (July 1988).

About the Book
and Editor

In this multidisciplinary volume, leading scholars question the current euphoria over the rapid growth of the "Pacific rim"—as an economic region and as a political concept. "Pacific rim" (or its correlate, "Asia-Pacific") has become one of the most important components of geopolitical vocabulary worldwide. In the United States, it has come to define a crucial arena of political and economic activity. Academic institutions are organized around it, and constant references to "the Pacific rim" in newspapers, journals, and the titles of numerous books have rendered it a part of everyday language. Yet there has been little effort to explore what this ubiquitous term signifies.

The essays in this volume undertake two related tasks. First, they explore critically the meaning of "Asia-Pacific" as concept, in order to bring to the surface the relationships of power that dynamize but are disguised by ideological constructions of "Asia-Pacific." They suggest that much of the discourse on the region is highly ideological, focusing on its potential for capitalist development while ignoring the limitations of such development. Second, against celebrations of "Asia-Pacific" they seek to uncover fundamental contradictions in the region, including its human costs and consequences. In evaluating the idea of "Asia-Pacific," the book shifts attention from abstract relationships between capital and commodities to the human interactions that have played a formative part in the region's constitution.

Arif Dirlik is professor of history at Duke University. His most recent publications include *The Origins of Chinese Communism, Anarchism in the Chinese Revolution,* and with Ming K. Chan, *Schools into Fields and Factories: Anarchists, the Guomindang, and the National Labor University in Shanghai, 1927–1932.*

About the Contributors

RAMÓN DE JESÚS RAMÍREZ ACOSTA is professor of economics and Assisting Dean in the School of Economics at the Universidad Autónoma de Baja California in Tijuana, Baja California, Mexico. He is the author of *Temas sobre Mexico y su Frontera Norte* (1991) and coauthor of *Baja California hacía el año 2000* (1990) and a columnist specializing in economic issues and business trends of the Mexican northern border economy.

GLENN ALCALAY is a Ph.D. candidate in anthropology at the New School for Social Research and is assistant professor of anthropology at Dowling College, Long Island. Alcalay has been conducting research in Micronesia for the past eighteen years. He has written extensively and has appeared on numerous occasions before the United Nations, the U.S. Congress, and the British House of Commons as an advocate for the rights of the indigenous peoples of the Pacific.

VICTOR M. CASTILLO is a professor of the graduate program in international economics at the Universidad Autónoma de Baja California in Tijuana, Baja California, Mexico, and is an international trade specialist at the Southwestern College Small Business Development and International Trade Center in Chula Vista, California. He is the author of *Economía Fronteriza y Desarrollo Regional* (1991) and coauthor of *Ecology and the Borderlands* (1986).

XIANGMING CHEN is assistant professor of sociology at the University of Illinois at Chicago and a faculty associate with the Center for East Asian Studies at the University of Chicago. His research has focused on the interface between urban and economic development from a comparative perspective with a central focus on China. He recently coauthored "Urban Economic Reform and Public Housing Investment in China" in *Urban Affairs Quarterly* 29 (1), 1993.

BRUCE CUMINGS is professor of East Asian and international history at the University of Chicago. He is the author of a two-volume study, *The Origins of the Korean War* (1981 and 1990). His most recent book is *War and Television* (1993).

EDWARD FOWLER teaches Japanese literature and film at the University of California at Irvine.

GARY GEREFFI has been a member of the Department of Sociology at Duke University since 1980. His published works include *The Pharmaceutical Industry and Dependency in the Third World* (1983); *Manufacturing Miracles: Paths of Industrialization in Latin America and East Asia,* coedited with the late Donald Wyman (1990); and *Commodity Chains and Global Capitalism,* coedited with Miguel Korzeniewicz (1993).

EVELYN HU-DEHART is professor of history and director of the Center for Studies of Ethnicity and Race in America (CSERA) at the University of Colorado at Boulder. Her current research concerns the Asian diaspora in Latin America and the Caribbean.

TOMOJI ISHI is a founder and executive director of the Japan Pacific Research Network base in Berkeley, California, with a branch office in Tokyo.

DONALD M. NONINI is associate professor of anthropology at the University of North Carolilna at Chapel Hill. He is author of *British Colonial Rule and Malay Peasant Resistance 1900–1957* (1993) and of many articles on social theory, cultural critique, and the political economy of Southeast Asian societies.

NEFERTI XINA M. TADIAR is a doctoral student in the Program of Literature at Duke University. She is currently on leave from the University of the Philippines where she is a faculty member of the Department of English and Comparative Literature.

ROB WILSON is a professor of English at the University of Hawaii in Honolulu. A member of the *boundary 2* and *Bamboo Ridge* collectives and frequent contributor to *Korean Culture,* he is the author of two books: *Waking in Seoul,* a collection of poetry and prose anecdotes about the American presence in South Korea (1988) and *American Sublime: The Genealogy of a Poetic Genre,* a study of the American poetics of national power (1991).

MEREDITH WOO-CUMINGS teaches in the Department of Political Science at Northwestern University. Her publications include *Race to the Swift: State and Finance in Korean Industrialization* (1991), and *Past as Prelude: History in the Making of a New World Order,* coedited with Michael Loriaux (Westview, 1993).

ALEXANDER WOODSIDE teaches Chinese and Southeast Asian history at the University of British Columbia in Vancouver. He is the author of *Vietnam and the Chinese Model* and *Community and Revolution in Modern Vietnam* and a coauthor of the forthcoming *Education and Society in Late Imperial China.*

Index

Acapulco, 252
Aceh, 25
Acheson, Dean, 32, 39–40
AFL-CIO, 128, 240
African Americans, 123–124, 125, 128,
    129, 216
"Against Tests on Moruroa" (ATOM),
    245
Ainu, 216
All I Asking for Is My Body
    (Murayama), 290
Alliance of Small Island States, 247–248
Amazon, 261–262
America Is in the Heart (Bulosan), 324
"American Lake," 140, 238
*American Lake: Nuclear Peril in the
    Pacific* (Hayes), 241
"American Pacific," 287
American products, 171
*And the View from the Shore: Literary
    Traditions of Hawaii,* 290–293
Anderson, Benedict, 154
Anglo-Japanese Alliance, 37
Anjain, Liam, 242
Apocalypse Now (movie), 31
"aquatic continent," 235
Aquino, Corason, 188, 194
Arnold, Matthew, 23
Art'om, 110
Asan, 105
Asia-Pacific,
    and Asia, 6–7
    class formations in, 10, 23–24, 33–
        34, 164–165, 166–175, 199–205,
        214–215

contradictions of, 9–11
cultural production in, 11, 20, 41,
    281–300
and East-West cultural divides, 185,
    315–320
ethnicity in, 24, 34, 41, 172, 175
as fantasy, 9, 183, 235, 284
as gendered concept, 183, 185–187
in global capitalism, 7–8, 9–10, 18–
    19, 40–45, 51–66, 163–165, 184–
    185, 284–288
and hegemony, 6, 15, 38–40, 142–
    147, 171–173, 320–325
human interactions in the formation
    of, 4–5, 6–7, 9
as invention, 4–6, 9
as myth and utopia, 13–26
origins of, as discourse, 7–8, 30, 32
problems in the definition of, 1, 51,
    161–163, 305–307
in prophetic culture, 13–26 *passim,*
    29
and regionalism, 8, 10, 40–45, 111–
    112
Asia-Pacific Economic Cooperation,
    111
Asia-Pacific Economic Council (APEC),
    8
Asian Americans, 7, 281–300, 305–325
Asiatic Mode of Production, 31, 34
Association of Southeast Asian Nations
    (ASEAN), 8, 57, 75, 100, 152, 173–
    174, 189–190
Atomic Energy Commission, 237
Australia, 8, 23, 75

333